2006

SIGNED

1

CW01263655

≥50P&3

574576

The titles in this three-part work by Raymond Tallis, and published by Edinburgh University Press, are:

*The Hand: A Philosophical Inquiry into Human Being*
*I Am: A Philosophical Inquiry into First-Person Being*
*The Knowing Animal: A Philosophical Inquiry into Knowledge and Truth*

# I Am

*A Philosophical Inquiry into First-Person Being*

Raymond Tallis

To Rod
with best wish

Ray Tallis

May 2006

Edinburgh University Press

To Michael Grant, philosopher and confidant,
for many years of support, encouragement
and inspiration

© Raymond Tallis, 2004

Edinburgh University Press Ltd
22 George Square, Edinburgh

Typeset in Sabon
by Koinonia, Manchester, and
printed and bound in Great Britain
by Antony Rowe Ltd, Chippenham, Wilts

A CIP record for this book is available
from the British Library

ISBN 0 7486 1950 X (hardback)
ISBN 0 7486 1951 8 (paperback)

The right of Raymond Tallis
to be identified as author of this work
has been asserted in accordance with
the Copyright, Designs and Patents Act 1988

# Contents

# Acknowledgements

This book is the second volume of a trilogy. None of it would have been published or even produced in a publishable form had it not been for the enthusiasm, kindness and support of Jackie Jones at Edinburgh University Press. For this I am enormously grateful – as I am to her dedicated team at Edinburgh, with whom it has been a delight to work. My agent Jacqueline Korn, of David Higham Associates, has provided advice, guidance and reassurance at critical times – for which many, many thanks. Finally, it is a pleasure to acknowledge the help yet again of Ruth Willats, whose copy editing skills and general wisdom I have been lucky enough now to secure for a seventh time.

# Preface

The present volume is the second of a trilogy. Along with its successor,[1] *I Am: A Philosophical Inquiry into First-Person Being* is devoted to working out, or unpacking, a single idea about the unique nature of human beings. This idea was the main philosophical product of the – rather less single-mindedly philosophical – first volume of the trilogy: *The Hand: A Philosophical Inquiry into Human Being*. The idea is that human beings differ from all other living creatures in virtue of a distinctive mode of awareness transilluminated by what I have called the Existential Intuition. While we are of course descended from animals and have much in common with them, the multitudinous consequences of the Existential Intuition have enabled us to conduct our lives at a distance from organic existence.

The trilogy builds on the notion, developed in earlier books, of man as the 'Explicit Animal'.[2] While I emphasise the difference between humans and other creatures, I advance a naturalistic, rather than a supernatural, explanation for this difference, thereby avoiding, on the one hand, 'over-spiritualising' humans and, on the other, 'over-biologising' them. I implicitly dissent from two views of humans: either that they are free-floating spirits, trains of thought, only accidentally entangled with bodies; or that they are pieces of meat, dancing to the same tunes to which non-human pieces of meat dance. The trilogy addresses what I believe to be the chief job of philosophical anthropology, indeed philosophy in the present time: to picture humankind in a way that neither regresses into theology nor, in the name of tough-minded opposition to sentimentality and superstition, yields to scientism.

At present, the temptations of scientism seem more apparent among philosophers than those of theology. John Gray's recently published and widely discussed *Straw Dogs*[3] is only the latest of a thousand books advancing what is effectively the current orthodoxy: that humans are deluded in their belief that they are fundamentally different from beasts. After Darwin, we are told, we should set aside our humanism with its belief in the special nature and possibilities of human beings and its dreams of progress:

> To believe in progress is to believe that, by using the new powers given us by growing scientific knowledge, humans can free themselves from the limits that frame the lives of other animals. This is the hope of nearly everybody nowadays, but it is groundless. (p. 4)

Science will not set us free because it has not grown out of its origin in 'faith, magic and trickery' (p. 21). Nor will it ever grow up, for the Darwinian reason that 'The human mind serves evolutionary success, not truth' (p. 26).

Gray, like many others, leaves us little to hope for. It is tempting to dismiss *Straw Dogs* – and similar books that claim to show humans what they really are – as deeply insincere – as well as self-contradictory.[4] It seems unlikely that the Professor of European Thought at the London School of Economics believes that his Chair is occupied by a creature not importantly different from a chimp; or that he cannot see that there must be something fundamentally different between human beings – who have discovered, and argue about, the evolutionary process – and all the other animals that are merely its products. Unfortunately, intelligent people in the grip of an idea often overlook what lies in front of their noses. This, after all, is a period in which, under the influence of 'masters of suspicion' such as Marx, Freud, Nietzsche and Foucault, many intellectuals have felt obliged to defecate on the image of humanity in the service of some distorted ideal of honesty which requires us to believe that the truth about humans is to be found in what is worst about us, while, at the same time, decrying honesty and truth as self-flattering illusions.

This is why it is necessary to show that it is possible to forgo super-naturalised accounts of human beings without committing oneself to wall-to-wall naturalism; that one can acknowledge that we are not disembodied reasoning machines without embracing the notion that we are (rather nasty) meat moving under the influence of blind instincts, tropisms and reflexes; that it is possible to develop an account of human beings which sees us as both part of, and apart from, the natural world. To achieve this it is necessary to explain in naturalistic terms how human beings came to be so different from their nearest animal kin; to show how belief in the reality of the seemingly profound differences between humans and animals is consistent with Darwinian thought – at least in so far as the latter is founded in true science rather than unchecked assertion. Only if it can be shown that hominids escaped from their biological heritage by biological means will the claim that human persons are not to be understood as animal organisms be safe from the charge of being merely regressive or anti-scientific.

In the first volume of this trilogy, *The Hand: A Philosophical Inquiry into Human Being*, I examined the role of the hand in pointing human beings down their unique path. The central notion of the 'chiro-philosophy' advanced in Volume 1 was that the tool-like status of the self-addressed hand transformed the relationship of the early hominids to their own bodies, awakening a second-order awareness characterised by self-consciousness, a sense of agency and, eventually, objective knowledge. These are the themes of the present volume and the next. This volume investigates in more detail the nature of distinctively human first-person being, of the selfhood or personal identity and the agency uniquely enjoyed by human beings. Volume 3, *The Knowing Animal: A Philosophical Inquiry into Knowledge and Truth*, will examine knowledge, a mode of awareness profoundly different from the sentience enjoyed to differing degrees by all animals, which is unique to human beings.

The itinerary of the present book is not straightforward. Its 'inquiry into first-person being' does not take the form of a linear argument towards a particular conclusion or set of conclusions. It *begins* with a second-order philosophical intuition about the central place of the Existential Intuition in the creation of the 'species being' of humanity and then explores the implications of this intuition in a variety of contexts. While the Existential Intuition is offered as a key to the philosophical issues – embodiment, individuation, personal identity, agency – with which the present book engages, its role is in many case descriptive rather than explanatory. While I hope that what I have to say will contribute to a better understanding of first-person being, in several places the discussion simply casts the problems of the self and of identity in a different but, I hope, more interesting light.

Of greater concern is an instability of viewpoint that may seem to undermine some of the discussion in *I Am*. Much as one would prefer that it were not so, it is impossible seriously to address first-person being without engaging with Cartesian scepticism. To try to counter Descartes' methodological solipsism with the notion, the Existential Intuition, which presupposes a good deal of biological knowledge is, of course, heroically point-missing. A biogenetic account of first-person being takes a lot on trust, most notably that we humans are embodied. While from the Cartesian viewpoint the body is a vulnerable inference, from the biogenetic viewpoint the (animal) body is (by definition) the unquestioned starting point and it is Descartes' notion of a pure thinking 'I' that is questionable. One way of engaging with Descartes is to turn the tables on him. The idea that embodiment might be a fantasy of the dreaming 'I' is itself dependent on the idea of bodiless existence. Might this not be a fantasy of the thinking 'I', itself a late result of the unfolding of the Existential Intuition whose primordial form was the sense 'That I am this [body] ...'? Although there is probably no way, ultimately, of adjudicating between these two starting points, much of the first half of the present volume is taken up with 'chunnelling' between Cartesian and biogenetic foundations for the 'I'.

Although this is unsatisfactory, it reflects how things in philosophy often are. In the last century or so the indefensibility of decisions as to what is foundational and what is to be built on foundations, and in what sequence, has become a major preoccupation. While 'anti-foundationalism' is largely boring and to be avoided, it is difficult to escape the suspicion that the hierarchical ordering of problems – from prior to posterior, from most to least fundamental – will always be arbitrary and subject to fashion. The anti-Cartesian revolution, associated with Frege and those analytical philosophers who took 'the linguistic turn', demonstrated this. And as we shall discuss in Volume 3, the anti-Cartesian revolution, which made the theory of meaning and the philosophy of language more fundamental than the theory of knowledge and the philosophy of mind, itself had no firm basis.

Problems, what is more, have a habit of running into other problems: the tidy separation of philosophical sub-disciplines does not accurately reflect the nexus of concerns, puzzles and mysteries that is out there. Many of the themes of this volume are inextricably interwoven: the investigation of theme A depends on assumptions growing out of positions adopted in themes B, C, etc., whose investigation, in turn, depends directly or indirectly on the outcome of the investigation of theme A. All of which is by way of an excuse for the fact that the appearance of a linear argument passing through the chapters of this book is largely that: appearance. There is much criss-crossing and even backtracking: the key themes form a kind of syncytium. After the first chapter, in which I try to bring the Existential Intuition into focus, my unpacking of the central intuition is driven by those problems it seems to bump against: the scepticism triggered by Cartesian systematic doubt; the mystery of, and the necessity for, embodiment of the 'I' (made particularly mysterious by the dubious Cartesian notion of embodiment being an accident); the puzzle of enduring personal identity through change; and the miracle of human agency. The intuition – and my own intuition as to the fundamental importance of 'the Existential Intuition' in human identity and agency – with which the book begins does not operate merely as an inaugurating premise. Rather, it lies at the heart of the book; its centre illuminating (or otherwise) the themes with which the book treats.

The apparent trajectory of *I Am* may be very roughly set out as follows. In Chapter 1, I introduce the Existential Intuition, briefly reiterating its biogenesis as set out in Volume 1 and examining some of its key ingredients. In Chapter 2, I connect the quasi-tautological nature of the Intuition 'That I am this …' with a rereading of the *Cogito* argument. I adumbrate an anomalous 'bio-logic' of first-person identity that promises to release the Cartesian prisoner from the cell to which methodological solipsism has confined him. The uniqueness of the 'bio-logic' of the identity asserted in the Existential Intuition lies in its being at once necessary and, at the same time, contentful. This seems to be an advance on the *Cogito* argument, whose meagre haul of material rescued from systematic doubt is at most a moment of present thinking. The anomalous bio-logic of 'am' assertions and first-person identity looks to correspond to a unique category of *de re* necessity and to extend the realm of necessary truth beyond that which, prior to Kripke, philosophers usually allowed. (Kripke's own claims about the essential necessity of third-person identity statements are examined and rejected.) This leads to a rethinking of the true nature of the *Cogito* argument: it proves the existence of a singular ('I, René Descartes' or 'I, Raymond Tallis') by means of logical arguments only because it reflects the merging of existential (more specifically carnal) and logical truth, or existential facts with logical necessity, which is evident in the propositional form of the Existential Intuition 'That I am this …'. By this means, I turn Descartes on his head (a compliment he could, of course, return) by seeing the *Cogito* argument – or its premise – as a late expression of the Existential Intuition awoken in the human organism.

The existential component of the 'I think therefore I am' was obscured because it has been traditionally treated as an argument on the page rather than, as was first suggested by Hintikka, as a performative – or the recipe for a performative – that takes place off the page. The full implications of the *Cogito* argument being rethought as a performance are examined in the light cast indirectly on it by the Existential Intuition. The Existential Intuition incorporates both logical and existential – more specifically carnal – assumptions that are necessarily true. The objections to Hintikka's 'performative' interpretation of the *Cogito* argument put forward by writers such as Bernard Williams may be deflected by fully appreciating what happens when the type-argument (on-the-page) is realised as a token in an individual (off-the-page). How the *Cogito* argument connects with the biogenetic account of the origin of the Existential Intuition, however, remains unclear: the chunnelling between the biogenetic story of 'I' and the methodological scepticism looking out from 'within' 'I' remains incomplete.

Chapter 3 further explores the Existential Intuition by trying to define the scope of its necessary truth and examining the immunity from error that characterises some but not all first-person beliefs, assumptions and assertions. The scope of first-person authority proves very difficult to define in general terms. It is obvious that I can safely infer from the fact that I think I am that I truly am. It is equally obvious that I cannot safely infer from the fact that I think I am Napoleon that I truly am Napoleon. What is not obvious is how to characterise in general terms the line that separates assertions that capture first-person, existential necessary truths from factual assertions that are vulnerable to error. Such a line would define the boundary between the 'subject truths' or 'existed truths' (which tend not to be 'fact-shaped'!) of first-person identity and the empirical beliefs that are held by the empirical self.

Notoriously, it is even unclear – at least to the sceptic – on what side of the line lies the fact that I am apparently embodied. Descartes recognised that his body lay beyond the direct output of the *Cogito* argument. The latter delivered only the fact that he was thinking and (according to him though it was not accepted by many of his critics) that he was a thinking substance. He concluded that, for all that he was intimately entangled with his body, it was a contingent fact about him: disembodied Descartes was neither an existential nor a logical impossibility. This is clearly unsatisfactory, particular where (as in the present book) the 'I' is approached through biology. In Chapters 4 and 5, therefore, I mobilise two kinds of argument for the necessity of the embodiment, which is already presupposed in my biogenetic account of the origin of the Existential Intuition and first-person being. These arguments supplement work in Chapter 2, which showed that first-person identity statements may be both necessary and contentful, and that Descartes can be turned on his head, such that his foundational intuition 'I think' may be seen as a late derivative of the biologically-rooted Existential Intuition.

In Chapter 4, I draw on recent arguments, notably from Quassim Cassam – who himself builds on the earlier writings of P. F. Strawson – to the effect that the 'I' is necessarily embodied because embodiment is a necessary condition of individuation and self-consciousness, for developed first-person being and the sense that 'I am'. This argument is complemented in Chapter 5 by an argument for the necessity of embodiment based on identification of what is missing in Heidegger's account of human being as *Da-sein* or 'being there'. If *Da-sein* is to be regarded not as a category like 'mind', but as something personal (analogous to an individual mind), there has to be some means by which it is particularised. There can be no *Da-sein* without a complementary *Fort-sein*, or 'being here'. The body is the only plausible basis for *Fort-sein* – even though, as becomes apparent on closer consideration, it seems in some respects rather ill-suited for this role, except in so far as it is haunted by an 'I'. (There is a dialectic relationship, or mutual dependency, between the 'I' that makes the body's *de facto* position 'here' and the body that enables the 'I' to be individuated and 'here'.)

The embodiment of 'I' is not a simple matter, either conceptually or phenomenologically. The multitude of shifting relationships between the self-conscious creature and her body, and the wide variety of ways in which the intuition 'That I am this ...' appropriates the body as the existential referent of 'this', are explored in Chapter 6. Being, suffering, possessing, using and knowing are just some of the modes of embodiment. At the heart of embodiment are tensions, even paradoxes: that there is no part of my body with which I am completely or consistently identified and yet embodiment is a necessary condition of my individuated existence; that my body is in many respects entirely alien to me; that 'What it is like to be Raymond Tallis' is not the same as 'What it is like to be Raymond Tallis's body' (not the least because there is no such thing as 'What it is like to be ...' for a body approached objectively, from the third-person viewpoint); and that Raymond Tallis's experiences are not the 'low-down on' or 'inside story of' Raymond Tallis's body. While my body is the primordial referent of the 'this' in the Existential Intuition 'That I am this ...', it seems that a) I fall short of fully colonising my body or even part of it, and b) what I am far exceeds the bounds of my body.

This leads naturally to the issue of personal identity, the theme of the Chapter 7. Many treatments of personal identity focus on its persistence over time. The basis for this persistence has been sought in psychological continuity through memory. There are serious problems with this approach, not the least being the fact that the thread of memory does not persist through one's life. Another problem is that of authenticating memories from within. Psychological accounts have therefore to be supplemented by accounts based on the spatio-temporal continuity of the body, which provides the 'audit trail' allowing true and false memories to be differentiated and the link between true memories and the present to be objectively established. The body is central to personal identity for two other connected reasons. First, and most importantly, it is the source and complement of the Existential Intuition. Without this there is no moment-to-moment sense of personal identity, which latter is the necessary condition of the sense of identity over time. Second, as already argued, it is the basis of individuation, without which there is no kind of identity, personal or otherwise. While in the initial discussion of identity I separate its vertical dimension (identity-at-a-given-time) from the horizontal dimension (identity-over-time), I do this only to draw attention to the former, which has been relatively neglected in recent discussions, though it is the necessary basis of the latter. The two are merged in a 'diagonal' dimension – moment-to-moment identity that is haunted, informed, given meaning by, the extended self rooted in the past and reaching into the future.

The eighth and final chapter deals with human agency and the seemingly mysterious fact that we humans are free to a unique extent to *lead* our lives: we are not merely sites where biological mechanisms operate. I argue that the Existential Intuition 'That I am this ...' and the appropriation of one's body and its world as one's own provide the basis of human freedom. First-person being plants the flag of 'here' and 'now' in an otherwise boundless world of material causation and enables the individual to be a point of origin in the universe. The Existential Intuition, gradually expanding to a complex self, is the seed of an enlarging 'outside' from which it is possible to position one's self to exploit one law of nature rather than another – 'obey nature in such a manner as to command it' – and so deflect the course of events in a preferred or willed direction. I also argue that actual freedom always falls short of imagined freedom, but that this partial illusion is self-fulfilling: we in our individual lives and humans over history are increasingly free, increasingly distant from the script laid down by our biology.

I am conscious that there are things in this book, beyond its contents and its specific arguments, that will provoke hostility and suspicion from philosophers, including some whom I admire enormously. Unfortunately, I suspect that it will be the early chapters that provoke most concern. The notion of an anomalous 'bio-logic' as evidenced in the Existential Intuition may awaken memories of previous disastrous attempts to merge logic and existence – notably the 'misadventures of the dialectic' (if I may turn on its head the title of Merleau-Ponty's last book) in the hands of certain Marxist philosophers, whose name it would be kind to withhold for the sake of their families. I am conscious above all that one of the fundamental intuitions driving many of the arguments of this book brings me close to Kant-intoxicated writers in the German Idealist tradition. Foremost among them is J. G. Gottlieb Fichte. Fichte it was who linked the logical truth expressed in the law of identity (A = A) with actual existence. This link between necessity and existence was, he claimed, realised in the I, which is at once self-identical (I = I) and self-positing. Many contemporary philosophers believe Fichte's entire philosophy to be based on some pretty simple errors.[5] Doubts have been voiced about the way he expressed the law of identity. Of even greater concern has been his supposed failure to appreciate that the privileged self-positing of the I actually boils down to a reflection of the grammar of a first-person pronoun. 'I' is just one of those words, like 'here' and 'now' whose meaning, or reference, is determined by the circumstances under which it is used. The fact that 'I' is apparently guaranteed a referent when anyone uses it is merely a grammatical feature of the word. It does not prove the existence of any substantive or special being whose existence is self-guaranteeing. Against this, I devote quite a few pages to showing why 'grammaticalisation' of 'I' does not capture its essential nature and to defending my intuition that 'I' – *understood as a token used on a particular occasion* – does signify a point of intersection between necessity and existence. While I do not follow Fichte into the metaphysically and political dubious places that he took himself to, I am still profoundly sympathetic to his fundamental intuition.

Even so, some philosophers will be appalled that the crusade against psychologism inaugurated by Frege will seem to have passed me by. The postulation in Chapter 2 of an 'Existential Grammar' to supplement Philosophical Grammar in the treatment of first-person utterances will only confirm the impression of naivety and inveterate looseness of thought. I will deal with the misunderstandings that I believe underlie Frege's anti-psychologism (and the tendency to exclude living beings from philosophical logic and the investigation of thought) in Volume 3. For the present, I would like to suggest that, when we are thinking about propositions containing essential or irreplaceably indexical terms such as 'I', and when those propositions are envisaged as being asserted – used as tokens, not merely mentioned as types or to instantiate types – then it is not only difficult but wrong and point-missing to leave out the existence of the utterer. Revealing this inescapable point of intersection between logic and existence is what I believe to be the enduring value of the *Cogito* argument. The painstaking, rigorous and often brilliant work of writers such as Elizabeth Anscombe, Anthony Kenny and P. M. S. Hacker, while richly illuminating, has not succeeded in disabusing me of the intuition that makes the I (underpinned by the Existential Intuition) the knot at the heart of the human world. Nor does it cure me of the belief that it is a good point of access to what Bryan Magee has called the ultimate mystery: 'the relationship between the self and the empirical world'.[6]

Something else may annoy the philosophically sophisticated reader, especially in the chapter on embodiment: my tendency to dwell rather too lovingly on the phenomenon. For this I apologise – but not sincerely. As with its predecessor, the present volume has been motivated by two not entirely convergent intellectual appetites: not only to make certain things about humans clearer, but to celebrate the extraordinary richness of human being. If rigour and wonder sometimes contend for the upper hand, then I hope this will add to, rather than distract from, the pleasure of the sympathetic reader. My ultimate aim is to unpack astonishment at the fact that I *am* – and that *I am something in particular* – while engaging with the most interesting philosophical debates in closely adjacent areas. For this purpose, the nimbus of wonder – expressed through a tendency (in Nabokov's words) 'to caress the details' – should invest an inquiry that I hope some will find enjoyable and even persuasive.

## NOTES

1. *The Knowing Animal: A Philosophical Inquiry into Knowledge and Truth* (Edinburgh: Edinburgh University Press, forthcoming).
2. See Raymond Tallis, *The Explicit Animal. A Defence of Human Consciousness*, 2nd edn (London: Macmillan, 1999); and Raymond Tallis, *On The Edge of Certainty: Philosophical Explorations* (London: Macmillan, 1999).
3. John Gray, *Straw Dogs* (Cambridge: Granta, 2002).
4. Gray, for example, relies heavily on science to advance his argument about the non-truth of science and deploys quite abstract reasons to prove that we are beyond the reach of reason or our reasoning is mere rationalisation. This is standard throughout the pessimism industry, as I have discussed in *Enemies of Hope: A Critique of Contemporary Pessimism*, 2nd edn (Basingstoke: Macmillan, 1999).
5. Both Fichte's fundamental idea and the contemporary criticism of it are summarised with miraculous clarity and brevity in Roger Scruton, *Modern Philosophy: An Introduction and Survey* (London: Arrow Books, 1997), pp. 482ff.
6. Bryan Magee, *Confessions of a Philosopher: A Journey through Western Philosophy* (London: Weidenfeld and Nicolson, 1997), p. 579.

# CHAPTER 1

# The Existential Intuition: An Introduction

In the opening paragraph of his book on Kant, Stepan Korner discusses 'metaphysical moments'. While 'metaphysics', he says, is 'apt to suggest something difficult, unusual and remote', it also has its 'familiar side':

> Most of us have times at which, in reflection, we seem to be confronted not with any particular isolated problem or any particular aspect of our experience but with experience, or life, or existence, *as a whole*. These might be called our metaphysical moments.[1]

Of all such moments, one of the most intense comes from the realisation that *I* exist. No fact (and 'fact' is ludicrously inadequate in this context) could be more obvious, less deniable (as Descartes observed) and yet at the same time more inexplicable. Glimpsed as a (contingent) fact, the 'I' that I am seems both deeply familiar and overwhelmingly strange; inevitable and yet unoccasioned. The oddness of the fact(s) *that* I am and that I am the entity that goes by the name 'Raymond Tallis' is stalked by two (almost unthinkable and dubiously allowable) thoughts: that I might have been something (or someone) else; and that I might not have been at all. The revelation of myself to myself confronts me with two kinds of contingency: that I am; and that I am *this* (person, life, consciousness, body).

Such confrontations sometimes bring terror in their wake. If, as is evidently the case, my existence is accidental (with an almost negligible prior probability), this accident will sooner or later be cancelled by other accidents that bring other existents into being. But they sometimes awaken feelings that go deeper than terror: an astonishment bordering at times on joy. The dubious reflections that a) I might not have been, and b) I might have been something (someone) entirely different,[2] and the less dubious reflection that c) I shall one day not be, are undercut by the unassailable reflection that *I am*. Fear is transilluminated by wonder.

There is a Greek proverb: 'Each is furthest from himself'.[3] It is open to many interpretations, but this is what it means to me: because we look out from within ourselves at the world around us, we tend, in a rather fundamental sense, to overlook ourselves. We are the dark centre, or the invisible origin, of the world with which we interact. At the heart of our concern for ourselves is a taking-for-granted, which prevents us from noticing at the deepest level that we exist. 'I need this', 'I want that', 'I must do the other' distract us from the fact that 'I', the one who needs, wants, must do, is ourself; or that there is one who needs, wants, must do, and that one is I. In unremitting pursuit of our direct and indirect self-interests, and our responsibilities, we look away from the self that is interested and bears responsibility. It is presupposed but unvoiced.

The sudden encounter with the contingency of the self, with the one who I am and have to be but who I might not have been, is an epiphany of the fundamental *assumption* – a term that has two linked senses, as we shall discuss in Chapter 2 – underpinning our engaged, busy, responsible, fearful, joyful, boring lives. Our selves are the last thing we discover.

This book (and indeed the entire trilogy) is built on the argument that the intuition '[That] I am [this]' – which I have called the Existential Intuition – is fundamental to what it is to be a human being. Although the intuition is directly encountered and fully experienced only rarely in our lives, as a supreme instance of a 'metaphysical moment', it pervades human existence and marks the difference between animals that merely live and humans who both live their lives and lead them; between the lives of organisms and those of persons; or between the existence of humans and the mode of being of everything else in the known universe.

## I.2 THE BIOGENESIS OF THE EXISTENTIAL INTUITION

Let me briefly recap some of the arguments of *The Hand: A Philosophical Inquiry into Human Being* that led to a) the idea of the Existential Intuition as the key to the differences between humans and other animals, and b) a biological account of its genesis. Of the many differences between mankind and the rest of animalkind, two seem fundamental: sustained self-awareness and agency. These are, as we shall see, aspects of what, in an earlier book,[4] I termed 'explicitness'; and they underpin a third unique feature – objective knowledge – which will be the theme of Volume 3.

The Existential Intuition owes its origin to the unique features of the hominid hand. According to the standard account, true handedness begins with the migration, said to have taken place six million years ago,[5] of Australopithicene hominids from the safety of the trees to the dangerous savannah. (This may have been triggered by climatic changes that devastated the forests.) In the savannah, the upright position was of adaptive value. Standing up increased the range of vision, allowing the eyes to assume their full potential as early warning devices; bipedalism also liberated the forelimbs from the demands of locomotion.[6] They were, in Charles Sherrington's beautiful phrase, transformed 'from a simple locomotor prop to a delicate explorer of space'. The distal parts of the forelimbs were freed to make the most of certain anatomical developments that characterise handedness.

Foremost among these developments were those that enabled full pad-to-pad contact between the thumb and the other fingers: so-called *opposability*. Some other primates show a degree of opposability, but because their thumbs have limited powers of rotation and are relatively short, opposability is incomplete.[7] Only in humans is there a large surface of very intimate contact between the pulps of opposing fingers. Opposability, combined with the ability (inherited from primate ancestors) to move the fingers independently, made the hand a stunningly versatile organ for interacting with the world. There is nothing else like it in the animal kingdom. The hand is richly supplied with sensory endings, so that the multitude of grips it can draw on may be perfectly adapted to the objects it is exploring and manipulating and be exquisitely regulated during manipulation by very subtle feedback processes. There is, of course, some overlap with the paws of other higher mammals. However, the human hand, through the complete opposability of the thumb, has another feature: in the touching tips of the fingers the body communicates with itself, as well as with the extra-corporeal world, with unprecedented intensity.

This much is standard. The *biological* importance of the wholly opposable thumb, its adaptive value, has been fully appreciated. The profound consequences for the animal's self-awareness, without which humans might merely have become gifted chimps, however, have been overlooked. Opposability, through its impact on the possibilities of the hand, utterly transforms the hominid's relationship not only to the external objects it is manipulating, *but also to its own body* and this in turn feeds back on to the relationship with those material objects. These transformed relationships are the key to the central role played by full handedness in the transition from primate consciousness, which for all its complexity is not turned back on itself in any sustained way, to human self-consciousness, and from animal behaviour to deliberate human activity. The liberated hand, I have suggested, took humans over the threshold dividing consciousness from self-consciousness and unreflective instinctive behaviour from true agency. This may seem somewhat implausible and more elaboration is necessary.

Opposability makes available a very large number of grips that the hand may deploy during the course of its manipulative activity. Crucially, at any given moment, there is a *range* of possible grips and strategies, so we have a *choice*. At the same time, the range is restricted by the shape and properties of the object we are manipulating. Humans, through their hands, thus have '*constrained manipulative indeterminacy*' and this, and the intimate choice it implies – the opposite of stereotyped, programmed movements – is a plausible starting point for the intuition of the agency of our own bodies and, more profoundly, the intuition of our bodies as our own and, indeed, as *ourselves*, and hence of ourselves as embodied agents: the Existential Intuition that 'I am … [this]'.

To see the connection between the choice arising out of constrained manipulative indeterminacy and the intuition of self-conscious agency one must appreciate that manual choosing takes place in a setting of especially intimate interaction with the manipulated object, underscored by constant direct sensory feedback about the position of our hands, their relationship to the object of interest and the progress of whatever operation is being performed, through skin sensation, limb proprioception and vision. This means that there is a very special relationship to our hand when it is engaged in manipulative activity. Not the least important fact is that the hand is in relationship to *itself*: opposability, with the mutual touching of the tips of the fingers (as we shall presently discuss), builds a new layer of bodily awareness.

Less contentiously, the special manipulative power of the hand creates a background from which it may plausibly be seen as emerging as a *proto-tool*. This sense of our own hands – a part of our body – as a tool changes our relationship with our own body as a whole into something that is not seen elsewhere in the animal kingdom. And it is easy to imagine how the tool-like status of the hand would retroact on the body, which in turn would become (more diffusely) instrumentalised. The hand-as-tool would 'infect' the body with agency and awaken a sense of the engaged body as something 'I' in part use and in part (as user) '*am*'. First-person being one's body – 'am-ing' it – and using it are inseparable. The process, started by the hand by which I awoke to my body as *my* body, as *myself*, also awoke my sense of being an agent – one who *does* – which further instrumentalises my body. The dialectic does not stop there: the hand itself then becomes more explicitly the agent of a body that wills events – or rather of an embodied individual who wills events or outcomes:

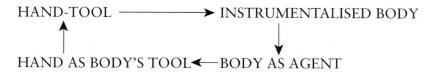

This is how deliberate action might begin to replace instinctive behaviour, tropisms and automatic responses to stimuli. Even though voluntary actions must still be fashioned out of, or built on, biological mechanisms, as we discussed in Volume 1,[8] there is an increasing contrast between the stereotyped mechanisms that make human actions possible and the non-stereotyped nature of those actions. Stereotyped mechanisms are deployed to non-stereotyped ends.

The sense of the hand-as-tool might not be fully awoken without 'meta-fingering' – second-order fingering in which the digits finger each other. The importance of this will become apparent as we address some of the objections that may be raised to the suggestion that it is handedness that awakens self-awareness and the intuition that, among the flow of events that take place, there are some – motivated by my appetites – that I *do*.

There is, first of all, the obvious objection that many non-human animals have organs that seem to exhibit a degree of manipulative indeterminacy: an elephant's trunk, for example; or a monkey's paw. The example of the elephant's trunk – along with the prehensile organs of any number of sub-primate mammals – is easily dealt with and casts light on what it is about the hand that makes it so special. We have to imagine that there is a threshold that has to be overcome in order for the sense of agency to emerge. Sub-primate mammals (not to speak of even lower creatures) are remote from that threshold. Even if the manipulative variability possessed by the elephant's trunk were as extensive as that enjoyed by the primates' paws, this would be available to a creature which does not have the level of consciousness that we may imagine is available, however fleetingly, to a primate. More specifically (and less contentiously) the grip of the proboscis does not incorporate the intimate interaction with the object that is seen in even the non-human primate grip. There is, moreover, a limited number of ways in which a trunk can seize an object and (more to the point) the variations of grip are largely accidental rather than chosen with respect to the particularities of the prehended object. The range – the degrees of freedom – of the variable prehensive strategies permitted to an elephant fall far short of the manipulative variability that is available even to non-human primates. Most importantly, the limited prehensile range of the elephant's trunk is in part due to *its not communicating with itself* in the way that the many-fingered hand with its opposable thumb does. The limited self-addressing of the elephant body would be insufficient to enable it to cross the very large distances that separate elephant awareness from sustained self-consciousness.

This last point is particularly relevant when we consider non-human primates such as monkeys whose paws *do* have an enormous variety of potential grips. Their range, however, still remains much more constricted than that available to the human – as is evident from the kinds of thing monkeys cannot do. Monkeys are not in the business of endlessly generating new kinds of grips as handed humans are. This also is because the organ engaged in prehension and manipulation is not addressed to itself in the way that the human hand is, via full pulp-to-pulp opposition. While there is some hand-hand (or paw-to-itself) interaction in the grips of non-human primates, this occurs to a much lesser degree than in humans. In humans, the interaction between the prehended object and the prehensile hand is modulated by an intense interaction of the prehensile hand with itself, which grows ever more self-aware as the infant human develops and uses its hands for a multitude of widely disparate tasks. We may think of the absence of opposability as being like a mittening anaesthesia, deadening (by comparison) bodily self-awareness.[9]

There remains, however, a third objection to our according the hand a central place in the instrumentalisation and 'first-personalisation' of the human body: we have considerable discretion over how we deploy other parts of our body such as our feet. Why not argue that the human foot, with constrained manipulative indeterminacy, lies at the root of the intuition of agency? While it is true that we may use our feet as instruments – as the incredible skills of foot-and-mouth artists testify to – this is consequential only on an already established relationship we have to the entirety of our body awoken by handedness. Foot-and-mouth artists and other people without functioning hands or arms are born into in a world created by Handyman and acquire a self-awareness forged in that world (just as congenitally blind individuals are shaped by and live in a world created by the sighted). When it is not freeloading on the skills established in a world the hand has built, the foot cannot act as a proto-tool because it lacks the dexterity, the self-addressing and object-customised manipulative indeterminacy of the hand.

The hand, which has exploratory and communicative as well as manipulative functions, is the chief organ of touch. The hand's touching is, as will already be clear, rather special: it takes place against a background of manual self-touching, through pad-to-pad opposition. The special nature of manual touching – and its momentous consequences – may be highlighted in a simple experiment. Slip off your shirt and let your bared shoulder cool. Touch it with your warm hand. You will find that you are divisible into at least two subjects and two objects. (That's leaving aside all the background bodily awareness and awareness of the things around your body.) Your hand (subject) is aware of the coolness of your shoulder (object). Your shoulder (subject) is aware of the warmth of your hand (object). There is therefore a double distance within you as an embodied person. This relationship, however, is not symmetrical: the hand has 'the upper hand'; it is manifestly the exploratory agent and the shoulder manifestly the explored surface. Although touch is reciprocated – the toucher in each case is also a touchee – there is a hierarchy of roles because the hand has come to the shoulder and not vice versa, and the hand has the established track record of being an explorer. The differentiation of roles, so that one part of your body is, as it were, 'superior' to another, sustains inner distances: the subject–object distance awoken within your body is not cancelled by an equal and opposite object–subject distance. Opposite, yes; equal, no.

These linked roles of the hand as an incomparable exploratory organ and peerless manipulative tool together create the sense of agency and, inseparable from this, the sense of oneself as a subject haunting (using, suffering, enjoying living and being) one's body:

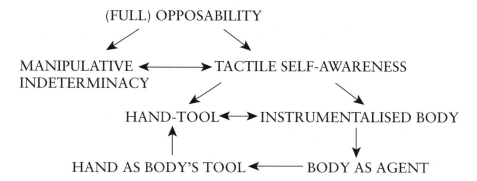

This, then, is how the hand awakens the intuition of *the agentive subject*.

The various tributaries feeding into the sense of self – or the sense that 'this body is mine' – may be set out in different ways. Here is one way:

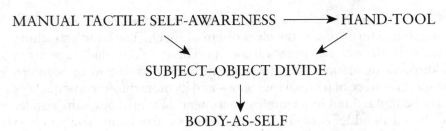

MANUAL TACTILE SELF-AWARENESS ⟶ HAND-TOOL

SUBJECT–OBJECT DIVIDE

BODY-AS-SELF

The subject–object, agent–patient, relationship within the body is many-layered. It is elaborated even within the hand, where every manipulation has a built-in hierarchy, such that part of the hand (for example, the palm and unmoving fingers) acts as a stabilising background and the rest is active foreground; and between hands, where, in bimanual activity, one hand may lead and the other follow, one stabilises, while the other manipulates; and between different parts of the body (as we shall discuss in Chapter 6).

While, therefore, it is also true that in much non-human animal activity one part of the body acts as a stabilising background for foreground activity, this is developed to an unparalleled extent in humans. As a consequence, humans are *subjects within*, *agents acting through*, their own bodies to a degree that other animals are not. And, to avoid misunderstanding, it is worth reiterating that, while differentiation into agent and patient, and subject and object, began with the hand, it does not remain there. In contemporary human beings, for example, we should not expect to experience a metaphysical difference between the hand and other parts of the body, except to the extent we have hitherto discussed. All parts of the instrumentalised body – the foot (as when I take a deliberate kick at a ball), shoulder (as when I charge a door), mouth (as when I break a thread between my teeth) – may become carnal tools.

It may not be easy to accept that the hand is the bearer of a higher level of bodily self-awareness, culminating in what is, effectively, an awakening of the organism to the status of an 'embodied subject' so that there is something (eventually *someone*) different from the body, that is aware of itself as embodied and has a gradually intensifying sense 'That I am this (body)'. Isn't it implausible to claim that something as contingent and as slight as a difference in the functional anatomy of the hand – which, after all, like the foot and the paw, is still only a piece of flesh when all is said and done – should have such momentous consequences? Actually, the hand didn't have to deliver all that much to start the process by which humans became evermore self-aware and distant from mere organic life and evermore clearly defined as subjects within their own bodies, for we may assume that other primates were close to the threshold that humans crossed. There is evidence of fleeting self-consciousness, nascent selfhood, in chimpanzees.[10] We are not therefore placing a huge metaphysical burden on the hand. It is not, for example, building self-consciousness from scratch. Rather it is consolidating the transient moments of primate self-consciousness into human sense of self. The hand enters a predisposing context: in a species that is already near to the threshold of sustained self-consciousness; which has assumed the upright position and is increasingly reliant on vision;[11] and which, because of the exigencies of the environment of the savannah, will benefit from increased dexterity. Moreover, the hand is required only to kick-start (or slap-start) the drift of humanity away from organic existence (although it is intimately involved in the many other developments that keep it going).

The question is not why, of all animals, man acquired agency and selfhood, but why humans were picked out from the other primates in this way. Sub-primates were not even candidates. While the self-addressing of human fingers is significantly different from the internal transactions of monkey paws, it is utterly remote from a cat scratching or licking itself. Not only is there a triadic relationship – finger-to-finger-to-object (which latter may be another part of the body) – but the meta-fingering is 'out there' at the end of the hand, and so remote from the implicit centre of the organism; visible as not-me and directly experienced as me.

Without the hand to open – and hold open – the gap between the body and itself wide enough to permit self-consciousness (the sense that one *is* this thing) and the linked sense of being an (embodied) agent, there is no plausible explanation as to why hominids of all the primates should have been the species in which agency and selfhood woke in the animal organism. The prehensions of the hand open the path to the apprehensions and comprehensions of self-conscious and consciously worlded humans beings. This is the path through which culture first trickles and then floods into nature.[12]

The notion of a *threshold* is intended to indicate how small a distance had to be crossed to start the journey that led away from animality. To mark how such a slight difference – the special characteristics of the human hand – could lead to such big differences – between human lives that are led and animal lives that are merely lived – we may imagine that non-human primates (unlike, say, elephants) have almost everything in place necessary to achieve bodily self-consciousness and the sense of agency. All that is needed is an extra margin of manipulative indeterminacy and of manual self-addressing, coming from full opposability, to lift the organism from bodily consciousness to bodily self-consciousness, with a consequent differentiation of agent and tool within the body. The special characteristics of the human hand are (to vary the metaphor) the coping stone that enables a previous unstable arching upwards of primate 'selfness' to hold up. The genius of manipulation is built on the genius of reaching, and the special awakening afforded by opposability is built on the near-awakening afforded by the fractionated finger movements of the primate paw. The latter is the highest expression of mechanism and beyond this we are in the territory of agency and at the beginning of the unique human pilgrimage through the material world. We are not able only to do more things with our hands than our nearest animal kin, but do them differently: dexterity delivers not only an increased range of skills, but truly deliberate activity.

To speak of thresholds, however, may be misleading, suggesting an abrupt and complete change. The process, however, by which a small difference leads to big differences must be envisaged as gradual – taking several millions of years. Though once the threshold is crossed there is no going back, the threshold marks only the *start* of a long process. The transition from the intuition of the agentive self to a fully developed complex human self confronting the kind of world we now inhabit was anything but sudden. We may envisage a feed-forward process, by which the consequences of self-awareness and the intuition of agency them-selves enhance self-awareness and sharpen and extend actual agency. Things that are fleeting in non-human primates – self-awareness, the use of the body as a tool, the use of tools to extend the body's tool-power – become increasingly securely established and have an ever-extended efficacy in humans. The relationship between human beings and the natural world will change progressively as a result of the different relationship humans have to one piece of nature – their own bodies.

Out of the Existential Intuition will grow a human world to rival the natural one. The precise details of the feed-forward unfolding of the agentive intuition into actual agentive power will be considered in Chapter 8. The unfolding of the self and its world will be discussed in Volume 3. For the present, we note that 'That I am this [thing]' marks the awakening of humanity within, to and out of the hominid body and the point at which human (cultural) development parted company from animal evolution. 'Am' separates the person from the organism and, when built over many thousands of centuries into a self, addressed to a world, that separation is stabilised. This escape from nature began as a natural process. As Erasmus Darwin (paraphrased by Roy Porter) argued:

Through such evolutionary processes, man had become lord of creation – his pre-eminence did not stem from a divine mission or any innate Cartesian endowments, but because of basic physical facts: highly sensitive hands, for instance, had permitted the development of superior powers of volition and understanding.[13]

## I.3 PRELIMINARY ENGAGEMENTS

This brief summary of the biogenesis of the Existential Intuition leaves much unexplained and much work to be done. Here are some of the most immediate questions. What is the *scope* of the Existential Intuition: what is it that is intuited that 'I' 'am' – or (to put it inescapably clumsily) that the 'I' 'is'? Is there a sense in which the Existential Intuition is 'true' and, if true, necessarily so; in short, incorrigible? To what extent is its scope coterminous with the body? How does the Existential Intuition connect with personal identity and selfhood as conventionally understood? Most importantly, if the Intuition is linked to the sense of agency, how 'true' is the feeling that we are agents? Does true (real, non-illusory) agency, at least to some degree, come bundled with 'amhood'? If selfhood and agency did not come all at once but evolved over hundreds of thousands of years, what are the means by which the scope of the self and the agent unfold during hominid history? How, in particular, does an organic life based on reflexes and pre-programmed instincts become increasingly replaced in human beings by a life shaped by deliberate activity and the push of causation become displaced by the pull of reason?

These will be the main concerns of the chapters to come, though some aspects – notably the unfolding of the knowing self (and its world) and the emergence of reason-based action – will spill over into Volume 3. For the present, we need to get the Existential Intuition itself more sharply into focus. Let me begin with a few comments about the term itself, which I settled on only after many vacillations.

## The Term

When I first started to formulate my views on the origin of humanity and the human hand, I referred to the intuition '[That] I am [this]' as 'the Existential Tautology'. This was a development of an earlier notion, 'the tautology of the self': 'I am what I am that I am'.[14] As several people have pointed out to me, however, the notion of a 'tautology' – a proposition whose negation is self-contradictory – is both too well defined and too narrowly understood to be used in this anomalous way.

While it is appropriate to explore the tautologous characteristics of the Intuition when it is presented in the form of a proposition, to speak of the Intuition itself as 'a tautology' is to give too many hostages to fortune. So Intuition it was.[15]

Nor am I entirely satisfied with the other word in the phrase: 'Existential'. For many people unfamiliar with the analytical literature and formal logic, 'existential' is indissolubly connected with 'Existentialism', the broad current of philosophical thought associated with a variety of figures, but most notably Martin Heidegger and Kark Jaspers in Germany, Jean-Paul Sartre and Gabriel Marcel in France, and numerous precursors such as Søren Kierkegaard and Friedrich Nietzsche. Existentialism takes its rise from theories about the mode of existence of human beings; most notably the idea that in so far as humans have an essence, it is individual and is created through actual existence. Human life does not consist in the unfolding of a pre-formed essence (revealed by biological science or theology or abstract theorising), but in the realising of projected possibilities that are not preordained. Essence is created in freely chosen activity: it lies in the past I have created, rather than in a past I have inherited, to be expressed in a future that awaits me. For those within the analytical tradition, 'existential' has a rather narrower sense, as a quantifier in first-order logic, with existential propositions being those that simply assert the existence of something – 'There is an x …'. In fact, 'Existential' as used in the present context has one foot in each camp, linking Frege and Sartre, as will be evident when we examine its 'bio-logical' properties in Chapter 2.[16] These properties come from the fact that its primary mode of existence is to be bodily lived or 'existed'.

It follows, given that neither of its components words is entirely right, that the phrase 'Existential Intuition' is far from satisfactory, though it has to stand because I cannot think of a better alternative.

## Formulation

Even less satisfactory is the formulation of what the Existential Intuition intuits:

'[That] I am this [x]'

This is unsatisfactory in both form and content.

Its form is that of an, admittedly rather anomalous, proposition. Propositions are, of course, rather slippery things. They slither between being the meanings of sentences, the meanings of speech acts that utilise sentences on particular occasions and the contents of beliefs or other propositional attitudes. The concept of a proposition belongs, as Steven Wagner has written, 'to a still rudimentary descriptive scheme'.[17] And attempts to liberate the concept from such rudimentary descriptive schemes are not wholly successful.[18] The presentation of the Existential Intuition as a proposition has problems in addition to those that arise from the uncertain nature of what propositions might express. For, since the awakening of the Intuition in hominids antedates the emergence of human language (and *a fortiori* utterances cast in propositional form) by several millions of years, this is wildly anachronistic. I 'proposition-alise' the Intuition thus for two reasons: first, this is the only way of capturing (necessarily in language) what it is; and second, this is an anticipation of one of its most important ultimate forms.[19]

So much for the form. As for the content of the proposition, it too is rather unsatisfactory. It hardly conforms to the most classical kind of proposition, which attaches general characteristics to particular entities. Instead, it links two indexicals – 'I' and 'this thing'. Worse still there is an initial term 'That' – which we shall inspect presently – which signifies something that usually goes without saying. As Wittgenstein observed, 'The general form of the proposition is: This is how things stand'.[20] It is not '*That* this is how things are' – because 'A proposition *shows* how things stand *if* it is true. And it *says that* they do so stand'.[21] It – or the sentence whose meaning it is – does not need to assert that it is asserting what it asserts. Equally awkward is the demonstrative 'this' and the uncertainty as to what it points out: entity? thing? body? conscious being? person? none of the above? all the above at different times? I have denoted this uncertainty by the variable or placeholder x, located in square brackets. This uncertainty is systematic and has a twofold origin additional to an intrinsic lack of clarity in what is expressed. First, the referent of the demonstrative is never entirely clear or sharp-edged at any particular time; and second, it will vary from time to time – at different stages in hominid history, and in the development of an individual person, and from moment to moment in the existence of a fully developed individual.

The Existential Intuition translates into a rather blurred and awkward proposition because one can clarify it and straighten it out only by simplifying it and giving it sharper outlines than it has: because, after all, it is rooted in *pre*-propositional awareness.[22] While it is the ultimate foundation of the propositional awareness that is unique to humans (as we shall discuss in detail in Volume 3), it is not itself entirely assimilated into that mode of awareness. It is at least as near to being something like a 'blush' of self-awareness – which suffuses a variable part of the world but always including one's body or part of it – as it is to being a proposition expressing such awareness. It is, to borrow a phrase of Wittgenstein's in a different context, 'a dawning over the whole', or a non-local realisation that is, none the less, rooted in the engaged body.[23]

The formula, then, and its propositional expression are both unsatisfactory, but they are, I hope, sufficient conceptual guides to illuminate our way towards a grasp of the distinctively human, which I believe has been insufficiently understood. Had there been such understanding, it would have proved a little less easy to overlook the vast space between humans and animals and to develop theories of human behaviour and existence (such as evolutionary psychology, sociobiology and neurophilosophy) that overlook pretty well everything that makes up a human being. But that is another story.

Two terms bracket the Intuition: 'that' and 'this'. They seem rather trivial and yet they are central to the argument, indeed the vision, of this book and therefore warrant separate attention.

### Concerning 'That'[24]

At first sight, 'That' seems almost redundant. At any rate, it lacks specific content: it merely has assertoric force. Just how negligible is the *content* it contributes may be judged from the observation that these two propositions:

a) 'That I am this [x or whatever]'

and

b) 'I am this [x or whatever]'

have identical truth conditions. This does not, however, justify the conclusion that it is redundant or empty; only that its contribution is not to be found in, or measured by, (empirical) content.[25] 'That' captures the transformation of what is into 'what is the case' or 'what is verifiably the case'. Far from being trivial, 'that' lies at the heart of the difference between human beings and animals: it denotes something that is central to the kind of being that is peculiar to humans, whom I have elsewhere characterised as 'explicit animals'[26] (I won't cover territory that has been covered at length there). The 'That' in 'That I am this' is the inaugural 'that'. But I am getting a little ahead of myself.

'That' denotes a certain highlighting or italicisation; or, more fundamentally, a making-explicit. It is a placeholder that signifies explicitness, notifying that something has been made explicit. We may think of it as a marker of a propositional attitude (belief, hope, denial, etc.), without that attitude being specified: marking a kind of undifferentiated, generic or ur-attitude. Clearly, then, although it is empirically empty, it makes all the difference in the world. Arguably, it marks the difference that is the 'worlding' of what is. In some respects, it overlaps with what Heidegger called 'disclosedness', the 'being-there' of those things that make up the world that characterises human being. This disclosure goes beyond that of mere sentience: it does not merely experience what is disclosed, but also acknowledges its (independent) existence; more precisely, it denotes that acknowledgement.

In the particular instance of 'that' we are considering – 'That I am this [x]' – the entity whose existence is acknowledged is identical with (indeed identified as) the one who acknowledges it. For Heidegger this reflexiveness is expressed in his characterisation of *Da-sein* as 'that being whose being is an issue for itself' and – closer to our present theme – as being 'constantly its "that" as care'.[27] In its most authentic form, *Da-sein* 'in its uncanniness, primordially thrown being-in-the-world, as not-at-home' is 'the naked "that" in the nothingness of the world'.[28]

It is evident that self-revelation and world-revelation are, for Heidegger, inseparable; and this will be a key theme of Volume 3. I shall argue that the explicitness of 'That I am this [x]' is closely linked with the explicitness of a material world: the emergence of first-person and third-person being (out of no-person being) are linked; and the explicit sense of being what one is is linked to the transition from sentience (in which the object of awareness is implicit) to knowledge (in which the object of awareness is distinct from the awareness itself and has explicit existence in its own right; has objectness). To put this another way, we are creatures who intuit – and later *say* 'That'. The 'this' that we are is the first element to be 'That-ed' in the world that is revealed to us. In other words, the 'that' of the world is rooted in, or begins with, the 'this' that I discover myself to be. It is here that the transformation of the environment begins and what is there is made *to be there* as 'That which is the case'.[29] The human world is everything *that* is [the case] – and also, as Richard Gaskin has pointed out, everything *that* is not the case.[30]

'That', in short, is neither empty nor redundant.

## Concerning 'This [x]'

'This [x]', too, seems empty at first sight. The demonstrative is like a linguistic pointer without a definite pointee – or a mere placeholder – given spurious specificity by an unspecified 'x'. Defining the 'this', the 'x' that I am, will occupy many of the pages to come. Here are a few preliminary comments.[31]

In so far as the Existential Intuition is viewed as a proposition – that is to say, articulated rather than merely being a blush of realisation – and 'this' genuinely does pick out *something*, its object – the x – is a singular rather than a type.[32] The kinds of things that it may pick out are: an individual human body; a 'phenomenal' body (in the sense associated with the writings of Merleau-Ponty, which we shall discuss in Chapter 6); a phenomenal body at any given time; an embodied self at, or over, time; a person; or (in its later Cartesian manifestation) a moment of thought. I shall argue that in its earliest form the x that 'this' is – both in hominid history and in the development of the individual – is the body as engaged in purposeful activity, as it presents itself in the consciousness of the engaged individual. Although the body *qua* active organism accounts for less of the 'this' in more developed human beings, it remains an essential anchor for the 'this', notwithstanding future transformations, spiritual refinements, abstractions towards bodilessness.

At any rate, 'this [x]' is necessary. The Intuition 'That I am ...'[33] is by itself incomplete, existentially unsaturated. There has to be a 'this' to specify *what* (or, more properly, *who*) I am; or to capture the specificity of first-person being. The 'this [x]' is not merely a particular (that I am given to be) but, as we shall, a particulariser of the personal existence I assume. For, as we shall see, that which I am is more than a mere presupposition of my being-in-the-world, more than a 'logical subject', like Kant's 'I think' which accompanies all perception. (Indeed, it is one of the main purposes of the present book to capture how first-person being can be something definitely and *meatily* there; how 'I' can transcend the third-person material world without thereby attenuating to Cartesian, Kantian or Heideggerian insubstantiality or nothingness.) The specificity of 'this [x]' – even if (for reasons we shall come to) it eludes precise specification, also reflects the biological provenance of the Intuition, which emerges in, and is an awakening to, the body in and by which 'I' feels embodied.

As we shall discuss in Chapter 6, the relationship between my body and 'what I am' – my self, or whatever it may be called – will vary enormously; in particular the extent and nature of the identity between them. In many cases, and not just in dualist or spiritual traditions, the extent of the overlap between the 'this [x]' that I am and 'my body' seems to be underestimated. Quassim Cassam, who argues that 'it is not possible to give an adequate account of self-consciousness without acknowledging the importance of certain forms of bodily self-awareness', points out that these 'have received surprisingly little attention in the analytical tradition'.[34] He notes how, by contrast, writers in the 'Continental tradition' have given much more importance to these forms of awareness; more specifically to 'the intuitive awareness of oneself as bodily or corporeal subject of consciousness' in self-consciousness. Not surprisingly, many writers steeped in neuroscience – such as Merleau-Ponty – and neuroscientists themselves place great emphasis on the body and various manifestations or organisations of the phenomenal body, such as 'the body-image', in the immediate intuition of the 'this' that I am. One of the challenges we shall have to address is the varying contribution of the body to the 'this' that I intuit myself to be – as when, for example, I am engaged in energetic physical activity, such as pushing a car; when I am simply busy (say, 'rushing around'); and when I am 'lost' in abstract thought. Even though complete, sustained bodilessness is never an option, there are times when 'Raymond Tallis' is identified with something less meaty – thoughts, projects, even a CV – than others.

The singular that 'this' picks out is more or less the entity that picks it out. This follows from the 'Existential Grammar' (a conception we shall examine in Chapter 3) of first-person identity statements. (There is some slippage and this is of immense importance.) There are both obvious and uninteresting reasons why this may be the case and less obvious and more interesting reasons. 'This' as used here is a demonstrative pronoun and as such is primarily deictic. ('Deixis' refers to the function of words 'which relate utterances to the spatio-temporal co-ordinates of the act of utterance'.[35]) In the case of the Existential Intuition, we are rarely (if ever, outside of philosophical discussions) talking about an *utterance* and, almost equally rarely, talking about a formulated thought. Nevertheless, inasmuch as the Intuition is experienced, it is tinged with deixis. This is the *force* of 'this'. For 'this' is most obviously contrasted with 'that'. The contrast with 'that' is with respect to its greater 'proximity to the zero-point of the deictic context'.[36] The unadorned 'this' captures unqualified nearness to the zero-point, the centre of egocentric space. One can almost imagine the Intuition being expressed through one's index finger pointing to one's chest.[37] But, more profoundly, it constitutes a small linguistic or conceptual journey away from one's self, which then makes it possible to return to one's self via reference: a super-position of one's self upon one's self.

Because the Existential Intuition is to a greater or lesser degree embedded in the singular, biological existence of the individual, and because it is to a greater or lesser degree experienced in propositional form, any analysis of it will oscillate between semantics and/or philosophical logic on the one hand and the phenomenology of the embodied subject on the other. It carries to the highest degree the peculiar and fascinating property of indexical assertions – namely, that they are twin-rooted in the (abstract) system of language and the concrete existence of the embodied person. 'This' in this context not only wobbles in terms of what it points to, but also in terms of its own status. While there has been a huge amount of work on demonstratives and other indexicals, the 'existential logic' or 'existential "bio-logic"' that is necessary to capture them has never been fully explored. We shall repair this omission in the pages to come. For the present, we note that 'this' seems to be empty only if we overlook the 'existential grammar' that underpins its use.

## NOTES

1. S. Korner, *Kant* (London: Pelican Books, 1955), p. 13.
2. Discussed in Raymond Tallis, '(That) I Am This (Thing)', in *On the Edge of Certainty* (London: Macmillan, 1999), pp. 155–88.
3. It is quoted by Martin Heidegger, but I cannot recall where. It seems to me to be close to his observation – quoted in Rudiger Safranski, *Martin Heidegger. Between Good and Evil*, translated by Ewald Osers (Cambridge, MA: Harvard University Press), p. 100 – that '[Philosophy] is a return into that nearest, which we invariably rush past, which surprises us anew each time we get sight of it'.
4. Raymond Tallis, *The Explicit Animal: A Defence of Human Consciousness* (London: Macmillan, 1991, 2nd edition 1999).
5. The date is uncertain because the fossil record between four and eight million years ago is missing. See Richard Leakey, *The Making of Mankind* (London: Michael Joseph, 1981). This is, of course, irrelevant to the present argument. The sequence of biological events is drawn from many sources, which are given in full in *The Hand: A Philosophical Inquiry into Human Being* (Edinburgh: Edinburgh University Press, 2003).
6. Although other animals assume the upright position from time to time, only man is overwhelmingly bipedal.
7. For a detailed account, see John Napier, *Hands* (New York: Pantheon Books, 1980).
8. See Tallis, *The Hand*, section 2.3: 'Mechanism and Agency'.
9. It is difficult to observe the awkward and severely limited manipulations of chimpanzees without feeling some discomfort.
10. For references to the evidence for fleeting self-awareness in chimpanzees, see Tallis, *The Hand*, p. 306.
11. This is important for the hand-driven transition from sentience to knowledge, as we shall discuss in *The Knowing Animal*, Chapter 4.
12. The candidacy of other agents, such as brain size, general intelligence and language as prime movers, is discussed and rejected in Tallis, *The Hand*, section 10.1. Even so, it is worth reiterating that the independent role assigned to the hand acting alone, while crucial, is relatively modest. By transforming our relationship to our own body, it inaugurated a process that very soon afterwards involved other things: increasing brain size and brain complexity, sociability and (finally) language. A dialectic between hand and evolving brain, a trialectic between hand, brain and tool,

a 'quadrilectic' between hand, brain, tool and sociability and a 'quintalectic' between hand, brain, tool, sociability and language are all envisaged. In short, the hand is not the sole repository of our smartness and only the trigger to the process by which we came to be so smart. Mary Midgeley (personal correspondence) has questioned my belief that language is a latecomer, pointing out with some justi-fication that the absence of evidence of language is not evidence of absence. This must be true: uttered air leaves no direct fossils. However, I think the argument in favour of language as a newcomer is quite strong; see Tallis, *The Hand*, sections 9.5 and 9.6.

13. Roy Porter, *Enlightenment. Britain and the Creation of the Modern World* (London: Penguin Books, 2000), p. 443.
14. In Tallis, '(That) I Am This (Thing)'.
15. In an earlier draft, I used the phrase 'Existed Identity'. Since, however, as Thomas Reid points out, as it is only persons who have an identity in any real sense, 'Existed Identity' would be close to a pleonasm.
16. I am tempted to speak jokingly of the Intuition as 'the Existential Qualifier'. Confining the joke to an endnote confirms that it was at least half-suppressed.
17. 'Proposition', in *The Cambridge Dictionary of Philosophy*, edited by Robert Audi (Cambridge: Cambridge University Press, 1995).
18. For example, the painstaking and scrupulous Introduction by Richard Gaskin to *Grammar in Early Twentieth-Century Philosophy* (London: Routledge, 2001) pp. 1–27, which still leaves a lot of unfinished business as to how much reference (as opposed to sense) can be incorporated in propositions. We shall return to this issue – and the relationship between facts, propositions, sentences and things-in-the-world (or on the surface of the globe) – in Volume 3.
19. I am not unaware of the extensive philosophical literature giving apparent reasons for denying that sentences such as 'I exist', 'I am conscious', 'I know that I am conscious' (and presumably 'That I am this [x]') mean or express genuine proposi-tions. According to A. J. Ayer, for example, 'statements like "I exist"' function merely as 'gesticulations' (*The Problem of Knowledge*, London: Penguin, 1956, p. 66) – presumably verbal self-pointings. That is why they enjoy the status of incorrigibility, but 'the price they pay for it is lack of descriptive content'. Against this, I want to maintain that the Existential Intuition is both more and less than a proposition. At any rate, Ayer simply identifies the complex nature of such assertions with their function of self-pointing, without noticing how extraordinary this is. Elizabeth Anscombe, by contrast, holds that while 'I am E. A.' is not an identity proposition, it is connected with an identity proposition, namely, 'This thing here is E. A.'. She then adds that the proposition 'I am this thing here' *is* 'a real proposition, but not a proposition of identity' (in 'The First Person', reprinted in Quassim Cassam (ed.), *Self-Knowledge. Oxford Readings in Philosophy*, Oxford: Oxford University Press, 1994). She then seems to contradict herself by translating 'I am this thing here' into 'this thing here is the thing, the person ... of whose action *this* idea of action ... is the idea' which sounds like an identity proposition to me. (We shall discuss Anscombe's deflationary approach to 'I' later.) Even so, the transcription of the Existential Intuition into propositional form is problematic; but the reasons for this are interesting, indeed profound, and not simply boring mistakes. My reason for not calling the Existential Intuition 'the Existential Proposition' – as something that is proposed, put forward – is that this suggests something too narrow (after all, it is one's self that is in question) and also would be to anticipate too much. 'That I am

this [x]' is primordially an intuition – this how it begins, continues and ends – and deeper than any individual proposition, though I am obliged to cast it in a narrow propositional form in order to get it on the page, indeed to make it a subject of discussion. I will argue in Volume 3 that it is the ultimate source of all propositions, the womb in which propositions develop, the start of the wandering 'That' that traces out the universe as an object of knowledge. Descartes' *Cogito* argument is an indirect discovery of this and a key moment in the development of human self-consciousness. Descartes places the Existential Intuition into the public domain for the first time in history at a certain level of self- awareness.

20. Ludwig Wittgenstein, *Tractatus Logico-Philosophicus*, translated by D. F. Pears and B. F. McGinness (London: Routledge & Kegan Paul, 1963), 4.5.

21. Ibid., 4.022.

22. Kant's 'I think that accompanies all my perceptions' is also over-propositionalised. It has other faults too, most notably (as we shall discuss) being bloodless, boneless and meatless, which makes it rather difficult to get a foothold on individuals. The notion of pre-propositional awareness – which embeds language more profoundly in the world – as the necessary context for the emergence of propositional discourse is an essential step in restoring language to its place in the consciousness of living beings after Fregean and other attempts to de-psychologise, indeed disinhabit, it, and treat it as a formal system that would work best in the absence of warm, sweaty users.

23. The global, or non-localised, nature of the Existential Intuition is connected with the fact that self-consciousness is not a subset of conscious experiences among others, but something that will seem to be implicit in other experiences – binding them at a particular time and over time. See Chapter 4 for further discussion of this.

24. In this section, I shall be dealing very briefly with topics that I have addressed in considerably more detail in other books, notably: *The Explicit Animal*, passim, but especially pp. 2–4 and 238–40; *On The Edge of Certainty*, especially pp. 2–17 and 155–88; and *A Conversation with Martin Heidegger* (Basingstoke: Palgrave, 2002), especially pp. 113–15.

25. Some readers may be prompted to recall F. P. Ramsay's deflation of the notion of truth: To assert 'p is true' is the same as to assert 'p'; therefore the concept of truth, or the predicate 'true' is empty. This is point-missing on a grand scale and we shall return to this in Volume 3 when we consider the nature of truth and, in particular, modern deflationist or minimalist theories.

26. In Tallis, *The Explicit Animal*.

27. Martin Heidegger, *Being and Time*, trans. Joan Stambaugh (New York: SUNY Press, 1996), p. 162.

28. Ibid., p. 255.

29. In Chapter 5, we shall distance ourselves from Heidegger's views, which overlook the centrality of the body. The inaugural 'That' has to have a home in order to be located and disclose a particular bit of the world. As we express it in that chapter, there is no *Da-sein*, being there, without *Fort-sein*, being-here; no 'That' can be naked: it has to be robed in flesh.

30. Gaskin, *Grammar in Early Twentieth-Century Philosophy*, p. 20.

31. Some of what follows has been stimulated by correspondence with Howard Robinson, for whose generous criticisms of an earlier version of some of these ideas I am grateful. I am not certain that I will have allayed his distrust of the Existential Intuition.

32. It is not, as Robinson suggested, merely a dummy universal or sortal doing nothing.

33. 'This' on its own would be insufficient as a complement of 'am'. As Anscombe ('The First Person', p. 148) points out, while demonstratives such as 'this' and 'that' 'are … non-names which function logically as names', 'I' could be neither reduced to a demonstrative nor merely linked to a demonstrative. The self-pointing of 'this' would still require further specification to identify *what* or *which* 'I' is – what is pointed to. (The use of 'is' and 'what' in this last sentence, shows how far off the mark we have drifted from 'I'.)
34. Quassim Cassam, *Self and World* (Oxford: Oxford University Press, 1997), p. v. I have been enormously stimulated by this remarkable book and have been prompted by it to articulate many of he most significant arguments of this volume.
35. John Lyons, *Semantics* (Cambridge: Cambridge University Press, 1977), Vol. 2, p. 636. I have discussed other aspects of the issues addressed in the next few paragraphs in *On the Edge of Certainty*, pp. 155–88. See especially pp. 165–9.
36. Ibid., p. 646.
37. The term 'deixis' comes from the Greek, meaning 'pointing' or 'indicating'. C. S. Peirce introduced 'indexical' to mean pointing. Indexicals point both inwards and outwards: outwards to the referents and inwards to the circumstances in which they are used, so that the referents can be determined. In the case of 'I' or other first-person indexicals, the pointings inwards and outwards are identical. Hence (perhaps) Perry's term 'the essential indexical'.

# CHAPTER 2

# 'Therefore I Am ...' The *Cogito* Argument and the Bio-Logic of First-Person Identity

## 2.1 FIRST-PERSON BEING AND THE EXISTENTIAL INTUITION: SOME INTRODUCTORY OBSERVATIONS

In the previous chapter we developed two distinct approaches to the Existential Intuition: one deals with its biogenesis, the other examines it as if it were a proposition of sorts. The former describes its biological provenance, the latter its philosophical logic. In this chapter, I want to see whether, and in what way, these two approaches may be related; whether, at the end of two journeys moving in the opposite direction, they might be connected, with the one journey moving inwards from a (remote) empirically-based 'outside' and the other moving outwards, under the pressure of logical argument, from the most intimate inside.

The endeavour in this chapter to investigate the 'bio-logic' of first-person being may be regarded in advance as fundamentally misconceived, driven by muddled thinking analogous to that which inspired psychologistic attempts to ground the meanings of terms in the processes by which speakers acquired them or the psychological accompaniments of their use. My constant cross-cutting between existential and logical approaches may make some philosophers feel that everything that has been gained since Gottlieb Frege is here forgotten or overlooked, and that we are back with J. S. Mill's *System of Logic* and Edmund Husserl's disastrous early attempts to psychologise arithmetic.[1] The analogy, I believe, is not entirely just. Anyway, the hazardous enterprise of linking the two approaches to first-person being – setting out from, respectively, Cartesian and bio-genetic starting points – is central to the purpose of this volume. My aim in this and the next few chapters will be to further understanding of the connections between logical arguments to the effect that the Cartesian 'I' must be embodied and the biological account that begins with living body and sees the 'I' arising from it. The twin facets (logical and existential) of the *assumption of self* that is the Existential Intuition will, I hope, cast further light on the embodied subject. This in turn will provide us with an approach to the two key characteristics of first-person being: (personal) identity and agency.

Philosophers in the analytical tradition in the twentieth century were very keen to make 'I' less mysterious: it may have been grammatically complex, but it was ontologically uninteresting – simple to the point of emptiness. For the earlier Wittgenstein, 'The subject does not belong to the world: rather it is a limit of the world'.[2] The subject, in fact, was dismissed along with the soul:

> there is no such thing as the soul – the subject etc. – as it is conceived in the superficial psychology of the present day.
> Indeed, a composite soul would no longer be a soul.[3]

And, for the later Wittgenstein, the notion of a substantive self having or housing thoughts, etc., to whom 'I' and other terms refer, is even less attractive: its mysteries are largely pseudo-puzzles created by philosophers ignorant of the philosophical grammar of natural languages.

To this viewpoint, we shall return. For the present we note that 'first-person being' is associated with various rather confusing entities, ideas or concepts: the self (or selfhood), the human subject, the person (or personhood), identity (or personal identity), the agent – to name just the few that immediately come to mind. These are in turn connected with other (higher-level) entities, ideas or concepts; for example, those of the actor, of the citizen, of one who bears responsibility and assumes duties, roles and offices, has a certain character, and leads a life in a world to some extent of her own choosing and accumulates a CV. At a more fundamental level, 'the first person' qualifies a lived, individual, 'private' viewpoint, which is contrasted with the public, collective and to some extent notional, third-person viewpoint: 'a view from somewhere', at the heart of egocentric space, or of an individual world, contrasted with the 'view from nowhere', the viewpointless view, that is the asymptote of objective science.[4]

While not denying the complexity of any of these entities or ideas – not to speak of the rather confused and confusing relations between them – I want to argue that the (relatively simple) Existential Intuition lies at the bottom of every manifestation of (truly) first-person being; without this Intuition, which is unique to mankind, there is no self (or selfhood) and nothing corresponding to personal identity or agency. The Existential Intuition is (implicitly) presupposed in them both, which is why it has tended to be overlooked; and this is also why, I believe, philosophers have found selfhood and agency so elusive, with the self apparently melting away on close inspection and agency seeming to have no place in the physical world. In Chapter 7, I shall argue that John Locke's account of personal identity, and neo-Lockean stories of the self, inevitably failed to grasp their object because they looked past the Existential Intuition and tried to locate selfhood in the connectedness of psychological contents that seemed somehow ownerless. In Chapter 8, I shall argue that the Existential Intuition lies at the heart of agency, explaining how, in particular, human beings can be 'a point of origin', a source of true actions, and consequently be able to change the course of nature.

I want, however, to begin by looking at something even more fundamental: the *logic* of first-person being; indeed, the 'bio-logic' of first-person identity already alluded to. This 'bio-logic' has, I believe, some interesting properties; in particular, an ability to generate new kinds of truth that are at once necessary and empirical, owing this property to the fact that they straddle existence and language, being direct intuitions of the speaker's existence cast in propositional (or pre-propositional) form. I shall examine this ability in the present chapter, while in Chapter 3, I will try (with limited success) to define the scope of those necessary truths and the limits of the incorrigibility of first-person assertions and of first-person authority.

## 2.2 THE PERMANENT SIGNIFICANCE OF THE *COGITO* ARGUMENT

The obvious place for this inquiry to start is with Descartes who, through the *Cogito* argument, placed first-person being at the centre of philosophical inquiry. Obvious, but perhaps best avoided. Over forty years ago Jaakko Hintikka, wrote:

> The fame (some would say the notoriety) of the adage *cogito, ergo sum* makes one expect that scholarly industry has long since exhausted whatever interest it may have historically or topically.[5]

Even if this was not true in 1962, it must surely, several thousands, perhaps tens of thousands of articles and books later, be true now. Not so. Hintikka's next sentence, 'A perusal of the relevant literature, however, fails to satisfy this expectation' may or may not be true. One would have to devote several lifetimes to check out 'the relevant literature'. Even so, it seems that the *Cogito* argument is inexhaustible because, both consciously and unconsciously, it touches on something absolutely fundamental about what we humans are.

I think: 'I think therefore I am'. As the argument seeps through my mind, it seems a perfect exemplar of philosophical thought: at once rigorous and profound, combining iron logic and an overwhelming sense of strange truth. When the excitement from the brilliance and unassailability of the argument settles down, however, disappointment creeps in. Descartes' *example* as a thinker – as someone committed to questioning everything, taking nothing for granted or on trust – comes to seem more impressive than this crucial and first positive result of his 'project of pure inquiry'. The validity of the *Cogito* argument seems beyond doubt. But what does the *Cogito* argument actually yield? What does the conclusion 'therefore I am' actually contain? What, how much, is placed beyond doubt?

This question has been posed many times since Descartes first published his argument. Some of the earliest objections were directed against his claim that immediate and indubitable awareness of his own thoughts allowed him not only to know *that* he was, but also *what* kind of entity he was; that he could proceed without loss of certainty from the (certain) knowledge that he was thinking to the belief that he was *a thinking being*; more precisely an immaterial substance whose essence was thought. Descartes' unassailable conclusion that he could not be deceived as to his own existence since the very fact that he was thinking (or doubting) that he existed necessarily implied that he did exist – his doubting put his existence as a doubter beyond doubt – did not deliver the larger conclusion 'that there is nothing which is easier for me to know than my mind'.[6] He was not justified in concluding from the infallibility of the *Cogito* argument that he could discover the essence of his self and know with certainty what he was. There was no reason to suppose that the self could be transilluminated by the introspective gaze of the thinking moment. His argument did not justify the assumption that he knew his own mind.

It was Gassendi who pointed to the fallacy in Descartes' step from 'knowing that he was thinking' to 'knowing that he was an immaterial substance whose essence was thought'. Because this step was fallacious, Descartes had failed, Gassendi argued, in his quest; namely, 'to discover not that you are a Thinking thing' (which even then is apparent only so long as you are thinking) 'but of what nature you, the thing that thinks, are'.[7] As Cassam expresses it: 'knowing that one is thinking does not give one *substantive* knowledge of what one is'.[8] The 'that' does not yield the 'what'.[9] Descartes, thinking that it did, concluded – crucially for his dualist ontology – that the indubitably existing I given in thought is a thinking substance who, given that he could not directly extend the same certainty to his body, could just as well be bodiless.[10] Unfortunately, it doesn't seem to include much of the 'thinking I''s self, even less his world, beyond the moment of thought.

It is difficult not to agree with Gassendi that Descartes has not delivered on the programme he had set out. The outward half of his journey – towards comprehensive doubt – seems (initially) more impressive than the return half – gradually widening certainty. This becomes even more apparent when Descartes goes beyond trying to find out what kind of creature he himself is and tries to place out of the reach of doubt many of the things he already believes and which have carried him through life hitherto. He cannot manage this without helping himself to one or two rather large free gifts, notably the assumption that the universe has been created by a God Who, being benign, would not be inclined systematically to deceive the thinker. Invoking God in this way looks like a way of getting back, free of charge – and clear of all charges – many things that systematic doubt had put in the dock. And the arguments for the existence of such a God – for example, the cosmological argument that only a God could have been the cause of our idea of God (because the cause must be adequate to the effect and we ourselves, who are imperfect and finite, could hardly be an adequate cause of the idea of a perfect, infinite being) – are even more vulnerable. All of which is very unsatisfactory, as many commentators have noted over the centuries.

Even so, the *Cogito* argument continues to attract – and seems to deserve to attract – intense interest. There is something in Descartes' argument, quite separate from his search for an unassailable bedrock for his beliefs, and independent of his unsatisfactory dualism, that draws one back again and again. For our present purposes, that something is the light it casts on the nature of first-person identity; more particularly on the *logic* of first-person identity or first-person identity statements (the inseparability of the two is central to that logic and opens the way to 'bio-logic'); more particularly still, on a profoundly interesting species of necessary truths that arise out of the intersection between logic and existence in the self-conscious existence of the thinking 'I'.

'I think therefore I am' is a thought that, being thought, supposedly demonstrates the existence of a thinker – the one who is thinking it; for, if there is thinking, there must be one who thinks. There can, Descartes argued, be 'no act or accident without a substance for it to belong to'[11] and hence there must be an I who is thinking.[12] While Descartes' belief that the I was a *thinking* substance, an *immaterial* mind, goes beyond what his argument actually delivers, the form of the argument is sound. If I am thinking (or arguing, or doubting) – even or especially thinking (or arguing, or doubting) that I *am* – I must exist; for the existence of such thinking is predicated on the existence of the thinker that is me. So much is incontrovertible. But as soon as the argument is used to generate, or derive, content, as soon as we assign referents to 'I', or impute substance to 'the one who is thinking' or whatever, the argument loses its immunity from doubt: it has gone beyond the scope of necessary truth.

As has often been observed, the more closely we scrutinise the *Cogito* argument the less it seems to establish. Indeed, it seems to shrink to a kind of tautology without empirical consequences. This could be expressed in different ways:

'I am now thinking therefore there is someone who is (now, thinking)'

or

'I am (now) thinking therefore I am (now) thinking'

and so on.

This is the essential disappointment of the *Cogito* argument: that it seems impossible to get more out of the conclusion than was put into the premises. Nothing new is generated, secured, guaranteed, placed beyond doubt. On the contrary, the uncharitable gaze might conclude that the right-hand side of

'I think therefore I am'

contains rather *less* than the left-hand side, since 'that I am' is somewhat less specified, informationally rich, than 'that I am thinking'. For to know merely that something exists is to know less than to know that it is in a particular state – namely, thinking.

This uncharitable view may miss the fundamental point of what Descartes was trying (at least initially) to achieve through the *Cogito* argument: to find just one unassailable, certain truth that will be proof against all doubt. And even if the doubt-resistant residue is minute, all that matters is that it should be *something*; that there should be an unyielding point from which the comeback campaign, which will reinstate the world razed by doubt, can be mounted. The uncharitable view, however, is justified once Descartes reveals his hand and uses this residue as the foundation of a reconstructed world-picture, similar in most important respects to the one that systematic doubt had razed. By default, however, this helps us to see where the continuing significance of the *Cogito* argument lies: not for its providing incontrovertible evidence for the reality of anything in a putatively objective world; but for its illuminating the nature of first-person being and the authority that such being enjoys.

Fully to appreciate this, it is necessary to see the *Cogito* argument from the first-person point of view – imagining it from within – and as something that exists not as a type, but as an indefinite number of token proofs actually being undertaken (experienced, undergone) by an individual and as providing grounds for resistance to particular doubts experienced by particular individuals at particular moments, rather than as an objective proof or the proof of some objective fact. As such, it imports much more than a mere tautological iteration. In many ways, the argument as it is usually set out on the page – as an argument-type – is best seen as a *recipe* for philosophers to demonstrate something to themselves. Something, in short, that indicates work to be done off the page.[13] It is not the thought 'He is thinking' or 'Someone is thinking' that carries the argument, but the thought 'I am thinking' or 'He – understood as an "I" – is thinking'. This central point – which has been made by many recent philosophers such as Hintikka, Kenny and Anscombe[14] to whom we shall return – is one whose full significance has not, I believe, been fully appreciated. Suffice it to say for the moment that the fact that the *Cogito* argument does its work as *a performative realised in a token rehearsal to one's self*, makes it a unique but revealing point of intersection between language and world, logic and existence.

Descartes invites you, the reader, fellow philosopher, fellow rational animal, not merely to follow an argument and to assent to a proof, but to undergo, and then to be rescued from, an ordeal: to be engulfed with doubt and then to be saved by a single certainty – which is available as soon as you recall that you are doubting.[15] The thought that you are drowning dries up the sea that threatens to engulf you. It is in the context of this lived, *token* doubt, this doubting-act (cf. speech act), that the *Cogito* argument imports content. Its content belongs to the first-person world, a world signalled by the 'I' that is posted at its entrance and reiterated within it.

Of course, it is possible to talk *about* 'I', as if from outside, in the third person – as 'the ego' and even 'the I' or 'the Cartesian I' – but in the present context this can be seriously misleading. Third-person 'I' is 'I' merely *mentioned* as a verbal type rather than being *used* as a verbal token to signify a particular individual who is the speaker, who is me. When 'I' is, as it were, in action then it cannot be separated from (first) persons. When it is on duty, doing its business, 'I', it hardly needs saying (though, as we shall see, some will deny this), refers to the person that is using it: while it has a general function, it has a singular reference in use;

its general function is to make that singular reference – to the person who is using it.[16]

It is easy to overlook this when discussing 'the' *Cogito* argument as it were from the outside: the 'I' under such circumstance is the general 'I'. The Cartesian demonstration, in which the word 'I' is tokenised, truly at work, in use rather than being referred to, employed in the context of an act of doubt followed by a saving realisation, is a first-person experience not a third-person fact or proof. For the force of the *Cogito* argument to be properly understood, and for its proof to be seen to rescue more than an extensionless dot from the universal wreck of universal doubt, it must be viewed 'from within', from inside the experience of the individual engaging in it. The 'I' that is the twice repeated subject of the argument must be recognised as being identical with the 'I' who is imagined to be rehearsing the proof.

In due course, I shall argue that the essence of the Cartesian invitation is to remember – repeat, rehearse – the Existential Intuition; more specifically the intuition of *one's own* existence. I want to argue that the latter, being a self-realising (or self-fulfilling) realisation, is unassailable. That is where the *Cogito* argument gets its necessity. What is more, given the biological origin, the rootedness, of the Intuition, this is where it also gets the content that eluded Descartes. This content is more defensible than the content Descartes attributed to the 'I' ('the thinking substance') he rescued from the whirlpool[17] of doubt and offered the ungrateful (to judge from the torrent of objections his argument attracted within a few years of its publication) philosophical community; and it has more substantive content than what most contemporary philosophers will allow that the *Cogito* yields.

Many will reject invoking the Existential Intuition as a way of augmenting the meagre Cartesian yield on the grounds that it assumes precisely the kinds of things – bodies, science, etc. – that Descartes set aside at the beginning of his *Meditations*. Accusations of indulging in an *à la carte* rather than an *à la Descartes* scepticism and of putting the horse (or the biological body) before the *Descartes* are to be expected. After all, it is no great achievement to get a more substantive output from an argument if one helps oneself to more generously provided input. This is perfectly true, but it does not take account of the fundamental point, which I shall develop in due course: that you cannot really begin where Descartes began. The Cartesian thinker cannot in fact drop as much as he pretends to do when he undergoes the ordeal of systematic doubt.

This latter point has been made by many philosophers – including in modern times Wittgenstein and Merleau-Ponty – but I believe that there is more to it than a denial of the possibility of the Cartesian *epoche*. For I believe that (to use a typical contemporary formulation of the *Cogito* argument) 'the belief that one has a thought is enough to justify that belief',[18] that there is no possible world in which a thinker can think without existing, is a late reflection of an equally unassailable intuition – the Existential Intuition – which gives a much more substantive yield.

I shall let this belief stand for the present and return to its defence later. First, I shall discuss a) the necessary truth of the Existential Intuition, and b) the content it derives from its biological origin. Together, these will provide the first hints of an 'existential grammar' of first-person being; of a logic of beings whose mode of being is 'am-ing' rather than 'is-ing'.

### 2.3 THE BORING LOGIC OF THIRD-PERSON IDENTITY STATEMENTS[19]

For many philosophers, the disappointing outcome of the *Cogito* argument – the meagre quantity of necessary or incontrovertible truth it really does secure – is exactly what might be expected, irrespective of whether one construes necessity as a (*de dicto*, modal) property attributed to propositions whose denial is formally self-contradictory or whether it is construed as a (*de re*) property of objects in the world.[20] Necessity at best sets limits in the broadest (and hence emptiest) sense to the actual, without in any way specifying what actually turns out to be the case. More narrowly, it describes the limits to co-occurrence of states of affairs – a surface cannot be both red and blue – or the concurrent truth of assertions – Not 'p and not-p'. The realm of the necessarily true has rather unexciting contents: in the *de dicto* department, propositions whose denial is self-contradictory; in the *de re* department, objects (part objects, events, etc.) that are identical with themselves. Another way of looking at the poverty of the realm of the necessarily true is that logical arguments do not yield new data, so that empirical beliefs cannot be rooted in necessity: they cannot be incontrovertible. Given that you cannot get something for nothing – empirical facts out of logical arguments – Descartes is very lucky to add (or seem to add) what little he does do to his initial premises.

How do we fare if we re-present the *Cogito* argument as an invitation to recall the Existential Intuition in the (propositional) form of a transparently necessary truth? How do things look if we repackage

  'I think therefore I am'

as

'That I am this [x]'

as an inescapable particular (indeed for each token instance, singular) truth; something which, despite being fact-like, cannot be denied?

'That I am this' appears, if 'this' is not further specified, to be both a necessary relationship and (not unconnectedly) an identity relationship. It looks a bit like a tautology and at the same time something a little more substantive than a tautology; at any rate trivial; a mere relation between two demonstratives – 'I' and 'this' – which, if not further specified, seems boringly unassailable because rather uninformative.[21] How much more substantive the Intuition is than a mere tautology depends on how we cash the [x] tucked away in the square brackets.

As we have just mentioned, *de re* necessary truths most typically take the form of identity relationships. *De dicto* necessary truths, beyond the general laws of non-contradiction

Not both p and not-p

or

p necessarily implies not not-p

can also take the form of identity relations. As an indirect way of getting hold of what is special about identity relations forged by 'am', it is useful to contrast them with those identity relations – or more precisely identity statements – linked by 'is', which have an overwhelming preponderance in the philosophical literature.

Here are two sorts of 'is' identity statements:

1. (transparent) assertion of the self-identity of singulars;
2. assertion of the identity of a singular accessed through two different referring expressions (different names, different descriptions).[22]

### 1. Referentially transparent assertion of the self-identity of singulars

This is the classical tautology:

A is A.

It says that (for example) an object is [identical with] itself.[23] This is a necessary truth, whose contradiction is impossible. It is true in all possible worlds and has no possible counter-instances. If assertions of this kind seem to be privileged in their immunity from error, this is because they are empty: they do not assert empirical truths; they highlight nothing factually new in the world. They are not strictly contentless – not at least when the variable 'A' is given a specific value, such as this pen in my hand – but there is no difference between the content of the left-hand side and the content of the right-hand side of the identity assertion. Nothing is added when we move from one side to the other of the equation and it is, moreover, *clearly evident* that nothing is added: it does not require a special knowledge of language or information about the world to know or to see that nothing is added. This emptiness is the key to their necessity: if anything was added, then the equation would be contingently true. 'I am this', by contrast, doesn't quite fit the model of such a tautology because there are readings of 'this' that make the identity relation informative.

## 2. Assertion of the identity of a singular accessed through two different referring expressions

There should, as W. V. O. Quine pointed out, be only one kind of identity relation: the identity of things with themselves. This is a bit disappointing:

> to say of anything that is identical with itself is trivial, and to say that it is identical with anything else is absurd. What then is the use of identity?[24]

Some of the philosophical interest in identity statements comes from those cases, first highlighted by Frege, in which the same individual thing may be accessed by two or more names or referring phrases that capture different sub-groups of its characteristics. The same referent may be accessed by expressions which have different senses. It may therefore be of use to assert the identity of the referent of two different expression. Under certain circumstances assertions to this effect may be non-empty, because the identity may not be apparent to everyone. The assertion is informative.

The surface form of this identity relation is 'B is (the same as) C' but, since B and C refer to the same entity (A), its underlying form is actually

A (= B) is A (= C).

Standard examples include the identity between the Morning Star and the Evening Star (which are identical, as the 'two stars' are the same star observed at different times of the day) and between Walter Scott and 'the author of *Waverley*'. The former we owe to Frege, the latter to Russell.[25]

In certain (so-called 'extensional') contexts which do not incorporate individuals' beliefs or knowledge about what is out there but deal 'directly' with what is out there, the identity of the Morning Star and the Evening Star (both are Venus) does not require saying; and saying it adds nothing to the sum total of asserted truths. Under other ('intensional') contexts it may count as a genuine empirical truth – something that someone did not know and could usefully be informed of. The identity in Frege's example holds, irrespective of whether the identity between the Morning Star and the Evening Star is understood to be either:

a) a contingent truth about language – 'That such and such a star has two names'; or
b) a contingent truth about the world –
   (i)   that there is a star which is visible in the morning and visible in the evening whose two manifestations are sufficiently different or sufficiently disconnected for it to be thought of as two stars – that leads to a truth about language;
   (ii)  in consequence of which the star has two names,

reinforcing the (false) belief in some people's minds that it is two different stars, so that (another empirical consequence) it is not vacuous to point out that the one is the same as the other.

The non-vacuousness of the identity *assertion* carries a price. While the identity relation is true in all possible worlds, in so far as the 'Morning Star' *is* the 'Evening Star', the substitution of one term for the other in a description of someone's beliefs may alter the truth conditions of that description. It does not follow from the fact that Fred believes that the Morning Star has certain properties that he believes that the Evening Star has those same properties. We may say that the identity holds at the level of the object but not at the level of discourse about the object. At this second level, the contingency of the underpinning facts – the apparent course of a particular star across the sky; what some people do and some people don't know about the apparent (interrupted) course of this star; how this star attracts two names because of this course; and what people do and don't know about this naming – reduces the scope of necessity. Just because I believe that the Morning Star has certain properties, it does not follow that I must (for consistency) believe that the Evening Star also has those properties. If, on the hand, I believe that 'A' (e.g. the 'Morning Star') has certain properties (such as appearing in the morning) it follows that I ought to believe that 'A' (the

'Evening Star') also has those properties. This is why it is not vacuous to point out that the Morning Star is the Evening Star and why, in this world, people actually do so.[26]

The fact that Walter Scott is the author of *Waverley* is apparently a more full-bloodedly contingent empirical truth about the world – about objects in the world rather than discourse about the world. Scott might still have been himself and not written the Waverley novels: he might have been killed before he did so. This identity between 'Walter Scott' and the 'author of *Waverley*' is contingent; and not only is it not true in all possible worlds, but its empirical vulnerability is not simply the result of certain empirical facts about language or of the knowledge and beliefs of language users or the definition and use of terms. It has necessity neither in virtue of definitions of terms nor in virtue of the properties of the object it describes. Its empirical payload is a reflection of the wider range of possible worlds in which the identity it asserts does *not* hold. The assertion of the identity relationship is more truly informative, and consequently its necessity is more deeply undermined.[27] (It could be argued, correctly, that the difference between the two cases is more apparent than real, more superficial than fundamental: after all Venus might have taken a less confusing course and not attracted two names, just as surely as Scott might not have written *Waverley*.)

These examples of 'is' identity relations that are necessary in all possible worlds ('A is A') and identity relations that are necessary in extensional though not in intensional contexts that involve beliefs ('The Morning Star is the Evening Star') have been invoked to illustrate the widely acknowledged principle that, as we move away from referentially transparent (and therefore rather dull) assertions of the identity of an object with itself, there is a trade-off between new information carried by the assertion of the identity relation (as measured as a difference between what is on the left and what is on the right-hand side of 'is') and loss of necessity and of immunity from error. Indeed, there seems to be an either/or: either vacuity or corrigibility. What we may call the net content of the assertion, the information it carries, reduces the range of worlds in which, or the conditions under which, it would be true. This illustrates a general principle: *You can't get something for nothing*. The choice is between:

a) the empty necessity of assertions which require no knowledge, either of language or of the world, of the lexicon or the encyclopaedia, to be asserted safely, in complete confidence of their truth, because they carry no empirical cargo at all, and are true in all possible worlds; and

b) content without necessity, which places us at the mercy of lexicons and encyclopaedias, of contingent facts about the knowledge and beliefs certain individuals have, or even their direct experience, which may refute any assertion one makes.

Assertions of identity are either void of factual content but true in all possible worlds or factually contentful but lacking necessity, being untrue in some possible worlds – in a world in which, say, language is differently structured and words have different semantic relations; or people have different knowledge and beliefs; or things are (contingently) different. The range of things that are necessarily true and so one cannot sensibly doubt them because one cannot be mistaken about them seems pretty unimpressive.

### 2.4 SAUL KRIPKE TRIES TO LIVEN THINGS UP

This argument may seem very old-fashioned, close to the empiricist or logical positivist position that necessity holds only in the propositions of mathematics and logic, and in semantic truths that express the translation of words into their synonyms. Most damagingly, it may appear to ignore the discussion of an entirely new kind of necessary truth – of the essential necessity of identity (the idea that, if x = y, then, *necessarily*, x = y) – inaugurated by Kripke's writings in the 1970s.[28]

Kripke examined the various characteristics of necessary and contingent truths and found them to be separable. For example, he challenged the standard assumption that the distinction between the necessary or analytic and the contingent or synthetic maps on to the distinction between the *a priori* and the *a posteriori*. He has argued that there are statements that are necessarily true which nevertheless can be known only through experience and be contingently discovered. As Baldwin has expressed it:

> The a priori/empirical distinction concerns the ways in which rational thinkers have come to knowledge of the world; thus it involves a conception of meaning tied to the process of understanding, to the ways of thinking of things characteristic of the words employed. By contrast, the necessary/contingent distinction concerns whether things might be other than they are; so it involves a conception of meaning that looks to the product of understanding, to the truth conditions of the sentence.[29]

Consider the proposition

Water is $H_2O$

This, it is argued, is both necessary (it would be true in all possible worlds) and *a posteriori* – in the sense that it is something that had to be *discovered*. Indeed, it has been known and generally accepted only for a couple of centuries or so. Kripke asserts that the necessity of this empirical identity derives from the fact that both 'water' and 'H$_2$O' are 'rigid designators'. A rigid designator is a word whose meaning is such that it designates the same thing in all possible worlds in which it designates anything: it is a term which stands for the same object in every possible world in which it has a reference at all. It is a linguistic instrument by which we can get hold of an object reliably in order to identify that different referring expressions may refer to the same thing: a royal or direct or privileged road to a referent that enables us to see that expressions with different senses are, indeed, accessing the same referent. The rigidity of the rigid designator is ultimately traceable to a baptismal moment of naming (of which more presently), which (apparently) is best mediated by direct ostension or pointing which, as it were, bypasses language – and its non-rigid descriptive phrases – in order to attach a name to an object. Using a rigid designator enables us to think about a thing's essential properties and by this means it is possible to see the necessary components of its identity; indeed the necessity of its identity inhering in its essence. According to Kripke, ordinary names – dog, rose, coffee – are rigid designators.

Disagreement with Kripke has taken many forms. Davidson, for example, has questioned the very idea of a 'rigid designator',[30] and it certainly seems very obscure. The notion that proper names, the paradigm rigid designators, acquire their rigidity through an 'original baptism' at which the name is introduced by ostension, an appropriate object being singled out for naming by a demonstrative expression such as 'this child' which has an unequivocal referent in a confined context, has also been questioned. While this seems an intuitively attractive way of pinning language to real referents in the real world – though Wittgenstein pointed out the naivety of this notion – it seems unlikely that names spread out from the baptismal font through an entire community of discourse like an infectious disease without the members of that community having to learn (contingent) things about the world in which designator and designated are connected. What is more, it is not clear that the spread of the name from the baptismal font of ostension does not result in contamination, or a softening, of rigid designation. If this is not guaranteed, then, given the limits (pointed out by Wittgenstein) to what can be individuated through ostention, Kripke's essential necessity of identity does not go beyond something that might be expressed in two stabs of an ostensive gesture accompanying the mantra

This is necessarily this

which hardly breaks new ground. In an attempt to clarify the notion of a rigid designator, and in support of the claim that water has an essential identity, so that 'water' could not mean anything other than $H_2O$, Putnam employed a thought experiment in which he imagined space travellers coming upon a planet, Twin-Earth, which appears in every respect to be like our own Earth, even down to its inhabitants. The water looks, tastes and in every other respect appears like our water. However, it proves to have a different chemical composition: XYZ instead of $H_2O$. Putnam argues that, although the Twin-Earthers call this stuff 'water', they are not entitled to do so: it is not water at all, because the reference of our term water is fixed by the fact that it is learned, and used, as a name for the aqueous liquid on earth, which is $H_2O$ and not XYZ.

As Baldwin points out, the scientific definition of water and other 'natural kinds' is not as rigid as it seems. Not only is it possible to imagine a world in which something with the experienceable properties of water turned out not to be $H_2O$ and yet was legitimately called water, we live in such a world. There are different kinds of water; even different kinds of the hydrogen that makes up the water molecule. All that remains true is that 'the ways in which sciences such as chemistry identify natural kinds implies that certain properties are characteristic of normal samples under standard conditions' – which represents a considerable retreat from rigidly designated natural kinds and a full-blown necessity of essential identity and identity assertions that are both contentful (to the point of being empirically discoverable) and necessary.[31]

The essential flaw in Kripke's claim to have discovered statements that are both necessary and *a posteriori* or synthetic is more easily seen in his revisiting of the Morning Star/Evening Star example. The truth of the assertion that 'The Morning Star is the Evening Star' is, he says, both necessary and *a posteriori*. If both Morning Star and Evening Star are Venus, then they must necessarily be identical with one another because Venus cannot merely contingently be identical with itself. Yet knowledge of their identity, far from being a free gift, was the fruit of a good deal of observation. This is not, however, proof that there can be truths that are both necessary and *a posteriori*, discovered only through experience. It is proof only that necessary and contingent truths may be closely associated – though not inseparable.

To demonstrate this, let us separate what is necessary and *a priori* from what is contingent and *a posteriori* in the identity of Venus:

a) Necessary and known *a priori*:
   (i)  That Venus is (identical with) Venus.
   (ii) That all the manifestations of Venus – its manifestations in the morning and its manifestations in the evening – are manifestations of Venus.
b) Contingent and/or discovered *a posteriori*:
   (i)   That the star called Venus exists.
   (ii)  That Venus is observed by, and so has manifestations to, human beings.
   (iii) That Venus has two sets of manifestations that are sufficiently separated in space and time for humans to believe that they are manifestations of a different star.
   (iv)  That these two sets of manifestations are so striking and so distinct that they attract distinct attention and receive different names.
   (v)   That this is sufficient to make people think that there is a Morning Star *and* an Evening Star.
   (vi)  That some people know that the Morning Star and the Evening Star are manifestations of the same state before others do and on the basis of this positional advantage make information-bearing statements to this effect to those who are still ignorant of this.

The observation of two phases of Venus that are so separate that they seem to be different stars, and the naming of those two sets of manifestations, create the contingent background to the contingent discovery that the Morning Star and the Evening Star are in fact manifestations of the same star.

While it is a necessary truth that Venus is identical with Venus and that all manifestations of Venus are manifestations of Venus, it does not follow from this that a) those manifestations should have been experienced; and b) they should have been dissociated from one another; so that c) they should have been linked in an identity assertion. For it is entirely possible that the star which has the manifestations of the Morning Star could have turned out to have been an entirely different star from that which had the manifestations of the Evening Star. The fact that they have been demonstrated to be two phases of the same star does not make it retrospectively necessary that this is how things should have turned out any more than it should have been necessarily the case that the spatio-temporal relationships between humans and Venus should have been such as to create the firm impression of their being two stars. Admittedly, now that we know that the Morning Star and the Evening Star are the same star, it appears necessary that they should be the same star, on the grounds that 'A' is necessarily the same as 'A': there is no world in which it could be 'not-A'.

Kripke seems to be making the mistake of reading back, or reinserting, into the object of which stargazers speak – which is necessarily identical with itself – the set of discourses about the object which have (relatively recently) arisen out of the relationship of humans to the object – which are contingent; of merging the contingencies of knowledge about an object with the necessary relationship to itself that can be imputed to it. This 'retrospective necessity' – or reinsertion of a *de dicto* necessity into things – is not equivalent to the prior (and posterior) necessity of the Cartesian assertion that 'I think therefore I am' or the necessary truth (and therefore justification) of the belief that I am at present thinking. And it is to this that we must now return.

### 2.5 THE ANOMALOUS (AND INTERESTING) LOGIC OF FIRST-PERSON IDENTITY STATEMENTS

We have travelled a long way from the Existential Intuition and our initial claim that first-person identity assertions are unique in combining necessity with empirical content. Our lengthy journey into 'is' identity was necessary in order to defend one half of this assertion; namely that, in the case of third-person identity statements, there is, notwithstanding Kripke's claims, a trade-off between necessity and content. Let us now return to the Existential Intuition and examine whether the iron law of the trade-off between necessity and empirical content, incorrigibility and content, still applies – whether, in short, Descartes was on the right track in pursuing necessary, indubitable and, because singular, empirical or information-bearing truths in first-person assertions. And whether we could follow him down the same track and get a little further than he did.

The identity relation asserted in the Existential Intuition

'[That] I *am* this [entity, something, thing]'

in which the elements on either side of the identity – 'I' and 'this' – are linked not by 'is' but by 'am', certainly *seems* to operate under more liberal rules than do 'is' identities. What comes out of the right-hand side is apparently different from what is put on the left-hand side and 'different from' must here mean 'more than'; for we do not lose 'I am I' when we gain 'I am this' and when 'this' gets specified as some x. At the same time, there appears to be a necessity about this identity: it does not seem to be the kind of thing that is open to disproof in the light of any conceivable future experience. (This will need to be qualified: the permitted ingredients of the right-hand side – the x that fulfils the demonstrative – will have to be specified carefully, as we shall do in due course.)

How is this breach of the fundamental rule of identity assertion – that if you get out more than you put in, you lose necessity – possible? It is because (to put it in a rather crude and vulnerable way) identity in an Existential Intuition is not merely *discovered* but *asserted* – and, what is more, *under such conditions that the assertion of the identity makes it true*. 'Am' does not merely report a pre-existing objective identity that has been accidentally found by the individual asserting/thinking/feeling the Intuition, but in some sense brings it about. The Intuition *establishes* or *lays down* the identity; indeed, it precedes any discovery of a factual identity relation. 'Am' is a mode of identification that is not merely epistemologically *a priori* but existentially *a priori*. It is a prior *assumption* – in at least two senses of the verb, as we shall explore presently – and is neither the mere product of a logical derivation nor a mere factual truth revealed by experience. It is self-realising; more precisely, it is 'a self-realising realisation'. In consequence, it seems to be a truth that is both necessary (as Descartes allowed himself to presuppose, believing that other philosophers would share this presupposition) and yet able to incorporate specific, empirical content. The Intuition affirms an identity relation that seems to be able to eat its cake logically and still have a bit of cake empirically.

We still haven't got to the bottom of this extraordinary property of first-person or 'am' identity. Let us look at it again. If I were to assert 'I am I' (or even 'I am that I am'), this would be a manifest tautology, not much more impressive than 'A is A' or 'A is the A that it is'. If I were to assert that 'I am this' – i.e. *a* this, or *some* this, where the demonstrative remains unspecified – I would still remain within the boundaries of conventional analytical statements. The assertion would simply be an iteration of the semantic rule that 'this' applies to whatever is more proximate to one's self (in contrast to 'that', which applies to whatever is less proximate) and nothing could be more proximate to myself than that which I am. Where, however, the assertion 'I am this' means a particular, specified this – for example, a particular living body, or a part of it – then we have something that escapes the iron law in accordance with which necessity and content are mutually exclusive. The latter would take one as far as 'I am *a* this', or 'I am *some* this', but not as far as 'I am *this* this'. The purely linguistic or logically necessary link is between 'I' and '*a* this' but not between 'I' and '*this* this'. To get from *a* this (some this, any old this) – which is a member of a class of 'thises' that has only virtual or notional existence – to a particular this, to *this* this, which has actual existence – we need to go beyond logical (and/or semantic) necessity as conventionally understood and which is available to third-person or 'is' or 'factual' identity relations. Logical necessity and semantic necessity, which legislate respectively over the general form of valid arguments and the general rules for the use of words, do not accommodate actual existence. To import actual (contingent) existence (and existents), an additional assumption is required: this is the assumption embedded in the Existential Intuition, which, at least when it is presented in a propositional form, straddles logic and existence, language and life.

In the Intuition

'[That] I am this [x]'

where x has a particular realisation or instantiation, logical necessity is welded to existential truth. The necessary truth of the Existential Intuition is not purely intra-linguistic – otherwise it would be empty – because it is not purely a proposition (and may only rarely, outside of philosophical discussion, take explicit propositional form). Strictly, we should talk about its 'necessity' only when we treat it as a pure proposition, as an assertion that has the form '*That* such-and-such is the case ...'. For the most part, we should remove both the prefixed 'That' and the quotation marks: it is simply what is assumed to be the case in a self-fulfilling or self-realising realisation, as syntactically unstructured as a blush. The Intuition is a self-realising realisation that does not move from left to right; and the propositional form is a distant, late, expression of this. Descartes' *Cogito* argument is a later, yet more distant, reflection of this late, distant reflection.

The propositional form we have imposed on the Existential Intuition in this discussion is, however, justified[32] – and for two reasons:

a) That which imports actual existence into the necessary truths of first-person identity may be described as an *assumption* (used in a double sense to be explored presently); and

b) The 'that' of the Existential Intuition is the origin of the explicitness which characterises the 'Explicit Animal' for whom sentience is supplemented by knowledge. As I shall argue in Volume 3, The Existential Intuition is the 'ur-proposition' which underpins the special consciousness of humans, the propositional awareness they do not share with any other creatures.

For the present, we shall focus on the (unassailable) *assumption* that imports necessity into the Existential Intuition which, when presented in the form of a proposition, looks to be contingent.

The existence of Raymond Tallis, and the form that existence takes, are just matters of fact; but when Raymond Tallis asserts of himself that he exists – or that he thinks he exists – this is a matter of necessity: it could not be untrue. When, moreover, Raymond Tallis asserts, under the aegis of the Existential Intuition, 'I am this ...', this too is necessarily the case, for the reason that the identity that is being conferred is being conferred *by* that *on which* it is conferred.[33] This identity of the donor and the recipient of identity is what I want to capture by saying that first-person identity is 'assumed'. It is assumed by a living creature; and it is this that gives it the content that its necessary truth leads one to expect that it should lack.

### 2.6 THE EXISTENTIAL INTUITION AS A BIO-LOGICAL ASSUMPTION

The Existential Intuition 'That I am [this] ...' – delivered to early humans by the hand-as-tool by the process described in section 1.2 – has two aspects: consciousness of self in the form of bodily self-awareness or awareness of the behaviourally engaged body; and the sense of this embodied self as an agent.[34] We may imagine that the initial intuition delivered to early 'Handyman' would be of the engaged organism (its body) interacting with its environment in a way that is objectively (for example, to the retrospective eye of the biologist who later emerged) purpos*ive* – for instance, serving a need (one experienced as a directed appetite such as hunger for a particular edible item) – though not fully purpose*ful* in the sense of being driven by, and explicitly addressed towards achieving, a goal that is explicit to the organism. (Hungers, unlike reasons, do not have to be formulated, assented to, understood or even intuited, to energise and shape behaviour.) The primitive self-consciousness of that early hominid could be captured by 'am' where the scope of 'am' is of that part of the body as it is experienced as engaged in the purposive behaviour; or the body in so far as it is thus engagedly experienced and experientially engaged. 'Am' would *suffuse* the engaged body. (We shall try to get a better grasp on this in Chapter 5 and especially Chapter 6.)

We may imagine this earliest form of the Existential Intuition as an unspoken (and decidedly pre-linguistic) 'That I am this' – a non-intellectualised analogue to the Kantian subject with its 'I think that accompanies all my perceptions', though crucially different from the latter inasmuch as it is a) fleshly and b) active in the empirical world. It shares with the Kantian subject the character of being an *assumption* (in the logical sense): it does not have to be 'proved' (nor could it be). But, unlike the Kantian subject, which is somewhat empty – 'a mere form of consciousness', a purely 'logical' subject of the 'universal representation of self-consciousness'[35] – it is also an assumption in a different sense: the active body is assumed in the way that one 'assumes an office' or The Son of God 'assumed flesh'. This second sense gives the 'am' the fleshiness and engagement with a specific, empirical world that is so difficult to understand in the case of the ethereal Kantian subject. Primordial 'am' is an assumption by itself of a meaty being engaged with the material world. It is the engaged organism assuming itself as 'myself'.

As such, it cannot be in error: this biologically-based self-assumption is a subject truth which, because it does not depend on third-person objective facts about the material world, is incorrigible. (Though *what* I am at present saying about it does depend on third-person facts and thereby hangs a tale – as we shall come to presently.) Indeed, it looks rather like a tautology: 'I am this' may be unpacked to 'I am that which I assume as me'. Or 'I am that which I *am*', where the second 'am' has a whiff of transitivity. The Existential Intuition is effectively a tautology that has a purchase on an existing being: it is a point of intersection between logic and existence, what must be the case and what actually is the case. Let us examine this a bit more and see how it differs from, and takes us further than, the incorrigible core – the 'I that thinks' – uncovered by the Cartesian meditation.

I cannot be mistaken that I am. That much is common to the *Cogito* argument and the present discussion. Beyond this there are fundamental differences. All that Descartes could really establish – so long as his argument remained out there, on the page, and did not present itself as an invitation, a recipe for something each of us has to do for ourselves – is that there is a moment of thought that 'I' can know with certainty is my thought. Cartesian incorrigibility does not extend beyond this. It does not, as we have noted, give me a guarantee that my present thinking is the manifestation, or proof of the existence, of a thinking substance that I am – if I am thought of as someone to whom such a thing *has to be proved*. Even less is it able to provide incontrovertible proof of the existence of my body. The Cartesian 'I' is cut off from the material world, even that part of it which he feels himself to be – his body – inasmuch as that feeling is seen to be an implicit claim which stands in need of proof or evidence. While the certainty of my own mind's momentary existence (so long as I am thinking) is beyond doubt for Descartes, that of my body is not; the reality of the body and the truth of my belief that I am embodied remain in question, unless they are guaranteed indirectly by a benign God Who would not deceive me.

By contrast, beginning from the standpoint of the Existential Intuition, I can hardly be mistaken that I am this engaged body; or to put it another way, that I am suffering the being of this body. I may be mistaken over certain details – for example, I may feel a limb that is not there (as when an amputee suffers from phantom limb pain) and feel that that limb is part of me. But I cannot be mistaken that it is I who am struggling, say, to manipulate a particular object. Or that it is I who am feeling malaise. 'Am' is irrefutable in part because it is global or diffuse: self-consciousness overarches specific contents of consciousness. It makes no particular claims about the referents of particular elements of my experience of myself. The Existential Intuition is not to be thought of as a matted block of propositions or implicit assertions.

Talk of incorrigibility may ring alarm bells. The assertion that I cannot be mistaken that it is I who am struggling to *do* something may suggest an attempt to sneak into the scope of irrefutable self-consciousness matters of objective fact. Isn't there something fishy about smuggling the body into the charmed circle of the incorrigible? For while it is not possible that I could be mistaken that 'I am' – the use of the word 'I' guarantees not only that it has a referent but also that it is present[36] and adding 'am' seems an innocent enough move, adding nothing – it surely remains possible that I could be mistaken in believing that 'I am this thing', where the thing in question is my engaged body. After all, one may dream that one is a flying creature with the body of a bird.

We may be tempted to bypass this objection by considering where we are beginning: with the existence of a creature – an early hominid (or a developing infant) – which then gradually assumes its body as its own. This assumption is an act of appropriation of its body as itself. It is not merely 'a statement to that effect' but an enactment of it; or, more precisely, a 'dawning to it'. The sense of 'am' that suffuses the needing, appetitive, engaged body is not a random alighting on a thing which one then chooses to be; nor is it a discovery that one is this thing (rather than some other thing), an act of identifying which bit of the world is oneself, a discovery, which could in theory prove to be mistaken. On the contrary, it is an engaged, aware body assuming itself as itself. It is difficult to see how this assumption could be open to correction. The body is *built into* the Existential Intuition and so cannot be mistaken; it is what I assume when I *am* in that quasi-active, quasi-transitive sense alluded to earlier.

From the Cartesian point of view, 'That I am this [say, engaged body]' would be an assumption in only one of the two senses given just now: it would be a starting premise, and a very vulnerable one at that. From the bio-logical point of view, by contrast, it is an assumption in a more profound sense which is not amenable to disproof (or even proof): an appropriation of the thing that one intuits that one is. It is a carnal assumption. The 'I' assumed in the Existential Intuition is not a given but a taken – or a given that is taken: its truth is brought about in its assumption. The assumption of the identity is by that whose identity is assumed. The carnal assumption, its existence conditions, also bring about its truth conditions. Proof is not necessary, nor is disproof possible, because we have living, or lived, proof of the Existential Intuition.

### 2.7 THE NECESSARY TRUTH OF THE EXISTENTIAL INTUITION

In Chapter 3, we shall subject the unusual logical properties of the Existential Intuition to further examination, with the primary aim of defining the limits of its incorrigibility in such a way as to head off concern that we may be going down a path that will lead to the absurd position that I am whatever I assume myself to be in the narrowly factual sense, so that if I believe I am Napoleon, I am Napoleon. For the present I want to defend the current arguments against a principled opposition to the direction they are taking.

It is usually (and usually correctly) regarded as a mistake to mix discussion of the logical properties of terms with discussion of their origin; to try to connect how they function with their genesis. Attempts to explain the operation of, say, connectives such as 'or' by referring to mental processes in individuals such as the uncertainties and hesitations of speakers give us no insight into what they do and how they function, into the work they do in their typical or proper settings, as in a truth-table. Likewise, explaining concepts in terms of the experiences that generated them tells us nothing about how they fit into the system of language: sense experiences, for example, do not give us the semantic fields of words or the relationships between them. This was why Frege was so averse to the psychologism of the early Husserl and why he tried to expel the contents of consciousness from the logical inquiry into thoughts.[37] To connect the logic of 'am' with the distinctive biology of the human species, as I have done, may seem to take the vice of psychologism to new depths. But the very fact that rooting the Intuition in biology is *not* a deep misunderstanding reaches the heart of the anomalous logic of first-person identity and to the intuitions that are at the heart of this volume.

Am, as we have said, is about the *assumption*, the positive *assertion* of identity: it is about the 'taken' as well as the 'given'.[38] To grasp this, it is necessary to understand the distinction, applicable to 'normal' assertions, between their existence conditions – the conditions that predispose to their being asserted – and their truth conditions; between the existence conditions that make a truth (or a falsehood) exist, that is, be made explicit or even be asserted, and the truth conditions that make it true (or false) – or what (to use the current popular phrase) we may call its 'truth-makers'. The existence conditions are what make the truth-makers be, count as, truth-makers: they transform mere states of affairs into truth-makers, into those things that have to be the case in order that the assertion should be true.

Let us illustrate this with Tarski's well-known example of an assertion,[39] the one he invoked to illustrate his semantic version of the correspondence theory of truth: '"Snow is white" is true if and only if snow is white'. This correspondence, truth, does not inhere in the whiteness of snow, or white snow, considered in itself. To put this another way – and one that connects more deeply with the arguments of this trilogy – white snow does not yield '*That* snow is white'. As Frege pointed out, sense-experiences do not of themselves yield truths, as 'being true is not a material, perceptible property'.[40] Assertions, even assertions that are true, are no more to be found in material nature than are quotation marks. The correspondence between the assertion 'Snow is white' and the whiteness of snow is not available to be unpacked from white snow as it is in itself.[41] While the whiteness of snow is the truth condition of 'Snow is white', it is not of itself an existence condition of the truth that snow is white; nor even, until the existence condition is created, does it *count* as – have the status of – a truth condition. Something additional is required to turn the whiteness of snow into something that is true, or into the truth *that* snow is white. This additional something is an assertion, or something like it, to the effect *that* snow is white.[42]

The existence conditions of third-person truths (for example, assertions or thoughts) and the truth conditions of the assertions that assert them are independent. It is possible to imagine a world in which there was white snow but no consciousnesses; or white snow and no articulate consciousness. In such a world, the whiteness of the snow would not have the status of a truth condition or a truth-maker. The independence of the existence conditions and the truth conditions of a truth is necessary in order that it should be possible that assertions or thoughts may be *either* true *or* false. Not all (possible) true thoughts exist and not all true assertions have been asserted; and not all expressed thoughts and assertions are true. Never-expressed (unthought, unwritten, unintuited) truths do not exist. Although it is true that my hand at the time of writing is a certain specified number of miles away from a particular brick in a building in New York, the truth corresponding to the exact distance will not exist until I think of it. While the exact distance in some sense exists (though whether it has independent existence – in what sense it can be said to exist – is another matter), it does not count as a 'truth' until I make assertions about it. Although 'Snow is black' is untrue (if snow is white), the potential truth that 'Snow is black' does exist if it is asserted. Indeed, this assertion turns the whiteness of snow into the falsity condition of 'Snow is black'.

This separation of the conditions under which truths exist from the conditions which make true assertions true applies only to those assertions that assert identity via 'is'. The key to the anomalous logic of 'am', however, is that the existence conditions and the truth conditions of the identity asserted in it are *not* clearly separate or independent in this way. The Existential Intuition which 'asserts' that 'I am [this]' provides both the truth conditions and the existence conditions of the identity asserted through it. In the case of 'am' identity, the existence conditions, if fulfilled, bring about, or bring with them, their own truth conditions: the existence conditions of the truth are also its truth conditions. This follows from the fact that the identity being asserted – the 'this' that I am – is being asserted by the 'entity' whose identity it is: what is being asserted is not merely a statement about a state of affairs but the state of affairs itself. The asserter and that which is asserted (to exist, to be the case) are inextricably linked.

## 2.8 THE SCOPE OF WHAT IS GUARANTEED BY THE EXISTENTIAL INTUITION

It is necessary to be a little careful here. I am not suggesting that *every* 'am' identity statement is true in virtue of being asserted; that, for example, if it is I who say 'I am Napoleon' it follows that I truly am Napoleon. We shall examine the limits to first-person authority and incorrigibility in the next chapter. For the present, it is necessary to note that the Existential Intuition is self-fulfilling to the extent that any proposition it may be formulated into is derived from a pre-propositional self-realising realisation. It is not, as we have said, a 'matted block' of implicit propositions. The Existential Intuition simply marks the ascent of a conscious entity to 'id-entity'. What entity is 'That I am this …', the blush of realisation, allowed to help itself to? Is it more than the output of the *Cogito* argument, which – without fudging, without taking on board massive assumptions such as a benign God – seems to amount to no more than a mere moment of thought?[43]

Well, it now seems to be. Given that the 'this' that is intuited in the primordial form of the Existential Intuition – a complement that is closer even than the most cognate of cognate objects, the most internal of internal accusatives – is the engaged body, interacting with its environment, then we seem to have a way of breaking out of the limits of the *Cogito* argument. What is immediately given in the Existential Intuition goes beyond thought, even beyond a putative thinking substance sealed off from the world of material bodies, and encompasses an engaged, living body from which it takes its rise. The self-realising realisation – 'That I am this [body ...]' – delivers to the 'I' a living and lived piece of the material world that is more than a mere moment of thought.

By now, the readers' suspicions will be thoroughly aroused: Surely the undeniable Existential Intuition escapes from the Cartesian prison only in virtue of my blindness to the power and authority of Cartesian doubt. Have I not simply drawn on the kind of knowledge Descartes felt he had to set aside when he listed all those things (as the title of the First Meditation has it) 'which may be brought within the sphere of the doubtful'? Does not the Existential Intuition deliver more than the *Cogito* argument simply because it lets more through 'on the nod'? If so much more is 'given', is it surprising that much more can be harvested? The story of the biogenesis of the Intuition, for example, rests on the unquestioning acceptance of facts that would scarcely survive the very first twinges of systematic doubt.

Do we in fact need to presuppose the biogenetic account of the Existential Intuition in order to escape the Cartesian prison? Can the Existential Intuition, irrespective of its origin, take us beyond the present moment of awareness to a living body? Or beyond a present moment of awareness of a living body to the body in itself? Does it offer us an entirely secure passage from

'That I am this ...'

to

'That I am this [living body]'

so that the Cartesian

'Therefore I am'

yields

'Therefore I am this [living body]'?

To put this another way, can the Existential Intuition, with its biological credentials, show Descartes' thinker out of the prison into which he has (methodologically) incarcerated (or, more precisely, *discarnated*) himself? Or, less ambitiously, is there some way in which the Cartesian Thinker can, without cheating, help himself to biology to get out of the mere iteration of the thought that he exists? Can the Existential Intuition provide a link between the airless interior (to which the meagre yield of third-person necessity confines him) and the world of living things (one of which is himself) outside?

I believe that it can, so that, far from ignoring Descartes' challenge, we are, by invoking the Existential Intuition, approaching it from another direction. This approach will make much of what follows a little difficult to map on to the philosophical agenda that has emerged in the wake of Descartes' moment of genius (including the post-Fregean, anti-Cartesian counter-revolution); indeed, many readers may have the sense of looking at a tapestry from the wrong side. And they will be half-right. We are looking at the tapestry from the other side, but I believe none the less that it is the right one.

In order to progress, we need to do two things: a) remind ourselves of what kind of going-on the *Cogito* argument is; and, connected with this, b) identify what it inadvertently (and inescapably) takes on board. In both these endeavours, I shall be building on the work that has been carried out on the *Cogito* argument in the analytical tradition but, in contrast to that tradition, do so not to debunk the argument but to uncover its true (and truly, vertiginously) thrilling nature.

## 2.9 THE POROSITY OF THE CARTESIAN PRISON

First of all, we need to remind ourselves of something we have already mentioned: the *Cogito* argument is a *recipe* – for others to follow. As many philosophers have pointed out, when Descartes wrote 'I think therefore I am' he was not simply talking about himself, demonstrating the existence of Descartes to reassure Descartes. This was not, that is to say, a first-person argument applicable only to himself which, from the standpoint of the present, is merely a third-person argument about a seventeenth-century 'he'. After all, it is hardly of great philosophical concern whether a particular person called Descartes existed. The *Cogito* argument is about everyone who reads and understands it: it is an invitation to each of us to observe ourselves in thought and to realise that, if we are thinking, we must be existing. As Elizabeth Anscombe has put it, 'the first-person character of Descartes' argument means that everyone must administer it to himself in the first person'.[44] It says: try to see if you can doubt your own existence or doubt, when thinking, that you are thinking. Or try to think the thought that you are not thinking, discover that you cannot think that thought and consider what must follow from this. It is an existential, not a purely cognitive purely logical argument.

This means, among many other things, that we must look beyond the argument on the page to the implied world to which it is addressed: the invitation implies invitees. The very fact that the *Cogito* argument is a disguised recipe or invitation means that it must deliver more than it says on the tin.

This is intimately connected with the fact that it doesn't start out as far back as is claimed. The implicit Cartesian starter pack is rather better provisioned than Descartes leads us to believe; for the existence of a recipe or an invitation presupposes many of those very things that are promised if the recipe is followed or the invitation accepted. The *Cogito* argument cannot itself be argued except from an assumed background certainty from which it will be possible to explore specific uncertainties, arising from the fear that one might be dreaming. These uncertainties cannot swamp everything: there must always be a large residue of the undoubtable, of the unquestioned, of certainty. The limit to would-be universal doubt does not come simply from the obligation to avoid logical contradiction: the limit is not purely logical. It is existential.

Because – to quote Anscombe again – 'the first-person character of Descartes' argument means that everyone must administer it to himself in the first person',[45] we are entitled to think of the *Cogito* argument as *a communication* and one of a rather special sort. It is a communication which invites the recipient to a) understand a certain meaning, and b) re-enact a certain argument. Or, more precisely, to accept a certain argument by replicating it; and to replicate it not merely cognitively but also existentially (for the argument doesn't merely impinge on, but encompasses the arguer) by acknowledging that he undeniably exists – an acknowledgement that I argue is descended from the self-realising realisation that is the Existential Intuition.

It may help to clarify the nature of the communication which has to be re-enacted in the recipient by using speech-act theory: there is a locutionary act, which is the rehearsal of the argument, with its rather limited pay-off; there is the illocutionary act, which asserts the argument and its outcome; and there is the perlocutionary act, in accordance with which both Descartes and I try to get someone (in Descartes' case himself and then his implied audience; in my case myself) to believe the argument and its consequences. It is to this perlocutionary act that most obviously the background certainty, the necessary survivor of universal doubt, belongs as an implicit, but none the less inescapable, assumption.

This implicit certainty is invisible so long as the argument is viewed as a series of symbols on a page, an entirely abstract argument (presumably abstracted from meaning; a purely syntactic argument, perhaps). It is visible as soon as the argument is seen as something that is argued *by someone* – especially if it is seen as being argued in response to an invitation issued by someone else. A putatively absolutely solitary Descartes may not be able to help himself to the background certainties, though it is doubtful whether such an individual is imaginable.[46] The argument is however available to an individual such as Raymond Tallis, who is aware of another individual such as Descartes, who has offered this answer to doubts that he (Descartes) has had (or at least entertained) and which he guesses (outside of his moments of absolute doubt) that others may have shared; an individual, Descartes, who has suggested this *recipe* for dealing with the doubts. The perlocutionary pay-off comes only when it is experienced in the first person; when Descartes' *Cogito* is tokenised as a speech act (or writing act) in 'my' rehearsal of the argument.

The fact that the *Cogito* argument is a *recipe* made available by one thinker for use by all therefore blows a large hole in the wall of the prison created by Descartes' methodological solipsism. Through this hole pours the *community* – of speakers, of enquirers, of philosophers – which must be presupposed in the very existence of the argument. We cannot, that is to say, ignore what Cavell calls 'the specific plight of mind and circumstance within which human beings give voice',[47] irrespective of whether they are talking to others or thinking to themselves. The Cartesian prison is therefore an impossible prison.

Wittgenstein covered much of this territory, especially in *On Certainty* where he brought together much of his lifetime's thought about the limits of philosophical doubt and the nonsensical nature of scepticism that transgressed those limits.[48] The formulation of doubts about other minds, the external world, and other fundamentals, are deeply insincere, not to say contradictory, because they hold in suspension those very conditions necessary for the formulation of such doubts. The thinker is like a speaker pretending to breathe in a vacuum. Doubting, as Wittgenstein said, requires that one believes something, at the very least that one's words have meaning; specifically, the public, stabilised, communicated meanings that words have – and hence the public world they belong to. A worldless doubt, or a pure-point thought, is therefore an impossibility. At the extremity of systematic doubt one could not *think* anything, for there would be nothing – no words, no signs – left to think with; nothing with which one could have differentiated thought.

Descartes, therefore, ends up by affirming what nobody (including himself) could have doubted, or expressed doubts over, in the first place. He ends, that is to say, where he began and the meagre yield of the *Cogito* argument is little cause for concern, since its output is superfluous. The *Meditations* illustrates the characteristic philosophical pastime which F. H. Bradley described metaphysics as being: finding bad reasons for what we believe on instinct – which we cannot unbelieve without losing everything we think with. Cartesian doubt, like the Husserlian *epoche* which tries to shed not only science but also 'the natural standpoint', would have to dispense with the very language in which its findings might be expressed and the community implicit in their being expressed.

So much for the Wittgensteinian critique of the Cartesian quest. While this draws out the implications of acknowledging the nature of the *Cogito* argument as a *recipe*, an invitation from one person to another, it does not get all the way to the point made by Hintikka and others after him that the argument has to be performed by *someone*; and these are very interesting indeed. Unless it is enacted by *someone*, it is merely *mentioned* rather than *used*. All third-person rehearsals of it are mere mentions; all uses must be first-person and the first person in question cannot be just an 'I-token' on-the-page: it has to be a person in the full-blown sense that is necessary when we think of a person as, say, a speaker. We are talking, that is to say, of an *individual*.

In *The Principles of Philosophy* Descartes argues that

> because each one of us is conscious that he thinks, and that in thinking he can shut off from himself all other substance, either thinking or extended, we may conclude that each of us similarly regarded, is really distinct from every other thinking substance and from every corporeal substance.[49]

The Existential Intuition, self-realising or self-affirming like the Cartesian 'I think', is not so separable. In particular, it is not shut off, or a shutting-off, from the body. Its assumption is not only existential, as the *Cogito*'s 'I think' is, but it is carnal. For it is not a piece of (factual) knowledge captured in a thought, an assertion, a piece of currently-being-thought knowledge. To put this another way: in its pre-propositional form as a self-realising realisation, there is no gap between use and mention: it is a standing token (cf. standing wave) where use and mention are inseparable. Indeed, as a self-apprehension, it is not separable from the body.

## 2.10 CARTESIANLY PREFERRED AND NON-PREFERRED THOUGHTS[50]

Why does Descartes privilege thoughts over experiences – so that he concluded that that which he knew with most certainty, that of which he had the clearest and most distinct idea, was the thought he was having that he existed and that, consequently, his essence was to be a thinking substance? If he had chosen some thought other than 'I think', might he not have come to a quite different conclusion as to the kind of thing that he was? While, as Gassendi has pointed out, the thought that you are existing proves that you exist, it doesn't prove that you are a thinking substance. Not only does it not prove that that you are any kind of *substance*, it also doesn't show that you are *only* thought. The certainty that I am thinking demonstrates only that I am at least a thinking entity, but not that I am *only* a thinking entity.

Gassendi was impatient with Descartes' 'pretence' that only thinking would deliver the certainty that he needed:

> When you come to the second Meditation, I see that you still persist in keeping your game of pretence, and that you recognise at least that 'you exist'; which thus establishes the 'conclusion that this proposition:– I am, I exist, is true each time that you pronounce or that you mentally conceive it'. But I don't see that you needed all this mechanism, when you had other grounds for being sure, and it was true, that you existed. You might have inferred that from any other activity, since our natural light informs us that whatever acts also exists.[51]

He could have taken this argument further. Given that, as Descartes had argued in the case of thought, there was 'no act or accident without a substance for it to belong to', and this had allowed him to move from the thinking 'I' to the 'I' as thinker and the 'I' as thinker to the I as thinking substance, he could just as well have moved from (say) 'I walk' to 'I am a walker'.

At first sight the preference for thought seems justified. The Cartesian philosopher is obligatorily engaged in thinking: one cannot, without pragmatic self-refutation, think that one is not thinking; one cannot think 'I am not thinking' and conclude from this that one might not after all exist. More importantly, one cannot be mistaken as to the fact that one is thinking. No proof or experience could demonstrate to me that I was not, after all, thinking when I thought that I was thinking. (It does not seem even to depend on knowing what the word 'thinking' means; for it is, willy-nilly, what the philosopher is doing, irrespective of whether he thinks that he is doing so.)

But is this certainty unique to thought? For example, the feeling that

I am uncomfortable/sweaty/cold is not something that could prove to be wrong. I could be wrong, at least on a particular occasion, as to the *cause* of my discomfort; the stuff that is trickling from my armpits may turn out to be blood or rainwater; and the feeling of cold may be due not to cold conditions but to a fever or a local anaesthetic. But I could not be wrong as to the feeling.

The attraction of thought as the material for the *Cogito* argument is also that it comes in propositional form, or is amenable to be cast as a proposition, whereas (for example) feeling uncomfortable is not: thought intrinsically has, or spontaneously assumes, propositional form and so looks like an initial premise. There may be less to this difference than meets the eye; for, while my thoughts may be propositional, the sense that I am thinking is not: unless one postulates a second-order proposition – 'I think "I am thinking"' – a Kantian 'I think that I think which accompanies all my thoughts'. This seems, to say the least, artificial; besides, a putative direct awareness that one is thinking is as remote from propositions, or from factual assertions, as the feeling of being uncomfortable. The sense that there are thoughts going on and that those thoughts are mine is not intrinsically discursive, or intrinsically a piece of knowledge.

Moreover, other indisputable awarenesses, such as the feeling of sweatiness or of being uncomfortable, seem to have a different virtue: they seem to be more decisively 'commingled' (to use Descartes' verb) with the body. At any rate, they are more ineluctably stitched into a location in space-time, and hence have co-location with a body. One feels uncomfortable in the very place where there is discomfort.

This difference, however, is also illusory: 'I sweat, therefore I am' is not an immediate outcome of the feeling of being sweaty: sweatiness does not incorporate a meta-sweatiness cast in propositional form that attests to one's existence. Perhaps all that one can say is that the feeling of sweatiness is closer to the most primordial layer of the Existential Intuition through which one apprehends one's body as one's own and apprehends through that body that one is.

We shall examine a few non-cognitive Cartesian sentences presently. For the moment, out of fairness, we must note that, in some discussions of his proof, Descartes did extend the scope of the starting premise of the argument, beyond what we may call 'cognitive performatives', to 'all operations of will, intellect, imagination, and of the senses' – for these, he says, are all 'thoughts':

> Suppose I say I *see* (or *I am walking*) *therefore I exist*. If I take this to refer to vision (or walking) as a corporeal action, the conclusion is not

absolutely certain. But if I take it to refer to actual sensations or consciousness of seeing (or walking), then it is quite certain; for in that case it has regard to the mind, and it is the mind alone that has a sense or thought of itself seeing (or walking).[52]

This does not, however, greatly extend the yield of the argument. When we replace the indubitability of the thought that I am having now with the indubitability of the sensation (or impression) that I am having now, the 'I' that is coterminous with the sensation is little if at all different from the extensionless dot of the 'I' of the 'I think' version of the *Cogito* argument. While I cannot doubt that I have the sensation that I am walking, this does not license my certainty that I *am* walking or even that I have legs – I might be imagining both. In other words, I am not licensed to attribute to the self that is put beyond doubt anything more than that which is mobilised to demonstrate the (very) bare existence of the self. The underlying form of the argument[53]

a) I am thinking and I cannot be mistaken over this because even to be mistaken over (or to doubt) the fact that I am thinking is itself an instance of thought.
b) Whatever thinks, exists.[54]
c) Therefore I exist.

remains unaltered, irrespective of whether 'thinking' is interpreted narrowly as 'rational thought' or in a wider sense that encompasses 'all operations of the will, intellect, imagination, and of the senses', in other words, all the contents of consciousness. And the yield is just as meagre. It is equally disappointing if we modify the *Cogito* argument to 'I am conscious, therefore I am'.[55]

Let us look a little closer at some 'bodily thoughts' as initial premises for the *Cogito* argument to see whether they give us a route out of the prison to which his systematic doubt – or, given that his doubt is impossible, his methodological solipsism – seems to have confined certainty, before we revisit his starting point to see what this does to the light in which we may look at the Existential Intuition rooted in the engaged, self-conscious body. We may characterise this as an attempt to extend the range of Cartesian thoughts; or as an attempt to see the *Cogito* argument as merely the first, and not necessarily the most helpful, of a whole class of such thoughts.

A Cartesian thought corresponds to a proposition that, like 'I think, therefore I am', has these two features:

a) It is necessarily true because self-affirming; and
b) it seems to contain empirical truth, to have actual content.

Here are some thoughts that have a bodily, rather than mental, premise:

a) 'I am cold, therefore I am'.
b) 'I am sweaty, therefore I am'.
c) 'I am heavy, therefore I am'.
d) 'I am in pain, therefore I am'.

Unfortunately, *understood as on-the-page arguments*, none of these delivers all of what is wanted: necessary truth that penetrates beyond the moment of its being entertained to establish beyond doubt the existence of an 'I' that is substantial, in virtue, say, of being embodied. To see how, why and that this is the case, let us look at each in turn.

### 'I am cold, therefore I am'

While it is not possible to deny the feeling that one is cold, it does not follow from the feeling of being cold that one is (objectively) cold. To be objectively cold implies that one's body would feel (to another person) colder than bodies usually feel. It is possible, of course, to feel desperately cold when one's body is objectively hot to the touch, as when one's temperature is rising in a fever. Suppose one confines the initial claim to 'I have the feeling that I am cold', this would be true irrespective of what one's bodily temperature is. It eludes any objective challenge. If it is seen as disconnected in this way from objective facts about the body, is it then reduced to a mental phenomenon? Is it divorced, that is to say, not only from any objective facts about a particular body, but from embodiment itself? The answer must be yes; from which it follows that this Cartesian sentence, which refers to an incorrigible feeling, does not include embodiment – or any substantive or enduring I – within the scope of its necessary truth.[56]

### 'I am sweaty, therefore I am'

At first, this seems promising, if only because one cannot be sweaty without having a body to sweat in or through. Disembodied sweating, unlike disembodied thought, is not conceivable. A closer look, however, dispels the promise. 'I am sweaty' is incorrigible only if it is interpreted as 'I feel sweaty' and not if it is interpreted as 'I am sweating' – that is to say, sweat is pouring off the body that I am/is mine. It is possible to dream that one is sweating when one is not. Moreover, in certain neurological conditions – such as spinal multiple sclerosis – it is possible to have the sensation of water trickling off parts of one's body, and so to imagine one is sweating, when nothing of the kind is happening. Sweating, while promisingly carnal, may be illusory, so it is not possible to place the existence of the body predicated in sweating beyond doubt.

### 'I am heavy, therefore I am'

If this looks promising as a Cartesian thought that is both undeniable and inseparable from the idea of bodily existence, it is because feeling heavy (like feeling uncomfortable) is global rather than localised. It seems impossible to excise – or indeed exorcise – it from one's body. While I may be mistaken in my belief that certain sensations really are *of* what I seem to sense through them, it hardly seems possible for me to be mistaken over something as non-localised as feeling heavy, with all the attendant consequences – such as the sense of effort I experience when engaging in activities that require movement of the body (walking uphill, etc.) – this has. It is, however, possible to be mistaken. Since it is possible to dream of flying and hence being weightless, it must be possible to be wrong about one's weight. The fact that people are more often reported as dreaming of weightlessness than of weightiness is not relevant: it is simply because the sense of being weighty does not deviate from the deliverance of waking consciousness and does not justify a report. Besides, Cartesian doubt is about the escape from what could conceivably be dreamed or a dream, not merely escape from what is in fact dreamed. It would be absurd if the allowable scope of doubt were to turn on what people actually get muddled over.

### 'I am in pain, therefore I am'

This seems most promising of all. I cannot be mistaken either that there is a pain, or that the pain is mine. While I may misinterpret a feeling of warmth or heaviness as standing for the real thing, I cannot misinterpret being in pain in this way because the primary thing about pain is not what it means (however important that is) or some putative cause it may have, but what it feels like. I may be wrong in thinking that my pain originates from a particular tooth and that it is due to a particular pathological process such as caries; but of my being in pain there can be no doubt. But disappointingly, even this Cartesian thought does not take us far beyond the present moment of experience. If it has the edge over the original *Cogito* argument, it is perhaps because pain is more rigidly nailed to the sufferer than thought is to the thinker. While Lichtenberg's and Russell's observation to the effect that 'I think' could be reduced to 'there is thinking' or 'it thinks' has a transient plausibility, the reduction of 'I am in pain' to 'there is pain' seems impossible. A pain without a suffering creature, a bearer, is unthinkable – perhaps because pains are inescapably tokens and 'off-the-page'.

Setting aside that difference, there does not seem to be much else to commend this Cartesian sentence over the one used by Descartes. For the existence of a pain, even if it cannot float freely, unattributed to a sufferer, does not bring anything along with it: there is no substantive 'I', even less a body, that is necessarily bundled in with it. The notion of discarnate or disembodied pain, while not readily conceived, is not (unlike that of 'unsuffered pain') self-contradictory. The 'I' that is imported via the 'therefore' is not guaranteed to be substantive.

### 2.11 THE ESSENTIAL IMPURITY IN THE PROJECT OF PURE INQUIRY

We must conclude, therefore, that no Cartesian thought, taken as the input to an on-the-page argument, delivers anything more than the original *Cogito* argument. Replacing thinking with grosser states – being in pain, sweating, feeling heavy, etc. – which seem more mired in the material world and, in particular, the body, does not augment the logico-empirical yield of the argument considered 'on-the-page'. No Cartesian thoughts, and not just the 'Cartesianly preferred' one used in the *Cogito* argument, will deliver very much, irrespective of whether they refer to mental or putatively corporeal attributes. They will start to deliver only when it is fully appreciated that these are arguments to be *rehearsed* and how much this latter requires, or presupposes.

Cartesian arguments, as they are usually interpreted, are disabled by having to generate *both* their necessary truth *and* their substantive content from an on-the-page *thought-type*. The combination of necessary truth and substantive content, however, can be delivered only through the *thought-token*, the *thought-being-thought*, the *thought-act* occurring off the page – in the token thought-act (or introspection) performed by an 'I'. The *Cogito* argument truly exists only through being enacted, through what Anscombe called 'self-administration': it is an *essential*, rather than merely optional, performative. It is essentially, as we said, a 'recipe' for something that anyone can do. But that anyone has to be a someone. It cannot *happen* in the third person. It could not – despite the old joke – be performed by a computer. While one could imagine a computer crunching symbols according to rules to produce 'I am' from 'I think', it would do so under precisely the same rules as would enable it to get 'It is' from 'It thinks' or 'Fred exists' from 'Fred thinks'. It would be an entirely 'on-the-page' argument: a performanceless, arguerless (and hence unargued) argument.

Descartes' argument is therefore not only in the grammatical first-person: it is in *the existential* first-person; otherwise it is not engaged in and simply does not happen. This is true of most arguments, but it has a particular relevance here because it is the first person that is in question. In its standard form, however, the *Cogito* argument is effectively third-person, though this is well hidden. While it has a first-person form, this is enclosed in an implicit third-person carapace, simply in virtue of being presented on-the-page as *argument-type*, a type of thought disconnected from any individual thinking it. If it is not a first-person *performative*, it isn't truly first-person at all.[57] It must be seen as a personal invitation to someone who is voluntarily cut off from the world and who, for the duration of the argument, is alone, accepting nothing on trust and seeking proof even of her own existence.

To put it in terms that speak to Descartes' aspiration, there is no Project of Pure Inquiry in the absence of an inquirer. The inquirer, however, is invisible so long as the argument is seen as being primarily an on-the-page thought-type which is being talked about rather than being argued or, more precisely, *thought*.[58] That is why the 'I' whose necessary existence has been demonstrated, the 'I' as the *product* of the argument (as opposed to the 'I' that is necessary for the argument to take place) is reduced to a dimensionless dot, or the present moment of thought: the actual existence of the thinker, the inquirer, the bearer of the argument, is suppressed.

Now this suppression of the thinker – the complex creature who relates to a society that underwrites the meaning of the words that are used in the argument and understands the point, purpose and context of the argument – is self-contradictory. That this does not seem so is precisely because the *Cogito* argument is envisaged as a third-person thought; or a first-person thought that is merely alluded to and so wrapped in an implicit third person; as something 'out there', somehow taking place without a thinker. So long as it is seen in this way, it will deliver very little.

Our understanding of Cartesian thoughts has, in other words, to be existential as well as logical, if they are to do the work that Descartes had hoped they would; indeed, any work at all. While the upfront ingredients brought to the 'pure inquiry' are somewhat lacking in substance, the irreplaceable need for the *inquirer* – from the point of view of the original project an impurity – smuggles in a good deal more substance. Just how impure the Thinker is and what form the impurity takes is something that will concern us in future chapters, notably Chapters 4, 5 and 6, where we examine the logical and existential necessity for embodiment and the nature of that embodiment. The necessary impurity is what gives substance to the output of the *Cogito* argument, fattening the 'I' from a mere moment of thinking to something like a self. The impurity that is the Pure Inquirer herself is the starter pack that she is equipped with when she is reconstructing the world after the nuclear attack of systematic doubt.

Given that the argument is an *essential performative* and not merely, say, a passage from one well-formed formula to another in accordance with the rules of logic, then the Pure Inquirer cannot deny that the 'I' that she establishes as necessarily existing must be an individual who can engage in such arguments – who is able to respond to Descartes' invitation; otherwise the performative would not be performed. Her intuition that the argument appeals to – and will carry any appeal the argument may have to her – is her contemporary *intuition* of her own existence. But what that existence is comprised of is much more than what the argument allows her to have: it is what she must be in order to engage in philosophical arguments; and that, as we have already observed, is much more than an isolated thought; or a succession of isolated thought-moments corresponding to repeated rehearsal of the argument.

How much follows from this is unclear. It is tempting to argue that if the philosopher is able to respond to Descartes' invitation, she must live in a world in which Descartes was an historical figure who truly existed; and an awful lot would follow from this. But this would be to miss the profound point of Descartes' methodological solipsism. She could still *imagine* that she lived in a world in which philosophical invitations (or challenges) were issued. 'Descartes' could be a coinage of her mind. It could be that her discussions with fellow philosophers (and, indeed, all her fellow creatures) were simply a polyphonic soliloquy. This is not, at first sight, a logical impossibility, though such a scenario might be excluded by the private language argument; namely that there would be no way of thinking to one's self using symbols with determinate meanings if there were no community-agreed rules underwriting the meanings of those symbols.

What, then, follows from the fact that the *Cogito* argument is an *essential* performative, that its intrinsic meaning is inseparable from a real, particular, first person thinking it (as opposed to a notional, general 'I' by which it gets thought), and that it exists only in token-realisations off-the-page? Certainly, it has a thinker – a real individual – bundled into it. But what is the minimum, necessary 'person spec.' of the Thinker? Does she necessarily have a body? Does she necessarily have a mind, a self, society, etc.? What does she have to be to think the *Cogito* argument? What does she have to have or to be in order to think 'I am'?

In putting the question in this way, I am perhaps already cheating a little, being intermittently a pick'n'mix sceptical – *à la carte Cartesian*. If I talk about the Cartesian thinker of the *Cogito* argument in the third person, am I not already assuming a 'world out there'? My use of 'she' presupposes a world that includes at least two people and, given that they are both philosophers, this brings quite a lot in its wake. Is it possible to think about the situation of the Thinker without slipping out of the Cartesian prison even before systematic doubt closes its doors? The truth is, it isn't; and this, as we have seen, has been the focus of much criticism of scepticism-driven epistemology over the last century. I shall re-examine this line of attack and, while I shall agree with its premises, I shall draw a different, and I believe more relevant, conclusion from them.

### 2.12 'I': FROM PHILOSOPHICAL GRAMMAR TO EXISTENTIAL GRAMMAR

Contemporary debates about the role of the first person transpose onto a linguistic plane the discussion of the essential nature of a human being that stems, in modern times, from Cartesian metaphysics.[59]

In philosophy, all that isn't gas is grammar.[60]

Wittgenstein's response to Descartes' universal doubt and philosophical scepticism in general is a complex, second-order scepticism: a scepticism towards philosophical doubt. This pervades his work. It is expressed most robustly and dogmatically in the *Tractatus*:

Scepticism is *not* irrefutable, but obviously nonsensical, when it tries to raise doubts where no questions can be asked.

For a doubt can exist only where a question exists, a question only where an answer exists, and an answer only where something *can be said*.[61]

It has its most subtle and elaborate expression in his last thoughts, collected posthumously in *On Certainty*.[62] The focus throughout is on what can, or cannot, be said: the bounds of verbal sense mark the limits of legitimate doubt, of what doubts can be entertained; and traditional philosophical scepticism, most notably Cartesian systematic doubt, lies outside those bounds.

In his early writings, Wittgenstein identified the source of the illegitimacy of philosophical scepticism (and equally of the reassurances, undeniable truths mobilised to counter scepticism) in the fact that they broke the rules of language. The latter was approached as if it were a symbolic system – with rules for the construction of well-formed formulae, and so on – similar to those formal systems which he had investigated in the wake of Russell's inquiries. In the later writings – notably in *Philosophical Investigation*, which acknowledged the way a language was embedded in, and inseparable from, the forms of life of the community of native speakers – the emphasis was less on the breach of formal rules and more on the disregard, inherent in philosophical discourse, of the way real languages function and assertions possess meaning. In his middle period, he was preoccupied with the notion of developing a 'philosophical grammar', which treated the linguistic constraints on the bounds of discourse that had sense, the distinction between sense and non-sense, as something that straddled both the internal (grammatical) rules of the putative system of language and the forms of our lives, worlds or consciousness.

Wittgenstein's notion of a 'philosophical grammar' has been usefully summarised by Gerd Brand:

> Grammar is the totality of rules which state in which connections words have meaning and propositions make sense ... It describes in such a way that it delimits what is describable. It describes the use of words in language and the conditions for the representation of reality through propositions.[63]

Philosophical grammar would show why it is correct to say 'I have a pain' but not 'My brain has a pain' or 'My hand has a pain'. It would show the proper use of words that would steer one away from unnecessary philosophical conundrums. Properly seen, philosophical grammar has its roots in formal rules of language and the way of life of a community of speakers, a community whose scope will vary according to the particular area of language being activated. A proposition, as Wittgenstein famously said, has meaning only in the stream of life.[64] In the case of Cartesian sentences, the living being is imagined as isolated, though the difference between the individual and the community will not be sharp-cut because the individual thinking to himself will be using the language of the community and responding to questions formulated within that community. Indeed, the notion of an isolated, innocent Cartesian thinker thinking to and for himself alone is a fantasy because the language in which he is thinking to himself is that of the community – in this case, rather a sophisticated philosophical community. There are no private philosophical languages.

Many of Wittgenstein's followers – and at times Wittgenstein himself – did not follow through the implications of the reference to the community necessary to guarantee the meaning of philosophical discourse. For all the critiques of the notions of 'private language' and so on, there was still a tendency to treat the Cartesian and comparable philosophical projects as illegitimate on the rather narrower grounds that they, as it were, broke the rules of language; as the arguments represented false moves in a system or an infinite network of interlocking language games. Traditional epistemological inquiry – scepticism and its resolution – was seen to transgress the fundamental grammar of language. The idea of a philosophical grammar reflected the aspiration to capture that deepest stratum of grammar: the implicit rules and assumptions that laid down the bounds of sense.

One of the most characteristic (and brilliant) examples of the 'philosophical grammar' approach in this area is the justly celebrated paper 'The First Person', by Wittgenstein's pupil Elizabeth Anscombe, which we have already cited.[65] This contribution, a *tour de force*, is important because it is also profoundly, even perversely, point-missing; and its character in this respect is connected with a quasi-moralistic impatience with Cartesian thoughts, or at least a desire to deny their profundity. One has the feeling that the author is irritated with the *Meditations* because they are deeply insincere: the starting point of the *Cogito* argument is actually an impossibility. It is 'self-impossibilising' and hence a fake. There is a feeling, common among Wittgenstein's pupils, that there is something culpably unserious about such philosophical mysteries, in particular those that arise out of puzzles about the nature of mind, self and certainty. The conundrum of the first person is one such unnecessary mystery, which can be cleared up by seeing how most approaches are mired in confusions about the grammar of the expression 'I'.

Anscombe examines various aspects of the behaviour of the word 'I' that have caused philosophers from Descartes onwards so much excited puzzlement. She argues that the apparently anomalous behaviour of 'I', and the perplexed commentary it has provoked, is the result of a misunderstanding of the function 'I' serves in language and the failure to develop a correct philosophical understanding of its grammar. This is in turn connected with 'the (deeply rooted) grammatical illusion of a subject'. Some of the erroneous ways of thinking of 'I' that she considers include: a proper name; the proper name of a self; an expression indicating singular reference; an abbreviation of a definite description; and a demonstrative. For different reasons, each of these interpretations fails to capture what 'I' does, or how it is used and the unusual properties it seems to have. For example, if it is a demonstrative, it cannot be an ordinary demonstrative, since it is guaranteed against reference-failure: 'Just thinking "I" guarantees not only the existence but the presence of its referent' (p. 149). This is true because, 'if thinking did not guarantee the presence, the existence of the referent could be doubted'. Similar arguments are mobilised against the notion that 'I' is a name because, unlike other names, it cannot be empty: while it is possible that there may be no object answering to the proper name 'Raymond Tallis' (cf. 'Pegasus'), 'I' cannot fail in this way.[66]

Anscombe invokes several other reasons for not treating 'I' as a proper name, or even as a logically proper name, or any other kind of referring expression ('a word whose role is to "make a singular reference"') notwithstanding that its syntactical behaviour makes us think that it should be treated in this way. For example, the reason that 'I' cannot get hold of the wrong object is not that it is guaranteed to get hold of the right object but that 'there is no getting hold of an object at all' (p. 153). And while, with true names, there are two things to grasp – 'the kind of use, and what to apply them to from time to time' – with 'I' there is only the use. 'I', then, is not a proper name, or any sort of name, and to treat it as if it were a name gets us into all sorts of problems.

Only if we resist ontological seduction by surface syntactical appearances and acknowledge that 'I' is not a proper name referring to an object shall we understand its true nature and avoid being misled into postulating the existence of some kind of object to which it refers. The seemingly magical protection 'I' enjoys against reference-failure is due, in short, to the rather unexciting fact that its use does not amount to an attempt to refer to anything. So long as we do not mistake it for a referring expression, we shall be spared a frustrating hunt for its object and the need for a 'correlative term … for its kind of object' (p. 147) – an example of a common illusion of an entity arising out of the shadows cast by the opacity of words, opacities that are thickened by grammatical misunderstandings. Indeed, if 'I' *were* seen as a referring expression, security of reference would evaporate: even a short stretch of a Cartesian ego would lie outside the scope of the guarantee; for, Anscombe argues, one could not be sure that, at any given moment of thought, one was not one thinker but ten thinkers thinking in unison. The assumption that 'I' is a referring expression opens a 'self-perpetuating, endless, irresolvable' dispute as to the nature of the referent, the selves, minds, persons to which it refers. A properly developed philosophical grammar of 'I' shows that it is neither a name nor, indeed, any other kind of expression whose logical role is to refer to something.

The effect of Anscombe's philosophical grammar is profoundly deflating and, indeed, contrary to the entire thrust of the arguments presented so far in this book. She asserts, for example, that 'I am E. A.

[Elizabeth Anscombe]' is not an identity proposition. It is, she admits, *connected with* an identity proposition – namely 'This thing here is E. A.' – and the first-person proposition 'I am this thing here'. The latter, however, is not a proposition of identity.

The reasoning behind this surprising assertion is quite difficult to follow. The proposition, she says, has the following meaning:

> this thing here is the thing, the person (in the 'offences against the person' sense) of whose action *this* idea of action is an idea, of whose movements *these* ideas of movement are ideas, of whose posture *this* idea of posture is the idea. And also, of which *these* intended actions, if carried out, will be the actions.

Or, to express it more simply,

> 'This body is my body' means 'My idea that I am standing up is verified by this body, if it is standing up'. And so on.

She then adds, 'Observation does not show which body is the one. Nothing shows me that.'

This last comment is particularly revealing when it is considered in conjunction with her assertion that propositions such as 'I am this thing here' are *not* identity propositions. The reason why Anscombe denies that, say, 'I am this body' is an identity proposition is that it is not the kind of proposition that is supported by observations; nor could it be disproved by observations. Just as nothing would show me which body is the one that I am, so nothing could show me that I had made a mistake over which body is mine. The reason that I do not require evidence or guidance in order to discover which body is mine is the same as the reason that I cannot locate myself in the wrong body or mis-allocate the wrong body to myself.

This, however, is not a reason that can be captured by philosophical grammar or, indeed, *any kind of grammar that treats Cartesian thoughts and the like as on-the-page thought-types rather than off-the-page token performatives or recipes thereof.* To put this another way, the grammar of third-person identity relations (such as, for example, 'This thing here is E. A.'), which are uprooted from the actual existence of speakers, cannot accommodate the necessary truths of first person identity statements such as 'I am this …'. Anscombe's dissolution of

'I am E. A.'

into

'This thing here is E. A. ...' plus 'I am this thing here'

denatures the first-person identity assertion by breaking it up into a contingent third-person identity assertion and a contingent first-person component that does not meet Anscombe's criteria for true identity.

The rejection of first-person identity statements as genuine identity statements, and the failure to recognise the need for a different kind of grammar to appreciate the true nature of sentences expressing Cartesian thoughts, are linked. First-person identity is real, but it is not contained within language: it is a point of intersection of discourse and existence, and for this what we shall call an 'existential grammar' is needed. When one passes from philosophical to existential grammar, one escapes the Wittgensteinian acid bath that dissolves the referent of 'I' into 'the grammatical illusion of a subject'.

The deflation of 'I' statements is an instance of a more general Wittgensteinian tendency to examine scepticism-driven epistemological discourse at the level of the thought-type and not at the level of occurrent thoughts which cannot be separated from the bearers. This signal oversight is an unsurprising consequence of the intense hostility to psychologism that gripped Wittgenstein and others influenced by Frege – to a degree that was not, perhaps, wholly conscious, being so deeply embedded in founding assumptions. The difference between the grammar-based critique of both philosophical scepticism and post-sceptical reconstruction and the present project is sufficiently marked to justify this new concept of an 'existential grammar' which does not deflate mysteries such as those that arise out of first-person being. Further justification, if any is needed, comes from the evidence in his last notebooks that Wittgenstein doubted whether scepticism can be completely discredited simply by invoking the notion of the bounds of legitimate discourse as determined by a philosophical grammar. The latter, moreover, was the name of an area of investigation and not a completed programme of thought or a discovered set of facts about the boundaries of sense-making discourse. It is possible that Wittgenstein might not have approved of the philosophical deflations carried out by his disciples.

At any rate, something more than philosophical grammar is required when Cartesian sentences/thoughts are seen for what they are, when they are liberated from the pages on which they are merely printed instances, rather than true first-person uses, of third-person thought-types, mere mentions rather than the realisations of the thought-type. When they, in short, engage, encompass and, indeed, engulf the thinker.

To capture the difference between existential and philosophical grammar, let us look at some passages in *On Certainty*[67] where Wittgenstein emphasised the impossibility of universal doubt:

> A doubt that doubted everything would not be a doubt. (para. 450)

because

> If you are not certain of any fact, you cannot be certain of the meaning of your words either. (p. 114)

as in this example:

> 'I don't know if this is a hand.' But do you know what the word 'hand' means? And don't say 'I know what it means now for me'.[68] And isn't it an empirical fact – that *this* word is used like *this*? (para. 306)

Sincere universal doubt would be (literally) unspeakable. But this reason (which justifies the belief that a fully developed philosophical grammar would liberate us from futile scepticism-driven epistemological inquiry) is rooted in a deeper reason why doubting cannot be universal:

> Doubt itself rests only on what is beyond doubt. (para. 519)

and

> The *questions* that we raise and our *doubts* depend on the fact that some propositions are exempt from doubt, are as it were like hinges on which those turn. (para. 341)

These locate the impossibility of universal doubt in the situation of the thinker, rather than in the rules of the language in which he thinks. To get a handle on this, we must go beyond an examination of the conventions of language – the kind of grammatical investigation exemplified by Anscombe's paper – into the human life in which language is rooted. This move beyond a philosophical grammar is mandatory in the case of first-person inquiry; for we are always and only talking about performatives, which are essentially, as opposed to accidentally, tokenised. The Pure Inquirer is, in the last analysis, an occurrent thinker and her thoughts have to make sense to herself. They can do so only so long as she remains within the bounds of sense and these are rooted in her life (in the widest sense), not narrowly in the terms in which she thinks to herself.

Wittgenstein does us a service by making it clear just how impure the starting point of Pure Inquiry is, given that it is always carried out by an

Inquirer. The things that Wittgenstein says the Inquirer cannot set aside or bracket off or doubt, if she is to remain within the bounds of sense or remain a human being in any sense, for us defines the luggage she necessarily brings with her into the *Cogito* moment. For Wittgenstein it bars the way into the Cartesian prison; for us, it shows the way out. Is there any difference? Probably not: if it was so easy to get out, perhaps it wasn't a prison at all. Meanwhile, the substantive mystery of 'I' – of the first person – remains undemolished by scrutiny of the grammar of the first-person pronoun. The hope of dispersing this mystery by developing a philosophical grammar of the first person depends on a question-begging confusion between first-person being and the first-person pronoun.[69]

The general case for replacing the philosophical grammar of the kind adumbrated by Wittgenstein (and invoked by philosophers influenced by him) by an existential grammar may not seem overwhelming. The specific case for such an approach in relation to understanding 'I' and first-person being is, as I hope is now evident, much stronger. It is connected with the unique nature of 'I'. 'I' is doubly indexicalised; like 'here' and 'now', it draws on the context of the speaker to determine who is indicated; but, unlike 'here' and 'now', the speaker is not merely that which specifies the region where the indicated person is to be found but actually is the indicated person. The speaker, in short, not only has a role in specifying the viewpoint by being the context of utterance which (implicitly) defines the universe of discourse from which the referent of 'I' will be selected, but is herself the referent. The speaker-dependency of the reference is tied into the speaker's identity with the referent and the speaker's guaranteeing that there is a reference.

This is why, as John Lyons has pointed out, the distinction between correct and successful reference cannot be drawn in relation to 'I': the correct reference of 'I' is determined (indeed guaranteed) by the deictic role of the person who says 'I'.[70] 'I' is indexical all the way down: the ultimate indexical. Whatever one says about 'I', it cannot exclude the utterer's point of view.[71] Deixis is where language and actuality meet, inasmuch as its referent depends on the circumstance of token-use; and 'I' is a special example where the piece of actuality in question is the speaker so that the point of origin of the utterance not only helps specify but *is* its reference. It is a unique tie between the spoken and what is extra-linguistically spoken of.

At the level of language, when I say 'I', the token is guaranteed to have a referent – and that referent is I who am saying it – *so long as my uttering the token is an instance of use rather than mere mention.* All of this may seem mere truism, but actually this is the nub of the matter. 'I' when uttered by one who is (necessarily) I – 'I' when it is 'I' – is a knot that ties language and the world.[72] The performative 'I think, therefore I am' enacts the passage from language – uttered language, or language imagined to be uttered – to the utterer, also imagined: it is one way (a very late and sophisticated way) of articulating self-encounter, the Existential Intuition. The link between language and extra-linguistic reality – between the utterance of words and something that is the case – is uniquely guaranteed. Because the reference of 'I' used on a particular occasion is specified through the person to whom it refers, it is guaranteed simply through being uttered, so long as the uttering is use rather than mention. Indeed, the *Cogito* argument could be presented as follows:

'I' therefore I am

In this form, its nature as a performative is shown more clearly; the first word stands for someone *saying* – or even ejaculating – 'I'. This underlines the nature of argument: it is not confined to the page, enjoying a virtual existence in a library, but here-and-now, where it is being undergone, in response to the Cartesian invitation.

This special tie between language and the world of space, time and (uttering) persons, which is seen in indexicals and, to a unique degree, in 'I', is not merely a dull consequence of the grammar of first-person pronouns, or a slightly less dull consequence of philosophical grammar, but is a key point in existential grammar, the grammar of the link between language and what is; and it is of particular interest because it makes visible the extraordinary situation of a (human) consciousness divided into awareness of what is the case and awareness of what is said to be the case. And it explains the enduring fascination of the *Cogito* argument: it reaches to the very bottom of what we are – though not for the reason, or in the sense, that Descartes intended – at least explicitly intended. What Descartes had stumbled on without fully appreciating it was an intersection between language and the world – which is not just a matter of language but a uniquely direct passage from language to the world. (The thought-to-herself 'I' of the Cartesian thinker is no different in this central respect from the uttered 'I', except that it is privatised.). Uttered or thought 'I' is self-consciousness placed in italics, concentrated to a pinpoint. We cannot examine 'I' statements from a third-person point of view; we cannot eliminate the speaker or thinker. If the special properties of 'I' are a matter of grammar, the grammar in question is the deep grammar of the human condition – of the propositional awareness that (as we shall discuss in Volume 3) distinguishes human from animal consciousness – and not an accident of a particular signifying system.[73] Only an existential grammar which spans the general, virtual existents posited by language and existence can capture this.

An existential grammar – rather than a merely grammatical reduction to system-rules – is necessary to reflect the actual status of the *Cogito* argument and Cartesian thoughts as occurrent tokens, with bearers or actors who *mean* what they say or think. The force of the *Cogito* argument is missed if we do not appreciate that it is something enacted, or imagined to be enacted, and that the 'I' in it is not a word-type, but a word-token, uttered at a given moment by an individual; it is still linked with the imaginary mouth of a given individual (even if thought silently).

Wittgenstein's scepticism-about-scepticism still obtains: the initial *epoche* cannot truly be performed in the way that Descartes envisaged it; the questioning of the entire universe outside the moment of thought is impossible. But the extent to which the denial fails (existentially) parallels the material that is imported with the *Cogito* beyond what Descartes envisaged.

### 2.13 CONCLUDING COMMENTS: THE *COGITO* ARGUMENT AND THE EXISTENTIAL INTUITION

The *Cogito* delivers more than Descartes' critics allowed, but for reasons that Descartes may not himself have been happy about.[74] Considered as a general, abstract argument, out there on the page, *Cogito ergo sum* yields very little: it could not, without a good deal of fudging, place more than a moment of thinking beyond the reach of doubt. If, however, we take it off the page and imagine it as an actual moment of thinking by which the Pure Inquirer saves herself from engulfment by uncertainty, then *Cogito ergo sum* can no longer be regarded as a general, abstract argument-type. We have to imagine it as a token argument – an actual thought or uttered sentence – being performed by being thought or uttered. And we have therefore also to imagine it being performed *by someone*. The existence of this someone cannot be doubted because she must be assumed in what we imagine is going on; and what we have *is* a going-on and not just a stand-alone allowable sequence of signs that it appears to be from an external or third-person standpoint, as when it is debated by philosophers. Even more obviously, it cannot be doubted from within – by the I who is thinking that her thought that she exists proves that she does exist. The external view allows the low-yield logical indubitability, and the internal view a higher-yield existential indubitability. The present view of the *Cogito* argument – the one I am developing on this page now –

encompasses both the inside and outside views; and the internal view enfolds the logical argument in the existential proof. Here, as so often when thinking about the *Cogito* argument, vertigo beckons.[75]

The most fundamental critique of Cartesian scepticism is not that its starting place is a grammatical impossibility or that it is based on a grammatical misunderstanding at some putatively fundamental level. It is that this starting place is an existential impossibility. While it is quite possible that 'Raymond Tallis' might not exist, it is not possible that 'I' (when 'I' is a token in use) might not exist or that Raymond Tallis might not exist if he is the I that utters 'I' and means 'I'. The standpoint from which the *Cogito* argument is conducted, therefore, is one on which there is nothing to stand. Descartes might protest that this was the precise point of his argument: I cannot unthink my own existence. True, but one doesn't have to appeal to a fact (the fact that one is thinking) to demonstrate this.

It is, of course, perfectly correct that, as Wittgenstein and others have emphasised, the putative epistemological vacuum from which the argument begins is one in which words would be void of meaning. Doubt, if truly universal, should actually withhold a presupposition vital to the *Cogito* argument – namely, that the words in which it is expressed should have meaning throughout the course of the argument. You cannot suspend the meaningfulness of the words in which an argument is conducted and still conduct the argument. If, however, we allow the words to retain their meaning even when Thought Zero has been reached after systematic doubt has supposedly razed every certainty, then we must also allow other things to be kept in place: society, the world, etc. For these are not only in the inescapable hinterland of the words the Pure Inquirer uses, they also guarantee their meaning, and that they have meaning. By making these points, however, Wittgensteinians have failed to dig deeply enough. For while they are right to criticise the assumption that words still have meaning after the epistemological zero-point has been reached, they have missed a yet more important target: the assumption that the Thinker can both entertain the possibility of his non-existence – sufficiently vividly to make demonstration of the necessity of his existence an accomplishment – and still exist in order to do so. Undergoing the *Cogito* argument requires the Thinker to distance himself from all of himself in order to encounter himself, as something whose certainty has been restored, at the end of a proof. The truth is that you cannot (logically or existentially) doubt your own existence sufficiently to make the resolution of that doubt a genuine piece of work that is done, because you need your existence in order to do the doubting and to do the resolving.[76] The Cartesian prison is inescapable because it cannot be entered by any*one*. This existential impossibility is a deeper flaw than the logico-linguistic possibility that Wittgenstein pointed to. It is also a more illuminating one; and it shows us the way back to the Existential Intuition and the connection between the latter and the *Cogito* argument.

The first thing that must now be clear is that the argument does not move, or certainly does not progress, from left to right. The starting premise – that I might not exist, so that my existence is worth proving – is a non-starter. While my existence is contingent from the third-person point of view, it cannot be contingent from the first-person viewpoint, where the first person in question is always, necessarily, myself. Systematic doubt *in practice* – tokens, instances, of the argument, actual performance, with the thoughts or sentences in real use rather than merely mentioned – has to fall so far short of being universal that the left-hand side carries as heavy a payload as the right-hand side.

With the *Cogito* argument, Descartes (like Victor Borge's uncle) has discovered a cure for which there is no disease.[77] The argumentative momentum of the *ergo* in the middle of the demonstration is spurious:

I think therefore I am

in practice amounts to:

I who am is thinking therefore I am

or

'I!' therefore 'I!'[78]

which gives 'therefore' no work to do. What we have, then, is not a journey but *stasis*. And this is absolutely right. For the *Cogito* argument is not an unfolding argument at all, with the right-hand side being better endowed than the left-hand side, but an intuition; simply an expression in words of the self-realising realisation that is the Existential Intuition. Descartes' proof of his own existence – and my proof of mine when I follow his recipe – is not an abstract demonstration, but a means of bringing one's own lived existence to a special form of self-consciousness. If the argument does any work at all, it is as a device for awakening the Existential Intuition to itself. *Cogito ergo sum* is a means for turning one's existence into living proof that one exists, for raising the immediate data of one's own consciousness to the level of a quasi-objective fact (which can then become a premise): elevating through introspection my thinking to '*That* I am (thinking)'. Such a blush of realisation, unlike the *Cogito* argument, does not move from left to right.

To be fair, Descartes himself at times thought this:

> when someone says *I am thinking, therefore I exist*, he does not have to deduce existence from thought by means of any syllogism, but recognizes it as something self-evident, by a simple intuition of the mind.[79]

Nevertheless, it was a proof that he seemed to offer of the certainty of his own existence; otherwise the *ergo* would not only be redundant but incomprehensible: the simple intuition of the mind is not an inference. Even so, it is the simple intuition that is accessed by means of the argument – or the performative that is addressed to oneself. This underlines our conclusion that the *Cogito* argument is not foundational, that it begins far from the foundations. Cartesian-preferred thoughts are higher-order, higher-level rehearsals of the Existential Intuition. The *Cogito* argument, a running-through of the preferred Cartesian thought – the thought that I am thinking – awakens the intuition that is the Existential Intuition to a higher-order awareness of itself. The preference for 'I think' over 'I feel sick' or 'I am sweating' is ill founded, as 'I am [anything] therefore I am' would have delivered what was required because the delivery does not come during the *course* of the argument, but from what is put in at the beginning (on the left-hand side) and which, of course, is still there at the end, as the sentence reaches its full stop.

Descartes had stumbled on a piece of language that seemingly had interesting properties at the level of the sentence type, on account of its being a first-person proposition. These and other more interesting properties really belong at the level of the token-utterance (out loud or in silent thought) because the latter necessarily presupposed the existence of the individual utterer. The seeming power of the *Cogito* argument was the result of illicitly borrowing for the argument-type (on the page) what in fact belongs exclusively to the token-argument off the page. The argument-type, unlike the token-argument, could place the 'I' in suspension; the token cannot do that. This is how it comes to seem as if the argument were delivering an 'I' – as a thinker, or at least as a something – that had been placed in doubt. The token delivers what the type places in doubt. The uncertainty as to whether the 'proof' is an argument, an intuition or a performance is not accidental: it is central to its power.

It is this slippage – between type-argument and token-performative yielding the moment of realisation – that enables Descartes to pull off the achievement of deriving a *de re* necessity (that a particular 'I' exists) from a *de dicto* one (that thoughts imply thinkers). Or, to put it another way, to merge undeniability (which is the psychological poor relation of logical necessity) with logical necessity. Elsewhere, this transition from *de dicto* to *de re* necessity is – notwithstanding Kripke – magic thinking. It is possible, and valid, only in the Existential Intuition, captured in explicit first-person self-references, where language and existence are merged.[80]

Linking it with the Existential Intuition does not increase the yield of the *Cogito* argument. The argument delivers only what is implicitly brought into it – which is exactly what one would expect from what is a statement of logical necessity. To put this another way, and to link it with our earlier claim about the Existential Intuition, will the link with the Existential Intuition answer to the need, created by the Cartesian starting point, to get beyond the extensionless dot which is all that the *Cogito* argument seems to deliver (if one forgets its very generous starter pack)? Will it show us the way to an intuitively self-evident, existentially self-verifiable assertion that will help us out of, say, uncertainties about the existence of our own body? Are there intuitions which are as undeniable as 'I think …' and which will not leave the 'I' confined to the present moment of thought?

Probably not; but then the whole thrust of our argument has been: Don't start from where Descartes started. It is an existential impossibility; a pretence that one can put one's own existence into question; to deny the very Intuition that lies at the heart of one's own existence as a human being. Don't imagine you can start there, where 'you' means any real person. Don't imagine you can *argue* anything from that starting point into necessary or undeniable existence. To put it another way: don't try, say, to discover what the Existential Intuition and its biological bearers give from a higher-level standpoint that begins by denying them. It would be like trying to rebuild a house without any kind of external scaffolding, from the roof downwards, when you have removed everything underneath the tiles. Don't look to the Cartesian level for the anomalous bio-logic that seems to yield more than the output of the *Cogito*.

'That I am this …' is both more than, and less than, a proposition; it is an ur-proposition between language and the material world that provides the necessary connection between the subject and her existence. It is here that – depending on whether one is envisaged travelling to a higher or a lower plane of reflection – upward movement from the biologically-generated Existential Intuition results in a parting of thought and existence – so that thought can imagine itself calling the thinker's existence into question; or downward movement from the *Cogito* argument to the Intuition results in a merging of thought and existence into the sense that one is and one (necessarily) is something in particular.

The ur-proposition 'That I am this ...' is in a mezzanine position between the kind of language in which formal logic operates and existence where it is simply not applicable. The Existential Intuition is a blush of realisation that may be presented in propositional form but not fully expressed or realised in it. At any rate, the performed inference, which is as it were 'existentially self-referential' – in which one over-hears or quasi-overhears oneself thinking or saying 'I think therefore I am' – at best places the Existential Intuition in italics. '"I", therefore I am' would deliver just as much: the through-and-through indexicality of 'I' delivers all that is needed to get across from language to world, and apparently to deliver existence out of a logical argument, to place beyond doubt something that is empirically the case.

By relating the Existential Intuition to the *Cogito* argument we may add force to our claim that the latter is 'self-impossibilising', but not everyone will be persuaded that this enables us to answer positively Anthony Kenny's question: 'May there not be some necessary relationship, unsuspected by Descartes, that will link his idea to that of extended body?'[81] Nor should it; for one should not be deceived into believing that one really can begin where Descartes began. Notwithstanding his claim to be creating a first philosophy, Descartes did not begin at the beginning: he began rather a long way down the track, far past the body, in sophisticated thought. But this preceding stretch of track was invisible: his existentially required starter pack was kept out of sight once the *Cogito* argument got under way.

In order to reimport the body into the world of certain truth, we need to look at the things that Descartes has bypassed on his way to his beginning: these, as we have noted, include society and a discursive community. More fundamentally, he has looked past what it is that is required to sustain the notion of the difference between appearance and reality ('my senses deceive me', etc.); and what it is that differentiates the subject into a particular 'I' with a particular world. Does this mean that the Pure Thinker's starter pack necessarily includes a body?

I shall argue in Volume 3 that the notion of error (and of truth) that drives Descartes' quest is itself rooted in our relationship to our own bodies, which permits knowledge to grow out of sentience, and that Descartes' scepticism, which presupposes a difference between knowledge and mere opinion, therefore requires a body. The intuition of the difference between reality and mere appearance is itself a product of the Existential Intuition in which one's body is revealed at once as that which one is and at the same time as only partly known. The Cartesian starting point, that 'I might be mistaken', is a late product of the special relationship we have to our own bodies that gave rise to the Existential Intuition.

We cannot, however, help ourselves to that explanation, which begins from the standpoint of biology, yet. For while the Cartesian prison is an imaginary one, allowable scepticism certainly encompasses the kinds of things we discussed in section 1.2 in accounting for the biogenesis of the Existential Intuition. It would be wrong to think of the latter as simply a more primitive version of the Cartesian 'therefore I am', which does not require derivation because it is directly experienced and is foundational. It is both these things, of course – and much more: it is the founding intuition of humanity, the self-realising realisation that set mankind on its distinctive course. Even so, it cannot be invoked as a way out of the Cartesian prison; rather it assists our understanding of the impossibility of that prison. In this sense, we may regard its anomalous bio-logic as casting an intense light on the way we bring to the prison the very world it is supposed to shut us away from.

But this is not the same as smuggling lived flesh into the prison by identifying the thinking moment that is the overt product of the *Cogito* argument with the 'this' in the 'That I am this' of the Existential Intuition and the 'this' in its turn with 'a living engaged body'. We shall need other arguments.

I will focus on the case for putting the body beyond the reach of doubt in Chapters 4 and 5. This case will not depend on allowing a large quantity of biological knowledge to pass unchallenged through the sceptical sieve – a dependency that would leave most philosophers very unimpressed. Instead, I shall invoke two cases for being unable to separate the Cartesian 'I' from bodies: a logical case, which will argue that individuation of the self (and the self's thoughts) requires embodiment; and an existential case, which will argue that the individuation of worlds is impossible without embodiment. The former will use ideas advanced by P. F. Strawson and some recent philosophers (notably Quassim Cassam) influenced by him; and the latter will be driven by an attempt to repair the deficiencies in Heidegger's ontology.

For the present, we note that if only thoughts are undeniable – in particular the thought that I am thinking – and that, on this account, we are distanced from, and certainly not identified with, our bodies, then there is no basis for individuation of the 'I' whose existence is delivered by the *Cogito* argument. It is also difficult to understand in what sense the thoughts that comprise the argument, and are appealed to in the argument, could be *occurrent*. There appears to be no place of attachment for them. The *Cogito* argument not only strips off everything that gives the 'I' substance or reference; it also denies it individuation; and without individuation, 'I' is empty.

The critique of the notion of the isolated thinking mind (consciousness, person, subject) as a starting point is particularly associated with Heidegger, for whom it represented a supreme example of the error of intellectualism, the idea that the primary way of relating to being is through objective knowledge of things beyond, or outside, ourselves. In other words, Descartes could not get very far past his starting point because he started too far down the track – indeed, towards the end of it. He tried to read back into what is primordial about humans something that is advanced, abstract and complicated. This is a view concordant with, but somewhat at an angle to, the one which has been developed here.

Descartes' most fundamental error therefore was not to postulate two separate substances – mind and body – but to begin his inquiries in the wrong place. His dualism was simply consequential on this (though even then his argument did not lead necessarily down that path). The place to begin is not the mind because the articulate Cartesian mind thinking the thought 'I am thinking' is a very late entry on the scene. While it has the advantage of on-the-page necessity, it has the profound disadvantage of being unable to deliver more than an extensionless dot; and even this nugatory yield is possible only by using a language that presupposes a world, a community, that, in the very same moment, it places beyond its own unaided reach. It cannot get past absolute certainty and transparency to the utterly real lived world of incomplete knowledge and intelligibility – the world in which we live, whose existence no one truly doubts. Its hybrid status as an on-the-page argument that makes sense only by appealing to off-the-page intuitions (abstracted forms of self-presence) makes it unable to move forward without moving away from the clear and distinct ideas to which alone it grants certain truth. By placing everything that makes the argument work at all, and make sense, off stage, it is self-doomed from the outset.

Asserting that the *Cogito* argument is in fact a late reflection of the Existential Intuition may seem, from the Cartesian standpoint, to be begging the question. What seems safe to assume is that the discovery that the standpoint cannot be adopted – that the Pure Inquirer has to bring to the *Cogito* argument the very thing that she wanted to put into question prior to the argument, in order to engage in it, that the existential precondition of the token argument is at odds with the logical presupposition of the argument-type on the page – is quite deeply connected with the nature of the Existential Intuition as an *unassailable* assumption. 'That I am this ...' is not something about which I can be wrong because the assumption is not merely logical but also carnal. In it, I assume my flesh as when God is said to have assumed human form when he came down on earth or (a little less dramatically) as when I assume an office. That the assumption *is* carnal, that it really is flesh that I assume in this way, cannot be doubted if I start from the biogenetic standpoint outlined in section 1.2. But this starting point is not available if one is going to take the sceptical arguments seriously. We still need to demonstrate, independently of the biological story, that not only is the Existential Intuition necessarily true (which I believe that we can accept), but that what is (existentially) assumed in it is a body. Before we argue this, we first need to look again at the scope of first-person necessary truths and (as a correlative to this) the limits to first-person authority and of its immunity to doubt.

## NOTES

1. For a general argument for readmitting the contents of consciousness into places where, since Frege, they have been forbidden entry, see Raymond Tallis, 'Philosophies of Consciousness and Philosophies of the Concept, Or: Is There Any Point in Studying the Headache I Have Now?', in *Enemies of Hope. A Critique of Contemporary Pessimism*, 2nd edn (Basingstoke: Macmillan, 1999). We shall return to these issues in Volume 3.
2. Ludwig Wittgenstein, *Tractatus Logico-Philosophicus*, translated by D. F. Pears and B. F. McGuinness (London: Routledge & Kegan Paul, 1963), 5.632.
3. Ibid., 5.421.
4. A phrase that, of course, Thomas Nagel made his own in *The View from Nowhere* (Oxford: Oxford University Press, 1986). It is inaccurate to contrast the 'privacy' of first-person being with the publicity of third-person being. The correct contrast is between a) the privacy of first-person being with respect to other first-person beings, and b) the publicity of third-person being with respect to first-person beings. It is important to make this point to avoid the notion that third-person being (strictly no-person being) has intrinsic publicity. Its being disclosed requires first-person being.
5. Jaakko Hintikka, 'Cogito, ergo sum: Inference or Performance?', *The Philosophical Review*, Vol. LXXI, No. 1 (January 1962): 3–32.
6. René Descartes, *The Philosophical Works of Descartes*, translated by Elizabeth S. Haldane and G. R. T. Ross (Cambridge: Cambridge University Press, 1967), Vol. I, p. 157.
7. Ibid., Vol. II, p. 150.
8. Quassim Cassam, Introduction to *Self-Knowledge. Oxford Readings in Philosophy* ed. Quassim Cassam (Oxford: Oxford University Press, 1994).
9. The observation made by Paul Valery's M. Teste – 'That we never think that what we think conceals from us what we are' – is very much to the point here (*M. Teste*, translated by Jackson Mathews, London: Routledge & Kegan Paul, 1973, p. 23). We shall return to this when we examine externalist accounts of mind and meaning in Chapter 3.
10. Though he does sometimes seem a little ambivalent about how absolute the

separation between mind and body, and thought and sense experience, is. In a rather surprising passage in the Sixth Meditation, he asserts that 'For all these sensations of hunger, thirst, pain, etc. are in truth none other than certain confused modes of thought which are produced by the union and apparent intermingling of mind and body' (*The Philosophical Works of Descartes*, Vol. I, translated by Haldane and Ross, p. 192).The inconsistencies in Descartes' dualism are helpfully teased out by Bernard Williams in his chapter on 'Mind and its Place in Nature' in *Descartes: The Project of Pure Enquiry* (London: Penguin, 1977).

11. Reply to the Third Set of Objections, *The Philosophical Works of Descartes*, Vol. II, translated by Haldane and Ross, p. 64.

12. Lichtenberg famously argued that all one could infer from Descartes' argument was 'it thinks' or 'there is thinking'. Bertrand Russell made a similar point when he argued that Descartes should not have allowed himself to begin with 'I think', but only with 'there are thoughts'. *History of Western Philosophy* (London: George Allen and Unwin, 1961), p. 550. Erich Heller, in *The Disinherited Mind* (London: Penguin, 1961), took this further and suggested an updated version of Descartes for alienated modern man – particularly as exemplified in the works of Franz Kafka – should be 'It thinks, and therefore I am not' (p. 177). When in 1641 Hyperaspistes wrote, 'You do not know whether it is you your self who thinks, or whether the world-soul in you thinks, as the Platonists believe' (quoted in Anthony Kenny, *Descartes. A Study of his Philosophy*, 1968, reprinted Thoemmes Press, 1993, p. 62), he could have been anticipating the observations made by psychiatrists on schizophrenic patients who have 'thought-insertion': 'I look out of the window and I think that the garden looks nice and the grass looks cool, but the thoughts of Eammon Andrews come into my mind ... He treats my mind like a screen and flashes his thoughts onto it like you flash a picture' (quoted in Gerard O'Brien and Jon Opie, 'The Multiplicity of Consciousness and the Emergence of the Self', in A. S. David and T. Kircher (eds), *The Self and Schizophrenia: A Neuropsychological Perspective* (Cambridge: Cambridge University Press, 2002)); or the famous passage from Rimbaud's letter (13 May 1871): 'It is wrong to say "I think". One ought to say "I am thought" ... I is somebody else' (quoted in Graham Robb, *Rimbaud*, London: Picador, 2000, p. 83). Bernard Williams (in *Descartes*), argues that this minimalist inference – 'there is thinking' – is not allowed because it adopts a third-person viewpoint, while the actual occurrent thoughts that Descartes is referring to have to be relativised to the first person. Lichtenberg and others are 'wrong in saying that the *content* of the Cartesian thought should be impersonal rather than first-personal' (p. 97). 'If we have no help from anything except the pure point of view of consciousness, the only coherent way of conceiving a thought happening is to conceive of thinking it' – and that must require *someone* thinking it. Ironically, he argues, the minimalisers (by claiming that they are in receipt of the objective fact that 'there is thinking') replicate Descartes' own error when he believed that he could derive an objective truth – in his case that there is a thinking 'I' – from the first-person perspective. Even so, 'It thinks, therefore I am not' is not existentially possible because the full form of this experience would be 'I am thinking: "It thinks therefore I am not", therefore I am not'. When written out in full (and taken off the page into the realm of someone actually thinking) even Lichtenberg's modest 'There is thinking ...' would not capture what Descartes had captured: 'I am thinking: "There is thinking"' would deliver the thinker, or at least his thinking moment. Even the patient who believes he has been the victim of thought insertion would have to

believe that it is *he* who is being made to think these thoughts and *he*, moreover, who has a suspicion that they have been planted on him. In other words, while his sense of self may be distorted, it is not attenuated.

13. This is not unique to the *Cogito* argument. G. E. Moore's 'Proof of an External World' (Annual Philosophical Lecture, Henriette Hertz Trust, *Proceedings of the British Academy*, Vol. XXV, 1939, pp. 3–30) is another (justly notorious) example. The basis of his proof is as follows: 'I can prove now that two human hands exist. How? By holding up my two hands, and saying, as I make a certain gesture with the right hand, "There is one hand", and adding, as I make a certain gesture with the left, "and here is another"' (p. 25). He insists that the proof of 'the existence of external things' is 'a perfectly rigorous one'. Indeed, 'it is perhaps impossible to give a better or more rigorous proof of anything whatever'. What he offers, however, is an account of a demonstration that took place during the course of a lecture. Philosophers are invited to imagine, or to repeat, the action for themselves. In short, we are offered a *recipe* for demonstrating the existence of the outside world to ourselves. As for the *Cogito* argument, John Cottingham emphasises how what the *Meditations* proposes are not 'a set of blackboard doctrines' and that it 'is not so much a book to be read as a set of exercises to be engaged in'. Interview in Andrew Pyle (ed.), *Key Philosophers in Conversation*, The Cogito Interviews (London: Routledge, 1999), p. 221.

14. Notably Hintikka, in '*Cogito, Ergo Sum*: Inference or Performance'. Kenny, *Descartes*, first drew this to my attention. The discussion in this section is indebted to Kenny's excellent book in other ways. When the time comes, I will use the word 'performative' rather than 'performance' because the Austinian term captures the 'speech-act' dimension of what is the rehearsal of an assertion or claim. Perhaps one could characterise the argument as 'an intuition-driven, performed inference, leading (back) to an intuition'.

15. This ordeal, the Cartesian journey, is something that all philosophers should go through and all philosophy should start from, as Husserl pointed out.

16. We shall say more about 'the existential grammar' of 'I' in section 2.12.

17. Though it can introduce whirlpools all of its own. 'I think therefore I am' opens on to an infinite regression: 'I think "I think therefore I am"', 'I think "I think 'I think therefore I am'"', etc. It is intrinsic to the nature of self-consciousness that it may become a hall of facing mirrors. It is not, however, a particular philosophically interesting feature of it, though it may be terrifying: 'The *Cogito* argument leapt off the page and I went mad'.

18. Donald Davidson, 'Knowing One's Own Mind', in Cassam, *Self-Knowledge*, p. 41.

19. This section has been greatly modified (and I hope improved) as a result of the very useful criticism of Quassim Cassam and Howard Robinson. They both generously read my script with great care, identified a large number of elementary howlers, pointed them out with extreme gentleness and tact, while at the same time being sympathetic to what I was trying to say. Whether they would agree with what follows, I am not too sure, but I felt that I could not justify further trespassing on their generosity: they, too, have lives to lead.

20. For some thinkers (for example, Rudolf Carnap and W. V. O. Quine) there is no such thing as *de re* necessity: necessity is a relationship between propositions. And it is certainly possible to read the classic examples of *de re* necessity – that, for example, a coloured surface cannot be both entirely red and entirely green or a coloured area must be extended – as *de dicto* necessity lightly disguised. If we link

necessity to truth – so that which is necessary is 'true in all possible worlds' – and if, as many philosophers do, argue that 'it is only such things as statements or propositions, or beliefs or opinions, which are expressible in language, that are capable of being true or false, certain or doubtful' (A. J. Ayer, *The Problem of Knowledge*, London: Pelican Books, 1956, p. 52) – then it follows that all necessity must be *de dicto*; or that *de re* necessity is a different tier of *de dicto* necessity. Necessity inheres not in the properties of things themselves but only in some of our ways of speaking. We shall return to this matter in Volume 3. It is possible to see belief in *de re* necessity as a form of magic thinking not so much in the standard sense of 'mind projected into things' but in a variant sense of 'words among things'. The Existential Intuition narrows, and at one place closes, the gap between *de re* and *de dicto* necessity, as we shall discuss later.

21. That 'I am *a* this' is clearly necessarily true in the conventional logical sense. That 'I am *this* this' which looks contingent has the 'existential necessity' which we shall discuss presently.

22. I am aware that this selection is somewhat idiosyncratic and the manner in which the different types of identity are symbolised is scarcely standard. Furthermore, in the light of the huge literature on identity my comments are necessarily rather superficial. I want, however, only to say enough about some kinds of 'is' identity to serve my very specific purpose of making the peculiar nature of 'am' identity more visible by contrast.

23. This, according to Quine, is the only true identity relation: 'But for all the looseness of common usage, the term in its strict sense is as tight as a term can be. A thing is identical with itself and with nothing else, not even with its identical twin' (W. V. O. Quine, *Quiddities: An Intermittently Philosophical Dictionary*, London: Penguin Books, 1990, p. 89).

24. More precisely: What is the *point* of asserting identity relations?

25. There are, of course, many other modes of identity. This truncated and simplistic treatment of types of identity may be forgiven, I hope, if only because, as Steven Wagner says, 'it seems likely our everyday talk of identity has a richness and ambiguity that escapes formal characterization' ('Identity', in *The Cambridge Encyclopaedia of Philosophy*, edited by Robert Audi, Cambridge: Cambridge University Press, 1995, p. 359). Besides, as J. L. Austin once remarked, 'one has to be a special kind of fool to rush in where so many angels have trodden already'.

26. We might be inclined to say that in worlds where there were several names for a particular star but these names were always learned together, identity assertions between the Morning Star and the Evening Star would not be made – there would be no point in doing so – rather than that they would be untrue. People would say, 'Why are you bothering to tell me this when you know that I already know what you are telling me?' In this sense – namely, with respect to their assertion conditions rather than their truth conditions – they are sensitive to different empirical realities, and they differ in this respect from the 'Scott'/'Author of Waverley' case, where the fact that Scott is the author of Waverley is unknown to many people.

27. There is a further category of 'is' statement: the identification of the kind of thing to which an entity belongs. These are not strictly identity statements in the sense philosophers use. They are, however, statements of the type-identity, or the 'what' – the *quidditas* rather than the *haecceitas* or 'thisness' – of a particular entity, and they are often regarded as 'identity' statements in non-philosophical discourses: we identify X as a Y. Identity in this looser sense is very potent in the wider world

outside of philosophy. The categorisations to which one is assigned by others lie at the heart of the debates around 'the politics of identity'. The central battle of identity politics is around the externally imposed versus the internally assumed (in a sense that we shall develop shortly) categorisation – between a 'what' that is self-assumed by a 'who' and a 'what' that is imposed on an 'it' by another who or group of whos. This loose use of 'identity' and the apparent paradoxes it may generate are wittily captured by Quine: 'When ... the ornithologist says "This is the same as that", pointing in two directions, it would be absurd to accuse him of meaning what he says. He means that the species of this bird is identical with the species of that one' (*Quiddities*, p. 91). There are other, even less clear, examples of 'is' identity. For example, the identification of two manifestations as phases of the same object, as when I assert that that acorn that was planted 100 years ago (of which I have a photograph) is the same as this tree that I am looking at now. Our hesitation in assigning a full identity relationship to the acorn and the oak tree is reflected in our tendency to assert:

This oak tree is the same [thing] as that acorn
rather than

This oak tree is this acorn

Since they are (rather more than somewhat) discernible, we hold back from bluntly asserting their 'identity'. We shall return to these issues when we consider 'personal identity' – as something sustained over time – in Chapter 7.

28. The need to refer to Kripke was emphasised in correspondence by both Howard Robinson and Quassim Cassam. The key reference is Saul Kripke, *Naming and Necessity* (Oxford: Oxford University Press, 1970). I was not unaware of Kripke, but insufficiently aware of the necessity of naming him in this work – partly because I don't believe that he has shown what he purports to have shown – as will become apparent in the next few paragraphs.

29. Thomas Baldwin, 'Exploring the Possibilities', in *Contemporary Philosophy. Philosophy in English since 1945* (Oxford: Oxford University Press, 2001), pp. 127–8. I have benefited enormously from Baldwin's lucid exposition of the Kripke's arguments for the necessity of identity and of the problems this runs into.

30. In 'Knowing One's Own Mind' he remarks: 'I realize that this remark, like many others in this piece, may show that I don't know a rigid designator when I see one. I don't' (p. 56).

31. Of even greater concern is the claim that the essential necessity of identity is manifested in an essential necessity of origin, an essential necessity of substance and an essential necessity of form. Let us examine the example that Kripke gives of the essential necessity of origin: that of the origin of a child. It is a genetic necessity, Kripke argues, that a child has the biological parents it does have. It seems impossible to disagree with this. While it is possible that my parents might not have met and had me, it is not possible that anyone else could be my parents. Likewise, while it is possible at my moment of birth I could have any number of futures ahead of me – I could have become something other than a doctor and other than the father of the children I actually have – the fact that I am a doctor and am the father of the children I actually have cannot now be untrue. This does not, however, place the fact that I am a doctor and the father of two boys on the same level as the fact that I am the son of Edward and Mary Tallis. These two earlier facts do not have the status of being part of my necessary identity. This should not lead us to conclude that my being the son of Edward and Mary Tallis is a necessary truth, or that it is not

possible that I might not have existed. The train of argument that leads in this (wrong) direction goes as follows:

a) I am the son of my parents
b) My parents are Edward and Mary Tallis
c) Therefore I am necessarily the son of Edward and Mary Tallis
d) Since I am necessarily the son of Edward and Mary Tallis, then they necessarily had children.
e) Since they necessarily had children, they necessarily had the children they did have, including Raymond Tallis.

This train of thought seems to foreclose my parents' future by forcing them to fulfil an inescapable destiny of meeting and becoming my parents. This is obviously nonsense. So where did the argument go wrong? It begins with the assumption that I exist. This assumption is inescapable because the argument is being put forward by me – it is in the first person. My existence goes without saying because it is I who am saying: I am both the subject of the sentence and the utterer of it. This assumption, however, is contingent. As Hector-Neri Castaneda has said, 'the first-person propositions belonging to a person X have a contingent existence: they exist if and only if X exists' ('On the Phenomeno-Logic of the I', in *Proceedings of the 14th International Conference of Philosophy*, iii, University of Vienna, 1969: 260–6). The invisible contingency on which the train of argument stands is buried in the first statement and in fact is there in 'I am'. Since the argument begins with a contingency, its conclusion also must be contingent. This helps to escape from the difficulties associated with the example discussed by Michael Dummett in his critique of Kripke: 'Note on an Attempted Refutation of Frege', in *Frege: Philosophy of Language* (London: Duckworth, 1973), pp. 110ff. (I think I agree with Dummett, but he is so determined to refute Kripke within the framework of the Fregean distinction between sense and reference that his argument is difficult to follow.) St. Anne is the mother of the Virgin Mary. The Virgin Mary could have no other parent. The conclusion that St. Anne was necessarily the parent of the Virgin Mary – this was a fate she could not elude – could be drawn only if it was a logical necessity that the Virgin Mary should exist and this is manifestly not the case. The opposite is thinkable without contradiction. The case is complicated by further considerations. Being Mary's mother is so essential to our idea of St. Anne (and at this distance of time she is primarily an idea), it is almost a defining characteristic because for most of us she is just a name attached to that single characteristic. St. Anne without motherhood of the Virgin Mary, while not logically unthinkable, is like *Hamlet* without the Prince or Shakespeare without his works – difficult to think. It is her place in history and her place in our consciousness. Her motherhood is the handle by which we take hold of her; a sense that is almost the canonical road to the referent; a definite description. As a result, asserting that 'St. Anne is the mother of Mary' feels like saying 'The mother of Mary is the mother of Mary'. This cognitive inertia, this near-unthinkability, should not be mistaken for evidence of necessity; to do would be to confuse psychological facts with logical necessity.

32. And far more justified than the cognitive propositional form that Kant imposed upon that which he believed secured the unity of apperception – 'The "I think" that accompanies all my perceptions' – as we shall discuss in Chapter 4.

33. This must not be taken to imply that whatever I say or believe about myself is necessarily true. We shall discuss the scope of the Existential Intuition and the limits of its incorrigibility in the next chapter.

34. These are inextricably linked. 'That I *am* this' and 'That *I* am *doing* these happenings' (or 'These happenings are my *doings*') are in their least developed form like the recto and verso of a sheet of paper. It is only subsequently that selfhood and agency differentiate, so that it then makes sense to link together, as if they were separable, the self and its actions, and to attribute the latter to the former. We shall leave discussion of agency until Chapter 8.

35. These characterisations of the 'I' in *The Critique of Pure Reason* are cited in Quassim Cassam, *Self and World* (Oxford: Clarendon Press, 1997), pp.15 and 16 respectively. We shall return to Kant, and to Cassam's discussion of him, in Chapter 5.

36. See G. E. M Anscombe, 'The First Person', reprinted in ibid., pp. 140–59.

37. Gottlieb Frege, *The Thought: A Logical Inquiry*, translated by Marcelle and Anthony Quinton, in *Philosophical Logic* ed. P. F. Strawson (Oxford: Oxford University Press, 1967). For an excellent account of Frege's critique of Husserl's psychologism and the middle period Husserl's own rejection of his early psychologism, see David Bell, *Husserl* (Oxford: Blackwell, 1990). See also note 1 above.

38. This is not, of course, the first time that this has been pointed out, though not in this form. The focus has usually been on the 'I' rather than the 'am', as in J. G. Fichte's assertion that the 'I' is not a fact but an act; that it is not something that is merely discovered or encountered but something that is *posited*. The Existential Intuition differs, however, from Fichte's 'self-positing I', from his 'fact/act' and his notion that the essence of selfhood lies in an active positing of self-identity, inasmuch as the I that 'ams' and 'is ammed' in the Existential Intuition is not transcendent. Unlike Fichte's 'I', it neither descends upon the material or natural world from some spiritual realm nor does it escape it; rather it is the assumption of a part of the natural world by itself, *as* itself.

39. Alfred Tarski actually talks about 'statements' rather than assertions (in Karl Popper, 'Comments on Tarski's Theory of Truth' (in *Objective Knowledge. An Evolutionary Process*, Oxford: Oxford University Press, 1972, pp. 318–40). Popper remarks that 'he finds uninteresting (because mainly verbal) the problem of whether we should speak of "sentences", "statements", or "propositions"'. He does not mention 'assertions', and so I do not know whether this is a legitimate term to use with respect to Tarski's theory. It is, however, important to me, not only because (as noted in Chapter 1) 'proposition' is such a slippery term, but also because 'assertion' seems to retain the link with human activity, intention and consciousness, which the other three words (in particular 'propositions') seem to have mostly lost through being depsychologised. Whether or not this last is true (and it probably isn't – I don't actually believe that even a proposition can exist outside of its token instances in which it is proposed, meant or understood – and this is important to the discussion in Volume 3, notably the critique of Fregean anti-psychologism), I wanted to retain 'assertion' as it captures what I believe is the deep philosophical significance of Tarski's Theory of Truth, which I am arrogant enough to believe escaped Tarski himself, and which we shall also revisit in Volume 3.

40. Frege, *The Thought*, p. 20.

41. Tarski, of course, didn't think that either. His theory aimed to rehabilitate the classical idea that truth is correspondence to *facts*. I think this is wrong. That the whiteness of snow is not *of itself* a fact (any more than the snow crystals are intermixed with '-ness' like a sherbert) is a matter of immense significance. We shall return to this in Volume 3, where we shall develop a version of the correspondence

theory that makes facts not one of the correspondents but a point in which correspondence inheres.

42. For more discussion of the distinction between the 'existence conditions' and the 'truth conditions' of true statements, see Raymond Tallis, 'Explicitness and Truth (and Falsehood)', in *On the Edge of Certainty* (Basingstoke: Macmillan, 1999).

43. More is placed beyond doubt simply in virtue of the limits to the initial doubt, as we shall discuss presently.

44. Anscombe, 'The First Person', p. 140.

45. Although, as Kenny has pointed out in *Descartes. A Study of his Philosophy* (1968, reprinted Thoemmes Press, 1993), p. 47, Descartes 'states the proof not only in the first person singular (*Discourse*, *Meditations*) but also in the first person plural (*Principles*) and in the second person (*Search After Truth*). In the *Principles* ... Descartes observes in the third person that "there is a contradiction in conceiving that what thinks does not, at the same time as it thinks, exist"' (p. 47).

46. It is in fact impossible to imagine such an argument occurring to an entirely asocial creature, and being addressed only to itself. (This, by the way, is the existential argument against solipsism: 'solipsism' as a theory would not occur to a creature for whom there was no outside world.) It is impossible to think of the *Cogito* argument as anything other than part of the great (public) conversation of philosophy. (Unless one believes that one has thought it up – and the books in which one has encountered Descartes' name and much else besides – oneself.)

47. Stanley Cavell, *Must We Mean What We Say?*, quoted in Barry Stroud, 'Reasonable Claims', in *Understanding Human Knowledge* (Oxford: Oxford University Press, 2000), p. 53.

48. For Wittgenstein's trajectory and the link between his earliest published works and his final thoughts, see the title essay in Tallis, *On the Edge of Certainty*. Interestingly, Maurice Merleau-Ponty made the same point in *Phenomenology of Perception*: 'I can evolve a solipsist philosophy but, in doing so, I assume the existence of a community of men endowed with speech, and I address myself to it ... Even that universal meditation which cuts the philosopher off from his nation, his friendships, his prejudices, his empirical being, the world in short, and which seems to leave him in complete isolation, is in reality an act, the spoken word, and consequently dialogue' (translated by Colin Smith, London: Routledge & Kegan Paul, 1962, pp. 360–1).

49. Haldane and Ross, *The Philosophical Works of Descartes*, Vol. I, p. 244.

50. I owe this nice phrase to Anscombe, The First Person', pp. 157–8. She argues that 'the Cartesianly preferred thoughts' – such as 'I am thinking' – are 'not the ones to investigate if one wants to understand the "I" philosophically' because, unlike, say, 'I am standing' they are so far removed from anything that might be checked, in part because they are desperately vague.

51. Haldane and Ross, *The Philosophical Works of Descartes*, Vol. II, p. 137. Gassendi could have gone beyond activity; for whatever *feels* also exists. What makes an 'I' exist, however, is the intuition the individual feels 'That I am this ...'.

52. Descartes, in ibid., Vol. I, p. 222, quoted in Kenny, *Descartes*.

53. If it is an argument, as opposed to a direct intuition. As Descartes himself points out, the knowledge that one exists, and the truth of the proposition 'I think, therefore I am', 'is not product of your reasoning, no lesson that your masters have taught you; it is something that your mind sees, feels, handles'. Quoted in Kenny, *Descartes*, p. 53. This compresses the entire argument into something close to the Existential Intuition – 'That I am this ...'. We shall return to this again.

54. This step is *not* dependent on the assumption that 'Whatever bears a predicate must exist'. This is a flawed assumption; after all, Pegasus (who does not exist) can carry the predicate 'has wings'. In other words, predicates may be attributed to non-existent objects. In the case of 'I am thinking', the attribution is of a very special kind; namely, self-attribution. This presupposes existence. Indeed, the attribution cannot be purely verbal, as it is with Pegasus: it is existential. This makes the form of the argument a bit suspect; for one does not discover that one exists by the application of a general principle – 'Whatever thinks, exists': the attribution is direct and directly particular. (Cf. All men are mortal; I am a man; therefore I am mortal. One can discover the truth that one dies but not the truth that one exists.)

55. It is interesting in this context to consider John Searle's argument against Dennett's denial of the reality of conscious experiences, of qualia in *The Mystery of Consciousness* (London: Granta Books, 1998): 'You can't disprove the existence of conscious experiences by proving that they are only an appearance disguising the underlying reality, because *where consciousness is concerned the existence of the appearance is the reality*. If it seems to me that I am having conscious experiences, then I am having conscious experiences' (p.112); 'where the existence of conscious states is concerned, you can't make the distinction between appearance and reality *because the existence of the appearance is the reality in question*' (p. 122). I cannot be mistaken that I am conscious as surely as I cannot be mistaken that I am thinking.

56. We are close here to the fundamental ideas of the trilogy. The double means of discovering one's bodily self – as, say, a feeling of cold, contradicted by discovering one's skin is hot (as in fever) – underlines the division between subject and object within one's own body and the differentiation within awareness between sentience and knowledge. The knowledge 'that' one's skin is hot is accessible to others; the feeling that one is cold is not (except indirectly through shivering). See Volume 3 passim, especially Chapter 4. The deepest link with the beginning of knowledge is through the exploratory hand that transforms the body into an object of knowledge revealed to a part of the body that has the status of an instrument – in this sense an instrument of cognition.

57. There are so many ways of depersonalising it; for example, by talking about 'The Cartesian "I"' and so on. This kind of talk conceals a fundamental misrepresentation of the *Cogito* argument.

58. The tendency to privilege thought-types, which are as it were 'bearerless' (as opposed to token-thoughts, which have to be thought by someone and so have bearers) will be discussed in Volume 3, where we subject Fregean and other anti-psychologistic accounts of thought, pushing the contents of the thinking consciousness to one side, to hostile examination.

59. P. M. S. Hacker, *Wittgenstein: Mind and Meaning* (Oxford: Blackwell, 1990), p. 472.

60. Ludwig Wittgenstein quoted in ibid., p. xiii.

61. Ludwig Wittgenstein, *Tractatus Logico-Philosophicus*, transl. D. F. Pears and B. F. McGuinness (London: Routledge and Kegan Paul, 1961), 6.51.

62. Discussed in the title essay of Tallis, *On the Edge of Certainty*.

63. Gerd Brand, *The Central Texts of Wittgenstein*, transl. with an introduction Robert Innis (Oxford: Blackwell, 1979), p. 137.

64. A position which, of course, undermined the notion that philosophical discussion could be brought to a halt – an end if not a conclusion – by elucidating the way words are used. The reduction of, say, the problem of perception and the mysterious notion of ways of 'seeing aspects' from a causal to a conceptual one (as is stated in

*Philosophical Investigations*, p. 213e) would not, in fact, be of much help in moving things on. If the grammar of words (and the associated logical geography of concepts) were a reflection of a way of life, then the latter re-enters philosophy as something that one has to clarify. *Da capo.*

65. Anscombe, 'The First Person'. The appeal to a 'philosophical grammar' approach in part overlapped with G. E. Moore's defence of common sense, though this had a rather more superficial origin than Wittgenstein's second-order scepticism and did not acknowledge the profounder third-order scepticism that Wittgenstein discovered in his last few months of life, which reunited him with his earliest most questing self.

66. Actually, it can. Imagine someone who has an insufficient grasp of English. He thinks that 'I' means what is meant by 'he'. Under such circumstances, it will fail to indicate what the speaker means by it. This, however, is only a verbal point; but it is, as we shall see, justified so long as 'philosophical grammar' overlooks the obligatory existential dimension of first-person reference.

67. Ludwig Wittgenstein, *On Certainty*, trans. by Denis Paul and G. E. M. Anscombe (Oxford: Blackwell, 1969).

68. Note that Wittgenstein doesn't allow knowing just what words mean 'now for me' as the necessary condition of sceptical thought; for, as he often pointed out, they would not have meaning for me unless that meaning was one that conformed to and was established, stabilised and underwritten by the community. Private languages – such as I might deploy in the Cartesian prison – not only have no point but also are a contradiction in terms.

69. We may characterise P. F. Strawson's position in the following passage as being half-way between philosophical grammar and existential grammar: 'There is no sense in the idea of ascribing states of consciousness to oneself, or at all, unless the ascriber already knows how to ascribe at least some states of consciousness to others ... The point is not that we must accept this conclusion in order to avoid scepticism, but that we must accept it in order to explain the existence of the conceptual scheme in terms of which the sceptical problem is stated ...' (*Individuals. An Essay in Descriptive Metaphysics*, London: Methuen, 1957, p. 106). The dissent from scepticism which comes from the standpoint of the Existential Intuition is deeper than implied by this passage, which still operates *within language*. The Existential Intuition is not, of course, in its primordial form an ascription, but an intuition, not a proposition or an assertion but an existential assumption, a lived reality. (We shall return to this key passage in Strawson in Chapter 3.)

70. John Lyons, *Semantics* (Cambridge: Cambridge University Press, 1977), Vol. 2, p. 645.

71. It is, as John Perry said, an *essential* indexical. See 'The Problem of the Essential Indexical' in *Self-Knowledge*, ed. Cassam.

72. Roland Barthes' observation (in *Elements of Semiology*, translated by Annette Lavers and Colin Smith, London: Jonathan Cape, 1967, p. 22) is relevant here: 'the *shifters* are probably the most interesting double structure: the most ready example is that of the personal pronoun (*I, thou*), an indicial symbol which unites within itself the conventional and the existential bonds: for it is only by virtue of a conventional rule that it represents its object ... but on the other hand, since it designates the person who utters it, it can only refer existentially to the utterance.'

73. It is important, in the context of this claim, to note two further observations made by Lyons: a) that there are no languages which lack first-person pronouns (p. 639);

and b) that person-deixis is something 'that cannot be analysed away in terms of something else' (p. 646).

74. I may have underestimated the extent to which Descartes knew what he was about; or at least the extent to which he acknowledged that *Cogito ergo sum* was more than just an abstract, decontextualised argument. Kenny (*Descartes*, p. 55) considers whether *Cogito, ergo sum* is an inference or an intuition and concludes that, while it may be plausibly interpreted as the former in Descartes' earlier formations, in its mature expression, it is both: intuition is necessary not only for seeing the truth of the premises, but also for seeing *that* the conclusions follow from the premises so that 'what is from one point of view intuited is from another point of view deduced'. In the context of philosophical argument, the appeal to intuition seems half way between an argument and an appeal to introspection. The intuition has the immediacy and self-evidence of introspection and the generalisability of an argument. In other respects, it seems like a telescoped argument. At any rate in this context, where the argument bears so directly upon what one is – and hence upon what one feels one is – argument and intuition are not easily separable.

75. In the version of the *Cogito* argument set out in *The Search After Truth*, it is a *Dubito* argument: it is doubting rather than thinking that cannot be doubted. Eudoxus, the spokesman for Descartes' view, argues as follows: 'Since, then, you cannot deny that you doubt, and that it is on the other hand certain that you doubt, and so certain that you cannot even doubt of that, it is likewise true that you are, you who doubt; and that is so true that you can no longer doubt of it any more' (Haldane and Ross, *The Philosophical Works of Descartes*, Vol. I, p. 316, quoted in Kenny, *Descartes*, p. 47). Doubting, like thinking, is something you cannot do without knowing that you are doing it, and hence without knowing that you exist – because you cannot do things if you don't exist. Doubting, that is to say, is a thought-act; it is a mode of thinking, where thinking is defined as – 'whatever takes place within ourselves so that we are conscious of it, insofar as it is an object of our consciousness'. It seems, then, like an innocent variation. It is, however, a version in which the abyss does yawn rather widely. If I have a second-order doubt that I doubt – indeed, if, as Descartes requires us, we are confident that we cannot doubt that we doubt – then this will undermine my first-order doubt and, presumably, challenge my certainty that I am first-order doubting. At any rate, the first doubt has been eliminated by the time we reach the end of the performance. That first-order doubt is, therefore, not indubitable at all but actually self-contradictory. The only way, in other words, that the argument can perform its work is if there is a temporal separation between the first half and the second half of the token enactment of it.

76. It is strange to think of a philosophy congress in which the *Cogito* argument and the systematic doubt that prepares the ground for it are taken seriously – while everyone present takes each other's existence for granted and assumes that there was a man called Descartes who discovered the argument!

77. Readers may object that I have forgotten the killer thought, which awakens the possibility of universal error and so justifies global if not total doubt: 'I might be dreaming'. The reason why dreams are so important philosophically is that we not only dream facts that are not true, we also dream the world around those facts, and are enclosed by those worlds. We are inside the false facts, instead of the facts being inside us. To dream is to be in a state of almost global error. The notion of a dream – and of being deceived as to the nature of the dream – is, however, parasitic on that of reality, as J. L. Austin pointed out. (Though this is not a matter of the meaning of

words of, say, 'unreal' rather than 'real' 'wearing the trousers' as Austin put it, but of the differentiation of types of experience.) The seeming reality of certain dreams is secondary to the actual reality of reality. Being able to entertain the very *thought* 'I might be dreaming' presupposes all of those things still to be in place if the thought is to make sense to me. The deeper point, however, is that the seeming reality of a dream – its realism – is parasitic on the reality of reality.

78. Or, as Michael Grant has suggested (personal correspondence): Not ('I!' and not-I).

79. J. Cottingham, R. Stothoff and D. Murdock (eds), *The Philosophical Writings of Descartes* (Cambridge: Cambridge University Press, 1985), Vol. II, p. 100.

80. One derivative form of this magic thinking is the magic thought that 'this body is me/mine', that this impersonal thing is the basis of my person. We shall discuss this in Chapter 6.

81. Kenny, *Descartes*, p. 95.

# CHAPTER 3

# First-Person Authority and Immunity from Error

we must … recognise that, as regards inner sense, that by means of it we intuit ourselves only as we are inwardly affected *by ourselves*; in other words, that, so far as inner intuition is concerned, we know our own subject only as appearance, not as it is in itself.[1]

## 3.1 WHAT DOES THE EXISTENTIAL INTUITION PLACE BEYOND DOUBT?

The temptation to move directly from the self-realising realisation 'That I am this …' to 'That I am this body …' by appealing to the biological story about the genesis of self-consciousness must be resisted. We cannot directly intuit the animal origins of self-consciousness – and the necessary embodiment of 'I' – from *within* the Existential Intuition. The novelty of the Existential Intuition (evident when it is cast in propositional form and imagined as realised in a particular bearer, in the least contentious case oneself) – that it expresses a *de re* necessity and that (notwithstanding Kripke) it is unique in this respect – is offset by uncertainty as to the scope of the necessary, empirical truths it uncovers.

We have described a putative early form of the Intuition in which the 'this' that I am is the engaged body as revealed to itself. To describe this form as 'primitive' carries the implication of 'earliness' which draws on a link with the bio-genetic story which we cannot presuppose. Perhaps we could describe it as 'minimal'. The body in question would not be the biological (or physical) body but the phenomenal body; the body as it is revealed to the embodied individual. The Existential Intuition does not yield any certain knowledge of what the body is itself – that it is made of flesh, that it has certain biological and other material characteristics, etc. – or even that there is a material body, which in some sense transcends the phenomenal body, that I am. 'Am', with its *de re* necessity, has limited penetration of the material world. Necessity extends only so far as the Intuition is inseparable, or at least incompletely separable, from what it intuits.

Whatever necessary truths it establishes, they cannot be facts, which *are* separate from the Intuition. To put it crudely: existed first-person identity is not fact-shaped. The Intuition 'That I am this ...' certainly places 'That I am' – indeed 'That I am this ...' – beyond doubt. But it does not place other things – such as that I am a particular, objectively specified, 'this' – beyond doubt. Just as the belief 'That I am Napoleon' demonstrates the truth of the belief 'That I am' but does not prove that I am Napoleon. 'Am' cannot use the epistemological privileges that attach to first-person being to buy certainties in the objective world of factual truth. The *de re* necessity realised in the Existential Intuition has a limited range. Yes, it is real, is immune from doubt and is about something that really exists, is a necessity that is not merely a *de dicto* limit on the bounds of possibility. It is all these things; but is it worth having? What do we derive from it? What, in short, is the scope of first-person authority?

Before we address this question, we ought to pause at this objection: How can the Existential Intuition *not* know that nature of what it is that it assumes as itself? If I assume my body as myself, surely I must in some important sense know what I am assuming. Alas, no. We have a problem here precisely analogous to the one that tripped up Descartes as he tried to exit from his imaginary prison. Indeed, our problem is potentially greater; after all, it seems easier to defend the idea that a self whose being is essentially thought knows itself through and through better than one whose being is in some sense identical with that of a body.[2]

Let us start with an examination of what I know about my own self and, in particular, my own thoughts. We shall discover that philosophers have found unexpected opacities even in them.

### 3.2 THE IDEA OF FIRST-PERSON AUTHORITY AND ITS LIMITS

There are several ways in which my authority on myself cannot be matched by others. There many things that I know about Raymond Tallis (RT) that are unknown to others. These things may be divided into those that I know and others happen not to know; and those that I know, or at least am aware of, and others could not know. In the former category are all sorts of experiences I have had or events that have involved me that may be articulated as statements of fact. There are several reasons why you may not know certain facts about RT that RT knows: I may have concealed them from you; you may simply have not been present when the events took place or I had the experiences; or the events or experiences are primarily 'inner' – as for example, the pain I suffered yesterday that I stoically kept mum about, the grudge I harbour against someone, the true motives for my actions, the worries that preoccupy me, the thoughts I am having now – and require my disclosure to make them evident to you. In principle, these could be communicated to others, at least at the level of factual truths.

That I am such an authority on myself in this sense is linked to the fact that I cannot but be present when things befall me, or I engage in activity. I have no choice but to be in the places that I have been in, to be present at the conversations I participate in, to have the thoughts that I have, to experience the pains that are mine, to entertain the hopes I hope. That I know things about myself that are unknown to others is, for the most part, then, the unsurprising consequence of the fact that those others do not occupy the viewpoint that I have. Usually, these things unknown to some, or all, others are so banal as hardly to rate as 'secrets'. They are simply consequences of the unbroken positional advantage that I have with respect to myself that no one could share.[3]

This is the least contentious, least interesting and least mysterious area of my special authority on myself. What I have privileged access to can be satisfactorily expressed in the form of factual assertions: they are things that I can tell others about. I do not have to tell myself about them because I experience them directly. No one but me knows what I am doing at present – that I am sitting in a hotel room, typing this page, looking up from time to time at the trees shimmering in the sunlight. But there is nothing to stop me from telling others, as the preceding sentence demonstrates. Or nothing to stop others discovering this for themselves, by finding me in this hotel room. There is, that is to say, an ignorance about me that others may have that may, if I choose, be alleviated: I can share some of my privileged knowledge of what is happening to me. It remains largely undisclosed, and hence beyond others' knowledge, not because I have any explicit intention to conceal it, but because there is no reason to reveal it: a comprehensive transcript of my life would be utterly tedious and, as Tristam Shandy discovered, endless. So there is nothing special about this authority: not only can my knowledge be shared, but I can also get things demonstrably wrong: experiences may be misinterpreted (those trees could be patterned curtains) and they may certainly be mis-remembered and I an unwitting font of false facts.

I have another form of privileged authority. I have access to things about myself that others could never know: 'awarenesses' that may be described as falling under the heading of 'what it is like' to be me. At the most obvious level, there are the basic experiences or sensations that I have and which you can at best vaguely guess at. Even if you had the same experience when you looked at a blue vase that I had, neither of us could be sure that we had the same type of experience.[4] At a higher level, you could not know what it is like to be put together psychologically like RT, what it is like to have my transitions, to pass from one experience to the next, from one thought to another, from one event to another, to be busy/sweaty/worried as I was when I was hurrying the other day to an appointment, etc.

We sometimes have a feeling that we have little inner knowledge even of the people with whom we share most daylight. Lying next to my wife the other night, she asleep, I awake, listening to her breathing, the deeply comforting sound of her presence, uttered in the ur-sound underlying all possible speech, I was aware as never before that I did not understand how she hung together. After thirty years being as close as two human beings can be, I still do not know what it is like to be Mrs Me any more than she knows what it is like to be Mr Her. I know as much, that is to say, of the organisation of her waking hours as I know of the content of her sleeping dreams. And yet this sort of tragic talk is absurd. Human beings in general understand one another rather well – rather too well at times. The drunk who says 'My wife does not understand me' is really complaining that her excellent understanding, rooted in a mountain of empirical data, does not accord with his rather romantic misunderstanding of himself. Specific misunderstandings stand out against a massive background of shared assumptions, understanding and knowledge. The chance-met stranger and I are able, if we wish, to engage in a way, with a subtlety of interaction, that would be simply impossible if we did not each have a pretty good idea of what each in some very important respects was like.

And yet …what? How many of our experiences have been truly shared in the sense of being similar? Take those dozens of eight-hour journeys down to Cornwall, when we were all four of us – two children, two adults – together in the same car, travelling along the same roads, listening quite often to the same stories on the radio, all downwind from the same rank odour of the dogs panting in the back. We had utterly different journeys. Our bodies felt different, the views made different sense, the structure of time in the long hours was different, our preoccupations, recreations and responsibilities were different. The car carried four different journeys. It is impossible for me to imagine, even less to express, how those journeys were experienced by the three others. (It's only slightly less impossible, now I think of it, to express, or even recall in a sustained way, how those journeys were experienced by *me*. But that's a different story.)

I suppose I could put it like this: I have as much objective knowledge as anyone about my wife and family. But the most detailed and informed knowledge of what they are like – the kind of information that permits world-sharing, communication, cooperation, imaginative interaction – falls short of what it is like to be them. When I try to imagine them from within – how they cohere, how their minds pass from one thought to the next, how I figure in their consciousnesses, what things loom large in their minds and what charge of significance they carry, what it feels like to be them – I can do so only in the very general terms that I might bring to my thoughts about a stranger. And yet we have been, and still are, very close. What this says about my familiarity with my world and the more or less casual acquaintances within it, hardly bears thinking about. The world of being-with others, this ordinary day-lit place, is in fact a zone of darkness.

This was captured by Joseph Conrad:

> It is when we try to grapple with another man's intimate need that we perceive how incomprehensible, wavering, and misty are the beings that share with us the sight of the stars and the warmth of the sun. It is as if loneliness were a hard and absolute condition of existence; the envelope of flesh and blood on which our eyes are fixed melts before the out-stretched hand, and there remains only the capricious, inconsolable, and elusive spirit that no eye can follow, no hand can grasp.[5]

This is perhaps part of a larger problem – and certainly part of a wider panic: the feeling that we pass through our lives without ever quite touching the sides; that we are never quite fully *there* – there to and for what is there. We humans hook together – like Lucretian atoms – briefly, share the same paths and then veer off. But even shared occasions are not quite shared and the single occasion is really as multiple as the participants, as the viewpoints that make it up.

At any rate, tragic sense apart, there are areas where I can be said to enjoy (or suffer) a unique, non-accidental authority on myself. Defining the scope of this second kind of first-person authority in a non-contentious way is not easy, particularly since its epistemic privileges are interwoven with what looks like epistemic *under*-privilege. It sometimes seems, for example, that others have a better idea of my motives than I do myself. Others may sometimes get a clearer view of what I look like than I do.[6] Behaviourists, for whom emotions are to be cashed out entirely in actions and inferred from the latter, may even claim (with little plausibility) that they sometimes see more clearly than I what I am feeling. There may be cases – as I am increasingly finding when I talk to my mother about my childhood – that much of my own past (at which we were indubitably present) is recalled more fully and more accurately by others. When Robert Burns exclaimed 'Oh to see ourselves as others see us', he implied that we would have not only a different but also a truer vision of ourselves. None of this, however, overturns the general truth that I know so much more about myself than others do – and that this is no great cause for self-congratulation. Being so well informed about RT does not make me some kind of scholar, if a rather over-specialised one. (It would not go down very well if I offered 'The experiences of Raymond Tallis' as my specialist topic on Mastermind.)

The most interesting, but most contentious, area of special authority is that in which I 'know what it is like' for me to experience something. For some, it does not make sense to speak in this way. At any rate, there is much argument about whether my knowing such a thing as 'what it is like to be me' or 'what it is like to have my experiences' counts as knowledge at all, especially where it is assumed to be something that a) I cannot be mistaken over, and b) something that I may not be able to communicate. Not only is it not intrinsically a fact – it is not directly experienced in factual form – neither is it something that lends itself to factual expression. Having said this, it is (unsurprisingly) difficult to capture exactly what it is that is incommunicable. While I may not be able to say what it is like to feel tired, I can say *that* I feel tired and thereby communicate something important about what RT feels like. If someone asks me what I feel like (or what it feels like to be me at the moment) I might say 'tired' and this, at one level, would be to answer the question. The inability to communicate what it is that is incommunicable about 'what it is like to be RT' raises justified suspicions as to whether there is anything to communicate. Some philosophers are reluctant to concede that there really is something in addition to 'tired' that RT cannot communicate; something corresponding to 'what is it like to be Raymond Tallis feeling tired', which remains as a nameless residue after he has said all he can say about his tiredness. There are good reasons for their reluctance but, even so, it would be odd to deny that there are certain things that one knows (or is aware of, or senses) about oneself that one cannot communicate to others; and that these are things that one has not arrived at by observation or are dependent on evidence. When I tell someone that I am in pain, I am informing them of something that they could not have got to know without my somehow expressing it – verbally or non-verbally. This seems to reflect something like knowledge that I have in virtue of my privileged access to myself. It is, however, not merely a matter of sharing the fruits of positional advantage. For the pain I am suffering, which makes my assertion that I am in pain true, is something I could not fail to experience; while the assertion that I am in pain falls short of fully expressing what I am experiencing.

Even so, if we accept that there is a form of first-person authority which is not vulnerable to challenge by others, then it is not senseless to try to define its scope. We could pose the challenge in a form that brings us closer to our earlier discussion: 'What do I know with certainty about myself?' In what areas do I not only have first-person authority but an authority that cannot be overridden? The Existential Intuition delivers an archetypal example of such authority: 'That I am this …'. The *Cogito* delivers another argument: that I am thinking cannot be denied by myself, the thinker. If we start from the *Cogito* argument, however, we do not get from the moment of thinking to a thinking entity (person, substance) – to *res cogitans*. Even more depressingly, some recent writers have argued, first-person authority not only fails to extend knowing with certainty what one is; it fails even to deliver certain knowledge as to what it is one is thinking.

It has been argued that we do not know our own thoughts. Not only does 'I think therefore I am' not deliver knowledge of what I am; it does not yield full knowledge of the thought we are having. Donald Davidson, for example, has argued that, while we do indeed have first-person authority with respect to propositional attitudes such as beliefs, the contents of those propositional attitudes are often determined by facts external to the person whose attitudes they are. Since these facts may be unknown to us, we may not know the contents they determine.[7] Building on Hilary Putnam's claim that the natural history of how someone learned the use of a word necessarily makes a difference to what the word means,[8] Davidson suggests that two thoughts that are the same to the thinker may have different meanings, depending on the conditions under which their constituent words were acquired. He concludes that their meanings are not 'in the thinker's head'[9] – or, come to that, in his mind; they are at least in part identified by events and objects outside of the person. I don't know my own mind because I don't even know my own thoughts, and I don't even know my own thoughts because the meanings of the words in which my thoughts are presented to me are rooted in things outside of my thoughts, indeed outside of my mind: 'the contents of our thoughts and the meanings of our words are often fixed by factors of which we are ignorant'.

Davidson cites, without fully supporting it, a view advanced by Andrew Woodfield. Referring to the claim that the contents of the mind are often determined by facts external, and perhaps unknown, to the person whose mind it is, he says:

Because the external relation is not determined subjectively, the subject is not authoritative about that. A third person may well be in a better position than the subject to know which object the subject is thinking about, hence be better placed to know which thought it was.[10]

This apparently overturns the Cartesian idea that 'the one thing we can be certain of is the contents of our own minds' (p. 50) and leads to 'the puzzling discovery that we apparently do not know what we think' (p. 50). If, at any rate, 'what we mean and think is determined by the linguistic habits of those around us in the way Burge believes they are, the first-person authority is very seriously compromised' (p. 54).

He rejects this conclusion – that although we can be certain *that* we are thinking we cannot know *what* we are thinking – because he rejects Burge's account of how social and other external factors control the contents of a person's mind. First, thoughts are not independent: my thoughts are interconnected with one another. This is an important observation. To rephrase it in a way that Davidson might not approve of: my thoughts belong together in the relatively private community of discourses with myself at least as much as they are rooted in the general community of discourse 'outside of my head'. This private community contributes to the individuation of my thoughts, to their identity, to the 'what' that they are thoughts about at least as much as the outside world. (Its influence is evident when thoughts are transcribed verbatim as in 'stream of consciousness prose', in which authors actually have to underplay that influence in order for the prose to be comprehensible to readers.) Second, speakers wishing to be understood must have some sense of how their utterances will be interpreted by others. We cannot mean what we say unless we are able to *mean* what we say and know *how* to mean what we say. This active meaning is possible only if the extra-cranial, or extra-mental, contribution to the meaning of our utterances is to some extent under our control and hence known to us. If we know what we say, then we must know what we think.

Davidson also, and more importantly, rejects the Burge–Putnam position on the grounds that it is committed (if unconsciously) to a discredited account of mind, in which there are 'entities that the mind can "entertain", "grasp", "have before it", or be "acquainted with"' (p. 61). Ordinary states of belief, desire, intention – and, of course, thoughts – seem 'polluted' by comparison with true inner states (qualia and the like) with respect to which it retains first-person authority, on account of their necessary connections with the social and public world. The way to accommodate the first-person authority of propositional attitudes is not to think of them as psychological objects at all; then they will not seem to be mental entities rendered comparatively opaque by contaminants necessary to individuate them. As Davidson argues: 'The source of the trouble is the dogma that to have a thought is to have an object before the mind'; for, 'if to have a thought is to have an object "before the mind", and the identity of the object determines what the thought is, then it would always be possible to be mistaken about what one is thinking. For unless one knows *everything* about the object, there will always be senses in which one does not know what object it is' (p. 63).

There are less esoteric defences of first-person authority with respect to one's own thoughts. If others were better placed to know what I was thinking than I was, it would be difficult to account for the routine observations that a) we usually require others to disclose their thoughts to us in order to know what they are thinking, and b) others cannot usually disclose our own thoughts for us. The observation that, sometimes, we ourselves really get to know our thoughts only when we have given them some form of external expression – 'How do I know what I think until I hear what I say?'[11] – does not after all support the notion that our thoughts have their primary existence in a third-person public sphere. Indeed, the latter notion opens all sorts of questions – 'How do I know what to say unless I first know what my thoughts are?' and 'How do I know that what I have said truly or accurately expresses my thoughts?' This question can be elaborated to any degree of tortuosity; for example: 'How do I know that the thought I have that what I have said matches my thoughts is accurate or true?'

Another defence that also mobilises the threat of infinite regression goes as follows. If you know my thoughts better than I do, how can this be possible, given that your understanding of my thought is itself another thought and one whose contents would be as unknown to you as mine are to me? If my meanings lie beyond me, your meanings lie beyond you, and the community's meanings to which my own meaning has ceded authority, exist outside every member of the community, then no one can mean anything. In short, your seemingly greater authority on my thoughts is upheld only so long as you do not think my thoughts; that is to say, receive my thoughts. It is an authority that exists only so long as it is not exercised! Third-person authority cannot exist if (as it must) it has ultimately to be realised in the first-person whose authority is discredited. To put this another way: I cannot know your thoughts better than you do – on the grounds that they contain ingredients of which you have incomplete knowledge – since my own thoughts, including the thoughts which express my knowledge of your thoughts, also contain such ingredients incompletely known to me.

A third defence comes from the fact that, in thinking to one's self – as

Descartes' Pure Inquirer is *ex hypothesi* – we do not lose control of the meaning of our words. When I utter my thoughts out loud for the benefit of another, there may well be a difference between what the thoughts mean to me and what they mean to my auditor. The difference is between what they mean 'out there' and what I mean them to mean. Where I am the auditor, the gap between what I mean to mean and what I mean is closed. In a way, the thought, along with its meaning, becomes less like an object of (uncertain, vulnerable) knowledge and more like (immediate, incorrigible) experience. The fact that the determinants of the meanings of the words that make up our thoughts lie outside of our heads, minds, selves does not mean that they are not transparent to us: in the isolation of the soliloquy, they mean what we mean, or take, them to mean. They mean to us what they mean to us and, for transparency, for knowing what we think, that is enough. As for not knowing what we think 'until we see what we say' – that, too, is not quite right. We know what we think once we hear our thinking. Which is the whole point of articulating our thoughts to ourselves anyway. If I had to see what I said until I knew what I thought, it would be impossible to explain how I would be able to recognise the thoughts I hear my lips forming as expressing what I think rather than being mere random vocalisations. At any rate, when we articulate our thoughts only to ourselves, we do not lose our unique authority over their meaning: they mean what we mean they mean. For this reason, we may reject the argument of writers such as Burge, Putnam, Fodor and Gareth Evans – as brilliantly characterised by Davidson – that 'propositions can't *both* determine the contents of our thoughts *and* be subjectively assured'.[12]

### 3.3 THE BOUNDS OF FIRST-PERSON CERTAINTY

We may therefore set aside this externalist assault on the first-person authority one has with respect to one's own thoughts. But 'I know my own thoughts – at any rate better than anyone else' is hardly a ringing endorsement for the certainties that may be mined out of first-person being, irrespective of whether it is a quasi-product of the *Cogito* argument or underwritten by the undeniable Existential Intuition. To say that one knows one's thoughts better than anyone else merely asserts a comparative, rather than an absolute, authority. This may be all the authority that is needed and it may be that – as I have just suggested – there is no real difference between being the best expert around and being expert period. For the experience of thoughts is not likely to be overturned by experience. It seems unlikely that my experiences showed me that I didn't know what my thoughts were. It may show me that my thoughts were wrong, but not that I was in error over what thought I was having. This, however, is cool comfort; for one's own thoughts hardly represent a huge extension of the territory of that which cannot be doubted.

And the externalist position on meaning does capture something very important: putting what is subjectively assured into propositional form for external consumption *does* render it vulnerable by taking it beyond itself. This applies even to seemingly undeniable assertions such as 'I am in pain'. While the fact that I am in pain is something I cannot be unsure about – especially if I present it as a composite of two quasi-facts which could not be doubted (that there is a pain; and it is I who am suffering it) – putting it in the form of a proposition makes the scope of its undeniability a bit fluffy. After all, it is perfectly sensible to say 'I've got this unpleasant feeling but I don't know whether or not to call it a pain/ whether it counts as a pain/whether you would call it a pain/whether the word "pain" would apply to it'. In other words, the extension of first-person authority beyond what we might call *Cartesian-assured* claims into the realm of propositions and assertions is fraught with difficulties, ambiguities and uncertainties. The passage from the certainty that one is feeling pain to the public assertion 'I am in pain' is a journey away from absolute certainty. The act of formulation creates a gap – which albeit may be very narrow – between the unassailable intuition and something which moves to the status of an empirical assertion. That is why we should look outside of formulated assertions to determine the scope of first-person authority.

This may be something of a relief. It spares us the task of finding some principled way of separating the corpus of self-affirming truths such as 'I am this …' or 'I am thinking …' and other, non-self-affirming claims, such as 'I am five foot eleven inches tall' or 'I am very intelligent' or 'I am Napoleon'. We know that:

a) there are certain things (very few) that I cannot doubt, expressed in what we might call Cartesian sentences;
b) there are certain things that (as Wittgenstein pointed out in *On Certainty*) I can *hardly* doubt – such as that I am living on the earth, and I share the earth with others, and that I did not come back from America a few minutes ago; and
c) there are certain things that are matters of fact and require evidential support – ranging from proximal facts about my body, to the great corpus of objective, empirical knowledge that I dip into in common with others.

It is difficult to define the plane of cleavage that separates the mass of things I can hardly doubt from those things I cannot doubt;[13] or the mass of things I can hardly doubt from things that might perfectly well be questioned and for which it would be clear what would count as evidentiary support. The scope of what I can hardly doubt does not correspond to the scope of unassailable first-person authority: it goes far beyond it. Its edges are drawn by more than one marker: roughly, my individual propensity to doubt (a matter of my personal psychology) and the patterns of belief in the community of which I am a part. ('Community' – the collective consciousness of which I am an unresisting part, or a part of in so far as I am unresisting – here is vague in the extreme.) Neither of these has much to do with the logic of necessity and impossibility as classically understood. The gradual loss of certainty as we pass from 'I am this' to 'I am this warm body' to 'I am standing next to the table' to 'I am Raymond Tallis' to 'I am a doctor' to 'I am someone who has been a doctor for many years' to 'I am someone who was born in 1946', and so on, is not segmented by sharp divisions between the impossible to doubt, the hard to doubt and the dubitable.

This difficulty of defining the boundaries of different levels or kinds of certainty becomes insuperable if we are tempted to proceed as if our task is to characterise three different subsets of declarative propositions about objective, empirical or factual truths corresponding to indubitable, scarcely dubitable and dubitable truths. The category of 'subject truths' which we discussed in Chapter 2 – and which are the immediate progeny of the Existential Intuition, being *assumed* in the double (logical and carnal) sense – should not be seen as a privileged sub-set of truths belonging within a homogeneous body of truths expressible in third-person declarative propositions of the form 'That such-and-such is the case'. What makes the 'subject truths' that grow out of the Existential Intuition incontestable is that they are existed or lived. The scope of first-person authority is the scope of 'existed being'.

This is even less clear than it seems at first sight and less helpful than might be supposed in helping us to separate that which I cannot be mistaken over from that which I can hardly be mistaken over, and the latter from that which I could (and, indeed, often am) mistaken over. Let us suppose, for example, that I translate my 'existed being' into 'my body'. Setting aside Cartesian qualms, this seems a reasonable suggestion since we are, as Cassam says, 'introspectively aware of ourselves as flesh and blood objects'.[14] How does this help us in our task of demarcation? Not as much as one might think. We express our difficulties by saying that our bodies have a) incomplete (and ill-defined) existential penetrability; b) incomplete (and ill-defined) cognitive penetrability; and c) – to make matters worse – an ill-defined boundary between what should count as existential and what should count as cognitive impenetrability. What my introspective certainty that I am a particular flesh-and-blood object actually says about what I am is uncertain. The mode in which I 'exist' in my body is extraordinarily complex and variable (as we shall see in Chapter 6), reflected in the wild fluctuations of the extent to which I as it were 'colonise' it. So much for uncertainties about the existential penetrability as viewed from the standpoint of the present moment assuming a posture of total scepticism. What about cognitive penetrability? The answer is equally disappointing. Introspection does not even yield the certain knowledge that I am made of 'flesh' and 'blood', except in so far as they are used in the vague everyday sense. The introspective certainty that we are made of flesh and blood tells us little about flesh – even about the flesh of which we are ourselves made. Pretty well everything about our own bodies is a closed book to us. The millions of facts that are common to our own and everyone else's bodies – such as those contained in textbooks of medicine, pathology, anatomy, physiology, biochemistry, molecular biology, etc. – are no more accessible to our introspection than they are to the introspection of a stranger standing next to me in the Tube. At any given time, I am aware of what the experience of some of that flesh (and less of that blood) is like, but even this is less informative than might appear. Experiencing the experiences of someone whose flesh that flesh is, and referring those experiences to that flesh, does not amount to a) experiencing the flesh in the sense of experiencing what that flesh 'in-itself' is; or b) experiencing what it is 'like to be that flesh' – for reasons that we shall discuss in Chapter 6.

In summary, existed being – such as 'existedly' being our bodies – does not, therefore, greatly extend the scope of certain knowledge. Experience of one's body is half-way between being and knowing: it is in itself neither knowledge nor ignorance. We do not, for example, enjoy, through in some sense being our bodies, 'noumenal' access to them.

These limitations apply to quite homely things as well as the things discovered by advanced science and written in textbooks. I could not, for example, discover my height or weight by introspection. The fact that I am 5 foot 10 inches tall requires to be established using measuring instruments whose operations make sense only in the context of complex institutions supporting the practice of measurement in feet and inches. Even the fact that I am 'tall' (which means having a longer body than is customary for the human group in which I move) is not immediately available to introspection. Indeed, the fact that I am above the average height for a particular reference group is no more given to me through the existed being of embodiment than is the fact that I am (or am not) Napoleon. With respect to these matters, however, I am not 'underprivileged' compared with others; only as unprivileged as they are.

The severely restricted cognitive privileges of the first person (rather than of first-person being) were widely discussed by philosophers in the twentieth century, who pointed out that the immunity of (uninterpreted) experiences – typically, sensations – from error was a direct consequence of their not making any objective claims.[15] We express this by saying that sensations exist below the threshold at which assertions, truth and falsity, emerge. In feeling this warm feeling I have now, I am neither right nor wrong. Only when I subsequently claim that it is due to my body actually being (objectively) hot or that the heating is due to the action of the sun can I be right or wrong, as subsequent sensations may reveal. Sensations may succeed sensation, but they do not correct each other. What one sensation may correct is an interpretation about objective reality that has been based on a preceding sensation: if the interpretation leads one to expect a subsequent sensation of Type $S_1$ and one actually has a sensation of Type $S_2$, then the interpretation of the first sensation is placed in question.

The warm, weighty, etc. bodily self-presence that is the introspectively most accessible and typical presentation of the Existential Intuition does not count as a piece of knowledge. It is a self-guaranteeing or self-warranting assumption that is prior to knowledge. (That it lies at the *root* of knowledge and the awakening of sentience to knowledge is something we shall discuss in Volume 3.) If it is not a piece of knowledge, is it therefore immune from error? Is it *pace* Descartes not merely one of those things that I can *hardly* doubt, but one of those things I simply cannot doubt or deny without running into existential or some other kind of self-contradiction? The answer must be yes, but there is a *caveat*: the feeling of being embodied is immune from error so long as it not offered as a piece of knowledge, as an objective fact – or as the site of an indefinite number of objective facts. To put it a little sourly: the experienced givenness of embodiment seems like a gift that is all phenomenal wrapping and no substantive contents. The inescapable feeling that I live what I designate by the term 'my body' does not mean that my living, the Existential Intuition, penetrates every aspect of that body or underwrites any objective truth about it. Beyond the cornerstone ur-proposition – the Existential Intuition – there is no guarantee that any specific proposition will be lived, assumed, and consequently proof against denial.

The fact that being RT means living a particular living body does not imply that RT has immediate or privileged access to all – or indeed any – truths *about* his body (so that they become existentially undeniable).

My awareness of being (in some sense) this body is not, as it were, the inner face, or the inner truth, of the objective facts of my body. Knowledge still has to be acquired and error is still possible. It may be available comparatively directly (as when I look at the back of my hand in order to interrogate a spot); indirectly (weighing myself or looking at a photo of, say, the small of my back or the back of my neck in a mirror); and very indirectly (as when I read about the kinds of cells there are in my bone marrow or the number of amino acids there are in the DNA in the cells of my body). There is no direct or certain path from immediate awareness to knowledge of one's body, even when the knowledge is of the same entity as that of which one has immediate awareness: my sense of altitude does not tell me my height; my feeling weightily embodied does not inform me as to, or translate into, my weight in kilograms; my pain in the lower right part of the abdomen does not yield knowledge of the migration of white cells as part of the inflammation of my appendix.

This all seems incontestable. *Knowledge* of the body (even where the body is my body and the knower is me) takes us beyond the curtilage of the Existential Intuition – where all is certain because it is made to be the case by a carnal assumption, where its truth, like that of an *a priori* proposition, does not require justification from other experiences – into the realm of objective knowledge, of the opaque, or partly scrutable, given. There are other cases where this is less clear. When I am in pain, I know not only that there is pain, but also whose pain it is and hence, presumably, the 'who' who is in pain. On the other hand, this does not give me knowledge of the 'who' who is in pain. I am not given, bundled in with my pain, objective facts about me; for example, social facts (which really belong to my whoness) such as that I am a doctor, that I am such-and-such an age, that I am not Napoleon; or material facts such as that I have appendicitis, or that I was born at a particular place, or that I am fated to die on a particular day. The facts that are not dissolved into the quantum of immediate 'who' that is bundled with my pain are what we might called '*quidditas*' knowledge, as opposed to '*haeceitas*' awareness. Such knowledge is not clearly connected with the moments of 'what it is like' to be me, though they contribute to the character and content of my life, the extended or macroscopic 'what it is like' to be me. And all knowledge, properly understood, is *quidditas* knowledge.

Knowledge is general, abstract, replicable: these are features of its objectivity and they are prior to its status as 'justified true belief'. Introspection, the sense of what I am, even where that sense is invested in a material, visible body (the living body of Raymond Tallis), does not reach into this territory.

## 3.4 THE BOUNDS OF CERTAINTY

The incontestable subject truths given in the Existential Intuition are not simply events, pieces of the world, facts one encounters. On the contrary: the Existential Intuition does not merely disclose something that is given: the 'I' is taken or assumed as well as given. But it is not simply or entirely assumed: I cannot assume any existent – Napoleon, for example – and become that existent. This is in part because, as we have remarked, existed identity is not fact-shaped. There are for this reason limits to first-person authority: I am what I am, not what I deem that I am. There is a given as well as a taken. And, as will be evident from what we were just saying, even within the body, many things – structures, events, processes – lie beyond the scope of what can be taken, assumed as what I am. When I assume my body, I do not also assume my stomach or my bone marrow.

That which is assumed may be assumed in different ways, at different points between 'thisness' and 'whatness'. The bounds of the assumable, and the kinds of assumption, will vary from moment to moment; and, as a consequence, what counts as lying outside of the scope of the Existential Intuition – empirical, objective, contestable and corrigible – will also vary. Different aspects of the world will fall into the realm of objective, propositional fact. This fluctuation is due to the fluctuations of the scope of the assumption of what I am.

At any time, however, what is encompassed in the Existential Intuition and falls within the curtilage of incorrigible first-person authority will always exceed what would be given through the *Cogito* argument because the latter overlooks what it assumes at its own start: the 'I' that thinks in order to prove that 'I am'. The I that thinks – the declared output of the *Cogito* argument – is not, and could not be, a mere isolated moment of thought, an iteration of sentences in an unextended vacuum of bodiless space. For Wittgenstein and others, as we noted in Chapter 2, the very meaning of Descartes' words require, and hence presuppose, a community of discourse, a world of speakers for whom the various terms deployed in Cartesian inquiry makes sense. This is not merely an accidental impurity in the project of pure inquiry, but a necessary one: it is the ground on which the inquiry must stand.

What we can take away from the previous chapter, and which survives the disappointing outcome of our search for first-person truths that are both objective and demonstrably true, is that the Existential Intuition, seen as a proposition – 'That I am this [x]' – is both contingent and necessary; or rather, as we have argued, has empirical content and is necessary. The empirical content refers to the particular 'this' that I turn out to be, which can be variously described as 'Raymond Tallis', 'Raymond Tallis's self', 'Raymond Tallis's lived being', etc. The necessity lies in the link between the personal pronoun (which under one description *pace* Elizabeth Anscombe could be regarded as a demonstrative) and 'this' which most certainly is a demonstrative. It teeters on the brink, that is to say, of various tautologies:

'This is this …'
'[This] I is this [I] …'

The importance, however, lies in the teetering: it does not fall over the brink. For the first I is not quite a 'this', as something pointed out: it is lived. And the second 'this' is not quite the I, because it is something that is inextricably caught up in e.g. a body or a life or a world that I cannot quite coincide with. This is how the identity that is asserted in this first-person identity statement is not an empty tautology, nor is it merely contingent: it is an essential identity – and one that is considerably more substantive (not to say more convincing, not to say more interesting) than the linguistically created essential identities that Kripke found, or thought he had found.

There is another way of capturing the contingent-necessity of the 'I'. Hector-Neri Castaneda notes that,

> anyone's 'I don't exist now' is a self-contradictory statement. Hence, 'I exist now' is necessarily true. Yet this seems wrong, for many of us are convinced that the statement one can make by saying 'I might not have been existing now' is true.[16]

This paradox can be solved, according to Castaneda, by arguing that,

> the 'I' is not a entity that exists either contingently or necessarily. It is not, in that sense, an entity *in* the world, but an entity outside the world that must be identifiable in terms of entities in the world (p. 166)

There is, however, a different (and, I believe, better) way of dealing with this seeming paradox. My current existence is necessary so long as it is I who am asserting it. It is contingent, so long as it is referred to by others. If John Smith says 'Raymond Tallis exists', this is a contingent truth. If Raymond Tallis says 'Raymond Tallis exists', this is a necessary truth because Raymond Tallis's existence is a necessary condition for Raymond Tallis's asserting that Raymond Tallis exists. If Raymond Tallis did not exist, he could not assert his existence (or, of course, his non-existence).

The necessity of the truth of 'Raymond Tallis exists' lies not within the proposition being asserted, but in the conditions necessary for the proposition to be asserted. Similarly, the Existential Intuition owes its necessity to its status as a subject-truth indexed to the subject realising it of herself and to its not being a mere objective truth. Its necessity lies in the existential conditions necessary for its being asserted.[17]

The notion of the Existential Intuition encompasses both components as it encompasses both discourse and existence. I have presented it here – on the page – necessarily as a proposition, with a grammatical structure, with a subject and a complement. It refers to something off the page that is not structured in this way. It could be described as 'a blush of me-this' haunting the world which presupposes 'me-this' – or any other fancy way. At any rate, it is extricable from existence only as a thought-type that is alluded to through verbal tokens; or printed words that tokenise it.

Some may be unimpressed by this claim to specialness. After all, the reality that is referred to in 'The cat is in the room' is not structured in the way that the grammatical sentence is: out there, there is not an unadorned cat to which there is attached a predicate 'in the room'. That is perfectly true: *the fact that* there is a cat in the room is not to be found out there, littering the earth. Reality outside language is not fact-shaped or decomposable into a definite number of facts which reflect the structure of sentences.[18] But we are not dealing with facts when we are dealing with the Existential Intuition. (On the contrary, 'am' cannot assume the shape of a fact: am-ing is not 'free-gift knowing'.) We are dealing with something that is not the case unless it is lived and its being lived – the *assumption* of identity, the awakening of 'am' into a (living) bit of 'is' – imports its necessity and its substantiality; or imports necessity into a matter of substance. We may describe the truth 'That I am this …' as a contingent necessity; or as a contingency that becomes necessary from the viewpoint of the contingency itself.[19]

The question that remains unanswered is whether the 'lived bit of "is"' that is the meat in the Existential Intuition, is the contentful necessary truth that is asserted in it, is actually meat. Can we demonstrate the necessity of the body so that we are then at liberty to adopt a biological account of the origin of self-consciousness?[20] The *Cogito* argument has inadvertently demonstrated that there is more to the 'I' that demonstrably exists than a moment of thought. The present chapter has caused us to be rather cautious in believing that what (by accident) it has demonstrated to exist is any kind of objective state of affairs. Is there some other way of demonstrating the necessity of the embodiment; of finding that the 'I' is an embodied subject; so that we can think seriously about biogenetic accounts of self-consciousness? It is to this question that the next two chapters are devoted.

NOTES

1. Immanuel Kant, *Critique of Pure Reason*, translated by Norman Kemp Smith (London: Macmillan, 1964), p.168.
2. This intuition is entirely sound. As we shall discussion in Volume 3, the encounter with one's own body as only partly scrutable lies at the root of the awakening of knowledge out of sentience, whose master-intuition is that there is a difference between how things are experienced by me and how they are in themselves.
3. This echoes Bernard Williams' notion of a *Purely Positional Advantage* – developed in *Truth and Truthfulness. An Essay in Genealogy* (Princeton, NJ: Princeton University Press, 2002) – which is 'the idea that a speaker can tell someone else about a situation because he is or was in it, while his hearer is or was not' (p. 50).
4. There have been numerous attempts by philosophers to deny or minimise this knowledge gap. Those for whom 'the experience of blue' is cashed out behaviourally, point to a) the public nature of behaviour, and b) the overall consistent relationship between experiences and behaviour as undermining the idea of important differences between 'private' experiences. An alternative strategy is to reject any approach that treats experience atomistically urging a holistic approach that sees experiences as essentially parts of indubitably shared world, one which is underwritten by the institutions, language, etc. that we have in common. In that sense, my experience of blue and yours, being both elements, occupying similar positions, of a common of world, are profoundly alike. Whereas I cannot be confident as to how 'blue' is experienced by you, there is no doubt that our experiences draw on, disclose, etc. a common world. While each of these attempts is successful in minimising the *practical* significance of the knowledge (or awareness) gap, it still does not close it.
5. Joseph Conrad, *Lord Jim* (Oxford: Oxford University Press, 1983 [1900]), pp. 179–80. Quoted in Christopher Hamilton, *Living Philosophy: Reflections on Life, Meaning and Morality* (Edinburgh: Edinburgh University Press, 2001).
6. The advantage that others have over me in this respect is twofold. For a start, there are parts of me that others can see directly that are hidden from my direct gaze – for example, the back of my head or the small of my back. Second, seeing what I look *like* is a matter of classifying me under some general third-person category and others who experience me in the third person are better placed than I – for whom RT is experienced in the first person. There is the fact that we cannot (usually) see our own faces, or our bodies, or our lives, because we look out from them. Hence, 'each is furthest from himself'; ourself is the last thing we discover because it is least thing-like. There is the deeper reason, first adduced by John the Scot, that 'it is impossible for any sentient being to know, in the sense of understand, its own nature' (quoted by Bryan Magee, in *Confessions of a Philosopher*, London: Phoenix, 1997, p. 443).
7. Donald Davidson, 'Knowing One's Own Mind', *Proceedings and Addresses of the American Philosophical Association* (1987), 60: 441–58. This is a view, incidentally, that echoes post-structuralist claims about the indeterminacy of meaning, the lack of transparency in our verbal intentions and the resultant speech acts, and the fact that 'language speaks us'. For a critique of this view, see Raymond Tallis, *Not Saussure:*

*A Critique of Literary Theory* (London: Macmillan, 1988; 1995), Chapter 6 'Walking and Différance'.

8. This is true only if one subscribes to something like a causal theory of meaning, itself a consequence or symptom of Putnam's functionalism. The case against both is set out in Raymond Tallis, *The Explicit Animal. A Defence of Human Consciousness*, 2nd edn (London: Macmillan, 1999): against the causal theory in Chapter 3 and against functionalism in Chapter 5. Opposition to the causal theory of meaning touches on the central arguments of this entire trilogy. It will be discussed in Volume 3. The suspicion that Davidson does subscribe to a causal theory of meaning is supported by this passage in his paper: 'The issue depends simply on how the basic connection between words and things, or thoughts and things, is established. I hold, along with Burge and Putnam if I understand them, that it is established by causal connections between people and parts and aspects of the world. The disposition to react differentially to objects and events thus set up are central to the correct interpretation of a person's thoughts and speech' (p. 56).

9. 'Meanings are not in the head' is not a very helpful slogan. It suggests that meanings are therefore extra-cranial. This is incompatible with the functionalism that Putnam espoused at the time when he was associated with this slogan. It should not be taken to imply that 'meanings are in society': they are (realised, instantiated) in ourselves in so far as we are socialised. This is true even of meanings I mean to myself, as in silent thought; though in this case, there is no clear gap between what I mean and how what I mean gets interpreted. Anyone who insists that meanings are in (or outside of) the 'self', will have to clarify things further. What I meant to mean may be in the self; what I actually succeed in meaning, or what I am taken to mean, is not an internal matter for the self.

10. Davidson. 'Knowing One's Own Mind', p. 49.

11. Or the Surrealist observation: 'Le pense se forme dans la bouche'.

12. Davidson, 'Knowing One's Own Mind', p. 63. There is an interesting question in this vicinity: Could I be mistaken in thinking that I am thinking if I do not know what the word 'thinking' means? Supposing, having seen people sweat when they struggle to think, I believe I am thinking whenever sweat pours off my brow, whatever the cause, shall I be mistaken in thinking that I am thinking? The answer is, of course, no. While I am mistaken in thinking that the sweat that pours off my brow is the essence of thought, I am not mistaken in thinking that I am thinking because the mistake itself is an occurrent thought. My error is in allocating among my conscious experiences the wrong one to the word 'thought' but the misallocation itself is an occurrent thought. My thought that I am thinking has the wrong grounds but is inescapably right. However ill-informed I am – about the world, about myself and about language – there is no way I can mistakenly think to myself that I am thinking. The thinking that is not present at the first-order level is present at the second-order level thought that I am thinking.

13. Cf. Wittgenstein: 'Is it not difficult to distinguish between cases in which I cannot and those in which I can *hardly* be mistaken? Is it always clear to which kind a case belongs? I believe not' (*On Certainty*, para. 673).

14. Introduction to *Self Knowledge*, edited by Quassim Cassam, Oxford Readings in Philosophy (Oxford: Oxford University Press, 1995), p. 5.

15. There are statements that are thought to be genuinely informative and yet logically immune from doubt. According to A. J. Ayer: 'The statements usually chosen for this role contain a demonstrative, but they are not wholly demonstrative; they also

contain a descriptive component which is supposed to characterize some present state of the speaker, or some present content of this experience' (*The Problem of Knowledge*, London: Pelican, 1956, p. 53). The examples Ayer gives are statements such as 'I feel a headache' which must have information content because one can assert them falsely. If I say that I have a headache and I do not have a headache, this is a piece of (objective) misinformation. The examples that involve others are irrelevant here since I am considering the amount of certain information arising from the sensations of one's own body. What one says to others about those sensations is, of course, informative, as we noted earlier when we discussed first-person authority. For myself, the possibility of error in the assertion 'I have a headache' is entirely verbal – as when my sister informed our mother that she had 'a headache in my knee'.

16. Hector-Neri Castaneda, 'On the Phenomeno-Logic of the I', *Proceedings of the 14th International Congress of Philosophy*, iii, University of Vienna, pp. 260–6, reproduced in Cassam, *Self Knowledge*, p. 165.

17. This is how the (sincere) assertion 'I am dead' – where the proposition is being used rather than merely being mentioned – is an impossibility. While it is not a logical self-contradiction it is an existential one.

18. This is something that we shall examine in detail in Volume 3.

19. I shall argue in Volume 3 that it is this subject truth that lies at the root of objective truths – not in the sense of guaranteeing them (that would be idealism) but in the sense of making what is the case be '*That* X is the case' and consequently objectively true. The awakening of 'that' in (according to the biogenetic theory) the human body is the origin of the differentiation of subject and objects, of the collectivisation of experience, and of objective truths, and a universe of facts. The 'That I am this ...' becomes the basis for the knowledge of the body, and thence for the body of knowledge, and finally knowledge about the body. The Existential Intuition is therefore the ultimate source of the kinds of inquiries, the 'active uncertainty' (to use Dewey's phrase) that culminated in the science postulated in the wake of Cartesian systematic doubt. The subject truth of the Intuition is the root of all truth (and falsehood) relations. The fundamental mistake of sceptical thought is to present as a propositional truth – and hence open to sceptical challenge – something that is pre-propositional, the underpinning of propositions thought. But we are here getting ahead of ourselves.

20. Among the many kinds of uneasiness that my style of arguing might awaken is one about the way in which I seem almost wilfully to confuse accounts of origins of certain notions with making a case for their truth. For many philosophers, the aetiology of a belief has nothing to do with its truth. For others, the fact that a belief has an aetiology actually undermines its truth. (These view range from the kind of *argumentum ad hominem* that says 'You only believe this because you were brought up badly/brainwashed, etc.' and therefore what you believe is untrue to the kind of metaphysical arguments that say, for example, that all perceptions are caused by interactions between objects and the nervous system and are therefore distorted, contaminated, illusions, etc.) My confusion of origins with truth content is not 'almost wilful': it is entirely wilful. There are certain circumstances where origins guarantee truths. This is a rather distasteful thought to those who have been brought up on anti-psychologism. We shall return to these issues in Volume 3.

# CHAPTER 4

# The Logical Necessity for Embodiment

## 4.1 ESCAPING THE CARTESIAN PRISON

If the primary purpose of the present volume were to find a way out of the prison created by Descartes' methodological solipsism, the reader might by now have become a little worried. We seemed to have escaped the Cartesian prison by two separate exits. Since the exits are far enough apart to seem hardly to belong to the same building, the story of escape is starting to sound a bit suspicious.

One escape story invokes the character of the *Cogito* argument, and of the systematic doubt that leads up to it, as a *performative*, involving an off-the-page token or occurrent argument. This imports the individual thinker into the prison and, along with her, all sorts of things – notably the discursive community necessary to give specific meaning to the words she uses (those in which she expresses, as well as those in which she attempts to limit, her doubts). While the argument 'I think therefore I am' delivers vanishingly little to the thinker famished for certainty, the *business* of getting to, and arguing, 'I think, therefore I am' delivers much more. The 'I' who enacts the *Cogito* argument must be much more than a moment of thought, for any moment of thought requires an infra-structure. By the same token, however good the grounds for systematic doubt, they cannot remove the grounds on which the doubter has to stand in order to mobilise, or to suffer, doubt, especially sophisticated philosophical doubt. Descartes' metaphysical slammer proves to be an extraordinary open institution in which the prisoner brings large parts of the extra-carceral world into gaol with her.

The other escape story places the *Cogito* argument – and the doubts leading up to it – firmly in an outside world, in which it figures as a derivative or late descendant or reflection of the Existential Intuition 'That I am this …'. From this perspective, Cartesian doubt seems existentially self-contradictory: something like a higher-level manifestation of the Existential Intuition denying the very body that was the first ground of that Intuition; or the thousandth floor denying the existence of the ground floor and, indeed, the ground.

Whatever one thinks of those stories independently, together they seem less plausible, rather as two alibis make a less impressive case for the defence than one – especially if they are incompatible with one another, in virtue of starting from different, conflicting sets of assumptions. Are they in fact compatible or are they, as implied in the second account, linked?

They do, of course, have something important in common. Both resist treating the *Cogito* argument as merely a matter of logic, of one proposition being derived from another: the existence of the arguer is brought into the argument and this means that existential and logical considerations can be mobilised together in the assault on scepticism. In the case of a first-person argument about the existence of that first person, the fact that, in order for the argument to be conducted, the first person has to exist (to be currently existing) is not irrelevant to the argument itself. This, after all, was what Descartes himself argued, though he seems to have underestimated the consequences of playing the existence of the thinker into the argument. Existential considerations can be brought into play because the grammatical subject of the proposition and the living originator of its realisation in an utterance are (whenever it is truly used rather than merely alluded to) identical. Since the utterer and the referent of the subject of the uttered statement are identical, it would not make sense to deny the existence of the former while maintaining that the latter had specific reference.

What follows from guaranteeing the existence of the thinker? Much more than the mere moment of thinking, which was all that Gassendi and others have permitted Descartes to take away from his argument. For the thinker could not be 'bare thinking': for to think anything as definite as 'That there is thinking' or 'Thinking is taking place' the component words have to have meaning and this implies the community of discourse that gives them meaning. Does it imply anything else? What, in addition, does the thinker have to be in order to be part of that community and to acquire the means of expression that it uses? To cut to the chase: Is the thinking 'I' necessarily embodied? If we accept the biogenetic story, then the answer must be yes: self-consciousness, and hence communities of selves, begin from the Existential Intuition which awakens within the human organism. Can we, however, arrive at the same conclusion without depending on the biogenetic argument?

## 4.2 'I THINK THEREFORE I AM EMBODIED'

Let us begin by reminding ourselves of the seemingly privileged status of thinking. 'I am' follows from 'I *any-thing* ...' More precisely: '*If* I any-thing', then 'I am'. If 'I any-thing' is thinking, the protasis is existentially self-guaranteeing, so that the apodosis is also guaranteed. The general form of the *Cogito* argument, that is to say, is as follows:

a) If I any-thing, then I am.
b) I any-thing.
c) Therefore I am.

Where 'any-thing', is 'thinking', b) is assured, it has a self-guaranteeing truth. As Ayer put it, 'If I believe that I am thinking, then I must believe truly, since my believing that I am thinking is itself a process of thought'.[1] The middle line of the proof is self-affirming in the case of thinking, not because the opposite would be self-contradictory (taken in isolation, on the page), but because it is existentially undeniable: the thinker cannot unthink it. My thinking that I think is itself an example of what my thought thinks exists. The *Cogito* argument therefore has this form:

If p ('I think'), then q ('I am')
p ('I think' – by self-affirmation)
Therefore q ('I am')

If, on the other hand, I think that I am embodied, my belief does not appear to be self-fulfilling inasmuch as my thinking is not an instance of my embodiment and so does not appear necessarily to entail it. Not, at any rate, if it is possible to be a thinking 'I' without being embodied. But is it? Does the undeniable fact that I am thinking also permit, indeed compel, the conclusion that I am embodied?

Let us look more closely at the grounds for the undeniability of the middle step in the proof. 'I think' comes free of charge. The undeniability of 'I think' is not merely the undeniability of 'thinking' or 'some thinking' which has the good fortune to attach itself to an 'I' on whose undeniability it can then hitch a ride: what is undeniable is not the thinking but *the thinking taken in conjunction with the 'I' that is doing it*.[2]

The question therefore changes in a small but important way. It is not whether thinking is, or is not, detachable from the body, but whether the 'I' who is thinking is thus detachable. An argument for importing the body in with the 'I' – so that if you allow 'I' you also allow the body –

has been based on some thoughts about identity (and identification) most famously developed by P. F. Strawson[3] and which has more recently been elaborated by a variety of thinkers, in particular Quassim Cassam.[4] The argument is that the existence of 'I' requires embodiment because without embodiment there is no basis for its individuation. It would seem that if 'I' has any characteristics at all, being an individual is one of them. It is its most basic feature.

Strawson argued in *Individuals* that a condition of our possessing a scheme of knowledge of particulars (such as we appear to have) is the ability to re-identify those particulars. Our inescapable world picture revolves around such re-identification: if we are to have any kinds of thoughts about particular objects, we must be able to identify those objects and this means identifying them on different occasions – *re-identifying them.*[5] We could put it this way: being this, rather than that, on one occasion implies being this, rather than that, on another occasion. Strawson further argued that identification 'rests ultimately on location in a unitary spatiotemporal framework of four dimensions' (p. 39). The attempt to found a system of re-identifiable particulars in the absence of such a framework proved, as he demonstrated, using a world constructed purely out of sounds, impossible. Since only material bodies could constitute that framework, such bodies were 'basic from the point of view of particular-identification'.

More relevant to our present discussion is Strawson's second category of 'basic particulars': persons. The case for the undeniable existence of persons – in whom are indissolubly combined a material (biological) body and psychological states – revolves around the notion of self-consciousness: the ascription of thoughts (and other mental phenomena) to oneself. Such an ascription has an interesting dual character: one's states of consciousness, one's thoughts and sensations, are ascribed *to the very same thing* as certain physical characteristics – such as height, colouring, shape and weight – of a particular body. It is the *same particular* that is five foot ten inches tall, sitting down and in a particular room as is thinking, or in pain. That particular is a person who has both material and psychological predicates. This person must, moreover, belong to a *community* of persons since, Strawson argues, the condition of ascribing material and psychological predicates to oneself is that one should *primarily* consider others as suitable for such ascriptions. We do not argue from self-ascription to ascription of predicates to others; on the contrary, 'there is no sense in the idea of ascribing states of consciousness to oneself, or at all, unless the ascriber already knows how to ascribe at least some states of consciousness to others' (p.106) because self-consciousness presupposes the ability to sustain the idea of the difference between oneself and others. This in turn requires that those others should be identified and such identification requires that they are picked out as individuals; and for this, they have to have the characteristics of spatiotemporally extended entities, like material objects, as well as being the ascriptees of states of consciousness. The inseparability of material and psychological predicates in those others makes 'persons' a 'logical primitive' or basic particular, like material objects.

Pretty well every element of Strawson's argument in *Individuals* (as well as aspects of it elaborated in his subsequent book *The Bounds of Sense*[6]) has been challenged and Strawson himself has conceded some of the validity of the challenges, in part by redefining what he was trying to do.[7] Even so, his argument remains inspiring and others have continued to work fruitfully in the field which he first cultivated. Cassam, for example, takes up the challenge of demonstrating necessary links between self-consciousness and the justification of the belief that one is embodied. Building on Strawson's thesis in *The Bounds of Sense* that to be self-conscious one must conceive of oneself as a corporeal object among objects, he argues in his *Self and World* that

> it is not possible to give an adequate account of self-consciousness without acknowledging the importance of certain forms of bodily self-awareness.[8]

Cassam's thesis has several components:

a) Introspective awareness of one's thinking, experiencing self as a physical object among physical objects is a *necessary* condition of self-consciousness (p. 3).
b) A physical object has a range of qualities, including shape, location and solidity. To the extent that one is aware of one's thinking, experiencing self as shaped, located and solid, one is aware of oneself as a physical object (pp. 2–3).
c) A self-conscious subject is one whose experience satisfies the *objectivity condition* ... awareness of oneself, *qua* subject of experience is a necessary condition of self-conscious experience in this sense (p. 28).
d) This 'objectivity condition' is met only if the object in question is an object 'in the weighty sense' – that is to say, it is capable being perceived *and* of existing unperceived; it is capable of *continued* existence, in the Humean sense of existing even when it is not present to the senses (p. 32).

If this complex thesis were true and the arguments for it sound, then it would provide a direct path from the Cartesian 'I' (whose existence is undeniable) to an embodied self, which is an – admittedly very special – physical object among objects. It would then provide a means of creating a passage between the closed universe of the 'Cartesianly preferred' thoughts to a world of living and other physical objects and would enable us to forge links between the *Cogito* argument and the biogenetic account that yields the undeniable Existential Intuition 'That I am this …'. It would allow 'this' to be translated as 'at least this body'.

Cassam's case combines phenomenological observations and abstract arguments about the nature of the human subject. The various twists of its complex and rigorous arguments cannot be followed here. I want, however, to rehearse some of its key steps. He argues that for one to be in a position to think of one's experience as experience of physical objects, it is not enough merely to think so – merely to have the appropriate conceptual resources; 'it must also be the case that one's experience permits or warrants conceptualization in these terms' (p. 52). This requires that experience should present itself 'as experience of a world of objects with, among other things, shape, location and solidity' and this, in turn, requires that 'one must be intuitively aware of oneself, *qua* subject of experience, as shaped, located and solid' (p. 52). In support of this last claim, he cites the observation of Brian O'Shaughnessy,

> the intuitive given-ness of the world to one is dependent upon one's sometimes veridically seeming to oneself to be a determinately shaped, determinately sized, determinately hard-or-soft something.

The sense of encounter with bodies requires, in other words, that one should have the sense of oneself as a body – shaped, solid and located. To put it bluntly: it takes one to know one. Or, to put it less crudely, an ethereal subject could neither experience, nor conceive of, a material object.

The case for one's status as an object is, it seems, somewhat circular: I feel my solidity through the solidity (the *obstance*) of the objects that I encounter, which in turn disclose my solidity. Perhaps this is not a problem. Cassam, however, points out that, unless one already assumes what one has to prove (namely, that the self and the body are in some sense identical or co-identified), observations such as that the space and solidity of our bodies provide access to the space and solidity of other bodies, do not provide conclusive support for the 'intuitive awareness of oneself *qua* Ego as a physical object' (p. 54). In particular, the argument does not deal with the lingering suspicion that there is a more subtle dualism between a 'core self', which is the thinking subject, and an empirical self which is (among other things) the centre of egocentric space and, as a perceiving or sensing subject, more plausibly seen as inextricably bound up with the body:

> it is one thing to show that the presented subject of tactile perception must itself be experienced as shaped and solid, but the idea that one is aware of the subject of one's thoughts as shaped and solid is an entirely different matter. (p. 73)

Indeed; and this is particularly relevant as it is the latter that seems closer to the subject of the Cartesianly preferred thoughts than the former. The thinker seems less like an object located in space – indeed at the zero point of egocentric space – than does the looker or, indeed, the perspirer.[9]

Cassam argues that while thinking, unlike perceiving, lacks spatial content, there are demonstrative thoughts (such as 'This monument is ugly') in which thought and perception interpenetrate. Moreover, one is ordinarily aware of one's thoughts and one's perceptions and sensations as belonging to the same self: 'talk of core-self is simply shorthand for a particular aspect of the life or functioning of the empirical or bodily self' (p. 76). To separate off a 'core self' of abstract thoughts is simply to create unnecessary trouble. It is hardly surprising that such an abstraction composed of abstractions cannot find a location in space.

Cassam argues that the sole way that awareness of the subject can be awareness of itself as a) one's point of view on the world, *and* b) the bearer of one's sensations, *and* c) the basis of awareness which makes it possible to make first-person statements that have a guaranteed and correct referent, is for it to be awareness of oneself *qua* subject as a physical object. We cannot disentangle our ability to think of our experiences as including perceptions of physical objects from our conception and our intuitive awareness of *ourselves as* physical objects.

This does not fully address the sceptical position and Descartes' uninhabitable prison. After all, it is perfectly possible that awareness of the world as containing objects in the weighty sense and awareness of the self as an object also in the weighty sense are linked delusions. Cassam meets this concern with what he calls 'the Unity Argument', deriving from Strawson. According to Cassam, 'the most basic notion of self-consciousness is one according to which a self-conscious subject must at least be capable of *self-ascribing* her experiences' (p. 91).[10] Strawson pointed out that the condition under which diverse representations may be said to be united in a single consciousness is precisely the condition, whatever that may be, under which a subject of experiences may ascribe different experiences to himself, conscious of the identity of that to which these different experiences, at different times belong ... unity of diverse experiences in a single consciousness requires experience of objects. (quoted in Cassam, p. 91)

In short, Cassam says, 'unity requires objectivity'. The stability of objects provides the glue to hold consciousness together across experiences as is presupposed in self-ascriptive self-consciousness.

According to the version of the Unity Argument that Cassam prefers,

self-consciousness requires unity of consciousness; unity of consciousness requires the ability to self-ascribe experiences; and the satisfaction of the full conditions of the possibility of self-ascription of experiences, which is constitutive of personal self-consciousness, requires experience of objects. (p. 112)

In particular,

the subject of self-conscious experience must be conceived of as a physical object. (p. 112)

More precisely,

self-consciousness requires the conception of oneself as a point of application for empirical criteria of personal identity and therefore as a physical object among physical objects. (p. 116)[11]

Cassam calls this the Identity Argument and it is underpinned by, among other things, the intuitively compelling notion that the capacity for first-person thought is not something that can exist in isolation: 'it can only be present in the context of a range of other cognitive abilities' (p. 169). The connection between the idea that something possesses these abilities and the idea that that something is an object among others in the world is as follows:

there is no level at which it is possible to abstract from the ownership of first-person thought while maintaining a fix upon its content ... the fact that I-thoughts are subject to the relativizing requirement shows that in the case of I-thoughts, the ascriptive and the content-specifying levels of description are inseparable. (p. 185)

(This is the underside of the observation made by Anscombe that whoever says 'I' guarantees both successful and accurate reference and the presence of the referent.)

This takes us far but does not quite take us all the way from the demonstrably indubitable capacity for I-thoughts to the conception of oneself as a physical object among objects. For this, we need to take on board this consideration: the ascription of I-thoughts can be correct only in the case of a being whose thoughts, perceptions and actions are organised in a certain way and this involves a capacity to conceive of oneself as temporally extended and spatially located; of a being which is a substantial subject, an object among objects. The argument that 'only subjects that are physical objects among physical objects can have what it takes to be capable of first-person thoughts' (p. 192) is supported by this claim:

> to be capable of I-thinking, one's I-thoughts must stand in certain relations to perception and action, and one must also be capable of remembering the basis of earlier present-tense judgements. Only something with shape, location and solidity can perceive, act or remember, so only subjects with shape, location, and solidity can have the internal organization required to sustain I-thinking. Since anything with shape, location, and solidity is a physical object, another way of putting this point would be to say that it only makes sense to ascribe I-thoughts to subjects who are physical objects among others in the world. This is a claim about the actual nature of I-thinkers, not a claim about how I-thinkers conceive of themselves. (p. 192)

Cassam concludes from this that 'self-consciousness ... is intimately bound up with awareness of the subject "as an object" – not as an immaterial substance but as a physical object in a world of physical objects' (p. 198).

I have given little indication here of the richness of Cassam's arguments, or of the numerous side-arguments in which he engages, and for the most part sees off, a variety of objections. Readers will need to consult the original before they decide whether they find his position as convincing as I do and feel that he has conclusively demonstrated the link between being conscious of one's self as an 'I' who is the subject of thought and experience and consciousness of one's self as a corporeal object among others. There are, however, at least three important pieces of unfinished business.

The first is to determine the extent to which Cassam is successful in establishing the necessity of embodiment and in seeing off the sceptical challenge. The necessary connection between consciousness of one's self as a subject of thought and experience and consciousness of one's self as an object in the weighty sense is not quite the same as proof that the self, or the 'I', is necessarily embodied. We shall re-examine this briefly in the next section by reflecting on the question of whether disembodied 'I-hood' is possible. The second is to follow out the connections between Cassam's embodiment argument and the bio-genetic account of the self that is central to this trilogy. This will occupy the final short section of this chapter. The third is to acknowledge that Cassam's thesis – and indeed the notion of the embodiment (necessary, accidental, or non-existent) of the 'I' – is less clear than it might seem at first sight. This will become apparent when we consider the extent to which the object which the subject is aware of as herself is identical to the biological body; more precisely, the extent to which the living body is the subject incarnate and the subject is, or lives, the life of the living body. This will occupy us in Chapter 6.

### 4.3 DISCARNATE EXISTENCE

If embodiment truly were a necessary condition of there being the kinds of subject that are referred to by 'I', then the notion of a disembodied 'I' should be impossible, self-contradictory, unthinkable, or all three. In *Individuals*, Strawson discusses the notion of a disembodied person and mounts two distinct arguments against it. The first relates more directly to his fundamental position that persons are basic particulars or logical primitives, with minds being derivative: 'the concept of a person is logically prior to that of an individual consciousness'.[12] This pre-empts the notion, implicit in that of discarnate continuation, of minds and bodies coming together by accident, so that their fates can be disentangled, permitting the former to enjoy a continuing existence independent of the latter. Strawson supplements this very general point by more specific observations about the contents of a disembodied after-life.[13]

If we imagine the disembodied 'I' a) now having no perceptions of a body related to her experiences as her body was when she was alive on earth, and b) having no power of initiating changes in the physical condition of the world, such as she did in her life with her hands, shoulders, feet and vocal cords, then all that seems to be left to her is a waning store of memories of her life when she was embodied. She must always think of herself with respect to the embodied person she was: as *dis*embodied, as a *former* person. In other words, disembodied existence is merely the fading wake of embodied existence. The notion of it is parasitic on that of ordinary human existence, which is (in Strawson's view) intrinsically embodied.

One could, perhaps, be a little more vigorous (though perhaps less rigorous) in dismissing the notion of a disembodied 'I'. It would have no location in space. It would not therefore be a viewpoint on the world. There would be no basis for new experiences of a putatively outside world. Nor would there be anything connected with action: action would be neither possible nor required. (It is difficult to conceive of the *needs* of the disembodied; though to say this may presuppose too much. The assumption that, for example, the needs of conscious creatures are rooted in physiological imperatives is self-evident only from a material-ist standpoint.) Such consciousness as might be imagined for it would be agenda-less: at best memories and thoughts disconnected from any kind of present. There is, at any rate, no future to be reached for, shaped by the past. There are neither lacks nor needs.

These are less obvious, deeper limitations and problems that throw into question the entire notion of disembodied first-person existence. I-thoughts, as Cassam argued, have to be relativised to an individual: they are essentially indexical. This is equally true of first-person memories (as we shall discuss in Chapter 7). The only way they can be thus relativised is by reference to something 'shaped, solid and located' – criteria hardly met by a discarnate 'I'.

There are, however, yet deeper problems. Can a disembodied 'I' that is not located in space be located in time? It seems unlikely to be located in *tensed* time as this is indexed to markers that it would not have access to; moreover, in the absence of new experiences and the anticipation of new experiences, there would be no basis for the differentiation between past, present and future. At best, there would be an eternal 'now-less now' of reiterated or recycled snippets of consciousness. But does a disembodied 'I' exist even in tenseless time? It is not located in space (though it may have a – progressively attenuating – sense of being so located). Is it possible for something to be temporally but not spatially located; to be located in tenseless, physical time but not located in physical space? That depends on whether we believe that space and time can be entirely separated. According to post-Einsteinian physics, space and time are inseparable: you can't have one without the other; or, to put it another way, if you don't have one, you don't have the other either.[14]

Disembodied 'I', therefore, seems condemned to exist neither in time nor in space and looks likely to be either immediately or eventually contentless. And an 'I' that has never been embodied would be entirely contentless because entirely 'untethered'. The notion of such an untethered (and contentless and certainly agenda-less) 'I' is entirely unspecified or undifferentiated. An undifferentiated and locationless 'I' is unintelligible

– or empty, a nothing. An 'I' that is free-floating in this way is not an 'I'; nor (to anticipate the last throw of scepticism) could it even entertain the *illusion* of being an 'I'. Its thoughts, moreover, would have no meaning to itself, because there would be no grounding for the meanings of the words that form its endless soliloquy. It would not have a viewpoint or needs or any unfolding in the time necessary to make a token, occurrent thought.[15]

This all seems quite obvious: no-where and no-when are eventless; and the locationless 'I' contentless. So where does this notion of a disembodied 'I' that can continue to suffer, or feel joy, come from? It is probably derived (as we shall discuss in Chapter 6) from our experience of our own thoughts, which have a certain transient independence of our body: they can be about nothing the body is currently environed by, or is suffering, and they are abstract. It is this that seduces us into imagining that there can be stand-alone thinking, independent of the world of bodies, and that thinking could be contentful and protracted indefinitely. We forget, of course, that all actual thoughts are parts of occurrent thinking: they occur to someone who is, or appears to be, in a particular material situation; at any rate at a particular point in space and time.

This, then, is how we might imagine that a disembodied 'I' seems possible. That such an 'I' is not only possible but is the only sure thing that we have – the outcome of systematic doubt plus the *Cogito* argument – comes from the apparently privileged nature of thought: that it is not only Cartesianly assured, but it could stand alone. This, as we have seen, is false. Thinking, even to one's self, presupposes, for example, a community of discourse to give meaning to one's self-communings. Moreover, the sense of the 'I' that the thinking requires presupposes some means of self-identification and re-identification – which, as Strawson, Cassam and others have argued, requires being aware of one's self as an object 'in the weighty sense'.

The ontological boot is suddenly on the other foot: the challenge is not to those who believe that the 'I' is embodied to prove it beyond all non-self-contradictory doubt, but to those who doubt this to demonstrate that their doubts are founded or even intelligible.

### 4.4 SCEPTICISM ABOUT THE NECESSARY EMBODIMENT OF THE 'I'

Even so, some would argue that the task of demonstrating the necessity of the embodiment of the 'I' – or conversely showing the very idea of a disembodied 'I' to be a logical impossibility – is incomplete and that neither Strawson nor Cassam fully meets the sceptical challenge, immunised the body from systematic doubt and allows the thinker an automatic passage from 'I am' to 'I am embodied'. It is still possible, they argue, that my sense of being embodied is an illusion.

Barry Stroud, for example, has criticised Strawson's attempt to overcome scepticism by appealing to concepts such as 'identifiability' and re-'identification'. Strawson, Stroud points out, assumes that we *can* identity and re-identify others – or, presumably, ourselves. Scepticism, however, begins by questioning that assumption – and indeed by questioning whether the very existence of others (external objects, other minds, etc.) can be taken for granted. The unquestionable given consists essentially of the experiences that I am having at any given time which may, or may not, be of the same objects and had by the same person.

In response to such criticism, Strawson[16] has redefined the nature of his project and of what it has achieved. He has emphasised the descriptive rather than the explanatory nature of his metaphysics, and has agreed that it does nothing to legitimate common sense. It is as if he has retracted the last sentence of *Individuals* (which echoes F. H. Bradley's rueful observation, noted earlier, that 'metaphysics is the art of finding bad reasons for what we believe upon instinct'):

> So if metaphysics is the finding of reasons, good, bad or indifferent, for what we believe on instinct, then this has been metaphysics.[17]

He would agree with Stroud that what he has done is to show

> only how one way of thinking is connected with another, and how our having one set of thoughts or beliefs about the world requires that we also have certain other thoughts and beliefs. It is to establish, in Strawson's words, 'a certain sort of interdependence of conceptual capacities and beliefs: e.g ... that in order for self-conscious thought and experience to be possible, we must take it, or *believe*, that we have knowledge of external physical objects or other minds'. It is not necessary to establish that there are such objects or minds.[18]

This apparently bypasses, rather than addresses, the sceptical challenge – a strategy Strawson himself defends on the grounds that our naturally implanted fundamental beliefs (that there are external objects, etc.) makes scepticism 'wholly idle' and not just in a practical sense.[19] As Thomas Baldwin has put it, 'the basic structure of our conceptual scheme lies so deep in our thought and practice that its legitimation is neither possible nor necessary'.[20]

The reasons that Strawson gives for conceding so much so easily are interesting. The claim that the sceptical challenge – to, for example, the notion of our identity, material objects or other minds – is 'idle', because no one could really entertain it as a possibility, should not itself go without challenge; or at least without examination.[21] It is similar to another argument Strawson uses against those who feel that human freedom is threatened by determinism: our practical feelings are not affected by any judgement as to whether we are free in the sense that determinism seems to place in question.[22] The determinist arguments against freedom are, therefore, 'idle'. In the same way, sceptical arguments about identity, the existence of external objects, and so on, are logically derivable but practically unthinkable, or unliveable. We can logically unthink the embodied 'I' – for anything is logically possible that does not imply logical contradiction – but cannot existentially unthink it.[23]

Even so, there is an argument to be had about why it is that 'the basic structure of our conceptual scheme lies so deep'. Could it not be because it captures something fundamental, real and true about what we are and the world is? If, for example, we believe that there are material objects and that we ourselves are, in some rather complex sense, caught up in, or identified with, material objects, isn't this most likely to be because there *are* such objects? Why, or how, could we have come to such a fundamental belief unless it were true? Likewise, isn't it most probable that we refer to a re-identifiable self as 'I' because there is such a self? 'I' would seem to be entirely redundant – 'idle', to appropriate Strawson's word – unless it had enduring referents opposed to, and immiscible with, the referents of 'you', 'he', etc. We are unlikely to have conceived of the world as containing such entities if it did not in fact contain them.

This is analogous to one of Descartes' most famous arguments. Descartes argued that God must exist, He cannot be a fabrication of the human mind, because a) He is infinite and perfect, and b) the human mind is finite and imperfect. Given that what is more perfect cannot proceed from what is less perfect, and nothing equals the perfection of God, the idea of God could have arisen only if there were indeed a God. While I am not tempted to mobilise a similar (flawed) argument in support of the reality of material objects and of the embodiment of 'I', the intuition that the mind, or minds, seems unlikely to have thought up, or come to believe in, material objects and its own embodiment unless both beliefs corresponded to reality, does seem to be a sound one. Kant's arguments notwithstanding, why would the mind concoct a story of objects if there were no objects? Why would it come to believe in an outside-of-itself if there were no outside-of-itself in the sense implicit in material objects? Why would it believe in its own embodiment if it were not indeed embodied? It seems a rather odd thing for a mind to do. We can, of course, be mistaken and our mistakes can be global howlers: we may dream that we are doing things in places when we are doing no such thing in no such place. But dreams and errors could not form the entire fabric of our world. Dreams and errors are local and parasitise reality and truth; the 'dream' or 'error' that there are re-identifiable objects seems a different order of departure from reality.[24] The various arguments that have been advanced – for example, that objects, though illusory, are handy ways of organising our experiences – seem to beg more questions than they answer. Why should it be useful to believe that we are embodied if we are in truth not embodied? And how should we arrive at that idea if it had no basis outside of our minds?

The most question-begging response to this is the suggestion that belief in objects – ourselves as embodied and our bodies as surrounded by material objects – is useful for 'survival'. Foregrounding 'survival' in this way is to buy into the notion of 'I's' as biologically rooted and hence as objects interacting materially with other (living and non-living) objects in a material universe. To presuppose this is to place the cart before the horse on a spectacular scale. This kind of error has been captured (with respect to evolutionary epistemology) beautifully by Anthony O'Hear:

> For, in doing epistemology, we are not entitled simply to assume certain results of science or any other field of enquiry ... Evolutionary epistemology ... invokes our biological knowledge in order to refute a particular brand of skepticism. We are asked to accord the deliverances of the senses some positive degree of probability because biology teaches us various things about the origins and past development of our sensory faculties. But, given that biology itself is a part of our system of knowledge, and in the end acceptable (if it is) because of its accord with sensory evidence, there is a massive circularity in attempting to justify or probability our sensory data by appeal to biology ... To invoke biology, and to see our perceptual apparatus as a biologically constituted device is not so much to refute skepticism or idealism as simply to side-step them.[25]

And that would never do.

It seems inappropriate, therefore, to dismiss scepticism as being 'wholly idle' just because it is at odds with the deepest level of our belief and because, at the deepest level, our beliefs are more than beliefs – with the assumption that their truth or falsehood is beside the point. Besides, Strawson seems to be conceding too much and too easily in concluding that we cannot, after all, place the body out of the reach of systematic doubt. His own attempt to demonstrate the necessary embodiment of the 'I', when developed by Cassam, seems to suggest that much progress can be made. We should not therefore accept his later epistemological pessimism and conclude that there is no way of getting from what we know with certainty – the kind of thing that the *Cogito* argument yields – to a confident assertion that we are indeed embodied. I believe he and his successors have given us good grounds for believing that without embodiment the intuition of 'I' cannot be individuated. From the point of view of objective knowledge, which after all is where scepticism takes its rise, and which is an essential precursor to the idea of error and justifies uncertainty, this seems undeniable.[26]

### 4.5 SELF-CONSCIOUSNESS, IDENTITY AND EMBODIMENT

The *Cogito* argument properly understood is, as we pointed out in the previous chapter, not about third-person knowledge but about first-person assumptions (in the double sense we have used). Seen in this way, 'I' is inseparable from 'I-dentity' and 'I-dentification'. If we accept that there is such a thing as identification and identity and that it has something at its core that is self-warranting, then the arguments that Strawson, Cassam and others mobilise to show that embodiment is necessary for these things are relevant and applicable.

Let us settle for this argument: if there is an 'I', I has an identity, understood as the well-founded and persistent intuition of something that is re-identifiable and which I am. I am a self-conscious subject who, at the very least, 'is capable of consciousness of his or her own identity as the subject of different experiences or representations'.[27] Self-consciousness is not a subset of conscious experiences among others, but something that is implicit in conscious experiences, binding them at a particular time and over time.[28] To say 'I' and at the same time to deny the existence of the only plausible mode of existence that 'I' might take is to contradict one's self. Given that material bodies are the only kind of re-identifiable things there are, then my identity is inseparable from the notion of a body – an object in the weighty sense – that I, in some sense, am. I am necessarily embodied.

It will be useful, finally, to connect the arguments in this chapter with the notion of the first person developed by looking at the connections between self-consciousness as Cassam and others conceive it and the Existential Intuition. There are interesting points of contact and of difference. While both acknowledge the necessary embodiment of the 'I', they arrive at this conclusion from different starting points. For Cassam and others, self-consciousness requires the body as a kind of tether or reference point to give the 'I' the basis for its sense of itself as 'the same being' – as 'this being rather than that thing' (me as contrasted with you) and as 'the same being now and in the past and in the future'.

It is as if the body is necessary to provide a criterion for re-identification, without which there is no identity and 'I' is unintelligible. While agreeing with his arguments vis-à-vis the necessary link between self-consciousness and being an object in the weighty sense, I arrive at the same conclusion setting out from a different starting point: the assumption that the (animal) body is the point of origin of self-consciousness: that self-consciousness in its most basic form is a realisation that passes across a conscious body that it *is* this body; the awakening of the body to itself.

These different conceptions of the relationship between the 'I' and embodiment are rooted in the fact that they begin from different assumptions, which we have already hinted at. Cassam and others start from – or take on – the sceptical viewpoint and the arguments of idealist philosophers. I begin with a body that is part of a natural world of living and non-living objects. My 'I' is (at least in the first instance – early hominid, contemporary newborn) the body's intuition of itself as itself – as 'myself'.

To caricature this difference, my 'I' *begins*, is rooted, in the identifiable object that Cassam's 'I' requisitions to tether its identity, to provide the necessary individuation at any given time and over time. Of course, both parts of the caricature are misrepresentions. For Cassam's 'I', the body is not just a crude marker pen to label successive phases or aspects of itself as phases or aspects of the same self. The label wouldn't do its work if 'I' and the body were not indissolubly linked. 'If it wasn't for the good fortune of having a (comparatively stable) body, I wouldn't be able to know who I was or that I was the same thing from moment to moment' is a travesty of Cassam's view of the relationship between 'I', identity and the body. It is expressed more accurately as follows: 'If it weren't for the body, there would be no intelligible way of underpinning anything corresponding to "I"'. The body, that is to say, is as deeply embedded in the 'I' in his account as it is in mine. And my own account doesn't really proceed directly from the awakening of self-consciousness to a full-blown 'I'. The issue of identity, that is to say, arises only further down the track when the 'I' has become sufficiently differentiated, elaborated and even (internally) distanced from the body for that relationship to have become a quasi-fact for which supportive evidence could reportedly be sought.

We approach the same conclusion – the necessary embodiment of 'I' – from different starting points. Is it, however, the same conclusion for both of us? We are both agreed that self-consciousness has somehow to be connected with something that transcends moments of experience to count as self-consciousness. 'That I am' is not enough to capture self-consciousness: it is, as it were, unsaturated. Self-consciousness must be consciousness of being something – that something's consciousness of being something. Hence 'That I am *this*'. Since, in my case, self-consciousness arises in the body, the Existential Intuition is self-saturating, self-identifying. 'Who/what am I?' comes later. For Cassam, self-consciousness too is consciousness of being something – an object in the weighty sense. However, it seems a contingent fact that this object is a living body. And this is connected with another important difference in the way embodiment is envisaged. Cassam's conclusion,

> that self-consciousness, and so the unity of consciousness, is intimately bound up with awareness of the subject 'as an object' – not as an 'immaterial' substance but as a physical object in a world of physical objects[29]

is curiously aseptic. 'Awareness of the subject as an object', even 'as a physical object in a world of physical objects', seems remote from the living, suffering, striving organism in which the Existential Intuition awakes. It is as if the logical necessity of embodiment – acknowledging that it is necessary for an intelligible account of the self-consciousness we assuredly have – were remote from its existential reality. Which is, of course, how it should be; and this is not a criticism of Cassam's approach, or of his argument, or of his conclusion, but of the place he is coming from. It reflects in part the unclosable distance between the sceptical challenge (which he meets head on) and the assumptions built into the biogenetic account of self- consciousness. There is no way that he could argue on grounds of 'the interdependence of conceptual capacities and beliefs' that the 'I' should be biologically embodied as opposed to being aware of itself as a physical object. The gap can be narrowed further, however. *The fact that the 'I' is aware implies that the object it is aware of being must presumably itself be aware.* It might be argued that the aware object it is obliged to think of itself as being is effectively the sentient creature that is my starting point. It is, however, a matter of faith to assume that Cassam's 'aware physical object' is a living organism.

There is another interesting gap in the very notion of embodiment, which I think is present in both the 'object in the weighty sense' and biological accounts. For Cassam, self-consciousness requires being aware of one's self as a physical object; but the very state of being aware of one's self *as* such an object both unites one with and distances one's self from that object. This raises questions about what it means to be identified with, and identified (by one's self and by others) *as*, something or other. Just how complex these questions are becomes apparent when we examine the whole business of actually being a body; of the standing realisation that one is (in some sense) that thing from which one's self-consciousness has taken its rise. 'Identification with some thing' is a matter of not quite being that something and of not being merely attached to, or labelled by, it. Being *em*bodied is not the same as being the body that one is. We shall attempt to examine the full extent of the complexity of the statement 'I am this', where 'this' is a living body, in the next two chapters.

We shall begin this task of making sense of what 'embodiment' amounts to by exploring another approach to the case for embodiment that eschews both the Cartesian and the scientific starting points: one that ultimately derives from Martin Heidegger, though this approach takes a course he most certainly would not have liked.

### NOTES

1. A. J. Ayer, *The Problem of Knowledge* (London: Penguin, 1956), p. 45.
2. 'There is thinking' is existentially self-guaranteeing in the same way because it could not be instantiated without being thought. One cannot separate the idea of the token-thought 'There is thinking' from the idea of someone thinking it.
3. P. F. Strawson, *Individuals. An Essay in Descriptive Metaphysics* (London: Methuen, 1957).
4. Quassim Cassam, *Self and World* (Oxford: Clarendon Press, 1997).
5. The relationship between having an identity and being re-identifiable is complex and will be discussed in Chapter 7.
6. P. F. Strawson, *The Bounds of Sense. An Essay on Kant's Critique of Pure Reason* (London: Methuen, 1966). In this book, he sees both his own and Kant's programme as 'determining the fundamental general structure of any conception of experience such as we can make intelligible to ourselves' (p. 44).
7. For example, Gareth Evans criticised the conclusion that Strawson drew from his thought experiment in which he imagined a universe consisting only of sounds and seemingly demonstrating that such a universe would have no basis within it for re-identification of particulars. ('Things without the Mind – A Commentary upon Chapter Two of Strawson's *Individuals*', in Z. van Straaten (ed.), *Philosophical Subjects: Essays Presented to P. P. Strawson* (Oxford: Clarendon Press, 1980).
8. Cassam, *Self and World*, p. v.
9. Although we shall question this in Volume 3, 'The Self and Its Own'.
10. And self-ascription does seem fundamental to I-hood. 'I' is one who crucially *says* 'I'. Which is not, of course, to imply that this is all she is. 'I' is not purely a linguistic activity – as some such as Emile Benveniste claimed – because that linguistic activity would then be empty. See Raymond Tallis, *In Defence of Realism* (London: Edward Arnold, 1988, reissued Nebraska University Press, 1995), section 5.2 'The Subject as Linguistic Artefact'. Benveniste's linguistic reduction of 'I' could have done with a touch of the Existential Grammar adumbrated in Chapter 2.
11. If I use the word 'I', I must enable someone else to know what 'I' is referring to – hence the need to have a perceptible body which the voice is coming out of. If 'I' was

routinely meaningless (or referenceless), it would not have emerged as a word. I would have no use for it.

12. Strawson, *Individuals*, p.103.
13. Ibid., pp. 115–16.
14. As Hermann Minkowski famously said: 'The views of space and time which I wish to lay before you have sprung from the soil of experimental physics, and therein lies their strength. Henceforth, space by itself, and time by itself, are doomed to fade away into mere shadows, and only a kind of union of the two will preserve an independent reality' (cited in Max Born, *Einstein's Theory of Relativity*, New York: Dover Publications, 1965, p. 305).
15. See also Volume 3, Chapter 1.
16. In, for example, *Skepticism and Naturalism: Some Varieties* (London: Methuen, 1985).
17. Strawson, *Individuals*, p. 247.
18. Barry Stroud, 'Kantian Argument', in *Understanding Human Knowledge* (Oxford: University Press, 2000), p. 164.
19. For the idleness or otherwise of sceptical thought, see Raymond Tallis, *George Moore's Hands. A Philosophical Inquiry into the Impossibility of Philosophy* (submitted for publication).
20. Thomas Baldwin, *Contemporary Philosophy. Philosophy in English since 1945* (Oxford: Oxford University Press, 2001), p. 176.
21. As, indeed, Stroud has challenged it, repeatedly in the beautiful essays in *Understanding Human Knowledge*.
22. P. F. Strawson, 'Freedom and Resentment', in Gary Watson, *Free Will*, Oxford Readings in Philosophy, 2nd edn (Oxford: Oxford University Press, 2003).
23. We may define classical philosophical scepticism as thought that occupies the space between the existentially and the logically unthinkable, the latter having a smaller territory than the former. This distinction casts a sidelight on the relationship between the systematic doubt that precedes the *Cogito* argument and the (undeniable) Existential Intuition. If the latter is seen as a pure proposition, then it can be logically unthought: 'I am not this ...' where 'this' stands for anything that one happens to be, is not logically self-contradictory. But, as it is put into play in the *Cogito* argument (seen as a recipe, or a performative – seen, that is to say, for what it is), it is not a pure proposition in this sense. The impurity – which is the 'I' who am 'this' – makes the Intuition impossible to unthink. The very business of unthinking it would be to affirm it. It cannot be 'unassumed' – least of all by someone engaged in higher-level philosophical reflection. The inappropriateness of separating out the (abstract, general) propositional content of the Existential Intuition from the sense that one *is* makes the existentially unthinkable period unthinkable. Which is, perhaps, what Descartes really meant to say, though he did try to unthink part (the bodily part) of his thinking 'I' and entertain the possibility that the thinker could exist without being embodied.
24. So much so that it may seem to undermine the very notion of getting things wrong. Without objects in the 'weighty' sense, it is not clear that there can be a realm of objective truth (or of objective falsehood) beyond that of 'subjective experience' so that the very process of entertaining scepticism about re- identifiable objects – and suspecting that things, globally, might be different from how they appear to be – removes the ground upon which it can, itself, stand. This is Wittgenstein's point, of course: we have to take so much for granted in order to entertain a doubt. Merleau-

Ponty also made a similar point, expressed by Eric Matthews as follows: 'Even our awareness of our own subjectivity is possible only if we are aware of a world that transcends it' (*The Philosophy of Merleau-Ponty*, Montreal: McGill-Queen's University Press, 2002, p. 89). This awareness lies at the root of knowledge and the awakening of knowledge out of sentience (as we shall discuss in Volume 3). Without it, there can be no grounds for scepticism because there is nothing to be sceptical about or with. The sceptical position, in short, assumes that there is a difference between how things seem to be and how things really are. That is to say, it assumes the existence of a viewpoint from which things – our errors, for example – can be exposed as errors. But the assumption of the difference between, say, reality and illusion is a rather unsceptical position!

25. 'The Evolution of Knowledge', *Critical Review* 2(1) (Winter 1988): 78–91. We shall return to this, and other fundamental flaws of evolutionary epistemology, in Volume 3.

26. To move closer to our present concern, someone might point out to the sceptic that a disembodied mind could not act upon the world. The sceptic would reply that he is not claiming that the disembodied subject does act on the world, but only that the disembodied subject could imagine that she is acting on the world when she in fact isn't. The reply to this is that if all actions are imaginary, then none is, because the difference between real and imaginary acts (a real difference, by the way) presupposes real ones.

27. Cassam, *Self and World*, p. 117. This is deliberately minimalist definition of self-consciousness.

28. Cf. Ayer, 'consciousness of one's self is not one experience among others, not even, as some have thought, a special experience which accompanies all the others. And this is not a matter of psychology but of logic' (*The Problem of Knowledge*, p. 48).

29. Cassam, *Self and World*, p. 198.

# CHAPTER 5

# The Existential Necessity for Embodiment: No *Da-Sein* without *Fort-Sein*

## 5.1 INTRODUCTION

Not all readers will be equally impressed by the arguments in the previous chapter for the necessary embodiment of 'I', such that if 'I' is given, then so too is the body. The pincer movement, combining the logical and biogenetic arguments, may arouse rather than allay suspicion, particularly as these two arguments come from such different directions and do not quite join up. To some, these difficulties will confirm the wisdom of those many twentieth-century philosophers, in both the analytical and existentialist traditions, who rejected the Cartesian project. Foremost among those who said 'I wouldn't start from here' was Martin Heidegger.

For Heidegger, Descartes was prisoner to a discredited mediaeval ontology; in particular he failed to conduct a necessary 'preliminary ontological analytic of the subjectivity of the subject':[1]

> With the *cogito sum* Descartes claims to prepare a new and secure foundation for philosophy. But what he leaves undetermined in this 'radical' beginning is the manner of being of the *res cogitans*, more precisely, *the meaning of being of the 'sum'*. (*Being and Time*, 21)

Descartes' mistake was to misunderstand where he was starting from, fully to realise what was implicit in the 'I'.

In a sense, this has been our position, too. For Heidegger, Descartes' error was both fundamental and, by default, illuminating. Partly in response to this, Heidegger develops an ontology that seems to dispose of the tradition of epistemological inquiry inaugurated by Descartes, in particular the examination of the adequacy of our grounds for believing in the existence of a world of objects outside our experiences or independent of our minds.[2] This ontology is set out in *Being and Time* (BT), Heidegger's unfinished masterpiece, an early work and still his most significant contribution to philosophy and, in the opinion of many, the greatest philosophical work of the twentieth century. Heidegger's ontology seems to offer a way out of the Cartesian prison – and indeed, side-steps at least three kinds of challenge (all tangled up with one another) that have lain at the heart of post-Cartesian epistemology:

a) extending certainty beyond the self-affirming 'I think'; beyond what we might call 'the *Cogito* moment';
b) explaining how it is that a material object – the human body or its brain – can 'gain access to' a world which contains other material bodies and acquire certain knowledge of them; and
c) explaining how the sensory experiences of a sentient entity (such as the human brain) gives a true, or at least a coherent, or partly satisfactory, account of the world outside of it.

Essentially, his ontology gives existence or lived experience priority over objective certainty in determining truth. In doing so, however, it runs into problems of its own. Even so, its deficiencies are as illuminating as Descartes' errors; indirectly they proved alternative grounds for affirming the necessity of embodiment, which is why we are examining Heidegger's ontology in this chapter, before we proceed to explore embodiment itself.

## 5.2 AN ONTOLOGY THAT BYPASSES DESCARTES: EXPOSITION

I shall not embark here on a full-scale exposition of Heidegger's ontology;[3] and my critique will focus narrowly on the failure of his attempt to bypass the Cartesian problem. I shall argue that, despite its robustly commonsensical outlook, the ontology expounded in *Being and Time* seems to work only because it overlooks, or at least glosses over, the role of the spatially located biological body in the specification or individuation of *Da-sein* ('being there') and the being-in-the-world that is 'constitutive of *Da-sein*'. He seems to miss the fundamental truth that the organic body is a necessary, though not a sufficient, condition of 'being there' and its necessary correlative, 'being here'.

The key notion in Heidegger's ontology is that *Da-sein*, or 'being there', is primordial – it is central to any account of 'what kinds of things there are', of any account of being. The primordiality of *Da-sein* permits us to focus directly on ontological questions, because *Da-sein* is the kind of being that we, who would inquire into the nature of being, are. We can approach ontological questions directly – and bypass questions about 'How we know' what is there – precisely because

> the constitutive attitudes of inquiry [such as] regarding, understanding and grasping, choosing and gaining access to ... are themselves modes of being of a particular being, of *the* being we inquirers ourselves in each case are. (BT 5–6)

> To work out the question of being means to make a being – he who questions – transparent in its being. Asking this question, as a mode of *being* a being is itself essentially determined by what is asked about in it – being. This being which we ourselves in each case are and which includes inquiry among the possibilities of its being we formulate terminologically as *Da-sein*. (BT 6)

> the being that has the character of *Da-sein* has a relation to the question of being itself ... certainly something like a priority of *Da-sein* has announced itself. (BT 7)

The first and final port of call, then, for anyone asking the question of being – of what is truly there – is the very being that (or who) asks the question, namely *Da-sein*. *Da-sein* is 'that being whose being is an issue for itself'.

Specifying what *Da-sein* is proves extraordinarily difficult. It seems at once obvious and elusive. *Da-sein*, 'being there', corresponds (very roughly) to human being. Whether it corresponds to individual human beings or to the entire category of human beings is an important ambiguity evident throughout *Being and Time* and will prove shortly to be a central issue for us. For the present, we note that, crucially, *Da-sein* does not merely 'gain access' to the world – through information, knowledge, experience, etc. It is *in* and *of* the world: being-in-the-world is 'constitutive of *Da-sein*'. Being worlded is not something that it acquires; worldedness is the very tissue of its being; it is primordial. *Da-sein* is quite unlike the extensionless Cartesian subject peering through an epistemological burkha at a world of spatially extended objects to which it does not itself belong. And the world in which it is worlded is not like the Cartesian world: it is not a collection of spatially extended physical objects, or 'objective presences', meaningless lumps of matter, such as physics describes. These latter are revealed to us (as subjects or knowers) only at a late stage, when we put ourselves in artificial states of detached contemplation or 'rigid staring'. They are not primordial forms of being. No, the world constitutive of *Da-sein* is composed of the 'ready-to-hand', typified by, though not solely made up of, tools. Tools, unlike the bits of matter that make up the extra-mental world of Cartesian dualism and the universe of physics, are not discrete and independent of one another. In the world, the discernible elements of the ready-to-hand are essentially connected: the hammer implies the nail, the hammer-and-nail implies carpentry, carpentry implies dwellings, dwellings disclose a human way of being, etc. The world of *Da-sein*, consequently, is a nexus of significances and not an array of physical objects made of matter.

As for knowing, far from being an inexplicable or dubitable mode of access of a subject to entities alien to it, it is 'a mode of being of *Da-sein* as being-in-the-world' (BT 57). Knowing itself 'is grounded beforehand in already-being-in-the-world which essentially constitutes the being of Da-sein'. Initially (before, that is, everything gets too intellectualised),

> this being-already-with is not solely a rigid staring at something merely objectively present. Being-in-the-world, as taking care of things, is *taken in by* the world which it takes care of. (BT 57)

Knowing is not a kind of reaching out to an unknown world whose existence lacks self-evident reality.

In summary, *Da-sein* does not 'discover' an 'outside' world, as an inner subject encountering an outer (physical) objective reality: the very being of *Da-sein* is 'disclosedness'. What is disclosed is not the neutral material objects, the 'objective presences', that physics investigates and that are the preoccupation of the intellectualising view of the abstract thinker who imagines that the world is primordially as it is revealed to theoretical inquiry. On the contrary, what is disclosed is the ready-to-hand, which is a web of significance, of meaning, which is neither 'subjective' in the Cartesian sense nor objective in the sense of the bits of matter uncovered in the truths, or putative truths, of science. One of the great mysteries, the origin of value in a world of objective fact, thus disappears: there is no puzzle as to how (meaningless) matter comes to matter so much because (meaningless) matter is not the basic stuff of the world. What is basic is being-in-the-world, which is constitutive of *Da-sein* which, since *Da-sein* is that being which is an issue for itself, has 'care' – mattering, heeding, meaning, etc. – built into its very fibres.

We are a long way from the Cartesian prison, built for himself by the Pure Inquirer furnished only with those thoughts that are the survivors of systematic doubt, trying to put together a starter pack consisting only of thoughts that cannot be doubted without self-contradiction. The gap between the *res cogitans* certain of his own existence and the *res extensa* (including the thinker's body) of which he is uncertain is eliminated.

Even space, that archetypically pre-human theatre of human activity, that firstborn of the physical world, turns out to be primarily part of this web of significances, this nexus of the ready-to-hand:

> the aroundness of the surrounding world, the specific spatiality of the beings encountered in the surrounding world is grounded in the worldliness of the world, and not the other way around, that is, we cannot say that the world in its turn is objectively present in space. (BT 94)

> There is never a three-dimensional multiplicity of possible positions initially given which is then filled out with objectively present things ... Regions are not first formed by things objectively together but are always already at hand in individual places. The places themselves are assigned to what is at hand in the circumspection of taking care of things, or else we come across them. (BT 96)

> The fact that what is at hand can be encountered in its space of the surrounding world is ontically[4] possible only because *Da-sein* itself is 'spatial' with regard to its being-in-the-world. (BT 97)

Egocentric space, the flag of 'here' and 'now', is not pitched in a pre-existent impersonal extensity.

No wonder Heidegger believed that he had 'annihilated' the 'problem of knowledge' (BT 57). By conferring primacy on being-in-the-world, itself constitutive of *Da-sein*, and making knowing 'a mode of *Da-sein*', he had apparently dissolved the post-Cartesian epistemological question of how it is that 'knowing inner subjects' gain access to 'outer objective presences'. Knowledge is rooted in, grows out of, being-in-the-world; there cannot therefore be any mystery as to how we gain access to, or can be sure of the existence of, an outside world. There cannot be a problem, for example, as to how I (who am here) am aware of that object 'over there', since the primordiality of *Da-sein* means that 'here' and 'there' are not in the first instance physical locations separated by empty space:

> 'Here' and 'over there' are possible only in a 'there', that is when there is a being which has disclosed spatiality as the being of the 'there'. This being bears in its ownmost being the character of not being closed. The expression 'there' means this essential disclosedness. Through disclosed-ness this being (*Da-sein*) is 'there' for itself together with the *Da-sein* of the world. (BT 125)

In other words, 'here' and 'there' are not external to one another. For example, when I encounter a tree, it is not a case of the tree (misunderstood as a lump of matter) and I (misunderstood either as a 'self' or an 'I-thing encumbered with a body') bumping into each from the outside, like two objective presences interacting, or one objective presence (the tree) encountering a localised subject (myself). That things seemingly outside-of-me are none the less disclosed to me is not surprising since the space that separates me from them is constituted primordially within the very being-in-the-world that is itself constitutive of the *Dasein* that I am.

This has profound, even exhilarating, consequences for those embroiled in the hopeless task of trying to solve the traditional epistemological problems. To those, for example, who might worry that, since everything we know about the outside world comes to us through our experiences, and our experiences are mediated through our sensoria, we have no certain evidence of a world outside our experiences; or cannot be confident that the world is in itself as our experiences tell us; or may feel, as Kant did, that the failure to demonstrate the existence of a world outside our experiences (and indeed to respond adequately to the challenge set by Descartes to get beyond the *Cogito* and its experiences), was nothing short of 'a scandal', Heidegger argues,

> The 'scandal of philosophy' does not consist in the fact that this proof [of the existence of things outside of me] is still lacking up to now, but *in the fact that such proofs are expected and attempted again and again.* (BT 190)

> Correctly understood, *Da-sein* defies such proofs, because it always already *is* in its being what the later proofs first deem necessary to demonstrate for it. (BT 190)

The existence of an outside world is precisely one of those things that cannot be questioned; for it is not a mere belief, but something presupposed in all belief. And this, not for the reason given by Wittgenstein that such a belief is a necessary condition for the language of doubting to have any sense, and for specific doubts to be articulated, but because 'outsideness' is part of the very fabric of the being of the world, and its existence needs no guarantee with respect to a knowing subject.

Being-in-the-world is primary; and the notion of an (isolated) subject facing a world of seemingly objective presences which it merely took on trust or constructed out of experiences, is derivative, a misbegotten product of a certain way of looking at the world; of an intellectualist, in particular a scientific, approach to what there is. The primordiality of *Da-sein* rules out in advance the subject – envisaged as 'an I-thing encumbered with a body' trying to figure out a world made of things that were utterly alien to it, which it could know only in so far as it constructed them or could not know at all.

This ontology, which gives primacy to *Da-sein*, thus enables Heidegger to bypass the Cartesian problem; in particular, the impossible task of finding an adequate proof of the existence of an external, extra-mental world, a certainty beyond the self-affirmation of the *Cogito* moment. Since 'knowing is a mode of *Da-sein* which is founded in being-in-the-world' (BT 58), it is absurd to try to justify our belief in the existence of the world through examining our knowledge and the grounds for that knowledge. That there is a world cannot be grounded in 'certain knowledge' because it is the ground from which knowledge grows and on which it stands. Being enworlded lies beneath human knowledge. The notion of the world as being primarily a nexus of meanings relevant to *Da-sein* also removes the difficulty of trying to find, or rediscover, indexicality in the viewpointless world revealed to, or presupposed in, objective science. The latter is not the real world but a second-order representation of the world relative to a particular intellectual stance characterised by 'rigid staring'.

### 5.3 AN ONTOLOGY THAT BYPASSES DESCARTES: CRITIQUE

Heidegger's ontology raises all sorts of questions, not the least about the respective priority of the 'ready-to-hand' and 'objective presences' and what the ontology may or may not tell us about the truth of science and of the place of *Da-sein* in the larger scheme of things if the ready-to-hand is taken as primordial. These are not directly relevant to our present inquiry and I have discussed them at some length elsewhere.[5] What is relevant here is whether Heidegger has successfully shimmied through the walls of the Cartesian prison and restored the lost certainties. I do not believe he has. I further believe that if he seems to have 'annihilated' 'the problem of knowledge', this is only because of a systematic ambiguity in the notion of *Da-sein*. He has got rid of the problem of knowledge not because he has taken certainty beyond the Cartesian limits – by demonstrating the impossibility of an asocial *Cogito* argument (as Wittgenstein did) or by uncovering the connection between 'I', identity, re-identification and embodiment (as Strawson and others have done). On the contrary, by making the world 'constitutive of *Da-sein*', he has not only bypassed the epistemological question, he has bypassed the body. In so doing, he runs the danger of being exposed as a closet idealist.⁶ More pertinent to our present concerns, Heidegger has inadvertently provided us with another reason for believing that the 'I', or the human subject, is necessarily embodied. Let us, therefore, examine this charge of suppressing the body.

Throughout *Being and Time*, '*Da-sein*' seems to alternate between two meanings, the first corresponding roughly to an individual such as a human being; the second roughly to a category of being.⁷ It must, of course, be one or the other; it cannot be both. Unfortunately, when it stabilises as an individual human being, it runs into one kind of trouble; and when it stabilises as a general category, it runs into another. In neither mode does it solve or bypass the Cartesian problem.

If *Da-sein* is interpreted as something equivalent to an individual human being, so that there is a different *Da-sein* for each person, and there is one *Da-sein* per person, it starts to look rather similar to the minds, or to the consciousnesses, or to the subjectivities, of individual persons – precisely the kinds of thing that Heidegger thought he had eliminated. Under this interpretation, we must assume that each person has – or is – his or her own being-there. Now the specific content of this being-there – what it is that is there – will depend on its 'location'. Bramhall is 'there' for me if I am in Bramhall. Cheadle is 'there' for me if I am in Cheadle. How then am I to be located? From what has been said in previous chapters, it must be assumed that my location will be tied to – borrowed from, identical with – the location of a very special object: my body. What is 'there' for 'my' *Da-sein* will be dependent (at least in part) on the location of my body: *Da-sein*'s content gets specified, is *of* a particular 'there', in virtue of its being determined by the location of the body which is my body. This fundamental state of affairs is not altered by the fact that I may sometimes ignore the place I am in because of preoccupations, memories, toothache: it remains the non-negotiable condition of my interaction with things, the most primordial mode of 'where'.

This raises all sorts of questions; for example, why should the 'there' of the *Da-sein* that is Raymond Tallis be located where Raymond Tallis's body is? How can Raymond Tallis's *Da-sein* help itself to the location of Raymond Tallis's body? Neurophilosophical and other impingement theories, which envisage interactions between the subject and the objects of which it is aware, at least offer some kind of account of this, however unsatisfactory. They propose that we are aware, are surrounded by, have a sense of being located in, the part of the physical world that impinges on our body: we are causally 'plugged into' a particular section of the material world.⁸ *Da-sein*, on the other hand, seen as unoccasioned 'disclosedness' rather than the result of materially triggered and materially shaped perception, seems utterly unexplained. In sum, if *Da-sein* is interpreted as corresponding to an individual human being, Heidegger's ontology inherits all the epistemological problems of neurophilosophy. At the same time, it has a problem of its own. While, like neurophilosophy, it cannot explain why there is such a thing as awareness or (to stick with Heidegger's term) 'disclosedness' at all (bodily (neurally) mediated awareness is utterly enigmatic), unlike neurophilosophy, it cannot even begin to suggest why awareness should be specific; why it should have one lot of contents rather than another; why disclosedness should disclose *this* world rather than another world; why being-in-the-world should be being-in-*this*-world (at present, Bramhall) rather than being-in-*that*-world (say, Cheadle). There is no reason why being-in-Cheadle (in the literal, unreformed physical sense) should generate being-in-Cheadle in the Heideggerian sense, unless the one is causally related to the other in the standard way assumed by neuroscience. If *Da-sein* is individualised, *Da-sein* philosophy may bypass the problem of how we come to be knowingly surrounded, but is then at a loss to explain how we come to have one lot of surroundings rather than another.

If, on the other hand, we think of *Da-sein* as a category, we can momentarily wriggle out of this seeming difficulty of the co-location of *Da-sein* and an individual body. This interpretation survives a little longer if we talk about 'disclosedness' – as a category – and forget about individual disclosings. The locationless category of *Da-sein* and the locationless category of 'disclosedness' pair off very satisfactorily. Unfortunately, the category of 'disclosedness' without individual disclosings of things in particular (and things in particular places) is entirely empty: a disclosure of nothing-in-particular is not readily distinguishable from a disclosure of nothing; and a disclosure of nothing is indistinguishable from non-disclosure.[9] Interpreting *Da-sein* as a category leaves it without specific content: we cannot explain how *Da-sein* does engage with, heed, care for, operate, live in, etc. individual, specific, different worlds.

If we seek an intermediate interpretation and think of *Da-sein* as a category with instantiations, this simply shifts the puzzle on. 'How does disclosedness differentiate into specific disclosings?' changes into 'How does *Da-sein* get instantiated?' Answering this restores the difficulties we encountered in interpreting *Da-sein* as *Da-seins* in the plural – as individuals. For we find ourselves asking how it is that the *Da-*, the 'there', of the instances is apparently so profoundly influenced by the locations of the bodies of instances that are 'there'.

Heidegger seems successfully to evade the subject-object ontology that generates the Cartesian, and indeed the epistemological, problems only by virtue of presenting *Da-sein* as the category of 'being-in-the-world', of uncommitted or non-specific 'disclosedness', and by evading the fact that *Da-sein* has always to be a 'being-in-*a*-world', to be that in virtue of which there are particular disclosings. Once we acknowledge that *Da-sein* boils down to individual *Da-sein*s disclosing this rather than that, we can no longer evade considering what it is that enables *Da-sein* to enjoy (or suffer) 'being-in-*this*-world' rather than 'being-in-*that*-world'. The traditional epistemological problems then return with a vengeance because the most plausible candidate for what it is that brings *Da-sein* down from a free-floating 'disclosedness' to specific disclosings and from 'being-in-the-world' (in general) to 'being-in-a-particular-world' is a body – an organic, biological, material body. This, we have seen, is the only coherent basis for individuation. *Da-sein* can seem to do its job of 'worlding' without a body only so long as the world it worlds is utterly general and unspecified and *Da-sein* itself oscillates between being a category on the one hand, and a set of individuals on the other. That would be persuasive if it were not for the small detail that we do live in particular worlds and that Raymond Tallis's world has particular locations and his world-line is different from that of, say, Martin Heidegger.

In summary, Heidegger's ontology leaves unaccounted for the fundamental feature of our conscious life; namely, that we experience the world from a certain point of view. Or that there is more than one of us and we experience the world from different points of view; that the 'there' for different *Da-sein*s is a different 'there', relative to a different 'here'. His ontology lacks any basis for the localisation of our lives and the specificity of our experiences, of our life-lines, and our destinies.

There can be no *Da-sein* that is 'being-there-in-general'. The 'there' is always and must always be a particular 'there'. Our being-there may, of course, be projected on to many different maps: the same 'there' may be described as 'near to my hand', 'in the Duchy of Cornwall', 'in the Spring of 2004', 'at a particular point in the solar system', etc. 'There' has ultimately to be related to a 'here', notwithstanding that objective physical descriptions, or other deindexicalised descriptions such as 'Ten miles from London', may launder out the stain of the personal. *Da-sein* is always particularised. It lights up a particular world; and it does so in virtue of being localised, or co-located with something that can have a location and localise other things with respect to itself. This something is necessary to 'in-here' *Da-sein*, or to create the reference 'here'. For every *Da-sein*, or every moment of every *Da-sein*, there must be a *Fort-sein* or being-here.[10]

In the absence of plausible alternatives, we must assume that the ultimate, or primordial, basis of this being-here is the body (or something like it).[11] Bodiless existence is hereless existence: no body, no here; no here, no there; no *Fort-sein*, no *Da-sein*. If there is no here, then experience cannot be determinate, there is merely an empty 'That!' – a disclosing that discloses nothing; a dawning so general that it dawns on featurelessness. *Da-sein* will have no basis for its particular relationship to certain objects or events. (We came to this conclusion in Chapter 4, it will be recalled, when we discussed the impossibility of discarnate existence.)

The necessity for postulating the body (or something like it) in order to establish the 'here' that will specify the 'there' and so 'pin down' *Da-sein* from a general category to individual *Da-sein*s, and commit 'disclosedness' to those specific disclosings that comprise a world (any world), identifies the point at which Heidegger's ontology fails to escape the epistemological problems. The mystery of a subject who is not identical with the things she knows and who cannot, therefore – at least according to the Cartesian thought experiment – be certain of anything beyond her moment of knowing, cannot be dissolved by invoking 'disclosed*ness*' as a primordial ontological reality because knowledge boils down to particular knowings and these need rather particular explanations. Knowings must at some point touch on the sense experience of individuals positioned to have those experiences.[12] Disclosings, likewise. While it may be possible to think of 'disclosedness' in a rather airy fashion, disclosings are more down to earth: it is difficult not to think of them like the disclosure of *something* (a state of affairs or whatever) to a *someone* (a person, a body, an embodied person).

### 5.4 SOME PRELIMINARY REFLECTIONS ON *FORT-SEIN*

If it really is a case of 'No body, no specific here; no specific here, no here; no here, no there; no there, no *Da-sein*', then the body in which the here is assumed to in-here starts to look like a *viewpoint*, or, at the very least, the material (specifically, biological) basis of a viewpoint. This at once licenses our reopening the questions that Heidegger bypassed. These are some of them:

1. What is it about the body that enables it to be a viewpoint?
2. What, at any rate, enables the body to be self-locating, even if only in relation to things that it locates?
3. What is it in the body that allows it to be explicitly 'here'?
4. Which, if any, of its properties accounts for the fact that I, the embodied, feel myself to be 'here'?

We need to bring some of these questions back into the frame. While acknowledging that they have been (beneficially) transformed by Heidegger's endeavour to suppress them, let us begin by turning him, if not on his head, at least inside out, by looking for a philosophy of *Fort-sein* that recognises the necessity of a 'being-here' to complement *Da-sein*. *Fort-sein* seems likely to prove 'equiprimordial' (to use one of Heidegger's favourite terms) with *Da-sein* and to be just as closely connected with being-in-the-world.

The fact that I am 'here' seems to go without saying. It hardly seems a *fact* at all, least of all an empirical fact. It seems really to have the emptiness that haunts the Existential Intuition 'That I am this ...' taken purely as a proposition. Where else *could* I be but here, given that 'here' is defined by *my* location? And yet – like the Existential Intuition '[That] I am this ...' – it is an astonishing and fathomless truth. The first challenge is to make that truth visible; for without this much subsequent discussion may seem, to put it politely, under-occasioned.

Many basic truths of our condition are easier to make visible indirectly, rather than directly – by contriving to come on them from the starting point of a system of thought that does not, or cannot, contain or accommodate them. That 'I am here' is one such truth. For 'being-here' the relevant system of thought that makes it conspicuous by its absence is neurophilosophy. I have elsewhere argued that there is no material, or more particularly neurological, basis for 'here' – or indeed other ego-centric particulars.[13] (And if we can't find 'here' in the nervous system, we are unlikely to find it elsewhere in the body: a nephrology or a gastro-enterology of 'here' seems, to say the least, implausible.) Neurophilosophy is a manifestation of materialist monism – and has been espoused by many contemporary philosophers, for example, Daniel Dennett.

According to Dennett,

> There is only one sort of stuff, namely *matter* – the physical stuff of physics, chemistry and physiology – and the mind is somehow nothing but a physical phenomenon. In short, the mind is the brain ... we can (in principle!) account for every mental phenomenon using the same physical principles, laws and raw materials that suffice to explain radioactivity, continental drift, photosynthesis, reproduction, nutrition and growth.[14]

This ontology sees the uncovering of the true nature of things as a gradual approximation to Nagel's 'view from nowhere',[15] a comprehensively and exclusively third-person view, an account of things in which there are objects but no (first-person) subjects. Russell characterised this with his usual clarity and eloquence:

no egocentric particulars occur in the language of physics. Physics views space-time impartially, as God might be supposed to view it; there is not, as in perception, a region which is specially warm and intimate and bright, surrounded in all directions by gradually growing darkness.[16]

Colin McGinn, who quotes this passage,[17] notes how physical science (and aspirationally those sciences that see themselves as ultimately reducible to physics) excludes 'indexicality', the feature of expressions whose meaning is, as we discussed in Chapter 2, at least in part determined by the context in which they are used; in particular, the location of the speaker. 'Here' is an obvious example: precisely *where* 'here' is (in, say, the statement 'I'm here') depends on the location of the mouth that utters it (more precisely, the person who *means* it). Indexicality, McGinn says, is often cited as a paradigm of that which a properly objective conception of the world would exclude: the physicist, we are told, refrains from indexical description of the world. The intuitive reason for this exclusion is that the use of indexicals involves treating oneself as somehow a *centre*, as a privileged coordinate; and objective description should not be thus invidious in its depiction of reality – it must be impartial. Indexicals flout this requirement of objective centreless description because they are semantically relative in their interpretation (pp. 15–16).

It is from the would-be viewpointless viewpoint of physical sciences – whence 'hereness' is problematic – that the fact that 'I am here' becomes visible and substantive. 'Hereness' is one dimension of the 'indexicality', which the aspiration to objectivity first tries to set aside while (non-subjective, universal, general) truths are pursued and then cannot recover when the object of study is consciousness and the subjective view.[18] If subjectivity (e.g. the 'I') is given, then 'here' follows as part of the package; but if it is withheld (as in an account of a world seen as primordially or intrinsically material), then, by contrast or default, the character of 'here' as something definite becomes evident.

That 'I am here', therefore, is by no means a free good; or not, at least, something that comes free with the material world. It is something additional to whatever it is that is yielded by the materialistic world picture; it is not nothing.[19] Its status, however, is difficult to pin down. In an attempt to do so, let us examine the statement 'I am here' as a token utterance – that is to say, as uttered by a particular someone on a particular occasion.

We are looking for someone in the dark. She shouts, 'I am here!' This, viewed as a proposition, as a type rather than a token, should be entirely uninformative. It is part of the analysis of the concept of 'I' to be 'here'.

'I' am 'here' just as much as 'I' am 'me'. But it is not, of course, uninformative. Thanks to her shout, the sound of her voice betraying where she is, we are able to locate her: we now know where she is. She is where we locate her voice to be coming from: at the point of origin of her voice.

If, on the other hand, we were to read in someone's autobiography that all her life she had been 'here' (in the literal sense), we would feel we had been told nothing. This bit of non-information would not differentiate her from any other 'I'. In contrast with the token utterance, for the sentence in the book (effectively a sentence-type) to have informative content, 'here' would have to be further specified. This could be provided in one of two ways:

a) explicitly in words, as in 'I am here, in Cornwall'; or
b) implicitly, where the localising context has been established by means of previous sentences.[20]

### 5.5 THE BODY UNDERWRITES *FORT-SEIN*

The implicit or existential specification of 'here', when the voice in the dark reveals the location of the one who says 'here', seems closer to the fundamental nature of 'here' than textual heres. Existentially specified 'here' highlights the unbreakable link between the body and the 'here', which is in turn founded on the non-negotiable connection between being embodied and being located; between corporeal being and being present (to, next to, in) *a* (particular) world.

My body, then, underpins my *Fort-sein*. Given this fact, what sort of assertion is 'My body is (always) here'? It is not a necessary or analytic truth unless a) 'here' is defined by the location of my body, and b) the location of my body is identical with the location – or source – of any token sentence uttered by me. Under such circumstances, we would be inclined to say, 'Of course your body is always here because "here" is defined as "where your body is"'. The failure of 'here' and the location of my body to achieve full coincidence is at least in part due to a) the vagueness of the notion of 'here' – it can mean this room, this town, this country; and b) the variability of the extent to which the parts of my body are pertinent to my sense of my location. My eyes may be more important than my appendix (unless the latter is inflamed); my appendix may be more important than my toenails; and my toenails are more important when they are attached to my toes than when they are clippings in a distant wastepaper basket.

There is some smearing, that is to say, of the relevant notion of my body and even greater smearing of the notion of 'here'. The vagueness or size of 'here' will depend on the vagueness or size of a putative 'there' to which it is opposed: 'here' will be this room when it is opposed to a 'there' that is another room in the house; it will be 'Cornwall' when the person we wish to be sharing our lovely time on holiday is in another county; and it will be England when 'there' or 'over there' is, say, France. And there are 'heres' that are smaller than the resolution of one body – as when I ask you to scratch me 'here' at the upper part of my back, rather than just an inch or so below.

The hereness of my body, that is to say, is conceptually quite complex and, in practical use, rather volatile. This should reassure us that we are dealing with more than a merely analytical truth: that 'I am here' seems fact-like because its shape and size, its blurredness or coarseness of *resolution*, change from moment to moment. Consequently, a given uttered assertion of this seemingly empty proposition will convey existentially or contextually much information. (The volatility of 'I am here' is not the same as the vagueness of general terms, which have ill-defined semantic fields and which may enter into straightforwardly analytical statements.) Even so, the assertion that my body is here does seem to have the emptiness of a statement of things that could not be otherwise. My body could not be anywhere but here – with the dubious exception of certain, highly atypical, moments in which we have out-of-body experiences and we seem to be able to look down on our own body from outside of them; when our bodies are seemingly *over there*, while *I* am here.[21] But these experiences are rightly regarded as delusory: the feeling that 'here' is anywhere other than where one's body is is abnormal, pathological, *wrong*.

The possibility of slippage, which dissociation between the location of one's body and the sense of where one is reveals, shows, however, that particular assertions to the effect that 'My body is here' carry empirical information and express more than empty necessary, analytic truths. The latter do not allow such slippage. While 'I' am necessarily 'here' – here being defined as where 'I' am – my body is not necessarily 'here', or even the basis of 'here', though it is so for the most part and, indeed, it is necessary that it should be so in the vast majority of cases.

It is arguable that when we think to ourselves, there is a dissociation of the 'here' where I am from the 'here' where my body is located. We ordinarily say of people who are preoccupied by thoughts – about the origin of the universe, about a slight they have received, about their summer holiday, about someone they are missing – that they are 'miles away', 'withdrawn', etc. It is clear that the thoughts even of a deeply preoccupied person are not located in, or even constitute, a rival 'here' side by side with the one constituted by her body. They do not mark, or use up, a point in space, and the elsewhere to which they direct the attention of the thinker is, strictly, nowhere – even in the case of singular thoughts with singular referents, unless we confuse the location of their thoughts with that of their referents. When I am thinking of my cat, the cat (if alive) has a location, but the cat *qua* referent does not.[22] Drifting away is only temporary and the master-here, to which any slippage relates, and which is always in place and underpins all others, is that of the body. (It may have been sufficient, however, to have inspired the notion of a dualist separation of mind and body and of thoughts being the essential being and location of the human being with the body rather awkwardly commingled. We shall discuss bodilessness in the next chapter.)

The bodily underpinning of here – that 'I am here (where my body is)' – is substantive, existential rather than emptily logical. This is the underside of the observation that there is nothing in the body *qua* material object that seems to guarantee that it is 'here': there is, as we earlier noted, no 'neurology of here', for example. 'I' and 'here' are linked necessarily with each other, but not with my body. (Of course when I die, both 'I' and 'here' leave my body: the corpse that was once the body of Raymond Tallis is both 'I-less' and 'here-less'.)

Is it perhaps rather overstating things to say that 'Here is where my body is', as if 'here' were a kind of absolute; or a positive rather than a comparative? Might we not more accurately say that '"Here" is defined as "closer to my body" compared with "there" which is "further from my body"'? 'Here' and 'there' would then be comparative terms for which the location of the body provides the yardstick. The body would not so much be 'here' as that by which 'hereness' (as opposed to 'thereness' – or 'over-thereness') would be underwritten. This may be the case; but it would not fully capture the role of my body in underpinning the truth of, or carnally instantiating, the assertion 'I am here'. If 'here' were merely a matter of definition – 'closer to my body' – we would still be left explaining why that definition was arrived at.

It is the body, then, that gives both content and truth to the assertion that 'I am here'. This may be seen as a facet of the way the body, or more precisely the embodiment of the I, in some way guarantees or underpins the truth and content of the Existential Intuition 'That I am this ...' and gives this the basis for a specific realisation. Without the body, the assertion 'I am here' would be empty, for there would be no location for the 'I'. We could express this a little differently by saying that the localisation of sensations, of body parts and of places is localisation with respect to other sensations, other body parts and other places. The possibility of a regression, whereby locations locate each other, is forestalled by the suffusing 'am' that is the primordial form of the Existential Intuition.

Let us summarise. The body underwrites 'here' (and, by contrast, 'there'). While this seems self-evident, it is, as we have seen, nothing of the kind. Of course my body is 'here', someone might say, where else could it be? There? Over there? Elsewhere? Nowhere? And the answer is that, with the exception of nowhere, it could be in any of these locations. Considered as a material object, the body is not *de facto* here any more than it is *de facto* there. Indexicality cannot be derived from objective facts or found in the third-person world of the scientific imagination. There is no *de facto* here because there are no *de facto* – objective, impersonal, viewpointless – indexicals. 'Here' is not part of any (objective) fact of the case. After all, another person's body – which I see from a third-person standpoint – can be here(-ish), or over there, or elsewhere, so why should my body be an exception?

There is, therefore, nothing in the body *qua* material object that makes it be 'here'. A pebble (by itself, alone, intrinsically) is not 'here' (nor come to that 'there' or 'elsewhere') except in so far as it is in relation to me, or to something like me. It is no more intrinsically 'here' or 'elsewhere' than it is intrinsically 'being seen' or 'out of sight'. There is nothing in the material properties of the body that make it be here and make everything there or elsewhere relative to it. It is only true of the body that it is 'here' so long as it is *my* body. My body is 'here' courtesy of its being mine; and it is mine only inasmuch as it is in some sense me, or what I am. 'Hereness' and 'thereness' and 'over there' and the rest are secondary to the 'me-ness' and the 'mine-ness' of my body.

This insight lies at the heart of what is right about Heidegger's understanding of the nature of the 'there' in *Da-sein*. It is not, he points out, primarily a region of physical space. Space, initially and for the most part, is bound up with mattering, with 'Care'. *Da-sein*

> is 'in' the world in the sense of a familiar and heedful association with the beings encountered within the world. Thus when spatiality is attributed to it in some way, this is possible only on the basis of this being-in. But the spatiality of being-in shows the character of *de-distancing* and *directionality* ... *Da-sein* is essential de-distancing. As the being that it is, it lets beings be encountered in nearness. (BT 97)

'De-distancing' is a difficult notion. It means 'making distance disappear, bringing it near' (BT 97): it is a way of making contact with something that is seen as both distant and other – as when I see something over there; or when I feel surrounded by things. Those things that surround me are *present*: they are part of the being-in-the-world that constitutes my *Da-sein* and yet at the same time they are 'away', 'yonder', 'over there'. It is important to appreciate that their being-at-a-distance is not being at the kind of distance that separates one material object from another:

> What is at hand in the surrounding world is, after all, not objectively present for an eternal spectator exempt from *Da-sein*, but is encountered in the heedful everydayness of *Da-sein*. (BT 98)

> *The circumspect de-distancing of everyday Da-sein discovers the being-in-itself of the 'true' world, of beings with which Da-sein as existing is always already together.* (BT 99)

So far, so good. Unfortunately, Heidegger then tries to evade the consequences of this – the central role of the (biological) body – by dismissing the problem that it poses.

> Bringing near is not oriented toward the I-thing encumbered with a body, but rather toward heedful being in the world, that is, what that being-in-the-world initially encounters. (BT 100)

And he simply asserts that:

> The essential disclosure of space lies in the significance with which *Da-sein* as heedful being-in is familiar. (BT 102)

And,

> Being-in-the world, as taking care of things, is *taken in by* the world which it takes care of. (BT 57)

This is a crucial step: because 'being-in-the-world belongs essentially to *Da-sein*, its being-toward-the-world is essentially taking care' (BT 53). It is because 'being-in-the-world belongs essentially to *Da-sein*' and 'its being toward the world is essentially taking care' (BT 53) that the beings *Da-sein* encounters are not objective presences, things merely present-at-hand, but things that are ready-to-hand. *Da-sein* is not just 'side by side' or 'alongside' its world: the being-with that characterises *Da-sein* cannot be reduced to the side-by-side of material objects which itself requires *Da-sein* to make them be together-with one another – to *be* side by side.

> Regions are not first formed by things objectively present together, but are always already at hand in individual places. The places themselves are assigned to what is at hand in the circumspection of taking care of things, or else we come across them. (BT 96)

This has implications for 'I' and 'here':

> This I-here does not mean an eminent point of an I-thing, but as being-in is to be understood in terms of the over there of the world at hand where *Da-sein* dwells in *taking care*. (BT 112)

Heidegger doesn't seem to acknowledge the difficulty of eliminating something like 'an I-thing encumbered with a body' or admit that there is a problem in trying to sort out a relationship between the 'I' that makes the body be 'here' and the body that gives that 'here' a content and the 'I' an empirical location.

And this is our essential difficulty. When we try to account for 'here', we cannot avoid invoking the body to give the 'here' specificity and actuality – to instantiate 'here'. At the same time we need something other than the body to make the latter's objective location into an experienced 'here'. While *Da-sein* without a body would have no 'there' because it would be nowhere in particular, a body on its own, understood as a material entity, cannot establish a 'there' or, indeed, a 'here'. We could be tempted to give up in despair at the inadequacy of bodiless *Da-sein* and the difficulty of encasing *Da-sein* in a body that will deliver the 'here' from which it will disclose a particular 'there'. This is clearly not something that is direct and straightforward; we need for this, and other, reasons to conceive of 'here' as being gradually and progressively established, constructed, enacted, through the body's own experience of itself and that self-experience as it is experienced in relation to other things. Those complex relationships – in which 'here' is in part founded on a body that 'I' 'am' – have to add up to a layered location of near-here, here, near-there, far-there, elsewhere and beyond. The 'hereness' of the body, far from being an empty tautology, is a working fact that has to be endlessly realised and is perhaps never fully achieved.[23] 'Hereness' is one of the most intimate consequences of the folded awareness of the human body;[24] of its relationship to itself as an object that it assumes as itself, though it remains only partially scrutable.

## 5.6 CONCLUSION

We might summarise our present position – and the difficulties in which it is mired – as follows: being embodied is a necessary condition of here, of being 'enhered' (*sic*); and an insufficient condition or explanation of it. The body underwrites here and gives here content – it has to do both – and yet it is not clear how it can do the first, so that we lack an explanation of how it pulls off the second. At the very least, an inquiry into first-person being should try to explain the here that underpins the there and the perceptions that disclose it and the actions that endeavour to change it. At any rate, it seems as if, while embodiment is necessary for localisation of the self, selving of the body is necessary for it to discharge this function of being here. The subject cannot be 'here' without being embodied and the body cannot be here without being haunted by the subject. This is a chicken-and-egg situation and, given that both chickens and eggs undoubtedly exist, not an impossible one or indeed uncommon.

To deny that such puzzles are serious, and to support one's denial by pointing out that these are not problems that bother us in the 'absorbed coping' or 'everyday concernful coping' (to use Hubert Dreyfus's apt phrases[25]) of daily life, is simply not good enough. In this respect (but no other) Heidegger proves himself to be as anti-intellectual as Dr Johnson when he 'refuted' Bishop Berkeley's idealism by kicking a stone. As someone once said, Johnson hit the stone but missed the point.[26]

We shall revisit the role of the body in establishing 'here' in Chapter 6 and find that things are even more complex and difficult to understand than we have found in this chapter. And in Volume 3, we shall explore the fact that 'here' in the sense that humans know does not come bundled with mere sentience. It is a child of *knowledge* – a uniquely human mode of awareness – and it becomes increasingly layered as knowledge (and the selfhood that develops in parallel with knowledge) becomes more complex. For the present, we shall settle for the conclusion that there is no being-there without being-here and no being-here without a body or something like it; that the philosophy of *Da-sein* cannot stand alone without a complementary philosophy of *Fort-sein*. No here, no there; no body, no here.

### NOTES

1. Martin Heidegger, *Being and Time*, p. 21. English-speaking readers (in particular virtual monoglots such as myself) are fortunate to have the translation by Joan Stambaugh (New York: State University of New York Press, 1996). This is a translation of the seventh edition of *Sein und Zeit* (originally published by Max

Niemeyer Verlag, Tubingen, 1953). I will rely on Stambaugh for the passages cited in this chapter. Not being a German scholar, I cannot judge the accuracy of the translation; I can only, as an impassioned reader, report with gratitude on its luminous clarity and expressiveness – and on the immensely helpful supporting material, notably the Lexicon of English Expressions, tracing the entire history of the terms used by the translator as they appear in the book.

2. He was not entirely alone in this, of course. Even Husserl went some way towards breaking down the object-subject divide by emphasising the intentional structure of consciousness, its character of being intrinsically outward-reaching. For Heidegger, however, this being-almost-in-the-world was not quite enough, since Husserl still began with the isolated consciousness as a kind of interior, even though its contents were phenomena, 'showings forth of reality'. Besides, as Husserl later discovered, the 'internal-externality' of consciousness did not break down the barrier between subject and object if the object were genuinely thought of as independent of consciousness: intentionality's reaching out was not enough to ensure that consciousness made contact with, and incorporated, the intrinsic nature of the object. Husserl's ambition, to unpack objective knowledge from the subjective experience of individuals, was never fulfilled; nor, as we shall see in Volume 3, could it have been. One of the reasons for this is that trying to find the component (immediate) experiences that are supposed to make up objective knowledge is like the project (undertaken by the professors in *Gulliver's Travels*) of identifying and counting the number of sunbeams that have gone into a cucumber.

3. There are many (hundreds, perhaps thousands of) accounts of Heidegger's fundamental ideas, most notably Hubert L. Dreyfus, *Being-in-the-World. A Commentary on Heidegger's* Being and Time *Division I* (Cambridge, MA: The MIT Press, 1991). Heidegger is a philosopher who provokes extreme reactions – contempt and idolatry – rather than measured appraisal; for the most part, commentaries tend to be uncritical expositions or superficial rejection. Dreyfus's book is neither. My own commentary (*A Conversation with Martin Heidegger*, Basingstoke: Palgrave, 2002) attempts to take his ideas seriously and sympathetically while remaining alert to the serious deficiencies, including the one that provides the present chapter with its theme.

4. 'Ontically' here is contrasted with ontologically. It relates to what is a matter of particular fact without reference to its way of being.

5. See the Appendix to Tallis, *A Conversation with Martin Heidegger*. This is an area of intense controversy among even his most sympathetic commentators.

6. See ibid., *passim*.

7. Ironically, this mirrors a similar ambiguity in Descartes. P. M. S. Hacker points out – in *Wittgenstein: Mind and Meaning* (Oxford: Blackwell, 1990, p. 472) – that Descartes equivocates on the word 'substance' (when he argues from 'thought' to the thinker on the grounds that there 'can be no act or accident without a substance for it to belong to'), 'signifying indestructible stuff' (material or immaterial) and also 'persisting particular'.

8. There are all sorts of problems with this neurological or materialistic way of generating a particular 'here' which I have discussed in various places – see, for example, 'The Poverty of Neurophilosophy', in *On the Edge of Certainty* (Basingstoke: Macmillan, 1999).

9. This critique of *Da-sein* as a category is analogous to Merleau-Ponty's criticism of Sartre's *Being and Nothingness* in his unpublished final work *The Visible and the*

*Invisible* as described by Eric Matthews in his excellent *The Philosophy of Merleau-Ponty* (Montreal: McGill-Queen's University Press, 2002, pp. 163–4). If all consciousnesses are Nothingness, how would they be differentiated? There is no way of distinguishing one nothing from another. The very notion of a pure Nothingness confronted with a pure Being is completely abstract: neither pure Being nor pure Nothingness can be found anywhere. The critique of Heidegger in this chapter also has much in common with Merleau-Ponty. Merleau-Ponty was tireless in his insistence that 'the subject of experience must be *an embodied person* rather than a mere "mind"' and that 'only a subject who was fully "embodied" could have 'being-in-the-world' (Matthews, *The Philosophy of Merleau-Ponty*, p. 55). This was, of course, directed against Cartesian thought even more than against Heidegger; but the application to Heidegger is clear. Merleau-Ponty would, I believe, have approved of the central thesis of the present chapter that the 'being-in-the-world that is constitutive of *Da-sein*' requires an embodiment that Heidegger does not sufficiently emphasise.

10. From the German *Fort* meaning 'here'. One anonymous reader of this manuscript wondered whether the oppositional pair 'da' and 'fort' was an echo of Freud's famous paper in which he reported observing his grandchild throwing away and retrieving a toy as if he were experimenting with 'here' and 'there' as a way of learning how to cope with loss by fantasising the certainty of recovery. There is no such echo.

11. The general specification of the entity that would deliver something like individuation of *Da-sein* has been discussed in the previous chapter and will be further examined in the next chapter.

12. Just how slightly knowledge is rooted in the direct sense experience of the knowing individual is a matter of supreme importance for our understanding of the distinctive nature of humans. This will emerge out of the discussion in the later chapters of Volume 3.

13. See Tallis, 'The Poverty of Neurophilosophy'. We shall return to this vexed question of the emergence of indexical awareness in the material world in Volume 3, Chapter 2.

14. Daniel Dennett, *The Intentional Stance* (Cambridge, MA: Bradford Books, 1987), p. 5.

15. Thomas Nagel, *The View from Nowhere* (Oxford: Oxford University Press, 1986).

16. Bertrand Russell, *An Inquiry into Meaning and Truth* (Harmondsworth: Penguin Books, 1962), p. 102.

17. Colin McGinn, *The Subjective View. Secondary Qualities and Indexical Thoughts* (Oxford: Clarendon Press, 1983).

18. This aspiration is evident at a superficial level in the typical language of the scientific paper, which is 'deindexicalised'. The authors do not write 'We did so-and-so' but 'So-and-so was done'. This assigns the findings to the scientific community as a whole and makes the experiments part of a general move towards objective truth. While it is a rhetorical device it does not, of course, reduce science to rhetoric, as the sociologists of knowledge would like to think. See Rom Harré, 'Some Narrative Conventions of Scientific Discourse', in *Narrative in Culture* ed. Cristopher Nash (London: Routledge, 1990).

19. The scientific world picture as I have presented it is, of course, a parody, though there are certain philosophers, such as Daniel Dennett, and certain scientists inclined to scientism, such as Richard Dawkins and Peter Atkins, for whom this parody is the

real thing. There are many sciences that can take account of things like conscious beings, and viewpoints – for example, social sciences – but they tend to be denigrated by those committed to scientism. See Mary Midgley, *Science and Poetry* (London: Routledge, 2001) for a definitive account of scientism, its aetiology and its dangers. Materialist reductionism fails because it cannot account for the fact that there are scientists, and explanations, and the desire to explain, etc.; in short, that there are inquiring observers. The scientist is hidden from view because he/she does not appear in person in the equations on the page. This deficiency can, therefore, be overlooked.

20. This explains the uselessness of asserting of someone, in a written biography, that 'So-and-so has always lived here' – where 'here' is not further specified. On the written page, 'here' loses the indexical force it derives from the implicit reference to a voice that utters it. A bare unqualified indexical is empty when it is decontextualised – that is to say de-indexicalised!

21. Even under such circumstances, it is not possible to imagine my (correctly) *saying* 'My body is over there' because the source of my utterance, which must be in my body, would define 'here'. One is not allowed to say 'I am not here' (though one might think it) even when undergoing out-of-body experiences.

22. It is a bit more complicated (and interesting) than this, as we shall discuss in Volume 3.

23. See 'The Difficulty of Arrival', in Raymond Tallis, *Newton's Sleep. Two Cultures and Two Kingdoms* (Basingstoke: Macmillan, 1995) for a discussion of the intuition that we are never entirely wholly 'here' in the sense of being fully in the place where we are or, more generally, in fully experiencing our experiences.

24. Perhaps 'Your hereness' would be an appropriate salutation for those whom we meet. 'Good morning, your hereness', etc.

25. See, for example, this passage, typical of many in Dreyfus's excellent book: 'Since we cannot take the traditional account of subjects knowing objects for granted as the basis for our investigation of being in the world, we must look instead at what we do in our everyday concernful coping' (*Being-in-the-World*, p. 61). In such circumstances – our usual circumstances – we are not confronted as isolated subjects by objective presences but engaged in using things that appear to us under the guise of the ready-to-hand, as 'equipment'.

26. Although it would be absurd to accuse Heidegger (of all people!) of being on the side of shallow common sense, his giving special authority to the world as it is presented in everyday awareness – so that beings ready-to-hand in 'absorbed coping' seem to be more primordial than beings presented to 'rigid staring', to scientific inquiry or to the disinterested beholding of the post-Socratic philosopher – does in some respects align him with such philosophers. He is not, however, a destroyer of philosophy like G. E. Moore, who is wonderfully demolished in Bryan Magee's *Confessions of a Philosopher* (London: Weidenfeld and Nicolson, 1997), pp. 54–5.

# CHAPTER 6

# Reports from Embodiment: On Being, Suffering, Having, Using and Knowing a Body

Nature also teaches me by these sensations of pain, hunger, thirst etc. that I am not only lodged in my body as a pilot in a vessel, but that I am very closely united to it, and so to speak so intermingled with it that I seem to compose with it one whole.[1]

If someone says 'I have a body', he can be asked 'Who is speaking here with this mouth?'[2]

## 6.1 THE CASE FOR EMBODIMENT: A RETROSPECT

We have made the case for the embodiment of the 'I' on several grounds. There is the quasi-logical argument that 'I' cannot be individuated without a body, so that the certainty that 'I' am – where 'I' is individuated in the token realisation of 'I' in the Cartesian performance – requires that we accept that an embodied 'I' is (am). Some may be unconvinced by this. There is the biological argument that links the sense of self with a particular state of a hominid body. Even fewer will be convinced by this; for if we can take biological knowledge for granted, then it can hardly be necessary to demonstrate the reality of something as fundamental as that I am embodied. There does seem to be, however, an interesting convergence between the path outwards from the Cartesian thought experiment and the path backwards from some pretty remote reaches of human knowledge. Even so, it remains uncertain whether we have secured a passage from the necessary existence of the 'I' (or that of the 'I' which is seen to be necessary) to the necessity (in whatever strict sense we wish to apply) of the embodied person. In the previous chapter, we took a different tack and arrived at a kind of demonstration of the necessity of embodiment via a critique of Heidegger's attempt to evade the Cartesian question. We observed that 'being-there' requires a 'here' to specify it and this requires a body.

Heidegger attempted to bypass the epistemological question in *Being and Time* by means of an existential analysis of *Da-sein* that did not seem to require the notions of the 'mind' or 'the knowing subject' on the one hand, or 'matter' and 'known objects' on the other – or not, at any rate, as primordial entities or categories. Arguing for the primordiality of *Da-sein* seemed at first very promising: knowledge was underpinned or guaranteed by 'existence', or being-in-the-world, which was 'constitutive of *Da-sein*'. There could be no post-Cartesian epistemological puzzle as to how we gained access to an 'outside' world. Moreover, the reality or the true nature of what we had access to could not be in question because we did not access it as it were from outside; or from an 'inside' that was outside of external reality. The world, very simply, was in no sense 'outside' *Da-sein*. Nor, on the other hand, was the world 'inside' *Da-sein* – *Da-sein* was not a kind of 'cabinet' housing the world, or 'its' world – so there was no question of *Da-sein*'s world being a potentially distorted representation, a model, or image of a real world out there, or even a fantasy constructed out of its experiences. *Da-sein* was 'disclosedness' in which subject and object were fused all the more completely for never having been separated.

We saw, however, that the post-Cartesian puzzles returned when we asked how it was that each (individual) *Da-sein*, each being-there, had a different 'there'; when it was recalled that the general category of 'disclosedness' had to be realised in each *Da-sein* in particular disclosings. This became apparent when the character of *Da-sein* was disambiguated; more specifically, when it was brought down from its vague status as a category and was recognised to be – or as having to be – a series of individual *Da-sein*s corresponding to individual persons, or something like individual persons, in individualised, if not private, worlds. When *Da-sein* was thus disambiguated, it became obvious that there could be no specific 'there' without a specific 'here': there cannot be a there without a here just as there cannot be a left without a right or an up without a down. What is more, there could be no here without a body, or something like it, pegging *Da-sein* to a particular world. The body was the only conceivable basis for the individuation of being-there, providing a being-here to engage with it in mutual individuation. While Heidegger did not deny the centrality of the body – after all, his category of the ready-to-hand implied hands for these entities to be ready-to – he failed to give it the prominence it should have or to acknowledge the implications of embodiment.

Heidegger's avoidance of scepticism, in short, was an evasion: it underplayed the necessary embodiment of *Da-sein* and made its individual bodies (of flesh and blood and bone) almost invisible. Once the body is made visible, the Cartesian problem of how this body knows what is there returns. If, moreover, its knowledge of what is there is mediated through the body – being based on, for example, perception courtesy of sense organs – how we can be sure that that knowledge is true and that what it gives access to is ultimately real? How do I know that the world that seems to me to be 'out there' is not a construction of my thinking self? How do I know I am not dreaming? In other words, the Cartesian worries return.

We shall postpone discussion of the *truth* of perception, and of bodily experiences, and such familiar epistemological questions until the third volume of this trilogy.[3] For the present, we shall focus on the more pressing question of the nature of the *Fort-sein* that the body underpins. The outcome of our investigations will be to make the 'hereness' underwritten by embodiment both more visible and more mysterious. We shall not, alas, succeed in explaining how the human body allows (and forces) human beings to be 'here' in the many different ways they are. Although being-here requires a body, the body (at least when understood as an organism or a material object, biologically or physically) does not seem to contain 'hereness' within it.

Just how complex – puzzling, fascinating, wonder-making – is the business of 'bodily here-making' becomes ever more apparent as we reflect on embodiment and the process of (actively and passively) living a body. The first part of this chapter will therefore be devoted to examining what might rather clumsily be described as 'the experience of embodiment'. The second will look at the suitability of a (necessarily) living body for the role of primordial underwriter of *Fort-sein* and find that it hardly meets the 'person spec.' for the role. The outcome of our discussion will be to banish once and for all the notion of the subject as essentially weightless, and its point of view as essentially that of a point with a view.

In many places we shall be mining the vein of thought already opened up by Merleau-Ponty (whose benign ghost haunts this chapter) and to develop his fundamental idea that the perspectival nature of human consciousness is profoundly connected with the 'ambiguous' (his word) character of humans as 'embodied subjects'.[4] As already hinted, the mystery of 'hereness' will remain largely intact at the end of our exploration, but I hope it will be more visible and even, perhaps, more amenable to investigation. It will open on to the concern of the next chapter: that of personal identity. While the body is a necessary condition of personal identity, and the Existential Intuition 'That I am this ...' has the body as its primordial substrate, there is a dialectic: the 'in-here-ing' of the body is elaborated by the multiple layers of the 'Identity' that characterises mature humans at the present late stage in the history of hominid existence.

## 6.2 THE MODES OF EMBODIMENT: AN INTRODUCTION

Our self-awareness is inseparable from our sense of ourselves as embodied. Self-consciousness and the sense of oneself as an object in the weighty sense are indissoluble.[5] Irrespective, therefore, of whether we have proved the essential embodiment of the 'I' – so that whoever self-affirms by saying 'I' also affirms her body – it is time that the 'I' of our inquiry into first-person being got a bit meatier. The question then arises in what sense, to what degree, and how, we apparently embodied creatures are related to our bodies; how and in what ways we are identified with them; what it is that the Existential Intuition 'That I am this [body or whatever]' actually appropriates; what, in its going beyond the Cartesian limits, it actually delivers. For, whatever one thinks of the Cartesian thought experiment, it does leave the lingering suspicion that we do not quite coincide with our bodies (as we shall discuss in section 6.8 on 'bodilessness'). While, as Descartes himself emphasised, we are not just lodged in our bodies like pilots in a ship, there is a slippage; there is distance. In fact, it is this distance that enables us actively to *live* our bodies. Let us examine this statement a little more closely.

Elizabeth Anscombe[6] asserts that '"The person" is a living human body', as opposed to a corpse, which is dead. It would be difficult, even perverse, to take exception to this. But this is unsatisfactory, not for what it says as for what it glides over. A person is not so much a living human body as a *lived* human body; more to the point, a human body that is lived in such a way that it can sustain a life that *is led*. This rather complex rephrasing signals the complexities to come. It should come as no surprise that appropriating the life of the body (much of which merely happens) for the human life that (unlike that of any other living creature) is actively led should involve many different ways of relating to the body and of being embodied. Our relationship to our body seems at times to be as complex as our relationship to the world – which is hardly surprising as it has to sustain, to underpin, our relationship to the world.

For a start, we are and we are not (identical) with it: our relationship fluctuates from an intimacy so complete that to speak of a 'relationship' is slightly bizarre – and the notion of 'intimacy' fails to be intimate enough – to a variety of distances, as when we contemplate our bodies with dissatisfaction or dismay, as if through the eyes of those we imagine judging our appearance, or when we go to the doctor in order to get a bit of our body checked or offer up our bodies to a surgeon to have a lump removed. To speak of an identity between ourselves and our bodies – not to speak of the body as the basis of our identity – therefore raises all sorts of questions. What, for example, are we identical with? All of our body? Our face, our eyes, our hands, our toenails, our spleen? Our body as a material object or our body as the seat of bodily experiences or our body as a viewpoint permitting experiences of things other than itself? Given that material objects do not have intrinsic qualitative properties – corresponding to a 'What it is like to be' those objects – it is difficult to conceive of an identity between something like a biological body and a self which seems to be composed of experiences of qualities and of entities such as thoughts and feelings. The equation 'I am this body' seems to have rather different things on its right- and left-hand side; and, while this is allowed for in the 'anomalous logic of Am' discussed in Chapter 2, it still seems awkward, given what we experience, and more important, fail to experience, of large stretches of my body.

It is these different modes and aspects of embodiment that we shall now examine. Although we shall deal with them under separate headings, they are not sharply divided as we shall discover when, for example, we think about 'using' and 'having' one's body.

### 6.3 BEING

The simplest, most straightforward, mode of embodiment must be one of straightforward identity between 'I' and 'this body'. It is the most direct mode of the Existential Intuition: 'That I *am* this body'. This apparent simplicity is deceptive. First, it is obvious that I am not identified with all of my body all of the time. I am only bits of it and am different bits at different times. Second, it is not clear what being my body (or bits of it) amounts to. Let me deal with these perplexities in turn.

### Being Bits

I am not all of my body all of the time. There is some of my body that I am much of the time (for example, parts of my oral cavity); some that I am some of the time (for example, my limbs, my forehead, my gut); and some that I am none of the time (for example, my bone marrow). What is it that makes a part of my body me; or (and this is importantly not quite the same question) makes me be part of my body? At the very least, I have to be aware of it. In order to be me, it has to be present to me; to signal its presence (which, interestingly, rules out the brain, which has no sensation of its own, though damaging or playing with the brain may create sensations referred elsewhere in the body). The awareness in question has to be immediate; not, for example, mediated via description. Being informed that an appendix I can see on a television screen during an operation is mine does not make it me. Indeed, it doesn't seem to qualify if my awareness of it has to be *mediated* – by external senses (or enteroceptors) such as vision, hearing, or even touch. If I truly am a part of my body, I don't have to *discover* that it is me (or mine). *Potentially* direct awareness is not enough. I could potentially be aware of my legs all the time, but in fact I am aware of them (or individual parts of them) only intermittently and some parts of them (for example, the marrow in my femur) not at all. They have to be *noticed*; and for this they have to be made noticeable. The fact that the oral cavity is relatively privileged in this respect is in part because something is always happening in it – salivation (of which more presently), talking and breathing, and eating. But that is not the whole story: it seems close to the centre of bodily consciousness (or its 'eminent point' – to use Heidegger's phrase); or at least seems so in the artificial circumstance of introspection like the present. Its seeming close to the centre may in turn be because it is where our words are formed and at the putative point of origin of the visual field.

The oral cavity is not always privileged and many other parts of the body come to prominence and seem closer to being my embodied self. Different parts of the body will be foregrounded in different circum-stances. Changes in temperature may make us aware of parts of our skin that hitherto had been unobtrusively there. Lovemaking may awaken dormant parts of the body as the object of the other's attentive gaze or stroking hand.[7] Effortful physical activity may make me be (or almost be) more of the large quantities of the meat that go under my proper name; as when, for example, I climb a hill, my straining legs and my panting chest become part of what I feel myself to be. (My thoughts, by contrast, lose their aura of importance as I climb and seem mere cognitive driftwood on a heaving sea of physiology.) Pathology may awaken sensation in otherwise silent places that will then become more or less part of what one currently is: an inflamed appendix may speak once in our lives and for a few hours become part of what we are forced to be. (Or almost: enteric sensations tend to be referred to places such as the abdominal wall, where we are used to getting sensations.) Less dramatically, my bald cranium rarely exists for me except when sun-burned. In short, there is a variable extent to which we colonise our own bodies.

The boundary separating what one bodily is and what one is not is rarely clear. The criteria to determine qualification for being something one is and, on the other hand, being something one suffers or has (both of which we shall discuss shortly) are nebulous. Importantly, the outline of bodily me does not match natural boundaries in the material body; for example, planes of cleavage separating named organs. One may, by itching, become in part one's skin; but there can be few, if any, circumstances where one becomes the entirety of one's skin. (This is an expression of the tension between the body one experience's one's self as being and the body that one knows or, more precisely knows of.) Moreover, whatever smorgasbord of giblets goes into one's moment-to-moment being-a-body, there is always continuity between them. The relevant parts making up the transient embodiments are unified in a body schema. There is, at some level, a single embodied 'I' at any given time; and the transitions between incarnations of the subject are smooth and imperceptible. In some cases, the unification is inherent in the contributory sensations: as in malaise, or fatigue, being bloated, or the sense of bodily effort. These are intrinsically diffused, even global and become a colouring of bodily being.

Unification comes in part from what one might call connective awareness: background sensations that infill between foreground sensations, or bodily noticings. I may be aware of certain things about myself as I am sitting here typing; most prominently the words in my head and the directed movements of my fingers and hands. But this reposes on a sense of where I am; and in particular a sense of my general deportment – the fact that I am sitting on a seat and am in a moderately but not perfectly comfortable position that makes the effort of holding my head in the right way a source of mild, diffuse discomfort in my mid-back. In a way, the rest of my body makes sense of the parts that are currently most prominent, rather as the perceptual field makes sense of individual perceptions. (It would be odd if my active hands were experienced in isolation, as it were floating.) The smile on my face as I type, unlike that of the Cheshire Cat, presupposes a face, the face a head and the head the rest of my body. The pressure on my buttocks, the minimal strain in my slightly too erect back, are also guarantors of a sort of the *reality* of my activity: this is something I really am *doing*. As we shall discuss later, we need a background hum to locate, or tether, the foreground active, or present, parts of our bodies. Even within the foreground agents, there is a kind of hierarchy, whereby some parts have a stabilising or assistive function and some have a protagonist role. (We shall return to *using* our bodies presently.) To what extent we are identified to different degrees with parts at a different place in the hierarchy is unclear.

We often have a rather ambiguous relationships to parts of our body. There are marginal creatures, such as our toenails. They clearly are no part of us when they are clippings on the floor and very little to do with us when they adorn our feet. They come closer to us – in the sense that we can be made directly aware of their existence – as we move towards the nail-base. We have similarly ambivalent relationships to that other horny outpouring – our hair. This may enter our immediate bodily self-consciousness through caressing us with its locks or when it tugs on our skull in a high wind. Mostly, however, the presence of our hair is mediated through the real or imaginary gaze of others. Some parts of the body come to prominence only in dialogue with others: legs may wake up to themselves and each other through being crossed. More rarely, breasts squeezed into a tightly fitting bra may be transiently aware of one another. There are other, even higher orders of complexity; for example, my awareness of my legs as part of me may be altered as a result of heightened awareness of my trousers when I resume them at the end of a fortnight's shorts-wearing on holiday.

Though my body is that part of the world that is more me than anything else, I am for the most part aware of its interior as dark in more than the literal sense. I have little awareness of what is going on inside so long as all is well. Indigestion – particular if recurrent and familiar – may make my stomach seem as much part of me as some more exterior and visible things, such as the limbs which struggle up hill. Indeed (and we shall return to this presently), abdominal discomfort may occupy the very places where the pleasure of thought or music is felt and pre-empt both. And there is a kind of interior coherence in this darkness, as if there were a plane constructed out of various incommensurate points: the back of the throat, the respiratory effort and the fullness or emptiness of the stomach. This interior, however, never quite makes it as part of ourselves. It is invisible (so that feeling is dissociated from seeing). Its invisibility means that it is not part of that by which people recognise me; it is too asocial to belong to the self. Even my usually invisible face is mine because others embed it in me with their recognition: 'That's Raymond. I can see his face!' The interior most often achieves presence, and enters the current account of the self, when it is a source of impersonal trouble. What's more, the stomach is full of vomit, the gut full of faeces, things which, if we encounter them, repel us; and it does not matter whether they are our own or someone else's.[8]

There is a creepy feeling that sometimes attends awakening to the fact that one is, incarnated, in this body. Sartre has recorded the astonishment of a man – Antoine Roquentin – catching sight of his own hand, which looked to him like a small animal.[9] This sense that 'I am this body' can be unbearable when, for example, one stubs one's toe or jams one's finger in a door. Almost as unpleasant is standing on a leg that has gone to sleep: it is and is no longer oneself. It makes 'being this body' seems like an ontological forced marriage. There is the unpleasant experience of catching sight of one's own smiling face in a crowded mirror and suffering a connected sense of one's own foolishness and unwilled particularity. There are patients who suffer from the so-called 'alien hand syndrome'. They cannot recognise their hand as their own and do not accept that its seemingly purposive movements emanate from themselves. There are even stroke patients who get to loathe their paralysed limbs. I had one such patient with so-called misoplegia who tried to throw his arm (which he had called 'Thatcher') out of bed.

The immediate feeling that a part of the body is oneself cannot be in error. It would, as Cassam points out,[10] be impossible to be mistaken in believing that a limb is one's own, at least if it is experienced in the appropriate way – immediately, as opposed to through a reflection in a mirror – just as it would be impossible to be sure that a pain is one's own. But here we have strayed into the having-relationship – showing how difficult it is to keep within the boundaries of different modes of embodiment. There is more work to be done with being before we move on to having.

### What is it to be these bits?

> Presuming that the object (that is, at least normally, the organism) with which one is concerned, is indeed conscious, then *being that organism* will have a certain definite complex quality at every waking moment ... Physical science makes no reference to qualities of this kind ... This use of 'be' ... though suggestive is most peculiar, for it is not the same thing to characterise the consciousness of the organism and to characterise that organism. (p.168)[11]

The embodied I is no stable thing, but a flurry of incarnations which, though they may have certain recurrent patterns, are never quite the same from one moment to the next. In order for a bit of my body to be me, and for a bit of me to be my body, it has at least to present itself through a sensation that fits it into a body schema. This is what is assumed or appropriated in the Existential Intuition. Well, not quite: what is assumed is the *engaged* body interacting with an environment and the assumption is connected with itself from moment to moment through the coherence of the engagement under some micro-purpose. We shall not address this complication here (it will be a theme of Volume 3). But it is noted for two reasons. First, to point to the basis for the connection between first-person being and voluntary action in the body-as-agent – the outlines of the active body are stretched over time and shaped by meaning as well as set out in space. And, second, to pre-empt one possible misconception: that the embodied 'I' is somehow identical with the body; that, for example, to be 'Raymond Tallis' is in some sense to be Raymond Tallis's body. That this is not the case should be obvious from the fact that the difference between two kinds of states of Raymond Tallis's body – living and a corpse – is not the same as the difference between Raymond Tallis alive and Raymond Tallis dead. Raymond Tallis alive is both existent and worlded; Raymond Tallis dead does not exist – or not at least in the first person. The difference between Raymond Tallis and nothing is not the same as the difference between living meat and dead meat.

To get a handle on this, it is useful to think of T. L. S. Sprigge's profound thought about conscious beings: that it can be said of them that 'there is something that it is like' to be that being. The point that I want to make is that 'What it is like to be Raymond Tallis' is not the same as 'What it is like to be Raymond Tallis's body': it is not the 'low-down' on, or inside story of, Raymond Tallis's body, for there is no 'What it is like to be Raymond Tallis's body' understood as a biological organism. Gut-ache or the sense of fullness, for example, is not a revelation of the intrinsic being of my colon. To put this another way, there is no third-person 'What it is like to be' anything or a 'what it is like to be' of objects construed as being third-personal. Raymond Tallis starts when the first person, ultimately rooted in the sense 'That *I* am this ...' which awoke in his remote ancestors, starts. For this first-person being is a second-order awareness taking off from the first-order awareness – the sentience – that humans enjoy or suffer in common with other creatures.

Sentience itself is not a revelation of the intrinsic nature, never mind the physical nature, of the organism. As Sprigge said, in the passage quoted above, 'it is not the same thing to characterise the consciousness of the organism and to characterise that organism'; and this is doubly true when the organism in question is a human being, who is quite far removed from the status of an organism. By the time consciousness has risen to the kind of self-consciousness presupposed in the Existential Intuition, it has already in some sense gone beyond the body in perception. If 'what it is like to be a colon' is nothing like a feeling of colic, how much less is 'what it is like to be a retina' like a visual field.

Looking at my own body through third-person eyes, I could not imagine what it is like to be me: my joy at the prospect of being on holiday or my exasperation with the present Labour administration – or even my feeling of warmth on coming in from a frosty walk.

My being my body – or in some esoteric sense 'being the being of my body' (where the iteration of 'being' captures the reflexive nature of the Existential Intuition) – is deeply mysterious so long as 'I' am understood as a first-person being and 'my body' as a third-person object. The 'my', of course, betrays the incursion of the first person on the right-hand side of the identity; even so, there is a gap between being a body (in the way that Raymond Tallis is Raymond Tallis's body) and the being of that body (as revealed, say, to the biologist or physicist).[12] In this unclosable gap, much can grow. We shall now examine some of the relationships, the modes of embodiment, that proliferate in the space of this non-coincidence.[13]

### 6.4 SUFFERING (WITH A GLANCE AT ENJOYING)

For who when healthy can become a foot?
    W. H. Auden, 'Surgical Ward'

What makes it difficult to appreciate the gap between the organism that one is and the person one is, between consciousness of the body, the body one is conscious of, and the self- and world-consciousness that the body (ultimately) makes possible, is the propensity for the organism to overwhelm the person – for its 'itness' (including its location as well as its biological properties) to seem to call the shots, so that the life one leads gets pinned down to the life *it* has and the demands imposed on the person keeping that life going. Halfway between the identification with (or, depending upon how it is viewed, immersion in) our bodies, on the one hand, and being at different kinds of distance from them (as in using, knowing, flaunting our bodies), on the other, we suffer and enjoy them.

While we are never quite identical with our bodies, or with any particular part of them, our distance from them is narrowed almost to cancellation by physical suffering. Suffering approximates the intimacy of being the being of our bodies. It places the unchosenness of bodily being in italics. We could put it like this: suffering is halfway between being and having; or it is the most intimate form of having; or a form of having in which one is had. This is reflected in the different ways in which we describe it: 'I am hurting', 'I am *in* pain', 'I have a pain', 'There is a pain just there', 'It hurts'. The descriptions are attempts to recover the pain for knowledge, to reintegrate it into that world. We say, 'I have toothache'; after a while we might just as well say 'I am toothache' or 'Toothache has me'. We move from 'I have this pain' to 'I am in pain' to 'I am pain' – or as Freud described himself towards the end of his life after years with cancer of the jaw – 'A small island in an ocean of pain'.

Hunger and thirst, which are indistinctly localised in the body, occupy the midway position between being and having with even more equipoise. It is interesting, therefore, that while the supposedly stoic English say 'I *am* hungry/thirsty', the French say 'I *have* hunger/thirst'. The more hungry one is, the more the English seem to have got it right: as Henry Miller once said, a starving man is one large, unsatisfied stomach. Nationals from both countries, however, agree on their relationship to tiredness. Perhaps because it is intrinsically diffuse and is not localised to a particular part of the body, we *are* tired, rather than *have* tiredness, on both sides of the Channel.

Pain is bodily suffering in its classical form: focused, clear and utterly absorbing. The world sustained by the body is tethered to the pain, shrinks towards it and is eventually enclosed in it. The great spaces of meaning opened up by one's body are gathered back up into the body and fuse into a black knot of unmeaning. I am inextricably woven in with this sensation that, nevertheless, has nothing specifically to do with me. It is both impersonal and inescapable. We are fastened to something that has at best an accidental relationship to us. (Though it may seem to reveal the permanent condition of our being. As Jacques said in *As You Like It* – of 'the icy fang' and 'the churlish chiding of the winter's wind' – 'These are counsellors / That feelingly persuade me what I am'.)

The impersonality of pain is not only in its origins, and evident at the level of knowledge (where, for example, I am able to attribute it to a general process in my general body, such as the decay of a tooth or the inflammation of an inner organ); it is impersonal in its manifest content. It is anybody's, or anyone's, and yet it fills every crack and corner of my individual being, cancelling all the personal meanings that I have built up over my life, spraying paraquat over the am-soil of my self. Because it has no one's name on it and yet I have to live it out, because it is not me and yet I cannot get outside of it, it is not merely meaningless: it is anti-meaning. At first it seems to be an interruption coming between me and myself. I go to sleep and hope it will pass away and I will no longer have to live it out. Sooner or later, if it persists, it will no longer be outside of me: it will be me-as-outside, a harbinger of the pure outside that my corpse will be.

Physical pain – which is at once intimate, alien and inescapable – drags us back down into a mode of bodily being prior to the Existential

Intuition: it is an eruption of pure sentience into the world, the life, of the knowing self. Which is why it seems at once closer to what we are than anything else and yet further from what we have become: the outbreak of anti-meaning (pre-meaning, unmeaning) is an alien landing but a landing from within. Hence, perhaps, the deep familiarity of pain – as when you bark your shin: it links me with the animal from which I have awoken, with the infant I once was. Physical pain is outwith the self that I have become (it has no part in my life) and, at the same time, from within the very places where the self has its roots. At any rate, it signals both our propensity for regression to organic existence and the ultimate inevitability of it.[14]

Suffering reveals our ambivalent relationship with the body that we-not-quite-are. While our body is (to borrow an adjective from Heidegger – or his English translators) our 'ownmost' place, much of it is alien territory; or territory that can suddenly become alien. At any moment, it could force an unchosen agenda of concern on you, make you something you are not. And this is true even of the 'ownmost of ownmost' – for example, our mouths. That which is most intimately and most consistently your embodied self turns out to have properties that have nothing to do with you: daggers of otherness lie sheathed in our teeth. Even when we sleep alone, we sleep with a potential enemy.[15]

Before we get too gloomy, it is important to remember bodily delight: the pleasure of exercising one's bare legs when walking out on a summer morning; of a stomach getting filled with *à la carte*; of being caressed; of doing a somersault, enjoying a controlled loss of control. Compared with suffering, all of these things, however, because welcome and indeed wooed and solicited, seem frail, tenuous: carnal luck that will not hold out. And they seem less intense – both intrinsically and because they are willed. Suffering does not have to be arranged, which may explain why some people seek pain in lovemaking: it is an endeavour to make our bodies our own by seeking out sensations, rooted in the delight of carnal awareness, that are as compelling and all-engulfing and attention-commanding as pain.[16]

Suffering (and to a lesser extent delight, though the fact that it is willed does not make some of the sensations associated with it less strange) raises a fundamental question about the sensations associated with bodily self-awareness: to what extent are they ourselves or part of us? Sensations are and are not us. To experience a sensation is both to be it and not be it; and while the tastes in our mouths, the feel of touched things, seems more like us than sights or 'heards' mediated by external senses, they are still not quite us. This ambiguity would be pervasive, even if our body did not serve up so many manifestly alien sensations, which we try to interpret. At any rate, we never quite know what we are going to feel. I stretched just now and was rewarded with articular and muscular pleasure beyond anything I had expected. To be embodied is to make such discoveries endlessly. I had quite forgotten how my legs would feel when they were re-trousered after a fortnight of be-shorted holidays. These discoveries are also a warning: the thing that I am, the thing that I suffer, is made up of bio-materials with their own properties: physical suffering is the starkest possible revelation of the fact that the body I-not-quite-am is a body I am made up of. While pain is a reminder of the meat that I am forced to be, even little things demonstrate this: the cramp in my calf that makes me feel queasy, for example, is a reminder that the flesh I am and suffer has its own properties and causal destiny. I will argue in Volume 3 that this is crucial to the fundamental awakening of objective knowledge out of sentience: the sense that our body is and is not ourself; that our experiences do and do not reveal what is there; that there are realities beyond appearances. The large, stubborn residue of alien darkness that lies at the heart of the body we assume as ourself is the revelation that underpins specifically human consciousness.

To suffer is to be re-immersed in a body that we have appropriated as ourselves and as our own and find that we protagonists of our everyday lives are not at one with those bodies, for all that we cannot extricate ourselves from them. They do not have the same agenda as we do: our bodies were not created with the lives we have founded on them in mind. Some bodily suffering, however, may be intrinsically social or socialised – as when, for example, we are made to suffer the external appearance of our bodies. To take a trivial example, a spot on our nose (the product of a sequence of events of which we have only the slightest inkling) may make us feel as teenagers the helpless object of another's slightly superior gaze.[17] But this takes us into boundless territory.

## 6.5 HAVING AND USING

My weight. What a possessive!
Paul Valéry

Ownership and utilisation of a body are tightly connected. 'Having' and 'using', ownership and control, are intertwined in bodily self-possession. The many-layered modes of 'having'[18] encompass awareness of our body, or part of it, as an instrument, our carnal being as a tool-kit. This, as we have discussed, owes its ultimate origin to the sense of the hand as a tool. The 'toolness' of the hand invades other parts of the body, themselves used as tools. But the tool-hand not only instrumentalises the rest of the body (which both directly and indirectly through artefacts reinforces the instrumentality of the hand), it also awakens conscious ownership of the body. In the overwhelming majority of cases, it is only part of the body that is a tool – a tool that is used by the rest of the body, or by the body experienced diffusely as an agent. The body, in short, differentiates into tool and tool-user, effectively tool and tool-owner. It is important not to exaggerate the explicitness of this divide. We don't *use* our body when we are hurriedly and efficiently tying our shoelaces in the way that we might use a device for helping us to tie our shoelaces.

The instrumental mode of 'having' our own bodies is likely to become more evident when a new, or for some other reason difficult, task is being undertaken: when the task requires particular *efforts* of either precision or power. Under such circumstances my leg, for example, becomes manifestly a tool (and a resource and hence a possession) which it is not when I am ordinarily walking while absorbed in conversation. It becomes a tool in proportion as I will it to perform in a certain way; in proportion as it resists utilisation; in proportion as it is deficient. The toolness of the body may also become especially apparent when a different part is substituted for the one usually carrying out a task – as when I use my mouth not to eat but to break a piece of thread or to get a cap off a bottle or when I use my shoulder to batter down a door or my toes to hold a fishing net I am repairing.

Under some circumstances, as when I am trying to push, say, a broken-down car, differentiation between tool and tool-user becomes less clear-cut, as so much of my body involved in the task. There is something more like a division of roles, for example into actor and stabiliser – the upper limb and trunk as the pusher, with the legs providing the necessary counter-reaction to prevent the reaction of the car from pushing me over. Even then, this division is unstable; for the legs themselves may be straightened out at the supreme moment of effort to provide that extra push. It is, however, an important division: the allocation of different parts of the body to different roles in a task – background enablement and foreground doing – deepens and elaborates the subject-object divide within the embodied person.[19] This division of roles may be evident even within a part of the body, especially in the upper limbs, where the arm transports the hand to the manipulandum, and some fingers are engaged in gripping it (as background stabilisation) and parts are engaged in operating on the manipulandum thus gripped. This is made even more complicated when, for example, I bend down in order to bring my arm closer to the object to be manipulated. My bent trunk, my outstretched arm, my gripping fingers become, in sequence, the background enablers to foreground doers.

There is a staggering variety of the ways in which the body may be used very explicitly as a tool and become thereby somewhat distanced from me, the user. Think of the hand used in a letter-press jam in rock-climbing; of the Scottish heroine who employed her arm as a bolt to prevent the castle door being opened by the soldiers looking for her king; of the deliberate use of the weight of our bodies to close an over-filled suitcase; of the arm trained to deliver a punch and the leg to deliver a kick and the whole body to deal a flying head-butt; of the exploitation of the opacity of the flesh in covering one's own or one's child's eyes to avoid a horrible spectacle or in deliberately and maliciously blocking someone's view or in the concealment or protection of one's genitals or sheltering a chipped tooth from another's gaze or cold air; or of the visibility of the body in waving to draw to attention; or of utilising both opacity and visibility in playing peek-a-boo; of the exploitation of naturally occurring bodily sounds – breathing, footfalls, farting – to signify one's presence, to inform of one's state, to misinform as to one's state (as in heavy breathing to fake an orgasm), to subvert a situation; of practising for many years to perfect a dive or a jump – making one's body a self-propelled missile; the adoption of certain facial expressions to signal a state of mind or a state of affairs to the world.[20] There is an entire category of deliberate uses of the body in relation to actively seeking or excluding perceptions. We may move our head in a position to see something, as in peeping, or our whole body, as when we walk to the top of a hill to survey the land. We may cup our hands behind our ears to enhance hearing. We may train our 'palates' to discriminate tastes. Contrariwise, we may use parts of our body to protect ourselves against unwanted perceptions – as when we shade our eyes from dazzle or pinch our noses to seal ourselves off from a bad smell. This active manipulation of our sense organs is a crucial aspect of instrumentalisation of the body: it is a vital step on the road from the unfocused, unsystematic gawping of beasts to the deliberate, systematic inquiries undertaken by humans.

The body, then, is deliberately used as an instrument – so that the person becomes the 'used-user' of her body – in an astonishing variety of ways so that its passive physical properties and active capabilities are exploited as one might exploit the physical properties of a non-bodily material object. The more familiar I am with a task, and the easier it becomes, the less consciously I 'do' it and the less evidently is my body being used as a tool: the more does 'using' get absorbed into general 'being'. In conditions of illness, most notably when I have suffered some paralysing condition, the 'toolness' of my body becomes more apparent, as I make vain efforts to get my arm to move, to make it reach out for an object. Not only is the 'doing' more apparent in its effortful failures, the instruments of doing are more manifestly instrumental in their incompetence; they become (to borrow a phrase of Heidegger's) 'conspicuous in their unhandiness'.[21] We can become cross with our own stupid fingers or our recalcitrant legs rather in the way that we may become angry with an uncooperative or stupid fellow human being or with a useless implement. Even global illness – as opposed to focal paralysis or local damage – can make the body seem like a failing instrument, and the subjective experience of malaise, fatigue, etc. becomes a sign of this.[22]

Using literal tools can sometimes underline the instrumentality of the body. Body-plus-tool becomes a complex instrument. This is illustrated when one is riding a bicycle: the rider not only uses the machine but is also used by it: *l'homme machine* seems more than simply the master metaphor encountered only indirectly at the level of abstract knowledge of the body as a carnal machine, as a collection of mechanisms. This is particularly apparent when the tool is used effortfully; as when riding a bike against the wind as opposed to chatting while spinning downhill. The rider stands up on the pedals in order to exploit his own weight to push them down.[23] Such manifest instrumentality can be out of place, betraying a lack of grace. In clumsy lovemaking – which expresses mechanics undissolved into passion – caresses are rather explicit strokes, rubbings and gropes; and coitus requires the deliberate insertion of the penis into the vagina (an activity if tumescence is insufficient that has been likened to potting a billiard ball with a length of hose-pipe), so that the penis is, indeed, a 'tool'.

'Toolness' is close to objectness. There are various ways in which we acknowledge the objectness of our bodies, or parts of them. This is true when we seem to fight against their limitations as in effortful activity; but also in more low-key occasions, when, for example, we pull a pullover over our head, or insert our arms into the sleeves of a jacket, or ensleeve our legs in trousers. This is equally the case when we try to squeeze past someone without touching them or purposely make ourselves visible (if we think we look good) or invisible (if we feel we look stupid or are unwanted). This highlights another mode of possession our bodies: through my awareness of 'my' appearance to others.

My appearance – 'What a possessive!' as Paul Valery might have said – is something I may wish to flaunt, to conceal, to pretend to be modest about. I may manipulate it in all sorts of ways – preparing, like T. S. Eliot's Alfred J. Prufrock, a face to meet the faces that I meet. Assumed expressions or postures, make-up and jewellery, expensive clothes with designer labels – all of these reflect the notion of my body's visibility as an asset or a liability. Some parts of the body – of women's bodies in particular – are particularly likely to be seen as 'assets' (with breasts being described crudely as 'belongings'). In extreme cases, bodily presence shades into a self-presentation that is more or less pure asset management. The sense of my body as an object in other's eyes is matched by my operating on it as an object to be fashioned, shaped, improved.[24] Concern about 'my' appearance may have secondary effects: a scar may pervade my self-awareness in a very complex fashion. (Concern about appearance does not of course confine itself to 'looks'. We are equally concerned about how our body may smell, or, when we speak, sound, or even, when we shake hands, feel.)

The feeling that I look silly or in some other way deficient may cause me to blush. My blush may in turn become a secondary asset or a liability that needs to be managed. Blushing, a condition of the body, breaks up into blushes that may or may not be charming, depending on how close they are to the idea of female vulnerability and how far they are from looking like a physiological reaction and/or a rash. The complexity of blushing – such that in certain cultures a permanent state of blushing may be simulated through a 'blusher' powder – is a dramatic indication of the many layers of the possessive relationship to the body through a layered possession of the body's own appearance. It is worth examining this further.

The external appearance of our body can be both something we use – most obviously as a set of signals (as in facial expressions, postures, sounds that occur as if spontaneously) – and something by which we are, as it were, used, as the helpless prisoners of other's judging gaze. We may be cornered by our appearance: it becomes a possession by which we are possessed. Even where there is nothing particularly amiss with how we look, we cannot help being aware (when we are in the company of strangers) that our physical appearance may be construed as a set of symbols which have meanings we cannot even guess at. In order, therefore, to control this, we adorn, make up, dress, flaunt, position, etc. ourselves in order to approximate to some archetype or role model or general type whose meaning is (very roughly) known to us and corresponds to a desirable account of what we are. This is of particular importance to the young whose current account appearance matters all the more because they have less in the way of a deposit account CV and less preoccupation and responsibility to draw them away from concern with their own surfaces. Looking 'silly', 'a gink', 'uncool' – or even 'smart', 'cutting edge', 'cool' – is a mode of subordinating one's appearance to the judgement of (general) others which loops through so much of the world. Self-consciousness in this narrow, colloquial sense is a kind of denaturation of the Existential Intuition, a way of selling out one's self –

for Heidegger the mark of inauthentic being and for Sartre a sign of 'bad faith'.

Consciously being in relation to its actual or imagined appearance[25] is, like physical suffering, a mode of being our body in which possession and being possessed keep changing places. *What* is appearing, how I appear, is at least in part in the keeping of certain others, or the General Other. That is why even this blush, which is warm on my face, betrays me, and gives me over, to others. The dark, general, organic interior of my body that is relevant to physical suffering is replaced by the dark, general, social exterior in the case of 'my' appearance. My appearance is thus at once closest to me – inseparable from my surface – and furthest from me. While my body's appearance to others is necessary to make it the expression of my thoughts and feelings as well as that through which I realise some of my intentions, it is also the reason for its being a permanent source of inadvertent signals. Hence it remains exquisitely poised on the border between using and having (and being had by – 'we are possessed by our possessions').[26] Our appearance in the (uncontrollable) judgement of others can become an obsession. There is a character in Beckett's *Murphy* novels who has body odour, is aware of it (she has 'insmell' into her condition as Murphy says) and devotes the entirety of her life to trying different deodorants.

There is a further sense – the obverse or dark underside of the ones we have been exploring – in which my body is thought of and even experienced as a possession: I have (or some cultures believe I have) a right to 'dispose of' my body as I wish. I alone – or my next of kin, assumed to be acting as my agent by proxy – may donate my kidneys to another, make arrangements for the disposal of my body. In some cultures, I may dispose of my body-life through seeking euthanasia when the suffering associated with an untreatable fatal illness becomes more than I wish to bear. Killing ourselves is the ultimate expression of the notion that we, in so far as we are identified with our body, are also not identified with our body; that our body – and the life it sustains – is our possession to do with what we wish. This is the supreme expression of the paradox of 'having' a body that is an instrument of one's will, since it is not, in the last analysis, separate from the operations, or even the agenda, of that will. We are able to will the end of our willing. As Marcel says:

> Having as such seems to have a tendency to destroy and lose itself in the very thing it began by possessing, but which now absorbs the master who thought he could control it. (p. 179)

It is true – and not simply because without the body one could not possess anything – to say that the body is the ur-possession (just as the hand is the ur-tool) – though as we have seen in the case of appearance, possessions outside the body may retroact on and change the character of one's possessive relationship to the body. The possessive relationship to the body is, however, limited. As Marcel says, 'I can only *have*, in the strict sense of the word, something whose existence is, up to a certain point, independent of me' (p. 169). When we consider the body as a whole – and it is born and dies as a whole – the possessive relationship fades as possessor and possession merge. While I may possess parts and attributes of my body, I am not able to possess it as a whole; this is a level at which my body and I converge and my limits increasingly become identical with its boundaries. My body as a possession may possess me, as in the case of overwhelming illness. Multi-layered, multi-stranded 'having' comes to an end as it is reabsorbed into bodily being, rather as a multitude of rivers drowns in the sea. Having and using fade into the inutile corpse. That 'we are possessed by our possessions' applies absolutely to the primordial possession of the body.

Which thought may seduce one into the sort of question asked by the idealist thinker: 'What makes a given body *my* body?'[27] If we treat this question as a request for a phenomenology of bodily having, we have gone some way to answering it. Of course, it goes beyond this. It is indirectly another request for a way out of the Cartesian prison, in which the 'I' can know only that it is thinking and cannot be sure that it is embodied; that this body of which he may be dreaming, really is *his* body. The biogenetic approach, of course, bypasses this question. The present discussion shows what a poor question it is. It starts in the wrong place; from the misleading assumption that 'I' and a certain body, because they seem logically separable (at least according to the Cartesian thought experiment), are *in fact* separable, indeed separate, and have to be attached or united, following which it becomes my body and that certain criteria or conditions have to be fulfilled to justify the ascription of this body by myself to myself. But my body and I are not separable, irrespective of the third-person logic of identity that would separate them. The present exposition of the phenomenology of embodi-ment unpacks the way in which 'I' – irrespective of any biogenetic story about the origin of specifically human self-consciousness – *begins* with the self-assumption of the body: it is, in its primordial form, the living, conscious body's assumption of itself *as* itself. It doesn't require being hooked up to it – either in order to incorporate it in its *de facto* identity or in order to be *identified* by the owner of the body. The question shows, in fact, that 'my' is too distant, and that possession is too provisional, a relationship to capture the core of my relationship to my body. It is only from the viewpoint of the higher, more abstract realm of the self, e.g. the self-as-thinker (itself built on the lower levels which cannot be separated from the body) that the self seems to have to be linked with – in the sense of having to be *attached to* – a body.

Cassam makes this point when he says that the question is illegitimate, 'for there is no independent "I" whose ownership of a particular body can be in question'. He goes on to quote Wittgenstein:

> There is a criterion for 'this is my nose': the nose would be possessed by the body to which it is attached. There is a temptation to say that there is a soul to which one's body belongs and that my body is the one that belongs to me.[28]

Behind this, of course, is Cassam's general position that we discussed in 'The Logical Necessity for Embodiment' – namely that one would not be 'in a position to think first-personally if one has never been presented to oneself as a physical object' (p. 148).

### 6.6 CARETAKING

Medical insurance companies warn us that, since bodies have only one owner and the latter are allowed only one body, owners are well advised to look after them. Heidegger described *Da-sein* as 'that being whose being is an issue for itself', but he forgot that the body was necessary to give it issues; and while he plausibly asserted that 'care' was 'the most primordial, existential and ontological constitution of *Da-sein*',[29] he did not appreciate that, without embodiment, *Da-sein* would have nothing to care about. The self-apprehended body is the ultimate basis of 'heedful caring' and that basis must also care for itself. Possessors and users of bodies must also be their caretakers.

The technology of bodily self-care, of honing the ur-tool, dominates talk inside and outside the gym. 'You must look after your body', we are told again and again – or (fascinating double possessive) 'You must look after your body's health' as 'it is your most precious possession'. And so I use my body – 'use it or lose it' – in order that the body can change itself: I keep it fit, in tune, etc. so that it can be a more perfect instrument of my goals and my pursuit of happiness is least clouded by the anti-meanings of disease.

Caring for a body can be very complex. I respect 'its needs'. I order my affairs so that I can secure my beauty sleep each night. I train – in part so that I can be a more effective, competent, graceful instrument.

This may be specific: so that I can be a safer bicyclist, do more impressive cartwheels; be a more lithe swordsman. More generally, I may train simply to exercise my body. Bodily activity of a certain deliberate kind is thus reclassified as a kind of medicine. The medicine may be calibrated: I have been told that 'health gains' will not accrue unless the intensity of effort is such that I achieve a certain pulse rate or I start sweating. The simplest, and most direct, manifestations to myself of a change in the state of my body are utilised as signs that what I am doing really will bring 'fitness' – fitness, that is to say, for future doings in the unspecified future.

What a twisted by-way of 'having and using' we have wandered into here! The body is used in two ways: otherwise pointless activity is undertaken simply to 'put the body through its paces' so that it will be more enduringly useful – a more reliable and comfortable servant of my will; and the physiological by-product of such activity (e.g. sweat) is used to gauge its quantity. Exercising, say jogging, becomes a prescription taken, or enacted, or endured, in recommended doses, a certain intensity times duration, with the intensity measured by the outpouring of sweat and the duration by distances covered or hours put in.

The twists and turns do not end here, of course. In pursuit of bodily fitness, I can go to the doctor and, in doing so, take my body to be examined and judged fit and well, in need of care and attention, or unwell. This trip to GP is rather peculiar: I transport my own body to a place where it can be checked; it is itself the theme of the journey. I might even walk to the surgery instead of driving, in order to make a small donation (too little, too late perhaps) to the campaign to keep my body fit. The walking, because I am well and practised, is not something I use my body to 'do' – so it is 'I' not 'my body' that is walking to the doctor. When I get there, I hand over my body, though it is, of course, I and not my body that explains the purpose of the visit. The visit, incidentally, may provide me with numerous esoteric bodily possessives that we had not envisaged in our discussion of 'having': 'my' blood pressure, 'my' blood sugar, 'my' platelet count. Some of these possessives belong to my body's darkness and lie beyond the reach of my (direct) possessive powers. (Indeed, just how many possessives I gain as a result of the visit depends on how concerned or diligent or obsessive the doctor is.) This is a further reminder of how it is not only others' bodies that are opaque to us: our own body is an Area of Darkness. There are many ill-lit places within ourselves – the plane between the back of the eyes and the front of one's feeling of fullness – where one's fate is being brewed. Obscure possessives, like 'my' platelet count, warn me that my body-possession is not a possession like other possessions.

For a start it is not one that I can do without; for another, it has its own unfolding story that may – indeed eventually will – engulf me. It is, we note again, a possession by which I am possessed.

But it illustrates something else: caring for one's body is a way of exercising 'having' that reaches into quite a different way of 'being' one's body; or an entirely different, uniquely human way of being aware of it. 'Caring' for one's body takes one beyond sentience and the immediate self-presentation of the flesh that one 'is' into *knowledge*. We *know* our bodies: we have knowledge of them and we have knowledge that others have knowledge of them and we know, therefore, that we have ignorance of them.

### 6.7 KNOWING (AND NOT KNOWING)

We are made of many things that know nothing about us. And this is how we fail to know ourselves.

Paul Valery[30]

– for our flesh
Surrounds us with its own decisions
Philip Larkin[31]

What does it mean to know one's own body? It is obviously not the same as to experience it. As regards the latter, I seem to be in some kind of privileged position: I and only I can experience the experiences of (being, suffering) my body. Others may have an experience of my body – for example, seeing it – they do so, as it were, from the outside – as when they are staring at me and seeing me; or touching me and feeling my warmth; or being sat on by me and feeling my weight. In order to do so, however, they have to be in a certain position and, as they are in that position intermittently, they will have only intermittent and patchy experiences of my body, whereas I do not have to position myself because I am inescapably in that position; I am always where my body is. What's more, what others experience of my body is not identical with what I experience of it. My looks to you are clearly not how I appear to myself – for much of the time when you are looking at me, my face is invisible to me; or not even invisible. The warmth you feel when you touch me may not be warmth to me. And when you feel my weight as I sit on your knee, I am not necessarily heavy to myself. Or your experience of my heaviness will not coincide with my experience of my heaviness. The report from my bottom about my weight will not exactly coincide with the report from your knee and this will not just be because of the scale – bottom, knee – recording the pressure from which the weight is inferred. And your bottom will certainly not experience or report the particular destiny of unremitting effort my weight (or over-weight) condemns me to.

But my privileged access to the experience of my body is, rather like the privileges of first-person authority we discussed in Chapter 3, a doubtful one. First, everyone one has such a privilege with respect to his or her own body. It is a privilege that, equally distributed, cancels out. Second, it is one I cannot voluntary give up. I cannot help experiencing my body or experiencing the experiences of my body. In this sense it is no more a privilege than suffering (one of the sub-categories of bodily self-awareness) is a privilege. Third, there is much about my direct experience of my body that cannot be communicated. This is connected with, fourth, the fact that this direct experience of embodiment seems to fall short of anything that we could call, or expect to count as, knowledge.

A truly privileged consciousness would be one that had access to *knowledge* that others were denied. My being always perfectly positioned to experience my own body does not mean that I have privileged knowledge of my own body. My first-person privilege of being this body, and through the Existential Intuition of consciously being this body through assuming it as me, and of experiencing the experiences that are to be had through, in and of it as my experiences, does not give me privileged third-person information about my body. This observation has connections in all sorts of directions: it touches on many things we have dwelt on already (for example, the limits to immunity from error discussed in Chapter 3); and on many things we shall examine at considerable length – such as the nature and origin of knowledge, which will occupy Volume 3. What I say now, therefore, will be brief and in places very sketchy.

For merely sentient creatures, there is neither a first person nor a third person. Neither subject nor object is differentiated out of the 'blooming, buzzing confusion' (to borrow William James' famous phrase) of living being. The Intuition 'That I am this ...' in the first instance reveals the active or engaged body as 'myself'. In the assumption of the body as 'myself' an explicit opacity becomes apparent in the world. The body that I am is not entirely dissolved into me. The body becomes an object. The Existential Intuition opens up the world and divides it into 'I' and 'it', and 'it' is present within, as well as outside, the body. Unlike sensation, the mode of awareness that will eventually evolve into knowledge has a sense of things as only partly scrutable. The first partly scrutable entity – and, for this reason, the bearer of object-sense into the world – is, unsurprisingly, the body itself. The Intuition 'That I am this …', though the 'this' is in part concealed from me – that it has a reality, an in-itself, that goes beyond my immediate awareness – lies at the root of the uniquely human sense that the world is composed of objects and that we have incomplete apprehension of them. This sense is one of the bases of objective knowledge; the other is the tool-mediated pooling of sentience leading ultimately to a collectivisation of awareness in an intersubjective, or social, trove of third-person fact. The transformation of unfocused gawping, of sniffing around, into institutionalised, cooperative inquiry whose product is factual knowledge, involved, among other things, an increasingly pronounced sense of 'I' and an increasingly pronounced sense of 'it' driving each other upwards. Third-person knowledge, a sense of 'This is how things are' (independently of me), and the connected sense *that* they are independent of this 'me', eventually returns to the place where the possibility of knowledge first awoke – after an extended pilgrimage through artefacts (in which it was for a long time embedded), through susperstitions (whose origins require explanation), through social institutions, through the stars, and through the non-human things on earth – to the human body. The third person – or non-person, or im-person, or de-person – came back to the place where 'I-hood' awoke out of organic existence. Increasingly, the uneasy uncertainty as to what one's body would next serve up, the mere probabilistic sense of what might happen, formalised into a pattern of dappled knowledge and ignorance, into a network of facts about the body (my body *qua* any-one's body) one knew, facts that one did not know while others did (facts that were in the keeping of the collective), and facts-to-be that no one knew.

With respect to this world of knowledge, one does not have privileged access. We have discussed in Chapter 3 how, in some respects, one might be regarded as *under*privileged. In everyday life, we may be less of an authority on how we look than others around us: their judgement, being closer to the collective judgement (being, like that of the collective, from the outside), may be more reliable than that of ourself, trying to achieve an outside view from the inside. We are less able to adopt the view of others than are others, however heterogeneous that notional collective is. And when we go beyond surface appearances and ordinary judge-ments, the privileges of the first-person viewpoint become even more unimpressive – as was foretold in the very intuitions that attended the emergence of the first person: the intuitions that revealed the body not only as 'I' but also as (only-partly-scrutable) 'It'.

The body as an object of knowledge seems opaque to the one whose body it is. At the most basic level, this opacity comes from the classification that places my 'thisness' under various modes of 'whatness'. Where or how I am classified will differ in different circumstances. For example, where it is a matter of qualitative judgement – such as that I am handsome or ugly – the privileged voice will certainly be that of others. I am not handsome if nobody else finds me handsome or the generality of people thinks I am ugly. In the case of certain surface, everyday facts about my body, I can access them precisely as others do, though I may find it more difficult to do so. I can determine how heavy or how tall I am using a scale and scales that others would use in order to do the same thing. I cannot discover that I am 5 foot 10 inches tall by means of introspection. Even less can introspection tell me whether I am tall for my age or under average weight for my build. These facts are rooted in complex systems of measurement and understanding that lie far outside any direct bodily experience I might have. They are rooted in centuries of realisations, of argument, of experiment, of institutionalisation, of discourse, dialogue and negotiation. My direct sense of my weightiness, of my height, of my solid being here, is innocent of all this. The way in which I am or weigh 10 stone and the way my body is or weighs 10 stone don't quite match.[32]

And this applies *a fortiori* when the quiddities in question are those that have been uncovered by medical science – which have the double character of being absolutely central to our well-being, to our efficacy, to our very sense of being embodied and of being recent entrants to a very complex body of knowledge that has been the joint work of hundreds of thousands of hands.[33] The achievement of medical science is to bring the most remote knowledge and the most elaborate and developed social institutions into the very places where we have the most intimate and direct apprehension of our embodied state. Knowledge touches the very places where immediate awareness seems to have the last word. Knowledge of the body draws directly and indirectly on an almost limitless body of knowledge. Courtesy of such science, there are things I know about my body that my body cannot experience: that it does not know and I cannot directly live, though they may be vital to my leading a life of my own choosing. It has shown us again and again, in ever more detail, how every aspect of embodiment reposes on – indeed consists in – things of which we are unaware. To vary Pascal, we might summarise this by observing that 'the body has mechanisms that the embodied know not'.[34]

There are huge differences between what mankind (collectively) knows about the human body and is documented and available for us to read off the Net or wherever; and what individuals know directly through experience. Doctors who, by virtue of their training, know (or should know) more about human bodies than most are often resented by their patients. This knowledge seems to some to make their patients comparatively powerless, even if – as is usually the case – the knowledge is put to benign, empowering ends: if knowledge is power, to be known, especially with respect to things that bear so closely on one's well-being, ill-being, being *tout court*, is a form of powerlessness. Moreover this knowledge is difficult to translate into terms that make intuitive sense to the lay patient. Which links with this key feature of knowledge of the body: that it is remote from the body as directly experienced by the embodied person.

We are, of course, used to indirect awareness of our body; as when for example we discover that our appearance is judged to be rather odd by seeing the quizzical look in another's eye. Mediated awareness is harder to take when it is of something that is inside ourselves and not on the border between ourselves and others, like our external appearance. Not to know the state of our inner organs is a reminder that the darkness within is not quite ourselves, though it may provide central themes of our existence. It is odder still not even to know of the gross structure of our body: not to know where the bladder is in relation to the vagina; or even that one has a spleen – until a doctor tells you that you have got something wrong with it and it has to come out. The very notion of distinct organs with different functions, and possibly able to be dispensed with, is a dizzying elaboration of the composite nature of a body with two hands, two legs, etc. and at odds with the moment-to-moment experienced unity of the body-self.

Increasingly, our knowledge of our body is mediated through the findings of biomedical science – more or less mangled in the minds of individual body-owners. This body of knowledge becomes harder and harder to map onto immediate awareness of embodiment. Though few will question the relevance of my serum potassium level, or the active transport of hydrogen ions across the semi-permeable membranes in the kidney, or the left ventricular ejection fraction, or the firing patterns of neurones in my amygdaloid body, to how I feel, how I experience bodily existence, and to how much my being me is obtrusively embodied, the connections between how I feel and these physiological parameters are perceived very indirectly. The body we live, through which we lead our lives, is decomposed in the realm of knowledge into things – structures, processes, mechanisms – that are not conceivably liveable. My raised urea may be a cause of suffering, but it is not what is suffered; my normal sodium makes normal life possible, but it cannot be lived in its own right. To put this differently: 'I feel absolutely ghastly' and 'Raymond Tallis has a raised blood urea' may be causally related, but cannot otherwise merge with one another. They refuse even to be opposite sides of the same state of affairs; or two senses of the same referent.

This fleshes out Merleau-Ponty's observation that 'being embodied' means that 'our personal existence is necessarily rooted in an impersonal, physical world' and that 'existence as a person is rooted in something pre-personal'.[35] As a result of the advent and advances of scientific medicine and its increasing penetration into everyday talk, we are increasingly aware of the impersonal basis of our personal existence.[36] And it is interesting that medicine has become more effective – and consequently more humane in the sense of limiting the unwilled incursions of the inhuman body into our human lives – in proportion as it has acquired objective knowledge of our bodies as organisms. Scientific medicine works because it assumes a depersonalised (and desacralised) attitude to the human body and so understands better what makes it go well or badly.

But there remains an inescapable tension, which is best captured through Sprigge's suggestive observation that 'it is not the same thing to characterise the consciousness of the organism and to characterise that organism'.[37] This gap goes deeper than any introduced by the fact that our knowledge is of things we cannot directly experience encapsulated in a language that is not fully transparent to us. It is the gap between what it is like to be me and what it is like to be my body – to which latter nothing corresponds. I can say what it is like to be Raymond Tallis suffering from colitis, but it makes no sense to speak of what it is like to be his inflamed colon. This does not mean that there is a fundamental separation between Raymond Tallis as 'subject' and Raymond Tallis's body or his colon. No; Raymond Tallis is *essentially* embodied in the body to which his name is attached. He is, as Merleau-Ponty says, 'an embodied subject'. Raymond Tallis's subjectivity and his embodiment are not separable. What it does mean is that Raymond Tallis has, as Merleau-Ponty also emphasised, 'an ambiguous character':[38] an 'I-it' in which the ever elaborated 'I' and the ever better known 'it' – with its ever-increasing context of the not-known,[39] the forgotten, and the not-yet-known – are in a state of permanent, and fruitful tension.

Sprigge's further observation is here very much to the point:

> One may find it very difficult to imagine what it must be like to be another human being ... Actually, there are also great difficulties in imagining what it must be like to be oneself.[40]

You can't straddle first- and third-person viewpoints. To imagine what 'it must be like to be oneself' requires that one should immerse oneself in systems of general categories – with some of which one has only a passing acquaintance so that one may be uncertain as to how to apply them – and at the same time be that person that engulfs one and one is. It is difficult to know what one is like without leaving one's self behind – particularly as acknowledging one's general qualities alters the very self to which they are ascribed.

### 6.8 BODILESS BEING: A CARTESIAN FLASHBACK

as things are, we can think I-thoughts while quite unconscious of our bodies.[41]

Descartes' thought experiments begin with the assumption not only that bodiless human being is possible, but that all we can be sure of is disembodied (or unembodied, or never-embodied) thought. I don't want to exacerbate the reader's suspicions further by producing yet another critique of the Cartesian starting point. Instead, I want to turn Descartes upside down by asking how he ever got to imagining (as opposed to arguing) that his essential self – the substance of which he was made and which lay beyond the reach of doubt (two importantly separate things) – could be bodiless. His starting point certainly has a great tradition behind it.

This tradition sees the body variously as: a husk of the soul which is laid aside at death (or from which one can be sprung by achieving sufficiently concentrated, pious or enlightened thoughts); an unreliable lens through which the conscious human being receives distorted accounts of the world in which she lives and/or the (more blessed) world in which she will one day live, by the alchemy of whose senses reality is turned into appearance; or a place where sinfulness is brewed; or as a mixture of all three. Richard Webster has spoken of the 'moral theology' underlying much thinking about mind and body:

the view that the secrets of human nature can be unlocked only by a theory of mind is, although commonly held by secular philosophers and psychologists, essentially a Christian idea. The idea has its most significant source in the ancient Christian-Platonic belief that human beings are made of two separate entities: an animal body which was created by God, and a mind, spirit or soul, which was given by God uniquely to man.[42]

Notwithstanding the Cartesian revolution, Descartes was the unquestioning heir to this tradition. His main contribution was to change its emphasis: denigration of the (animal) body and elevation of the (immortal and non-animal) mind were less moralistic and spiritual critiques than purely epistemological ones. The ethereal thinking self was better informed – at least about its own nature – than any meaty being could be. Sensations were at best 'confused modes of thoughts'.[43]

At the heart of the tradition is the assumption that the notion of a sharp distinction between body and mind makes ready sense. Our examination of embodiment has undermined this sharp dichotomy: there seems to be an infinity of gradations between the extremes of pure 'bodiliness' and of pure 'mindliness' – between, say, feeling bloated and thinking about Plato. Moreover, at any given point on the spectrum, body and mind are closely imbricated, as a few examples will show.

Let us call first at the most obvious port: the emotions. The physical experience of worrying about a potential assailant (a physical threat) and a lecture in three weeks' time, or the potential threat of a hostile review of a book one is about to publish (an abstract or mental threat) will have enormous overlap: in both cases, I might break out into a sweat or feel my heart race. Exposure to simple physical danger or to very abstract ridicule – for example, at one's failure to comprehend Plotinus' true meaning – may express themselves in the same exocrine outpouring of saline. In chronic anxiety states, any number of different – physically present and/or absent – abstract things may be experienced through an identical racing of the heart. Not infrequently, illnesses which are associated with the physiological accompaniments of emotion will transform the contents of the world into the objects of such emotion. The rapid heart rate and sweating in thryotoxicosis will make many things a cause of anxiety: a free-floating fear alights on all sorts of things that would not ordinarily be a matter of great concern. Sometimes such changes demand an emotional explanation. Famously, Hans Castorp, the hero of Thomas Mann's *The Magic Mountain*, is able to come to terms with his persistent rapid heart rate (due to the high altitude in the sanitorium) only when he 'realises' that it is due to his being in love with the beautiful Claudia Chauchat. The irritability we feel in hot weather is due not only to discomfort, but to experiencing ourselves sweating and translating that into being 'on the edge' of anger or fear. Physical illness can take away our pleasure in physical activities; but they can also take away our pleasure in mental activities. When I have a cold, malaise blocks my delight in abstract thought. It does not stop me thinking, but I am conscious that I am saving up an enjoyment for the future. In my own case, indigestion seems to occupy the very places where I would feel the glow of discovery. Nietzsche's claim that Carlyle's rather too strenuous 'Yes-saying' – founded, he suspected, in a more spontaneous absence of delight – was a product of his poor digestion seems plausible. Even his suggestion (founded, I suspect, on a rather small series of cases: n = 1 = Nietzsche) that optimistic and pessimistic world pictures are explained by, respectively, good and bad digestion, does not seem entirely absurd. The gut may have no influence over the logical form of arguments, but it will certainly influence the premises that are requisitioned for logic to operate on. Any bodily self-observer will have noticed how abstract and complex pleasures – such as my delight the other day in an Edwardian house in the early morning sunshine, which invoked so many ideas about my own childhood and the lives of the past – depend on the places where they are felt not being already occupied by bodily discomfort.[44]

The intimate relationship between tiredness, physical and mental disinclination, lack of inspiration, level of thought and level of consciousness, is so obvious as hardly to need spelling out – except that it is often forgotten. And it contributes to understanding where the notion of bodiless mind comes from, to which we now need to turn our attention.

How do we arrive at the idea that our minds are, or could be, separated from our minds? Why, despite the moment-by-moment evidence that body-and-mind are imbricated, that mind has only a syncategorematic existence and cannot exist without the body, do so many philosophers imagine that we are essentially minds rather than bodies? Why, given the evidence all around us of pre-human organisms lacking minds, do we imagine that mind has ontological priority over bodies? First of all, it is easy to forget the body when all is going well. I lose myself in the world of my intentions. Except when the primary goal is physical pleasure (sex, exercise, eating), the body is transparent, unobtrusive. A busybody is almost bodiless: it is effaced to the status of a background presupposition. Second, we recall dreams in which the mind seemed to be operating independently of the body, because the content of the dreams seemed to have nothing to do with the location of the body, what it was actually doing, its present state. Dreams seem so deeply mysterious, no wonder they were thought to have prophetic value and the freewheeling mind thought to access to the real truths about things, and the dreamer to be transported to another place where he could live, bodilessly in a place a truth. In earlier times, when our days were less busy, less closely prescribed, we perhaps had more interesting dreams and more inclination to cultivate and believe them. Most impressively, perhaps, there is the constant patter of thought and of memory that accompanies our passage through the world and seems to be relatively loosely connected with it. I can be driving a car and thinking about Plato, or about the Battle of the Boyne, or recollecting my childhood.

These forays into apparent bodilessness, however, are only momentary episodes against a background of uncontestable embodiment. It doesn't take even toothache to bring our philosophising to a halt. The bodiless busybody encounters her body in all the small efforts of lifting and positioning and manipulating that even the lightest occupations require of us. While when I am involved in non-manual labour (for example, information services[45]) relatively little of my self-presence is fleshly, the very literal, opaque, body is always there – not merely waiting to return in tiredness, hunger, self-positioning to get a better view, or to squeeze past someone – but as the background hum (of which more presently) that makes everything, even thoughts and memories, really 'here', really occur. Nevertheless, the notion of the mind as potentially free from the body, and of the freed mind as our true selves, has immense seductive power. The belief that we are essentially self-consciousness – and that we are more human, less animal, more ourselves, less cognitively and even morally disabled the more disembodied we are, that the flesh is a prison, that we are better off without it – is one of the most enduring in human thought. Why then do we – like Kant's dove which, 'cleaving the air in her free flight, and feeling its resistance, might imagine that its flight would be still easier in empty space'[46] – so often imagine that bodiless existence is possible; that we could be minds, and better minds, without bodies; that even if thoughts are not deeper and more truly ourselves than toothache, the latter could exist anyway in a disembodied creature; and that, compared with our minds, our bodies are epistemologically uncertain?

The fact that this way of thinking is so enduring suggests that it goes very deep. I will attempt to explain it in Volume 3 when we consider man, 'the knowing animal'. For the present, a few remarks will have to suffice. Consider the transformation of bodily sensations in the wake of the Existential Intuition. An animal may feel cold. It does not feel 'cold' – that is to say, it does not classify its discomfort. In the case of a human, 'being cold' differentiates into 'I am cold' and 'It is cold'. The feeling of being cold, referred to the emergent subject that one intuits oneself to be, is transformed into the pre-factual sense 'That it is cold'. The suffering subject connects his suffering with a cause that will eventually be presented as a state of affairs out there. 'That I am ...' and 'That it is ...' co-emerge – in the history of humanity and in the development of an individual human being. The 'it' that lies outside of 'I' is an object of evolving knowledge but, not being me, it is only partly known: the quest for further (objective) knowledge is interminable. Uncertainty haunts objective knowledge; and active uncertainty drives inquiry. The world is uncertain; it is also unsafe, for the explicit 'I' knows that it is at risk; is aware of future possibilities. It is, as Heidegger says, 'an issue for itself'. It is conscious of its vulnerability and, in an inchoate way, of its mortality. The creature awoken out of sentience to knowledge awakes to a dangerous world outside of which is incompletely scrutable. It is not surprising, therefore, that it should arrive at the idea of a 'true' self that is so far 'inside' the body as to be insulated from the threats of the world, and the threats to that body, a self whose existence is potentially underwritten by a transcendent creature (e.g. a God) who is and knows and encompasses the inscrutable remainder of the inscrutable world.

The dream of mind–body separation, in other words, is a consequence of the knowing animal's encounter with its self and a world that makes incomplete sense. It is a way of rounding off the sense of the world and making that world safer. As we move from sentience to sentences, from feeling cold to the thought '[That] it is cold', so we become more aware of our bodily exposure and more aware of ourselves as an inner place where we might become, we may imagine, beyond exposure. Our sentences – whose meanings are separated from token utterances – posit a realm where (as Hopkins' nun, thinking of the Heaven-Haven she had chosen, described the after-life) 'flies no sharp and sided hail / ...where no storms come'. It is not surprising that, not long after the invention of writing, and soon after world-pictures became formalised as philosophical systems, there was postulated a Heaven of unchanging forms whose character was accessed not through the senses but through sentences. It offers the possibility of escape from suffering now (Buddhism) or later (Christianity), which gives meaning even to suffering now. The dream of becoming a thought or a mental something – inside or outside the mind of God – at the very least offers the idea of comfort for the suffering that, sooner or later, will come. To become a spiritual thing is to find the ultimate place of refuge in a world of shin-barking material things and hence to cancel the sentence of death.[47]

Let me end this brief exploration of the fantasies the embodied have harboured of bodiless being by looking once more at Descartes' choice of thought as the key to his essential self. We have discussed what Anscombe called 'Cartesianly preferred thoughts'. Descartes preferred 'I think, therefore I am' to, for example, 'I am sweaty, therefore I am' because while the logic of both the *Cogito* and the *Sudo* arguments, of the glowing and thinking arguments, is equally unassailable, the former is preferred because its premise is also unassailable.[48] I may be mistaken as to whether or not I am sweaty, but I cannot be mistaken as to whether or not I am thinking. 'I am thinking' is self-affirming while 'I am sweaty' is not. By using logical, rational certainty as a criterion for the unquestionable reality of something, he was therefore obliged to confer reality on his thinking and withhold it from his sweating. So even though he later concluded from the fact that God would not deceive him that he could not be mistaken as to a fact as fundamental as that he was embodied, he still stuck to the idea that he was essentially a thinking substance. He thought of himself not as a meaty, sweaty creature but as an odourless succession of thought-moments. The self of the philosopher is his philosophising self. And he was most apparent to himself – and hence most certain of himself – in the second-order thought that he was thinking; in the highest, most focused, narrowest self-encounter, in the most concentrated 'hereness'. Such are the destinations of the dream of disembodiment.[49]

### 6.9 BEING-A-BODY REVISITED

Even before we embarked on the examination of the many modes and aspects of embodiment – and in particular the dense and varied foliage of self-awareness that grows in the gap between the character of the consciousness of the organism and the character of the organism – we should have known that we would have to follow many twisted paths in our search for a philosophy of *Fort-sein*. For the very origin of 'being-here', in the manner in which we humans are here, located in the centre of explicit egocentric space, is to be found in the foldedness of bodily presences ('meta-fingering', etc.) out of which grows the sense 'That I am this body ...' – which is, of course, 'here'. The breakdown, which we observed in the previous sections, of the simple mind–body dichotomy to a more elusive, shifting boundary between 'I' and 'It', the move from a binary opposition between subject and object to parts of the world that I am, parts of the world that I suffer, parts that I use, etc., is in tune with the bio-genetic account of the origin of the self in the apprehension of the body as 'me' and 'mine'. The self-apprehension of the body stands at the origin of the emergence of self-consciousness, of consciousness of the self and the ultimate structuring of a world that pooled selves are conscious of. In the relationship between self and world, there is incomplete separation between the object and contents of consciousness.

In many ways all we have achieved is to shift the bump in the carpet. The body seems rather ill-suited to the role of quasi-pure, quasi-geometrical centre of egocentric space. The burden of this chapter is that being a body is far from a simple and undivided condition. At any given time, we experience both a multitude of fleeting and sustained bodily awarenesses – awarenesses of the body itself and awarenesses made possible in virtue of the body. (This duality is an important – and necessary – complication, as we shall see.) These awarenesses are difficult to capture and characterise. It is usually only when we wake up out of 'absorbed coping' in actions that we become explicitly conscious of its elements: the subliminal is helped over the threshold, the just-supra-liminal moves centre stage. It is only when I pause between bursts of writing, for example, that I notice the pressure of my buttocks on the seat reporting, and being reported by, the pressure of the seat on my buttocks; the warm glow in my hands, arrested above the keyboard; the pulsing of the blood in my right calf; the sensation of my socked right foot pressing down on the carpet; the slight dryness of the eyes; the tongue bathed in saliva touching the inner surface of the front teeth; the respiratory movements of my chest.

These, along with many other sensations that it would be tedious to list, sketch out an outline of my body – closer to what Merleau-Ponty would call the 'phenomenal', as opposed to the 'objective' or physical or biological body – *le corps propre*.[50] This is the body that is *presupposed* in action and in perception. Its nodal points, although seemingly joined up like the inter-wired lights on a Christmas tree, are not entirely separate. They are united through intervening stretches of near-threshold sensations – for example the liminal not-quite-tingling of the skin that may be woken by impingements at any time to actually sensations. Less egregiously, there are often non-focal experiences such as the sense of one's own weightiness. Warmth may be global; nausea may have no clear location or break out at various locations, as when there is an upwelling of waterbrash or a flurry of pre-heaves; and tiredness may be a mixture of clearly localised sensations, as in aching muscles, or localisations that are somewhat epiphenomenal, as in the slight throat-ache of permanent incipient yawns, or non-localised, as in the drift towards sleep and the disinclination to act.

The phenomenal body is not, as Merleau-Ponty emphasised again and again, a mere sum of distinct sensations: the presentation of the objective body in the phenomenal body is not an aggregation of separate awarenesses but an ever-changing whole against the background of more body and of the extra-corporeal world. An inventory of specific experiences, therefore, is inadequate as a rendering of bodily self-presence, especially since the contents of the inventory are highlighted and given prominence only by an artificial state of introspection. Moreover, localising individual experiences misrepresents them: they too are parts of a whole. While certain experiences (for example, itches) may stand out as isolated events, the basic unit of perception is, as Merleau-Ponty argued, a *whole*. In this, he was building on the work of gestalt psychologists,[51] who pointed out that what we perceive always forms part of a field. There are two levels of the gestalt: the object or array which is synthesised into one; and the world that enframes or enworlds it and acts as its background. This is as true of perceptions of the body as it is of the awareness of things outside the body. What it is that 'brings it all together', we shall address in due course.

For the present, we note that the more immediate modes of being our body or something close to it – directly and locally or directly and diffusely (my warmth, my weightiness) – are supplemented by indirect encounters. The body may reveal itself to itself through touch; it may catch sight of itself – either directly, as when I see my hand, or hear my breathing, or indirectly, as when I catch sight of myself in a mirror; or it may infer its presence from its effect on its physical surroundings (as when I glimpse my shadow on a wall or when I make a floorboard creak); or, most complexly mediated of all, become aware of itself through its (my) social impact – as when 'they' look up or stop talking when I enter a room and I become aware of my physical presence, or perhaps am reminded of a scar on my face or, less dramatically, of my recent haircut.

### 6.10 EMBODIMENT: CONCLUSION

We have examined the actual experience of embodiment in such detail because we are looking to the body to underpin *Fort-sein*, being-here. It is of concern that we have discovered that embodiment is far from simple and undivided. And things are actually more complicated than we have hitherto portrayed them. There is, for example, a balance to be struck between the amount of bodily self-presence required for the body to be here (explicitly here) and located at a particular place in the world, that which is necessary for it to be a point of origin or initiation of action and a point of disclosure of the world, and the amount that would occlude that same extra-corporeal world. Awareness of some parts of our body interferes with perception of, and action on, the world. Ideally, the seeing eye should be unaware of itself; dry, sore eyes neither look nor see as well as eyes that do not sense themselves.

Perception becomes more difficult, more of an 'action', where the body is obtrusive: just as walking becomes 'doing walking' when there is a problem with the legs, so seeing becomes deliberately looking and looking becomes peering. The body resists dissolution into the job in hand: the arthritic joints provide their own report on the act of walking and it is always the same report that has nothing to do with the meaning of the walk – to the pub, to a loved one, to a hated duty.[52] There are levels of self-presence where the background murmur rises to a full-blown self-narration of the body; as when, for example, gut-presence in repleteness modulates to gut-ache.

With illness, the body's narrative amplifies to a din; and perception of the body progressively occludes perception of the world which is anyway less well perceived as the sick body functions less well in supporting external perception. As a serious illness advances, so the experience of the body increasingly overshadows experience of the world: nausea, pain, shortness of breath cease to be merely the over-dominant background music of perception of the world outside the body and merge into an all-encompassing bodily awareness, a sea into which the perceiver, increasingly confused and decreasingly aware, drowns. The body, finally, becomes the last reef of the receding world, and here and there merge, cancel or collapse.

The role of the body in being the here from which a there is disclosed was never going to be straightforward – if only because we are, as it were, bodily folded over on ourselves: this, after all, is what has occasioned the Existential Intuition and started the process by which we became human subjects 'inside' our organic bodies, transforming both our bodies and the material environment into the world in which selves lead their lives. We are touched touchers who touch that with which we touch; seers who see our eyes; breathers who hear our breathing and are able to make it our own, as when panting is sculptured into speech. We are encounterable as objects in a world in which our own awareness provides the more-or-less obtrusive principle of coherence; in which, as the visible and invisible centre of our visual field, the presupposed tangible of our touchings, we are able to encounter ourselves. We are, as Merleau-Ponty says 'sensible sentients'.

### 6.11 DELIVERING *FORT-SEIN*: TOUCHING AND SEEING

The purpose of the foregoing account of embodiment was an attempt to characterise the way the body provides the here that was missing in Heidegger's existential analytic of *Da-sein*. As a clarification, it has been signally unsuccessful! Let us, however, press on, for an account of here is desperately needed: any there must be a particular there; so that *Da-sein* without the specification furnished by a complementary here would be there-less; in short, a *Da-sein* without a *Da*. It would be simply '*sein*', or 'being', itself; or perhaps an emptiness lacking even enough substance to wander.

We have spent so much time examining our relationship to our body because the basis of here seems in the first instance to be the body's awareness of itself or, more precisely, my awareness of my body: the way I experience embodiment. The body *qua* material object cannot establish here: it cannot exploit being *de facto* here because 'hereness' is not an objective fact of material, or indeed any other, objects; in short, material objects are not *de facto*.

This awareness, this solidity of presence, must – as we have seen – not be so pronounced as to occlude the world the body is to be aware of, act in and act on. The body, as Merleau-Ponty emphasised, is for the most part 'transparent' to us. This must be self-evidently so in the case of our sense organs: skin that asserted itself to us through constant tingling would lose tactile discrimination; the eyes see better through being themselves invisible; the ears are better listeners through themselves being inaudible. And, as we noted, the more efficient, the healthier, our bodies, the less obtrusive they are: busybodies are at times almost bodiless. Even so, some opacity is necessary for the body to furnish the hereness, which will, for example, locate the specific objects of which we are aware through our senses in a world as 'there'.

This there will, in turn, confirm the hereness of the body. While we have given here priority over there, this is to some extent merely a reflection of where the argument is coming from. There is what might be called a dialectical relationship between here and there. While there is no there without a here, there is no fully developed here without a there. The 'over-hereness' of my body places the desk lamp in the 'over there' of a world; but that 'over there', including the lamp, underlines the 'hereness' of my body. My proximity to you is inseparable from your proximity to me. The things that are there make me be here.

This is true at whatever level of complexity or abstractness here and there are specified; whether we are talking about a here that corresponds to 'near to my hand', 'in the Duchy of Cornwall' or 'at a particular point in the solar system'. There is, in short, an interaction between there and here so that each reinforces the other; the process, however, would not have begun without an initial here. Here has priority: it has to be in the starter pack. At the moment it dawns, however, it will relate to its cognate there – its internal accusative, as it were – and priority then becomes meaningless.

The interaction between here and there – like the two halves of an arch – is most directly and simply illustrated by touch, where the touched object touches the touching body so that the sense of the object being in contact with the body (and hence there) brings with it the sense of the body being in contact with the object (and hence, comparatively, here).[53] The active nature of exploratory touch brings into play more of the body, making more of it be here. Touch is of particular interest because, uniquely of all the senses, it has reciprocity built into it: we touch at the cost of being touched. This is why the 'meta-fingering' hand – with its immediate (as opposed to mediated) second-order awareness –

proved, as we argued in Volume 1 and in Chapter 1 of the present volume, crucial to the emergence of the distinctively human. The other proximate senses – smell and taste – do not have this reciprocity built into them: we are not smelt by the flowers we smell, the food we eat does not know what our mouths taste like. And the same is true of the distance senses: we can see without being seen, can hear without being heard.

The specially close interaction between here and there in touch is, in fact, dangerously close. Touch is exposure to the touched object. 'I' and 'it' are in direct contact. In touch you literally have to put your own hide 'on the line'. More than this biological risk, there is an epistemological risk that the touched and the toucher might not be fully differentiated as object (of knowledge) and subject (of experience): here and there are literally touching; at the point of experiencing the object, there is no distance between them. And the interaction too is dangerously democratic: the properties of the touching body and that of the touched body seem to contribute equally to the experience that results: the feeling of a pebble comes equally from the non-deformability of granite and the deformability of skin. We might contrast touch with vision by arguing that the former at best prehends the object, while the latter *com*prehends it.[54]

The danger of collapsing here-and-there into something that is not quite either is averted, however, by the fact that the object even in touch addresses several different types of sense organ: temperature, texture, pressure, weight, are all sampled and some of these, notably weight, are experienced at a distance from the object as well as at the point of contact. (For example, the weight of this pebble is experienced not only over my hand, but proximally in the arm that is supporting it.) The otherness of the pebble is thus established, while an intimate interaction between here and there is sustained. It is intimate without being mutually cancelling. In the case of human touch, of course, the toucher is, as it were, pre-differentiated – as a subject 'within' her own body. This is established by the processes, ultimately mediated by the hand, which we have already described in some detail and to which we shall return in the next two chapters.

The interaction between here and there in touch is highlighted by the reflecting on what is involved in the perception of solidity and location. According to Cassam, a crucial aspect of the perception of solidity by touch

> is the way in which it is bound up with a sense of the solidity of the perceiver. Solidity is typically felt as an impediment to one's movements,

and to experience a solid object as an 'obstructive something' (O'Shaughnessy, 1989) is at the same time to be sensibly or intuitively aware of that which is obstructed – the *subject* of tactile perception – as obstructed.[55]

This vividly illustrates the importance of touch to 'hereness': it plugs one more completely into here. It is almost as if there is a trade-off between the 'sufferedness' of here (as in touch and in the most intimate self-touch of proprioception), its felt reality, on the one hand, and on the other, the synoptic sense of it; between 'being' here and 'knowing that' [one is] here.

The array of in-world objects illuminated by, or that shows up for, an awareness that is bodily located in a here underlines the there which then retroactively locates the body. Like action and reaction, here and there are equal and opposite. In the case of the telereceptors – sight and hearing – the visible objects 'over there' make the visible body of the one who sees or hears a subject 'over here'. This interdependency is captured by Heidegger in his discussion of space to which we alluded to earlier:

> 'Here' and 'over there' are possible only in a there, that is when there is a being which has disclosed spatiality as the being of the there. This being bears in its ownmost being the character of not being closed. The expression there means this essential disclosedness. Through disclosedness this being (*Da-sein*) is there for itself together with the *Da-sein* of the world. (BT 125)

Unfortunately, as we can see, he gives there priority over here. Downplaying the necessity for a here in order to have a there, and hence overlooking the body, can result in a view that, as we earlier noted, sails close to idealism – especially when the relationship between the 'world' (of *Da-sein*) and the universe of material things is considered:

> the aroundness of the surrounding world, the specific spatiality of the beings encountered in the surrounding world is grounded in the worldliness of the world, and not the other way around, that is, we cannot say that the world in its turn is objectively present in space. (BT 94)

> There is never a three-dimensional multiplicity of possible positions initially given which is then filled out with objectively present things ... Regions are not first formed by things objectively together but are always already at hand in individual places. The places themselves are assigned

to what is at hand in the circumspection of taking care of things, or else we come across them. (BT 96)

The fact that what is at hand can be encountered in its space of the surrounding world is ontically possible only because *Da-sein* itself is 'spatial' with regard to its being-in-the-world. (BT 97)

The idealist reading may be unfair[56] but it is an inevitable, though most certainly unintended, consequence of his overlooking the body. At any rate, it obscures a real contribution to our understanding of being-in-the-world. For Heidegger is quite correct in saying that the 'things at hand of everyday association' which 'have the character of *nearness*' do not 'simply have a place in space, objectively present somewhere' (BT 95). They are not primarily located in the neutral, deindexicalised space of physics.

Heidegger's notion of 'de-distancing', already referred to, brilliantly captures the interaction between here and there: their mutual distance is created out of a relationship of accessibility that closes the distance. If this distance is to be crossed in fact – as opposed to merely in the sensing from here of that which is over there – physical space has to be traversed by a physical body. The apple has to be reached for; the door has to be walked towards; the journey to the shop has to be undertaken. The awareness that brings the object to the body shows what the body has to do in order to take hold of the object.

De-distancing – the experience of a crossable distance, of an open world – is based on a bodily underwritten *Fort-sein*, which differentiates there into a specific '*Da-sein*'. The re-importation of the body into Heidegger's system places that system safely out of reach of idealism. As O'Shaughnessy says, 'the space and solidity of our bodies provides the access to the space and solidity of other bodies'.[57]

The interaction between here and the actions that turn the potential 'de-distancing' into actual distance crossed – so that the ready-to-hand is actually placed in one's hands – is vividly portrayed by O'Shaughnessy. He points out, first of all, that tactile perception requires proprioception: sensing the other is in relation to being aware of oneself as a body. My touching, groping, manipulating hand knows itself in the course of knowing the object; or rather its awareness of the object it is grasping is inseparable from its awareness of itself engaged with the object. This is most explicitly true in the case of humans where sensing opens up into knowing. The body parts engaged in the actions must be such that one is aware proprioceptively of their position and movement in space: one must have a feeling for them; they must be part of 'an integrated bodily totality' (a concept significantly overlapping with Merleau-Ponty's 'phenomenal body'). In humans, they must, in addition, be implicitly related to oneself as instruments. The danger that de-distancing will collapse into mere immersion of a sentient creature in its environment, and here-and-there will deflate into something that is not quite either, is averted in humans by the complex relations they have to their bodies; ultimately by the Existential Intuition awoken by the hand.

Of particular interest is O'Shaughnessy's Lockean observation that one must not only have a feeling in the relevant bodily part but also a 'concern' for it. This reaches back to the fundamentals of Heidegger's ontology and his characterisation of *Da-sein* as 'that being whose being is an issue for itself' and the key characteristic of *Da-sein* as 'heedful being-alongside' or 'care'. O'Shaughnessy reminds us that we need something to have concern for. *Fort-sein* philosophy, which emphasises the priority of being-here over being-there, and the body as that in virtue of which one occupies a here, also highlights how, without the body, there would be nothing to care for; there would be no being to be an issue for itself. Bodiless *Da-sein* would be a nothing caring for nothing – which is what at times Heidegger makes it seem like.[58] The body, which imports here into a hereless universe, and so underpins the nexus of heres and theres that is the world, also gives the here something to care about. *Sorge* is made to care about something; care is made to care.

The integration of perception and action implicit in *Fort-sein* philosophy, in which touch has the status of the paradigm, or basic, sense, is consistent with Merleau-Ponty's line of thinking. Perception, he argued, is not a detached awareness of the world but an active involvement in it.[59] He emphasised how the senses and motor skills work together in a unified way in exploration and discovery. Manipulation, the very archetype of prehension and of human apprehension, is a process in which it is difficult to separate action from perception: the two are profoundly interdigitated (if this is not an over-determined word). When I am tying my shoelaces, finding out about the character of the shoelaces, their evolving relationships to one another as the knot is tied, the feedback on the position of my own fingers and the motor activity in performing the task (modified as always by exteroceptive and proprioceptive commentary), are inseparable.

The intimate relationship between motor activity and bodily self-perception is highlighted by the paralysis that may result when proprioception is severely impaired.[60] The 'veridical body', which O'Shaughnessy emphasised was necessary to make the 'animal body' 'actively employable', is lost. Without clues as to where the body – or the relevant limb – is, there can be no notion of what has to be done in order to accomplish an action; to cross over from here to there. We can get to a there only from an explicit here which will give our journey a starting point, a point of departure.⁶¹

## 6.12 FURTHER (EVEN MORE PUZZLED) REFLECTIONS ON THE BODY AS THE GUARANTOR AND CURATOR OF 'HERE'

This is the point at which we find ourselves moving from assertion and description to puzzlement. Our starting point was that *Da-sein* required *Fort-sein* and the only credible source of *Fort-sein* would be the human body. On further reflection, it looks increasingly difficult to see how the human body could actually deliver what is required of it. There is merit in spelling out some of the outstanding difficulties, even if we shall make little progress in solving them. If the outcome is wonder, this is not a bad result.

### The body is at risk of being too obtrusive

In order that a place should be established as (a) 'here', it is not enough that the body should simply be at that place. 'Here' cannot be derived from *de facto* location of an object considered objectively. The objective fact that the body, considered as a physical object, happens to be at a particular spot does not make either the spot or the body here – for there is no here for either to be at. The flag has to be planted and the centre to be proclaimed. (To look at this from another angle: being-here cannot be an 'objective fact' – only a subject-reality, a reality founded on an established subjectivity, because here varies from subject to subject and without subjects there is no here.)

The body has therefore to be present to itself; or an 'I' has to be present to herself through her body. This bodily self-presence, the explicit experience of embodiment, has proved, we found, to be extraordinarily complex, with many dimensions of 'having' and (more intimately) 'being' a body. The sensation of bodily being is necessary to make the body's being 'anywhere' into a being-here.⁶² The bodily being-there that is necessary to perceptions (as well as, more problematically, to thoughts and memories) – comprised of things such as the warmth of the body against itself, the pressure against the surfaces that support it, the formation and re-formation of the pool of saliva in the mouth, as well as even less distinguished presences, such as what the physiologists refer to as the 'neuromuscular ghost', etc. – is a kind of low-grade 'hum'. It is this presumably that establishes the here, which is in turn the necessary counterpoint to the there of the world. This is, as it were, the flag planted in the world, making this object over here be here, and that object over there be there. Once the there has been established, this will feed back into the here.

This last is an important point. While the starting point of this chapter is that there is no there without here, the not-quite-converse is also true, as we have already hinted: there can be no fully developed here without a there derived in turn from the ur-here of bodily self-presence. Only the ur-here has primacy; after that there is a dialectic between here and there in which each drives the other to greater complexity. Although the 'body-hum-here' would not have a location if it were isolated from everything else – it becomes a specific, contentful here in relation to an encompassing there, to particular objects – it is necessary that it should pre-exist there in order that the there should be *received*.

The experienced here also makes what lies before us not only be there but also be *really* there. To be established as an experiencer of a real world, one has to have a here. Without the here in the centre of things, one is a mere spectator – as when one is watching a film.[63] The link between the body that is suffered and the there that gives access is itself important for making what is there real. We need to be embodied in order to be embedded to reveal a real world: the self-revelation of the body is the ground, the underpinning, of this embedding.[64]

This is at first reassuring: the embedding of experience of the there in the toils of the body-here seems as self-evidently necessary as friction is necessary for walking or the resistant air for the flight of the dove. This is the condition of there being *there for someone* so that its contents are truly *experienced* and connected with other experiences in the cumulative, structured, archived, realm of the self. (The question of there being truly experienced arises only when we have moved beyond sentience, which does not differentiate appearance from reality, itself from its objects, so that the reality of the latter may be put in question.) In other words, the here, if it were humless, an extensionless point, would not deliver what is needed: not only because an extensionless point would have only a notional existence, but also because the opacity of the embodied here is necessary to stop everything passing straight through. The here has to be a bit solid in order to 'field' the there. This reassurance, however, turns to puzzlement when we consider the kind of things that make up the background hum necessary to confer specificity and substantiality on the here.

For a start, the inventory of rather random bodily sensations and experiences, and the evanescent shoals of carnal self-appropriations, which we found earlier when we looked at embodiment, hardly seems to amount to a unified or coherent being-here. Hereness-via-embodiment is at best a being 'locally all over the place'. One can make oneself acutely aware of this if one concentrates on the various deliverances of the body as one lies flat on one's stomach (a dead man's float) and turns into a dropped meat – like a side of Francis Bacon. The inventory of the sensations of this 'fallen' self is complex indeed and, while some of them may plausibly be said to be (spatially) related to one another – the feeling of the weight of the head on the pillow at the top, the warmth of the shoulder in the middle, the tingle in the calf near the bottom and the itch in the toe at the very tip – others cannot. For example, there is no clear spatial relationship between the sound of one's breathing and the itch in the toe or between the effort of thought and the tingle in the calf. Nor do these fragments have a clear relationship to the unified body schema that informs my engaged body 'absorbedly coping' with daily life.

While the inventory may be dismissed as an artefact of an artificial state of bodily attention – the kind of puzzling entity that emerges when, as Wittgenstein would say, the 'engine is idling' or the product of what Heidegger called 'rigid staring' – its components cannot be dismissed entirely. For they are only partly assimilated into the body schema, and yet any one of them is available to be thus assimilated. There is, at the very least, a question about the relationship between the awarenesses that are assumed into a body schema, the explicit sense of here, and the things that are observed in the body when the engine is idling. It is even arguable that the things that are picked out in an artificial state of attention might be the grit in the 'smooth machine' of busyness that makes being-here real.

As well as being spatially patchy – being referred to scattered but specific locations on the body – the patchwork-hum of bodily being-here is also highly volatile. What is more, it is made up of heterogeneous types of experience. So while we accept that the extensionless point of hereness, subjectivity, or whatever does indeed need to be clothed in something and a body is just the thing to give it the necessary substance to confront or address and (in the form of perceptions) to 'field' a there, what it is actually composed of seems worryingly haphazard. It lacks the unity that one might expect of a point of disclosure, an underpinning of here. Moreover, it seems at times rather too obtrusive. While an extensionless point, a transparency, would be quite inadequate as a basis for here, for reasons already given, the obtrusive sensations of the body – even when the body is not ill, or seeking sensation for its own sake as in lovemaking or sunbathing – seem as liable to *occlude* as to *field* the there that it has to receive.

Both the lack of unity and the obtrusiveness of bodily experiences are illustrated by an ordinary bodily sensation such as an itch – at least as it is experienced by humans. (Animal itching is metaphysically less interesting.) An itch is manifestly far too obtrusive to establish the presence of here through the self-iteration of the body. While it is self-disclosive, it is too 'noisy' to be disclosive of a there – or not an extra-corporeal there, anyway. Moreover, it illustrates the body's dividedness against itself and the division of 'here' that this would seem to produce. When we scratch, we first of all *locate* the itch. This involves a *search* – sometimes short to the point of implicitness and sometimes prolonged and explicit. At any rate, we have to find a place on our own body, a process that divides the body into the searching hand which is here and the searched-for itching place which is there or 'over there'. The itch, in other words, underlines or modulates the division of the human body into subject and object; and the job of relieving it affirms the differentiation of agent and patient within the body, with the motor activity in the transporting arm and then the scratching hand, creating spatial referents of here with respect to the there of the itch. This simple example illustrates the multiplicity of heres and theres within the body.[65]

This would seem to distract the body from, even actively unfit the body for, its role in providing a 'point of disclosure', a means of drawing down *Da-sein* from a category to a particular, so that disclosedness differentiates into disclosings, by establishing a here. (One could become quite nostalgic for the simplicities of the self as an extensionless point and for the discarnate metaphysics of traditional subject-object epistemologies!) At any rate, we face serious difficulties when we try to imagine how the body's deliverances to itself connect with, rather than occlude, the body's awareness of the world whose there it establishes through its here; how, in short, the here-hum and the there are kept apart and yet connected and integrated. To put this another way: How the body's presence to itself – essential for the here to be asserted as a localised here – squares with the body's role as that in virtue of which things are present. How the body's revelation of itself to itself – this feeling of warmth diffused through my frame, this pressure of the seat on my buttocks, revealing the pressure of my buttock on the seat – does not get in the way of its role in revealing the world that surrounds itself. Disclosedness demands transparency; specific disclosing requires a partially opaque here to field a particular there. The conflict seems unresolvable. No wonder philosophers have so often been suspicious of sense experience.

## The body has too many jobs to do at once

We could rephrase the concern of the previous paragraphs as follows: there is a potential conflict between the body's role in i) creating the viewpoint which makes the there be there and the here be here, and ii) its role as the recipient of the perceptions received at that viewpoint. Two roles seem one too many. The suggestion that these two roles are one and the same, or that they are each supportive of the other, has to be set aside when it is appreciated that experiences of things 'over there' are perspectival and located, while experiences that create the here are not, collectively, perspectival and are (possibly) location-supporting, rather than located. One does not experience one's body, inasmuch as it is the basis of here, perspectivally. Nor indeed does one experience it as located in an objective sense. For the here is the precursor of both existential and objective location. Of course (to add to the complexity), the body has to paint itself into the frame: it has to be all three – perceiver, the basis of perception and a thing that is perceived; to be that which gives us access to space and solidity while at the same time presenting itself as spatially extended and solid. It has to be the basis of perception as well as the source of perception's here. This is an even tougher assignment than Merleau-Ponty's description of embodied subjects as 'sensible sentients' would suggest.

The situation is yet more complex. In its capacity as the viewpoint underpinning the view that is presented to (encircles, immerses) me, my body is the epistemological or metaphysical centre of my world. It is certainly its functional centre; and – though this is to anticipate more abstract modes of consciousness – it is its geometric centre. And yet I am able to experience myself as being on the margin – at the edge of the room, on the fringes of the occasion, in the dark or ill-lit places of exile. I can sustain this double awareness: the viewpoint on the view and the viewpoint on the viewpoint. I can, that is to say, see myself at least in part, fleetingly and incompletely, in a perspectival way.

The two main roles we have identified are not the end of the matter. There are other jobs the body has, and these take it beyond being the basis of here. It is an actor as well as an existential coordinate; an originator of events as well as a point of origin of events. This fits with the relationship of 'having', of possession, to our bodies, which fundamentally is one of instrumentality. We 'employ' or utilise our bodies; or rather, we employ parts of them in the service of other parts of them or in service of the body as a whole. This instrumentality, 'ownership', is never, of course, complete, even in relation to body parts – though (as we noted earlier) it may be particularly apparent under certain circumstances, as when I use my shoulder to batter down a door or use my foot to prevent a door being closed in my face or my hand to lift a forkful of food to my mouth or when my body is in some way disabled so that I see it as 'not working', 'not doing its job'. This job as an agent might also be expected to curdle the here that the body brings to the world, and to place the body at odds with itself in its role as a point of disclosure.

The body also, finally, has its own agenda: it has to care for itself and the world it reveals is subordinated to its needs: it is surrounded by consumables, tools, predators, threats and promises. It has to survive in order that it can continue to be a point of disclosure and the condition of its surviving is a self-preoccupation which infects its here with something other than mere disclosure and takes the latter yet further from disinterested beholding. Being a continuing point of disclosure requires regular dinners.[66] And nearly all of the body consists of 'inner workings' – even the skin, which is simply the outermost reaches of the inner workings. The body as a steward of here for the sake of its own survival seems almost to cut across the notion of the body as a steward of here for the sake of the truth; or at least for getting things right. Or at least as a point of disclosure.[67] It seems in danger of disappearing into its own cognitive navel.

The role of the body as the steward of the past is another source of bafflement. How can the body both support being the underpinning of here (which requires that it be something not too complexly differentiated) and, at the same time, support the archived, complexly layered self amid the modulations of the 'hum' short of illness and the current needs and ambitions of everyday life – as we seek the pleasures of food and drink, of being caressed, of sunshine? How can the enteroceptive and proprioceptive components of consciousness, as well as the telereceptive (sights and sounds) ones be brought together with, and kept apart from, the abstract (memories, thoughts, gossip, conversation) contents? It is difficult to understand how the instantaneous experience of the body both adds up to and connects with the archived experience that is implicit in the self and keeps the current and deposit account separate. We touch on this in Chapter 7; suffice it to note, for the present, that here is experienced by an individual who at any given time (other than at the putative first moment of her life) is 'already' here – and hence literally in a position to have, and also to have had, one set of experiences rather than another. This being-here is characterised not only by the present location, but also by prior experiences which are relevant to what made being in *this* here possible and also give depth of meaning to this here: now's instantaneous here is embedded in a continuous narrative, in a more or less stable archive, which stretches back from the preceding few moments to the earliest months, or at least years, of one's life.

'Here', in other words, is both synchronically and diachronically established. This necessary temporal depth of here is in part captured in this passage from Gareth Evans:

> self-location cannot in general be a momentary thing. For ... self location depends crucially upon the axiom that the subject moves continuously through space; and that axiom can be brought to bear upon particular questions of location only if the subject has the capacity to retain information about his previous perceptions, and to use that information in making judgements about his past, and thereby his present, position.[68]

Being here must be informed by a sense of how I got here (just as now is informed by what led up to now) and, indeed, by a sense of where here is in relation to other heres: here is ultimately located on a spatio-temporal map. At the very least, it is immersed in 'hodological' space – a fabric of routes and viewpoints – traced out by our lives. There is, therefore, no truly instantaneous here; but, on the other hand, there can be no enduring here without the instantaneous appropriation of something, the background bodily hum, to establish ur-here.[69]

The fundamental problem, therefore, of a body-based philosophy of *Fort-sein* is that the body needs enough of a 'hum' of background, typically proprioceptive, activity to make its here explicit, but this hum (much of which may be rather confusingly lodged in unconsciousness or made to cohere through unconscious continuities) must not be too obtrusive. Nor should the surplus of bodily self-awareness or bodily self-concern (as reported in, say, hunger pangs and the activities that seek to salve them) itself occlude the here and interfere with the body's role as a transparent locus of disclosure. The body's need to be self-present in order to provide the 'here' threatens to occlude the there, as does its need to look after itself.[70]

These are complex, difficult areas beset with unsolved problems to which there seems to be no sensible approach.

### The body seems the wrong kind of thing to do any of these jobs: there is no basis for in the body for self-disclosure or here-bearing

The body, it seems, has so many roles that it is difficult to see how it could carry out what from the point of view of our present discussion is its primary job: to deliver the basis of a here which will pick out a there. Its many other roles seem to interfere with this central role. But that is not the end of this particular puzzle of embodiment. For the body seems to be the wrong kind of thing to provide a here. Let us look again at this background hum.

We have described this as the body's presence to itself; more specifically, it is the body's self-disclosure. But is the body the kind of thing that one might expect to be able to disclose itself? We shall argue in Volume 3 that even the most likely candidate for the organ of self-disclosure – the brain – does not deliver what is needed; and the most plausible mechanism – neural activity triggered by events in the body – seems unintelligible. A brief rehearsal of some of the arguments that will be put forward there is in order here.

First, given that the brain is regarded as the final common pathway of all modes of awareness, encompasing awareness of the body, awareness of the things around the body and more abstract forms of awareness such as memory and thought, it is impossible to understand how it could differentiate these. Correctly assigning distinct awarenesses to the body, to the extra-corporeal world and to the inner world of the past or thought, seems to require mechanisms that the brain, with its monotonous or homogeneous response to all events, could not provide. There seems to be no conceivable way in which neural activity could differentiate, say, the neuromuscular ghost that haunts my body from the thoughts that counter-haunt my body. And yet it not only has to do that; it also has to link the two in a unified sense of 'me-thinking-here-now'.

Second, and more profoundly, the body's self-disclosure could not be captured in the brain's self-disclosure in neural activity because that activity would not, of itself, disclose anything. For what is neural activity *in itself*? According to the physicalist theory, which provides the framework of neural theories of consciousness, they are at best collections of primary qualities – mere size, number, shape and location. They are void, empty of qualitative content. Even if they were able to disclose themselves, and through this, the causes of which they are effects, what they disclosed would not correspond to what the body seems to disclose in *its* self-awareness.

Third, and yet more deeply, the body itself, seen as a material object, would, like neural activity, have no secondary qualities to disclose. This, it seems to me, is what lies behind Sprigge's observation we have already cited that, being a particular organism (e.g. a human body), 'will have a certain definite complex quality at every waking moment', but this is not the same as the properties of that organism: 'it is not the same thing to characterise the consciousness of the organism and to characterise that organism'.[71] In other words, there is no reason to expect that the objective properties of the organism will be mirrored in the waking consciousness of that organism. After all, these objective properties – as described by science – will include the experiences of the organism which all are agreed on – for example, that it has rose-red cheeks, and that it has such and such a texture. These will themselves be secondary to their being experienced – *qua* biological material, cheeks are not in themselves red, brains are not in themselves like slop.

There is therefore an even more complete dissociation between the consciousness of the human organism and the properties of that organism than we envisaged when we discussed this earlier. The organism in itself, being a physical body, does not have any qualities. Even if it did, which properties would be selected as representing the organism? The body could not declare all of itself: every element at every level of discrimination (molecule, cell, organ, limb, whole body, etc.). Indeed, there is no way of defining what would be an accurate, comprehensive or adequate self-declaration of a material body in self-awareness. We might express this by saying that there is a deeply puzzling but total disconnection between the phenomenal and the objective body.

We should not imagine, therefore, that there is a *canonical represen-tation in experience* of the being of the human body. (To put this another way, there are no qualia necessarily connected, in a bond of correspondent truth, with a particular body.) This compounds the problem of allocating experiences to different categories: experiences of the body and experiences by the body of the world; or bodily experiences and experiences made possible courtesy of the body. (There is nothing that could bear the unmistakable mark of being authentically from or of the body.) It seems that such a basis for assigning the origin of sensations to the body or to the extra-corporeal world – to the there or to the body which counterpoints it – can be found only after the body has been claimed for a self and certain rules established for differentiating the deliverances of, say, telereception from those of proprioception or enteroception. Those rules, however, presuppose certain assumptions which need prior characterisation.

It might be objected that to describe the problem in this way is to miss the fact that the body does not declare itself in isolation: the body is self-declared in relation to an outside world, ongoing activity, a track record of acting and perceiving, etc.; in short, in a *situation*. This, while importantly true, may simply move the bump in the carpet elsewhere. If the self-declaration of the body is interactive, or at least in relation to things both outside the body and in the past of the body, then there is the problem of 'unscrambling' what belongs to the body, to its present and to its past, and what belongs to the world outside of the body. The conscious, here-bearing and there-positing body it seems would be faced with solving a simultaneous equation in which the individual values of none of the variables is given.

Against this background, it is easy to see how attractive functionalism – which bypasses the contents of consciousness altogether (though this is not always admitted) and focuses on input (events impinging on the animal body/brain) and output (responses of the animal body/brain) – might be. Nothing has to be sorted or unscrambled because the beast is merely a way-station in event-chains that pass through it and it is automatically locked into patterns of behaviour that will ensure its survival. But it will be evident from what we have just said that, if one accepts that there are such things as contents of consciousness (or, less vulnerably) a 'what it is like to be this creature' or 'what it is like to be this creature here in a world that is there', no physicalist theory, functionalism included, will deliver anything that accounts for how things are for us.

If it were argued that sensations and perceptions are not given, or unscrambled, in isolation, it remains an article of faith that a collection of perceptions gives enough information for us to unscramble the experiences derived from the interaction between the body and the outside world and determine the contributions of the body and the world outside of the body.

And if it is extraordinary that we should have a sense of both the object out there (as the object of experience) and the body here as the subject of experience (even though both of those intuitions are mediated by the body), it is even more extraordinary that we are presented with:

a) both the body and the object as separate objects;
b) the relation of the body and the object to one another; and
c) each of these objects (body and thing out there) in a perspectival manner.

They are linked; but this makes it more, not less, amazing that they can be experienced, or attended to, separately. The presentation of the body in a relational mode to the perceived object – 'I am so many feet from the window' – is a particularly remarkable turning of the tables, in which the body experiences itself as an object on all fours with other objects. This is a long way from the body as the underpinning of a transparent here.

Even if there were some way of accounting for this structure of ordinary perception – how the simultaneous equations are solved while they are kept in play in both solved and unsolved forms – we should still be left unable to explain where the secondary qualities that make up the hum of (bodily) here are derived from. Not from the physical body, that is for sure. Or not anyway as it is described in physicalist thought.

We could characterise the explanatory gap in other ways. For example, the body does not seem to provide any basis for the ownership that is deeply implicated in human corporeal self-awareness, for the implicit 'my' in sensations, perceptions and thoughts; or for the ownership that has to be present inchoately in the elements of bodily consciousness in order that it may emerge explicitly in our sense of our embodied selves. This is an especially difficult puzzle to tackle because sensations are nascently, and human perceptions explicitly, of something other than the sensor: 'my' experience is of something that is 'not me'. The body, therefore, has to provide the basis not merely for here but for 'me-here' ('that it is I who am here') and 'me-here experiencing not-me-there';[72] and this is in the very structure of human consciousness: it cannot be put together or tacked together *a posteriori*. To put this another way: *consciousness* cannot *establish* here; it must *presuppose* here, possibly not as Kant's logical subject is presupposed in all perceptions, but in some respect.[73]

### 6.13 HERE AND I: SOME FINAL THOUGHTS

Experience of the world, ordinary life, requires that what is there should be there for someone who is here. Notwithstanding that it is a traditional mistake to conceive of 'what is there' as being primordially something like a material object and the basis of the here as being something like the bodiless (but by some mysterious dispensation located and localised) Cartesian subject, we do need an account of our existence that acknowledges the polarisation between myself and the world. While we may agree with Heidegger's view that the world we engage with is a nexus of meaning-saturated readies-to-hand rather than a sullen array of opaque meaning-free physical objects, the physical nature of the world – or the difference between the 'I' and much of the material of the world in which human life is lived – must be accommodated somehow. While we cannot get a here by inserting a disembodied subject in the material world, and while the conscious (or self-conscious) body is the only candidate for establishing the necessary here to address a specific there, to enable *Da-sein* to get a purchase on a particular *Da*, there is nothing in the body viewed as a physical organism to lead one to expect that it should be experienced, that it should be the basis of the experience of the world, or that it should have *those* particular experiences, and by this means pull *Da-sein* down to a particular *Da*. The 'hereness' of awareness must be connected with the body of the experiencing person but we do not know how.

The reason for making this connection between the 'I', 'here' and the body goes even deeper than the deep reason invoked by Strawson:

> for each person there is one body which occupies a certain *causal* position in relation to that person's perceptual experience, a causal position which in various ways is unique in relation to each of the various kinds of perceptual experience he has; and – as a further consequence – that his body is also unique for him as an *object* of the various kinds of perceptual experience which he has.[74]

This is to understate the depth, the intimacy, of the relationship between experience and the body. Without a body, there is no rationale for the location that is experienced and there is no basis for the reality of, ownership of and responsibility for the experiences. Since discarnate existence would establish no here on the basis of which things could be there, the notion of the person as a pure (bodiless) experiencer is nonsensical, even self-contradictory; for the experiencer would have to be in receipt of a set of experiences relevant to and constitutive of a view from a particular point in space and time and yet would not exist at a particular point in space and time. There would seem therefore to be no grounds for the individual to enjoy one set of experiences rather than another; nor (as a correlative of this) any restriction on the scope and content of that set of experiences.

So, the body is the essential bearer of here and yet seems very poorly qualified – or, in some respects, actively disqualified – for the job. Since, however, it does in fact do what is required of it – I am here as I type these words and, seemingly, courtesy of embodiment – there is interesting work to be done to make sense of the body's providing this essential condition of everyday life. One possible task for future epistemology is to try to understand how having, suffering (and enjoying) and being a body can be squared with, indeed underpin, being here. To put this in the terms that we associate in particular with Merleau-Ponty: we need to think how we might account for the fact that the living body is *lived*; how it is the basis of someone's being enworlded.[75]

Just how far we are from understanding this is demonstrated by the fact that we cannot identify what it is in the body that makes it the basis of the experience or why it should have those experiences – of colour, of warmth, of hatred, of hope, etc. To put this more accurately: we cannot connect our third-person knowledge of the (general) body with our first-person experience of embodiment and the experiences that are made possible apparently through embodiment. There is a gap in our knowledge: we lack knowledge of how knowledge and experience are connected with one another; how the former, perhaps, arose out of the latter. We shall have much more to say about this in Volume 3. For the present, we note that we cannot rule out the possibility that the body is *explicitly* here only through some other means that makes its physical location into its world; that, while the body 'tags' here, it is not of itself able to turn the physical coordinates of space into 'here' – a here that co-locates thoughts, bodily sensations, objects experienced as 'surrounding', etc., and the body itself.

The fundamental error in trying to find 'here' in the body, especially the body as seen through the eyes of objective science, for example, neuroscience, is that 'here' is an indexical that has no place in the third-person world of material objects. 'Here' cannot be understood except as one pole – the near pole – of egocentric space. No body, no here – that is certainly true. Equally, and perhaps more fundamentally, true is this: No ego, no here. 'Here' is inextricably linked with 'I'.[76]

In this context, this passage from *Being and Time* is of the greatest interest:

> W. V. Humboldt has alluded to certain languages which express the 'I' by 'here', the 'thou' by 'there' and the 'he' by 'over there', thus rendering the personal pronouns by locative adverbs ... It is controversial whether the primordial meaning of locative expressions is adverbial or pronominal. This dispute loses its basis if one notes that locative adverbs have a relation to the I qua *Da-sein*. The 'here', 'over there' and 'there' are not primarily pure locative designations in space but, rather, characteristics of the primordial spatiality of *Da-sein*. The supposedly locative adverbs are determinations of *Da-sein*; they have primarily an existential, not a categorial, meaning. But they are not pronouns, either. Their significance is prior to the distinction of locative adverbs and personal pronouns. The true spatial meaning of these expressions for *Da-sein*, however, documents the fact that the theoretically undistorted interpretation of *Da-sein* sees the latter immediately in its spatial 'being-together-with' the world taken care of, spatial in the sense of de-distancing and directionality. In the 'here' *Da- sein*, absorbed in its world, does not address itself, but speaks away from itself, in circumspection, to the 'over there' of something at hand and means, however, *itself* in its existentiality. (BT 112)

This is a brilliant exploration of the intimate relationship of 'I' and 'here'; so intimate, in fact, that they cannot be separated from each other: 'I' and indexical spatiality are inseparable because they are aspects of that *Da-sein* which is 'being-in' or 'being-in-the-world'. 'Here' cannot be isolated from the existence that is *Da-sein*.

It is hardly surprising that the neurophilosopher's attempt to find 'here' in an 'I-less' body – or a body approached from the viewpoint of deindexicalised objective science – is doomed to failure. The body will not form the basis of here unless it is someone's – namely, 'my' – body. There is one immediate, rather obvious, consequence of this: that the relationship between primordial 'here' and 'there' will be linked to the relationship between 'I' (or 'the self') and 'the world'.

This opens up a more important line of inquiry: whether, in fact, the 'I' has priority over the 'here'. While, for Heidegger, it is evident that 'I' and 'there' are equiprimordial, we may ask whether the sense of self takes the lead in the development of the 'I-here' pair. Or whether, at least, if we are to understand how the body comes to plant the flag of here in 'hereless, thereless' space, or to root *Da-sein* in a *fort* to give its disclosedness specific contents, we should lead with an investigation of the origin of the self or the I in the body.[77]

This is a question of pre-eminent concern for the overall inquiry of this book. The absolutely key notion is that of the Existential Intuition – 'That I am this ...', an affirmation of identity whose sides are linked by am, which does not have to be logically derived and cannot be empirically proved (or disproved). This may seem like a knockdown case for leading with 'I', as opposed to 'here', or giving the establishment of 'I' in the body priority over the body as the basis of 'here'. The prior establishment of 'here' seems at best to affirm a circularity – 'Here is where the body is and where the body is, is here' – whereas, as we shall see, the Existential Intuition reaches beyond the manifest circularity of 'I is I' to a quasi-synthetic, but none the less incorrigible, identity, 'I am this'. It is arguable that 'this' incorporates not only the body but also 'here'; for what is 'heremost' – or 'thismost' – other than the body which I am? In the 'this' of the Existential Intuition, here and the body are not clearly differentiated: they are given at once and as one.

We shall have much more to say about the Existential Intuition and its relation to the body as the basis of identity and of agency in the next two chapters. For the present, we note that, while we may envisage it in its primordial form as immediate, it unfolds (in the history of humanity and in the development of individuals) into a self with its cognate worlds that have many layers of here-there pairings. This Intuition, which lights up in and has, as its immediate content, the engaged human organism, takes humans far beyond the organic world. It is the moment of explicit indexicalisation (from a putative pre-indexical animal awareness) that leads, ultimately, to the deindexicalised or propositional awareness that is (as we shall discuss in Volume 3) the knowledge that humans alone possess. This deindexicalised, factual knowledge greatly expands the scope of here – from this body to this room to these streets to this country – and its correlative there that constitutes the almost boundless world in which we humans act out our lives. In its extreme form, it dispenses with 'here' and 'there' altogether. This extreme form is the deindexicalised discourse of science. It is hardly surprising, therefore, that we cannot find 'here' in the body looked at through the eyes of science.[78]

At any rate, we shall not find the basis of 'here' in the body so long as it is unhaunted by the identity of the embodied person. 'Here' and 'I', *Fort-sein* and identity, are inseparable. It is to identity, therefore, that we shall now turn.

NOTES

1. René Descartes, *Meditations on First Philosophy: Meditation VI*, in *The Philosophical Works of Descartes*, Vol. I, translated by Elizabeth Haldane and G. R. T. Ross (Cambridge: Cambridge University Press, 1967), p. 192. Some eminent Descartes scholars emphasise his backtracking on a sharp separation between body and mind. For example, John Cottingham: 'But if we want to understand what a human being is, as opposed to a kind of bloodless angel which just happened to be using a body (and this is a distinction Descartes often discusses), then we have to focus on bodily sensations and passions as key sources of evidence for the fact that we are not just minds inhabiting our bodies but are, as Descartes puts it, intimately united with them' (interviewed in Andrew Pyle (ed.), *Key Philosophers in Conversation*, The Cogito Interviews (London: Routledge, 1999), p. 224).
2. Ludwig Wittgenstein, *On Certainty*, ed. G. E. M. Anscombe and G. H. von Wright, translated by Denis Paul and G. E. M. Anscombe (Oxford: Basil Blackwell, 1969), para. 244, p. 32e.
3. I shall argue that to question the truth of sense experience is inadmissible because the contrast between truth and falsehood arises only when sentience has given rise to knowledge.
4. Like Heidegger, Merleau-Ponty rejected the schism between the subject and object of experience. Unlike Heidegger, he did so by embedding the subject in the body. For him, subjectivity is inseparable from embodiment. Merleau-Ponty was concerned that Hume, Kant, Sartre and many other philosophers overlooked the body: they were more Cartesian, more intellectualising, than they realised. He was not alone in this, of course. Dilthey too complained, as Peter Rickman has pointed out ('From Hermeneutics to Deconstruction: The Epistemology of Interpretation', in *The Challenge of Philosophy*, London: Open Gate Press, 2000, p. 128), 'as he looked at the history of epistemology culminating in Kant – that "no blood flowed in the veins of the cognitive subject"'. Merleau-Ponty's emphasis on the perspectival nature of knowledge is meant as a corrective to the Cartesian (and indeed post-Cartesian – Kantian and Husserlian) notion of the human subject as extricated from, transcending, the grubby world of things. We are on all fours with the things of the material world. As Eric Matthews has put it: 'the human subject [is] not a detached Cartesian "ego", but human beings who are part of the world that they experience, and who experience it, not in the form of pure contemplation, but in the course of active involvement with it' (*The Philosophy of Merleau-Ponty*, Montreal and

Kingston: McGill-Queen's University Press, 2002, p. 29). While Merleau-Ponty's influence on this chapter goes beyond any particular acknowledged borrowings, I disagree with him at key points. In particular, in his wish to reassert 'The Primacy of Perception' – embodied, perspectival – he underestimates the gap between sense experience and knowledge and the extent to which the latter has liberated itself from the former. Knowledge aspires to being aperspectival and sentience is pre-perspectival. I will discuss this in the final section of Volume 3.

5. And for Quassim Cassam, as we discussed in Chapter 4, this indissolubility is logical (or perhaps ontological) rather than merely psychological, and hence necessarily the case.

6. Elizabeth Anscombe, 'The First Person', in Samuel Guttenplan, *Mind and Language: Wolfson College Lectures, 1974* (Oxford: Oxford University Press, 1975), p. 61.

7. See Raymond Tallis, 'Carpal Knowledge', in *The Hand: A Philosophical Inquiry into Human Being* (Edinburgh: Edinburgh University Press, 2003).

8. This is true even of saliva. Paul Broks, in *In the Silent Land* (London: Atlantic Books, 2003), recounts an experiment one of his teachers asked him to take part in. He had to fill a glass with his own sputum and then consider whether he could bear to drink it.

9. Jean-Paul Sartre, *Nausea*, transl. Robert Baldick (London: Penguin, 1965).

10. Quassim Cassam, *Self and World* (Oxford: Clarendon, 1997), p. 63. Cassam cites an interesting passage from John Locke, where the latter argues that what makes a part of one's body a part of one's self, is that it is 'vitally united to this … thinking conscious self'. *Thinking* conscious self? When you touch my arm and my trousers touch my leg, are they both touching my thinking conscious self?

11. 'Final Causes', *Proceedings of the Aristotelian Society*, Supplemental Volume, (1971), pp. 149–70. See also Raymond Tallis, *On the Edge of Certainty* (Basingstoke: Macmillan, 1999). If, incidentally, the neural theory of consciousness were true, and neurones really were able mysteriously to import into our lives the qualitative experiences we actually enjoy, though they have no place in the material world of which (according to neurophilosophers) we are a part, we should have to conclude – more in sorrow than in anger – that the brain was a means by which the body was induced to lie to itself about itself!

12. John the Scot famously asserted that it is impossible for any sentient being (including God himself) to know its own nature. This makes intuitive sense. First, sentience as it were looks outwards: its objects (if there are any) are other than itself. Second, sentience is interactive and any awareness is it were contaminated. And third, and most importantly, knowledge is at a higher level than sentience and sentience cannot therefore arrive at knowledge of the knower. The Existential Intuition is not a piece of absolute knowledge: it settles for what it feels to be itself as itself. This is true not at the level of empirical knowledge but at the level that *gives rise to* or *creates the possibility of* knowledge. (We shall elaborate on these points in Volume 3.)

13. Material existence is not sufficient to be something in the way that I am my body. A pebble is entirely a pebble, but it does not know a pebble. Obviously. But more than this, it *is* not a pebble: it doesn't exist pebblehood.

14. And this is the deep meaning, and bottomless evil, of torture: the reduction of a human being to a suffering body; to a howling piece of violated meat.

15. And some times we inadvertently collude with the enemy through carelessness. The exquisite pain of a bitten tongue is particularly envenomed because it is inflicted on

one deeply personal part of our body (the chief sculptor of our words) by another that is, by virtue of its location, part of ourself and by virtue of its mineral insensibility and dispensability, part of the outside world, and the act takes place in the mouth which is, of all the accessible insides of our body, most ourselves.

16. It may be *inflicted* for the same reason: to make the person be as totally present as is possible, by reducing them to their tangible bodies. To say this is to glide over many issues of power – of humiliation and other abuses.

17. The layers of the appearance we suffer are multiple: feeling one is rather red-faced; appearing shifty while waiting for someone; looking old-fashioned; seeming foolish on a podium. In our 'take' on our appearance to others the mind and body merge.

18. See Gabriel Marcel's wonderful essay 'Outlines of a Phenomenology of Having', in *Being and Having* (London and Glasgow: Fontana, 1965). The translation is not attributed, which is a serious injustice because the translator has done an excellent job.

19. See *The Hand: A Philosophical Inquiry into Human Being* (Edinburgh: Edinburgh University Press, 2003), especially pp. 279–82.

20. This last example illustrates something that lies at the beginning of a long chain of developments in which natural events are exploited as signs; signs are made to be signs of the situations in which they are found; these meta-signs are used to signify signifying behaviour, etc. For a brief discussion of this, see *The Hand*, section 3.1.

21. Martin Heidegger, *Being and Time*, transl. Joan Stambaugh (Albany, NY: State University of New York Press 1996): 'When we discover its unusability, the thing becomes conspicuous. *Conspicuousness* presents the thing at hand in a certain unhandiness' (p. 68).

22. The following observation by Bernard Williams – from 'Mind and its Place in Nature' in his *Descartes: The Project of Pure Enquiry* (London: Penguin, 1977), p. 289 – is pertinent: 'Now it is a notable feature of our experience that our control over our limbs is not ballistic: we do not, unless partially paralysed, throw our arm at something on a desired trajectory, but rather reach out for a thing.'

23. Animals sometimes use their weight in this way (as in compressing foliage before settling down for the night); but this is simply part of a limited portfolio of tool-like behaviours that are not mediated though bodily self-consciousness that utilises the body-possession as an all-purpose instrument.

24. The following (Marcel, 'Outlines of a Phenomenology of Having', p.188) is of great interest: 'I really think that the idea of autonomy, whatever we may have thought of it, is bound up with a kind of reduction or particularisation of the subject. The notion of personal autonomy and the narrowing of the subject to a focal self are connected – through the instrumentalisation of the body.'

25. Just how complex bodily self-identity mediated through appearance may be, even when we are in solitude, is beautifully captured in this passage from Trollope's Miss Mackenzie: 'She moved up her hair from off her ears, knowing where she would find a few that were grey, and shaking her head, as though owning to herself that she was old; but as her fingers ran almost involuntarily across her locks, her touch told her that they were soft and silken; and she looked into her own eyes, and saw that they were bright; and her hand touched the outline of her cheek, and she knew that something of the fresh bloom of youth was still there; and her lips parted, and there were her white teeth; and there came a smile and a dimple, and a slight purpose of laughter in her eye, and then a tear. She pulled her scarf tighter across her bosom, feeling her own form, and then she leaned forward and kissed herself in the glass.'

26. Of course, there are many other less public ways in which we relate to our body as an object; as when, for example, we examine parts of it for signs of disease; or when we try to locate an itch by a method of trial and error; or when we deliberately warm a frozen part; or when we seek to give ourselves bodily pleasure by 'playing' with ourselves.
27. Cassam, *Self and World*, p. 67 points out the illegitimacy of this question.
28. Ibid. The quotation is from *Philosophical Investigations*. The use of the possessive with respect to the relationship between the body and its nose, by the way, strikes me as a little loose!
29. *Being and Time*, p. 211.
30. Paul Valery, *Monsieur Teste*, transl. Jackson Mathews (London: Routledge & Kegan Paul, 1973), p. 49.
31. 'Ignorance', in *The Whitsun Weddings* (London: Faber and Faber, 1964).
32. I have discussed one aspect of this mismatch – the gap between the ideas of (verbalised) events and the actual experience of them – in 'The Difficulty of Arrival', in *Newton's Sleep* (London: Macmillan, 1995).
33. Just how much knowledge is behind the minutest medical or biomedical fact is discussed in Raymond Tallis, *Hippocratic Oaths: Medicine and its Discontents* (London: Atlantic Books, forthcoming), where I compare a fact to one of the *nunataks*, little splinters of ice in the Antarctic that signal Everest-sized blocks beneath.
34. It is easier to be scornful about the claims I have to knowledge about, of, my body than it is to determine in a principled way the boundary between where I am and where I am not an authority on Raymond Tallis's body, Raymond Tallis's experience of his body and Raymond Tallis.
35. This is how Matthews expresses it in *The Philosophy of Merleau-Ponty*, p. 83.
36. This is not, of course, confined to the organic substrate of our lives. We are latecomers to, and belong to, a collective that has been evolving over many hundreds of thousands of years. Merleau-Ponty's central notion that 'humanity' is not just the name of a biological species but a term that stands for an idea that has to be created in the course of history, captures this other source, or dimension, of the impersonal in our lives.
37. Sprigge, *Proceedings of the Aristotelian Society*.
38. There is one very striking area of mismatch between knowledge of the body and the state of embodiment: the sense of the discrepancy between the size of one's body and the size of the world that one knows. This has always been apparent to humans looking on others from heights. The growth of science, however, has put figures on our relative insignificance – adding galaxies and billions of years to the framework within we have our spatio-temporal bodily being. The tension between the objective view of physical science and the egocentric view of the living human is captured in Valery's retort to Pascal's famous 'the eternal silence of the infinite spaces terrifies me'. Hmm, said Valery, 'the little hub-bub in the corner comforts me'.
39. It is interesting that an explicit awareness of the incompleteness of awareness lies at the heart of active inquiry. The sense of not-knowing, of there being something more to know, haunts knowledge. While a sense of ignorance permeates knowledge, the feeling of insentience does not permeate sentience – numbness does not permeate touch. This is because knowledge is linked with the sense of incompletely scrutable objects of knowledge – objects that exist in themselves. (Our own body, as we first noted, is the first such partially scrutable object.) Even our ordinary sensations

become, retrospectively, permeated by a sense of ignorance seeping in from the realm of knowledge. The caresses of 'knowing animals' are tactile inquiries.

40. Sprigge, *Proceedings of the Aristotelian Society*, p. 167.

41. P. F. Strawson, 'The First Person and Others', in Quassim Cassam, *Self-Knowledge*, Oxford Readings in Philosophy (Oxford: Oxford University Press, 1994), p. 214.

42. Richard Webster, *Why Freud was Wrong. Sin, Science and Psychoanalysis* (London: HarperCollins, 1995), p. 461.

43. 'For all these sensations of hunger, thirst, pain, etc. are in truth none other than certain confused modes of thought which are produced by the union and apparent intermingling of mind and body' (*Sixth Meditation. The Philosophical Works of Descartes*, transl. E. S. Haldane and G. R. T. Ross, Vol. I Cambridge: Cambridge University Press, 1967, p. 192). If only sensations *were* confused thoughts: toothache could be treated by allowing one's attention to drift. Alas, sensations command attention in such a way that one cannot disobey.

44. The reader might be interested in an account of the influence of Wittgenstein's fatal prostate cancer, and in particular its treatment with hormones, on his propensity to thought, in Raymond Tallis, *On the Edge of Certainty* (Basingstoke: Macmillan, 1999). All philosophers will have known that state of chronic tiredness in which one merely alludes to, or cycles, one's thoughts rather than thinking them.

45. I have discussed 'the progressive disembodiment of life' (including – or especially – labour) in 'The Work of Art in an Age of Electronic Reproduction', in *Theorrhoea and After* (Basingstoke: Macmillan, 1999).

46. Immanuel Kant, *Critique of Pure Reason*, transl. Norman Kemp Smith (London: Macmillan, 1964), p. 47.

47. I have here touched on matters that deserve much less superficial treatment than they have received here, if only because they are close to the fundamental preoccupations of the entire trilogy. I shall endeavour to treat them at the proper level in Volume 3, when I ask the question why it was that collective human awareness had to pass first through a theological phase before it arrived at scientific understanding.

48. I could not be mistaken as to who it is that is feeling sweaty but I could be mistaken as to whether it is sweatiness I feel.

49. A passage already quoted from Cassam is particularly relevant to the connection between the fantasy of disembodiment and the notion of the self as a succession of thoughts: 'it is one thing to show that the presented subject of tactile perception must itself be experienced as shaped and solid, but the idea that one is aware of the subject of one's thoughts as shaped and solid is an entirely different matter' (*Self and World*, p. 73).

50. Maurice Merleau-Ponty, *Phenomenology of Perception*, transl. Colin Smith (London: Routledge & Kegan Paul 1962), especially pp. 105–13.

51. Though, as Matthews points out, he criticised them for treating this as a contingent, empirical fact about perception, when it is necessary condition for calling anything a 'perception'.

52. There are, of course, many activities whose primary purpose is bodily experience. But even these so-called 'pleasures of the senses' are not entirely subsumed under the bodily sensations with which they are associated. Eating a meal, for example, is a social activity and the accompanying conversation may be as important as the tastes, textures and fragrances of the food. True lovemaking, the supreme expression of the pursuit of bodily self-enjoyment, is at least as important as a mode of communication between persons, and as a succession of highly symbolic interactions (signifying

acceptance, power, privilege, acknowledgement, etc.), as it is as a source of pleasurable bodily sensations. (See Raymond Tallis, 'Carpal Knowledge; Towards a Natural Philosophy of the Caress', *Philosophy Now* (September/October 2001): 24–7, for an account of this.) Other activities, such as sport and exercise, may be pursued at least in part for the bodily sensations with which they are associated, but these are also subordinated to their social or personal *significance*. In short, the pleasures of the senses, the delights of the flesh, are not simply about the sensations served up by our flesh. All pursue a mixture in varying proportions of proprioceptive experience, exteroceptive experience and symbol-mediated social interaction.

53. This is even more clearly evident when the 'object' touched is (the body of) another person. The signs of the person's awareness of the touch – so that they are touched in the sense of being *affected* – reinforce one's sense of being a toucher as well as of 'being in touch'.

54. Is this the intuition behind what Marcel referred to as 'the hegemony of the visual' for the Greeks? Touch is grubby and compromised in the way that seeing is not; the latter, moreover, is closer to an asymmetrical beholding, which leaves the beholder in a dominant position. Vision is further than touch along the path from sensation to knowledge; it is a 'purer' perception. This difference will be of great importance when we come, in Volume 3, to consider knowledge, a form of awareness unique to human beings. Vision, it must be added, can become comprehending only on the basis of the subject-object relationship awoken within the body by the tool-like hand.

55. Cassam, *Self and World*, p. 52. The older philosophers had a nice word for this: 'obstance'.

56. For a discussion of this – and for references to writers who defend Heidegger against the charge of idealism – see Raymond Tallis, *A Conversation with Martin Heidegger* (Basingstoke: Palgrave, 2002), in particular the Appendix.

57. Quoted Cassam, *Self and World*, p. 54.

58. See Tallis, *A Conversation with Martin Heidegger*, especially 'Darkness in Todtnauberg'.

59. This is in contrast to factual knowledge, which, as will be discussed in Volume 3, is a uniquely human mode of awareness, in which the subject is 'uncoupled' from the world to engage with it on more favourable terms.

60. Jonathan Cole, *Pride and a Daily Marathon* (London: Duckworth, 1991) describes paralysis experienced as a result of almost complete loss of proprioception. Another, more homely example of the interaction between sense of limb position and the initiation of movement is that of itching. Relieving an itch requires the involvement of motor activity in another part of the body to create a referent (Y. Iwamura, M. Tanaka and O. Hikosaka, 'Cortical Neuronal Mechanisms of Tactile Perception Studied in the Conscious Monkey', in Y. Katsuki, R. Norgren and M. Sato (eds), *Brain Mechanisms of Sensation*, New York: Wiley, 1981, pp. 61–73). According to standard neurophysiology, the reverse is also true: somatosensory activation is mediated by motor activity; stretching, etc. wakes me through feeding into the reticular formation of the brain stem which, in turn, activates the cerebral cortex.

61. Before leaving Heidegger on 'here' and 'there', it is worth noting this passage from *Being and Time*, which reminds us that the opposition between 'here' and 'there' does not map directly on to the contrast between 'nearer' and 'further' either in the objective physical sense or even in the sense of existential space: 'What is supposedly "nearest" is by no means that which has the smallest distance "from us". What is

"near" lies in that which is in the circle of an average reach, grasp and look. Since *Da-sein* is essentially spatial in the manner of de-distancing, its associations always take place in a "surrounding world" which is remote from it in a certain leeway. Thus we initially always overlook and fail to hear what is measurably "nearest" to us ... For someone who, for example, wears spectacles, which are distantially so near to him that they are "sitting on his nose", this useful thing is further away in the surrounding world than the picture on the wall across the room' (BT 99). The presence of here, or the basis of here, may not therefore be of something that is explicitly nearer than something that is there. This does not mean that here is not nearer than there but that the things that constitute the here, and pin thereness down to a particular there, may be less obtrusive than the elements of the there. Just as the 0,0,0 that establishes a frame of reference may be less obtrusive than the positions that acquire numbers within that frame of reference. Almost by definition, the background that platforms the here needs to be unobtrusive: the here is what is (almost but not quite) overlooked. This is why, in the discussion to come, we shall be so concerned that the body seems a little too obtrusive to provide the basis for here.

62. For the phenomenologists and for Heidegger this is not simply – or perhaps not at all – a matter of turning the objective location of the body into a subjective location, since objective location is a late entry on the scene. It belongs to the world of 'objective presences' at least in part brought into being by a 'rigid staring', and intellectualising gaze. I am not sure whether or not I agree with this view as to the respective priority of existential and physical space. See Tallis, *A Conversation with Martin Heidegger*, Appendix.

63. Actually, this is not quite accurate. The filmed spectacle is a there uprooted from a here; however, its presentation is dependent on another here – the here of one's body located in the room or the auditorium where one is watching the film. So the principle still stands: 'the hereless there' would be unreal.

64. This is crucial to the search for a non-circular way of differentiating real from pseudo-memories, which is in turn key to the notion of personal identity being based upon psychological continuity mediated by memory. (See Chapter 7.)

65. The itch itself, even unscratched, is complex: it is apodeictically 'my' itch, which captures its indeterminate position between 'here/me' and 'there/it'.

66. This is one of the most telling respects in which embodied I-here is different from the logical subject. The latter does not have any basis for engaging with particular places and particular times – especially if it is seen as transcendent.

67. The body's 'getting things right' and its caring for itself are regarded as two sides of the same coin in Darwinian and other biologically based pragmatist theories of truth. Truth is whatever promotes survival. I have criticised these views in *On the Edge of Certainty*, Chapter 1 'Explicitness, Truth and Falsehood' pp. 28 ff. and will return to them in Volume 3. At this juncture, it is relevant only to note that, if establishing here through bodily sensations and verifying the truth of the there and, on the basis of this, identifying and serving the needs of the body *were* fused, the human body would be like any other material body simply coupled to its material environment: the relationship between here and there would be collapsed.

68. Gareth Evans, quoted in Cassam, *Self and World*, p. 39.

69. The temporal depth of the here is also connected with the constraints on passage between heres. Cassam (ibid.) refers to Christopher Peacocke's noting the '*inter-temporal restrictions*' on self-location. There has to be a plausible audit trail linking the here one is in now with the here one was in a moment or two ago, an hour ago,

a day ago, and so on. To use Peacocke's example, this monument I am looking at now must be the one in London and not a similar monument in Dallas because I was in London a second ago and no feasible spatio-temporal path connects my being in London a second ago with my being in Dallas now.

70. The body is unsatisfactory as the basis for here for this further reason: sensations, like bodies, have too many things to do at once. For example, the rapid oppressive beating of my heart when I am anxious will make me be here as nothing else will; and yet at the same time, as the basis of an emotion, it has to refer beyond itself to something else, something possibly quite abstract – for example, the lecture I have to give in a few weeks' time. This dual role of sensations is, of course, exploited in psychoactive drugs: there is a significant overlap between the sensations associated with, say, the glow of satisfaction (appropriate to one who has achieved something or done a good deed), and those, say, associated with opiates. Drugs may therefore substitute for more conventional happiness: therein lies their potency; and therein lies their profoundly corrupting effect. They enable sensations or bodily experience equivalent to those associated with happiness or justified self-satisfaction to be uncoupled from any grounds for self-satisfaction or the right to happiness. It is interesting to speculate how exteroceptive, and even more particularly proprioceptive (especially visceroceptive), experiences are interwoven so closely with emotions that they comprise their immediate content. The relationship provides an interesting puzzle if only because the bodily accompaniments of emotions – for example, worry and embarrassment about a *faux pas* one has made or slight irritation at a sound one cannot easily interpret made by a nextdoor neighbour – seem only distantly connected with the meaning of the emotion, or what might be roughly called its referent, especially if that referent is conceived in propositional terms. This is reflected in the fact that the repertoire of physical accompaniments of emotions is greatly reduced compared with the almost infinity variety of things that may provoke emotions and which emotions may be 'about'. It is possible to arrange the emotions along a scale ranging from free-floating panic, which has predominantly physiological accompani- ments (fast heart beat, sweating palms, dry mouth, etc.) through to very specific, complex ones that chew themselves over in words and may be described as almost purely propositional. In between are emotions such as irritation which may have specific triggers (a file wiped off the computer) but which are not reducible to propositional attitudes. At no point along the scale is the relationship between the modes of heeding and their physiological or verbal accompaniments fully intelligible.

71. Sprigge, *Proceedings of the Aristotelian Society*. The lack of correlation between the physical appearance of the body and how it is experienced – what it is like to be it – is noted, at the most superficial level, by lovers who feel this uncertainty as a dark and frustrating mystery enveloping the beloved. It also frustrates those who would read character from bodily appearance and who discover as did Shakespeare that 'There's no art to read the mind's construction from the face'.

72. Made all the more complex by the fact that, in the 'musical *chairs*' we described earlier, the same bit of flesh may be at one time of the subject's party and at another an object.

73. One could be forgiven for patronising the body for doing such a good job of making 'I' be here considering how poorly designed it has been for the task imposed upon it. No one creating a basis for the sort of heres humans inhabit here would have started from here! This is not proof that we did not start from the body – only that very little

of our body had our humanity, with its multi-layered heres in mind. We are outposts of the biological world but biology gives very little clue to what we are now.

74. P. F. Strawson, *Individuals: An Essay in Descriptive Metaphysics* (London: Methuen, 1959), p. 9.

75. There is another twist in the tale, which I shall assign to a footnote lest I weary the reader by labouring too many complex amazements. We have noted the difficulty of finding the origin of secondary qualities – such as weightiness, warmth, colour, etc. – in the body. But our sense of being here is made even more secure (or weighs on us more heavily) in virtue of higher order qualities: tertiary qualities, such as feeling of pleasure and pain; or even quaternary qualities such as those that colour in emotions, propositional attitudes, factual knowledge, and so on. Where on earth they come from, Heaven alone knows. There is nothing in the body that would seem to qualify it as the place where matter should learn to matter so much and in this complicated way.

76. Or with the origin of the 'me' in my body, which may be thought of as 'I' arrived at as if from the outside, from the standpoint of another's gaze, half-objectified, as when I refer to myself in the course of saying something like 'Nobody likes me'. Or with 'myself' which makes of the 'I' a somewhat egregious possession of the half objectified I – sufficiently objectified, at any rate, to be able to have possessions, even if the possession in question is only itself!

77. I have said nothing about 'now' – the temporal indexical, analogous in some respects but not others to here. For Heidegger, time is more fundamental than space: '*Only on the basis of ecstatic and horizontal temporality is it possible for Da-sein to break into space*' (BT 337). 'The temporality of factical being-in-the-world is what primordially makes the disclosure of space possible ...' (BT 383). The temporal-isation of the body is no easier to understand than its localisation. The generation of 'now' is just as resistant to neurological or objective-physical understanding as the generation of 'here'. The absence of a discussion of time is therefore an omission – but not an accidental one. It is just that, at present, I have nothing useful to say about 'now'.

78. What extraordinary adventures of the spirit and of thought are to be had from just being ordinarily alive, if one thinks about one's own body in a manner that is free of scientism and theological prejudices.

# CHAPTER 7

# Personal Identity: What I Am

## 7.1 INTRODUCING PERSONAL IDENTITY

The outcome of the discussion so far has been disappointing; we have ended with even more questions than we faced at the outset and many more than we could answer, even in a preliminary way. We have come no nearer to dissolving the clot of mystery at the heart of embodiment; on the contrary, embodied *Fort-sein* seems more densely clotted – or tightly knotted – the closer we examine it. More worryingly, we have ended with something close to a paradox. On the one hand, we found it to be necessary, in order to establish *Fort-sein*, and thus be specified, that *Da-sein* should be inextricably associated with a material body; in fact, a living human body. On the other hand, it was not easy to see how such a body could actually create the basis of 'here'. 'No body, no here' – certainly; but the human body did not seem to have the wherewithal in itself to create a here: 'to plant the flag' in whatever there is prior to *Da-sein* and identify itself as the centre of the *lebenswelt* of an individual. Something else was needed to make this body deliver 'here'.

This 'something else' is the *appropriation* of the body by the sentient creature whose body it is as *itself*. The here-ness of the body is rooted in the 'I-ness' of the body; that is to say in the Existential Intuition through which the engaged, aware human body assumes itself as itself; through which 'I' starts to awaken in the body so that it ultimately encounters itself as 'embodied'. The body can become here – and its background hum underwrite 'here' – only if it is already the body of *someone*. The body cannot underpin here unless there is an additional (more fundamental) intuition that 'I am this' – more precisely, I am this (phenomenal) body within the objective body. Deixis, the indexical view, the particular world, does not otherwise come packaged with the body: the organism *qua* organism does not provide it. 'Here' is an aspect of 'me-here', established through the *appropriated* body, and cannot exist independently of it. This body is 'here' only if *I* am, in some degree, this body which then defines (to a greater or lesser extent) the 'here' where I am.

Characterising in precisely what sense I *am* this body has proved rather difficult. Happily, it is not the purpose of the present chapter to take this any further, though it is crucial to an understanding of ourselves as both human agents and biological entities and much important work remains to be done. Our focus in this chapter will still be on 'I', but we shall approach it through the elusive notion of 'personal identity'. In the course of an attempt to characterise this rather slippery phenomenon (concept/entity), I shall correct what I believe to be a misplacement of emphasis in the writings of some philosophers who have addressed this mystery of first-person being. Centrally, I shall argue that a philosophical account of personal identity must focus not only on the endurance of the 'I' over time – the preoccupation of much of the literature – but also what it is that makes the 'I' be something that is here and now, that exists at a given time, and that the latter should be given priority. However disembodied the self – viewed as a mode of human being enduring over time – may become, enduring selfhood is unthinkable without instantaneous, moment-by-moment selfhood, and the latter is rooted in bodily existence and the special relationship of human being to the human body.

In philosophical discussion, 'personal identity' does not have a single, clear-cut meaning and the 'problem of personal identity' (or of the self or personhood) encompasses more than one puzzle. These meanings and puzzles are difficult to disentangle, not the least because they have deep connections. Attempts to characterise, or give an account of, or defend the notion of, personal identity try to answer a variety of questions.

## What thing am I?

This question is different when it is something I pose of myself – when I am looking at the problem from within – from when it is posed of selves in general. Philosophers are concerned, of course, with the general question. If we settle for the general (third-person) form of the question – 'What x corresponds to an 'I'? – this can elicit different sorts of answers, depending on whether one is asking 'Which particular x am I?' (numerical identity) or 'What kind of x am I?' (type identity). There is another sort of answer if one asks a general question – What sorts of things are persons? – as opposed to a singular question about me, asked as it were, from 'within'.

### In virtue of what am I the same x over time?

This, too, can have different sorts of answer, depending on how the question is interpreted. It is important, for example, to distinguish criteria for sameness of identity from criteria for identification of something as the same thing and these from 'sufficient clues' to enable one to be confident that this is the same thing (and not, say, another thing like it). Here are some interpretations:

(i)   What enduring *de facto* characteristics make me the same x?
(ii)  What makes others believe/think I am the same x over time?
(iii) What makes *me* think/feel I am the same x over time?

And these, in turn, prompt other questions, such as:

(i)   What makes it justified for either me or any one else to think that I am the same x over time?
(ii)  Is such justification necessary or even possible?

This can prompt yet further inquiries. For example: Am I 'the same x' if I think that I am? If I believe that I am the same I, can anything overturn that belief? Is this belief invulnerable in the way that the Existential Intuition is invulnerable – because it is a manifestation of the Intuition? If it is invulnerable, is it because it is self-affirming in the way that Cartesianly preferred thoughts are? Or is the self-affirming truth of the belief something to do with the internal relationship between the senses and/or referents of the three instances of 'I' in the sentence 'I believe that I am the same'?

I have no ambition to answer these different questions or even to determine the relationships between them. They are listed only to reassure the reader that I am not unaware of the complexity of the territory we are entering. This complexity was prefigured in the unsatisfactory discussion we had on the scope of first-person authority. It seems difficult, perhaps impossible, to determine where the last word is to be found on a) which particular I am, and b) what kind of thing that particular is. This is especially so, since the 'what' questions are of many different kinds: they may range from 'Am I a body or a succession of thoughts?' to 'Am I a male human being?' to 'Am I a citizen of the United States?' to 'Am I the tallest person in Stockport?' They include, in other words, all-encompassing constitutive features of me, certain apparently key characteristics, and accidental attributes. As we move from the former to the latter, the locus of authority naturally moves from the first person to the third person: we leave the realm of existed identity for that of third-person facts.

The problem, of course, is that there is no principled way of drawing a line between essential constituents and accidental attributes, between those judgements about oneself that fall under first-person authority and those where the last word is to be had elsewhere, between those that are true in virtue of existential assumption and those that are vulnerable to empirical challenge. Nor, to compound the problem, do we have secure reasons for assuming that, even if we could define these dividing lines, all three coincide. While it is obvious that the authority I enjoy as to the fact that I am embodied does not extend to the fact that I am male; what authority I do enjoy over that fact (which has extended in recent years; 'identity politics' has construed 'maleness' as an aspect of identity that the individual has the final say over) does not extend to my citizenship of the United States or my being the tallest person in Stockport.

What follows, therefore, is necessarily simplified and, in our discussion, we shall glide over many of the more difficult questions as to the *scope* of first-person identity.

## 7.2 ENTITY AND IDENTITY

Since Thomas Reid, many philosophers have pointed to what they believe to be a crucial difference between the notion of identity when we use it with respect to humans and the notion when we use it with respect to things, events, collections of objects, abstract objects, etc. Humans or persons have an identity that has an inner aspect and this 'inner aspect' is primary: personal identity is, in some sense, self-creating. As we have already noted, 'amhood' is rooted in an assumption that is unassailable (though the limits of what it unassailably specifies are difficult to define), such that external criteria are secondary. Third-person objects, by contrast, have an identity that exists only through being *conferred*.

Consider this conferred identity of material objects. The heap of matter on the table over there can be specified as 'a bowl full of pebbles' or specified pebble by pebble. The category under which this matter falls counts – or, more precisely, *is counted* – as one or more objects. The conferred general identity then determines the number of entities that we are talking about: one bowl of pebbles or, say, a dozen objects, consisting of one glass bowl and eleven pebbles. No physical object comes packaged with its own boundaries, except in so far as it is experienced or described as falling under a certain category; that is to say, except in so far as it is a referent or an intentional object. The general category under which it falls selects which of its many possible boundaries are relevant. It is this boundary that makes it count as *one*, as individual (that is, undivided as well as singular), and as the individual that it is. This is not a nominalist, even less a linguistic idealist, position. I am not saying that the material world does not dissect itself; only that it has many planes of cleavage and that categorisation is necessary to select which one is to be operative. This identification of the object as an individual, its uprooting from a number of possible configurations, in some of which it counts as a part, in others as a whole and in yet others as more than the whole, therefore in part generates the criteria for determining whether identity has been preserved or lost over time. (I say 'in part': the Sorites Paradox, of which more presently, underlines the systematic vagueness of objective criteria for the identity of objects that do not pick themselves out.) Once an externally imposed general identity – a 'what' – has been picked out as an entity, the entity thus dissected out – the full bowl of pebbles or a single pebble – has an identity which can be sustained by relative persistence over time or lost through change. Lack of change, inertia, is sufficient to secure enduring identity. This renders it amenable, too, to be identified and re-identified. To put this another way: only when we have defined the general kind, the 'what' of the 'this' we are referring to, does it count as one thing that can then be tracked, and carry a history which may be a history of its endurance or disappearance.

Strawson makes an interesting point when he argues that 'we need ... general principles of identification for *particulars* because *particular* individuals do not have *individual essences*',[1] which could be used to settle identity questions, such as whether this object is or is not a tree (type or qualitative identity) and whether it does or does not count as the same tree (token or numerical identity). The criteria will not be the same, though the reason for having to apply such criteria will be: one could think of an individual object, as some philosophers have claimed, as amounting to an entire class of token appearances. What is rather more contentious is Strawson's assertion that abstract or general things do have individual essences which are in most cases 'captured by, or are identical with, the *sense* of some adjective or common noun or verb, or with that of the relevant abstract noun, if there is one'. Because the individual essence of the general thing constitutes its individual identity, 'there is no need of a *common* general principle for all the general things of some more general kind to which the given general thing belongs'.[2]

Denying intrinsic identity to individual objects is fine; but ascribing intrinsic identity to general types is rather odd in several ways:[3] it 'tokenises' these types; it overlooks that they are intensional linguistic meanings expressed in general terms rather than extensional referents; and, above all, it seems to personalise them. I would like to argue that it is as true of general types as it is of material objects, that, since they do not *experience* or enjoy their identities, they do not *have* them either. To put it another way, they do not, of themselves, have an identity: the boundary is drawn from without and is not internal or internalised; it is neither asserted nor even received. The general principle this illustrates – it applies as much to words and their meanings as it does to lumps of matter – is that identity (and the presumption of the possibility of identification and re-identification) arises only in the context of the prior determination of *entity*. Intrinsic identity belongs only to self-identifying entities and the latter presupposes self-identification. To anticipate, neither the pebble nor the bowl of pebbles has a *self* or (to remove any ambiguity) even an *itself*. To ascribe (intrinsic) identity to material objects or general types is, effectively, to ascribe selfhood to them.

Consider my identity, my being Raymond Tallis. This has, and necessarily has, an inner aspect. The identity that I have, the persistent feeling that I am myself, cannot, moreover, be conferred from without. The Existential Intuition cannot be substituted for by external attribution – though an external aspect may be important for the stabilisation of the content of my sense of my identity, not least by depositing that sense in others' expectations of me, and so enabling me to encounter it in part from without. Ultimately, however, the boundaries of personal identity – of identity *tout court* – have to be self-drawn. This essential characteristic of moment-to-moment identity will also characterise identity over time: mere continuation, lack of change, pebble-like inertia, will not suffice to underpin continuing personal identity. While *something* has to endure, the (objective) endurance of something will not be enough to secure continuation of identity: some degree of unchangingness will be a necessary but not a sufficient condition of retention of identity, because it will not be sufficient for having identity at all.

The ultimate source of personal identity is the Existential Intuition: it will have therefore to be continuously *assumed* (in the twin senses we introduced in Chapter 1), asserted, lived. Without this assumption, endurance of some*thing* (for example, Raymond Tallis's body) cannot count as the endurance of some*one*. This is in part captured in Fichte's assertion that 'the "I" is not a fact but an act'.[4] 'Act' is too strong – something like a 'middle voice' is required; but Fichte correctly senses that the continuation of some objective state of affairs is not sufficient to underwrite the continuation of personal identity *over time* because it is not sufficient to underwrite personal identity *at any given time*. Not only is it insufficient; it is in a sense irrelevant: I do not confer identity on myself, or have the notion that I am a self, that I am I, as a result of my observing that I meet certain (objective) criteria for being a self or for being I or for being the same self or the same I.

'That I am (this thing)' is an assumption – in both logical and existential senses – that is close enough to 'That I am I' to require no instantaneous external validation. There is no gainsaying the Existential Intuition, even though its contents are not voluntarily chosen: there can be no question that this pain is mine. The Existential Intuition lies at the root of the transformation of the body from a something into a someone, from an organism to the embodiment of an I or a self.

### 7.3 INSTANTANEOUS AND ENDURING IDENTITY

What makes for personal identity (over time) must grow out of what it is that makes a self be a self *at any given time*; for without the instantaneous self there would be no enduring self. To put this another way: the enduring self is built up out of the moments of the instantaneous self. Not in the literal sense of course; for beyond (as we shall later discuss) a very primitive stage of development, the moments of the self are implicitly or explicitly lit from many corners of the experienced past, the imagined future and the surrounding world. Even so, the enduring self cannot be envisaged without presupposing instantaneous 'selving'. An investigation of the notion of personal identity that focuses exclusively, or even primarily, on what it is that makes me have the same identity, or count as being the same person, at two separate times – the focus of quite a bit of the philosophy of the self in recent decades – will miss the essence of personal identity.

Here is a typical expression (by Richard Swinburne) of the philosophical inquiry into personal identity:

> There are two philosophical questions about personal identity. The first is: what are the logically necessary and sufficient conditions for a person $P_2$ at time $t_2$ being the same person as a person $P_1$ at an earlier time $t_1$, or, loosely, what does it mean to say that $P_2$ is the same person as $P_1$? The second is: what evidence of observation and experience can we have that a person at $P_2$ at $t_2$ is the same person as $P_1$ at $t_1$ (and how are different pieces of evidence to be weighed against each other)?[5]

In his piece on 'Personal Identity' for the *Cambridge Encyclopaedia of Philosophy*, Sydney Shoemaker, who has profoundly different views about the nature and origin of the self from Swinburne, none the less agrees with him on this central point: he defines personal identity as 'the (numerical) identity over time of persons'.[6]

Questions about how the self or the person endures over time must be secondary to questions about the instantaneous person or self which may then endure or not endure. Even if this ordering of priorities is rejected, as simplistic, or unintelligible, it must surely be recognised that the self or personal identity has two dimensions: (i) the instantaneous, and (ii) the enduring. These I shall designate as the 'vertical' and 'horizontal' dimensions of personal identity.

The vertical dimension of personal identity is an *assumption* of identity with something. Because it is assumed rather than discovered, derived or proved, the instantaneous self neither has, nor requires, criteria. It is invulnerable to disproof by the same token as it is not susceptible of proof. I am what I feel myself to be – within the (indefinable) bounds of what we called in Chapter 3 'subject truths'. I cannot be mistaken over the fact that I am (that is to say that I am a self, that I have an identity) or that 'I am this ...' where 'this' is whatever is experienced directly as opposed to mediated through knowledge or discourse. The horizontal dimension of identity – endurance of personal identity over time – may also be *assumed* by the individual in question. 'That I am *the same* this' may, under some circumstances, or in some senses, be open to correction and, unlike instantaneous identity, is the kind of thing to which it makes sense to apply criteria. (What those criteria are and how strictly they should be applied and who shall apply them are other matters to which we shall return.) As a thousand thought experiments have demonstrated, we may be mistaken as to whether or not a particular criterion for having an unchanged objective identity is met. The kind of evidence that philosophers suggest may be invoked to support the belief that the criteria *are* met includes a) the inner experiences of the person of herself; b) her 'outer' observations – of her body and its circumstances; and c) the necessarily 'outer' observations of others, which will include observations not only of her bodily appearance but also of her behaviour. None is immune from error. My (fallible) judgement that I am the same person at time $t_2$ as I was at time $t_1$, in other words, must therefore be separated from my (ungainsayable) sense that I am 'myself' now, notwithstanding that 'now' has continuously changing temporal coordinates. At any given time, I am my self, I am I; but the extent to which the self, or the I, at any given time is the same self as at another time, may vary, depending on external criteria to be applied. 'That I am this' is invulnerable. 'That I am *the same* this' may be vulnerable, depending on the criteria deployed to determine what counts as 'the same this'. While instantaneous identity is assumed, continuing identity is (in some sense) *conferred* after the judgement that something has not changed. By the same token, it may be withheld.

My own (moment-to-moment – we never miss out on a moment of our own lives!) sense of my identity is therefore both of something changing and of something unchangeable; your judgement of my identity, on the other hand, may be of something relatively unchanged or relative changed or, indeed, changed out of all recognition and no longer there at all. The unchanging element is not guaranteed and is never absolute. We may represent these two dimension of identity as follows:

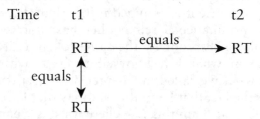

Distinguishing these two dimensions of personal identity shows why enduring objective characteristics are not sufficient on their own to underwrite enduring personal identity. They cannot underwrite enduring identity because they do not of themselves create instantaneous identity. That is why a pebble, which has exemplary steadfastness and would always be recognised as the same pebble, does not have an enduring intrinsic identity because it does not have intrinsic identity. Its identity or identities is/are entirely *conferred* and are relative to the viewpoint of others, and *a fortiori*, relative to the way it is described: 'a pebble', 'a paperweight', '[part of] the beach', '[part of] desk clutter', etc. Left to itself, the pebble is identityless and, for this reason, not a definite entity. Lacking instantaneous selfhood, its unchangingness does not qualify it for enduring selfhood or unchanging identity.[7] By contrast, a human being can retain identity in the face of radical changes that would make her unrecognisable to others or even to herself, in every waking state – to the edge of sleep or coma or to the very end stages of Alzheimer's disease, so long as she has not been reduced to mere sentience.[8]

We could summarise by saying that the vertical dimension of the instantaneous self is necessary if we are to find the 'id' in 'id-entity'. Without this, we have at best mere 'entity' and it remains questionable whether even 'entityhood' exists without an external viewpoint to dissect the bearer of entityhood as 'one thing' as an in-dividuum.

### 7.4 THE EXISTENTIAL INTUITION AND THE ENDURING SELF

As we discussed in Chapter 1, the Existential Intuition can be formulated in a variety of different ways. Likewise, the instantaneous self could be captured in a variety of formulae:

'I am'
'I am this'
'I am this thing'
'I am this entity'.

None of these is satisfactory, if only because the instantaneous self is not a proposition or to be captured in one.

The first formulation, however, seems especially deficient: the self that I am at any moment must be *defined* in some way. Hence the need to add something to the right-hand side of the assertion of existence. The subject needs a complement. A complement is not, of course, an object – that would be too 'external' – nor is it a mere predicate – that would be insufficient. It is close to an internal accusative or a cognate. The verb 'to be' is not fully transitive nor is it fully intransitive: it does not take an external object, but hangs unsatisfied without alighting on some kind of object. (These observations are meant not as observations of conventional grammar but as points of existential grammar.) To offer the verb only the reiteration of its subject – 'I am I' – seems too purely tautological: this is a tautology with no content, a bare logical form, like 'A is A'. It does, however, capture the *iterative* element in identity.

'I am myself' is likewise a little too sealed off from specificity. While it seems to offer more than bare tautology and to import something like substance into the left hand of the equation from the right hand, the formula does not move far enough away from mere iteration that would entrain nothing substantive or definite, unless 'myself' is further specified. The 'I' has to get a purchase on something definite if the Existential Intuition is not to shrink to a bare tautology. Hence 'I am this' or 'I am this thing' or 'I am this entity'.

'This thing' and 'this entity' are to be preferred to an unqualified 'this' because they highlight the demonstranda beyond the demonstrative. There is more than unfocused, or uncommitted, word-waving. While 'this' puts out a little way from the 'I' – it appears to offer a kind of reflexive pointing – the loop of the reflection, however, is not long enough to enclose anything. We need something more. 'Thing' and 'entity' provide this: they are placeholders that designate in the most general sense what 'this' is. They designate, in the most general sense, what it is that is assumed in instantaneous person identity.

The question then arises as to the nature of the 'thing' or – so as not to pre-empt the outcome of the discussion – the 'entity' which is assumed in the instantaneous identity. Whatever the thing/entity is, identification with it must be absolute, otherwise the tautological nature of the relationship is lost and identity goes begging. This raises a central problem: What am I able to assume, to appropriate to myself, *in toto* in order to specify my instantaneous identity? Our discussion over the last few chapters has pointed to one very obvious candidate: my body. The trouble with this is, as we have discovered, that my relationship to my body is rather tortured and complex. To oversimplify for the present: I am not the whole of my body at any time; nor am I at any time any part of my body wholeheartedly. The next most likely candidate would be certain bodily sensations or (given the need for self-consciousness to identify the self with an object in the 'weighty' sense) my body as revealed in an instantaneous cluster of sensations. This seems plausible if the sensations are seen as somehow merging into a single entity, which may be roughly identified with the 'phenomenal body' or 'the instantaneous body schema'. This, however, does not address the fact that we are never entirely identified with our body: our body, as we noted, all but vanishes in 'absorbed coping' (which is more often than not addressed to rather complex, abstract, frames of reference) and there is something called thought which, for all that it cannot survive prolonged toothache, is very difficult to dissolve without residue into something like a body schema.

We shall set aside this problem of delineating the instantaneous complement of personal identity to avoid going round the same circles we started to lap in the previous chapter; for the present, we need only note that the identity is absolute rather than relative: I am that I. Diagrammatically, we may show it like this:

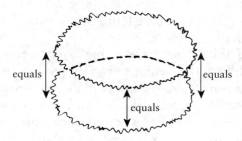

*The Absoluteness of Instantaneous Identity*

The Existential Intuition has no truck with rough approximations. Iteration in *id*-entity is complete, even though what it is that is iterated is volatile and blur-edged. 'I am (absolutely) this' not 'roughly' this. Identity permits no relative identification, no degrees of realisation. (This was first pointed out by Reid, with respect to personal identity – the only true form of identity according to him – and we shall return to it.)

At the same time, what is iterated has to have some substance, if the self is not to end up as something like a mere logical subject.[9] The iteration 'That I am ...' which is necessary to transform a mere entity into an identity has to assimilate a slice of the *de facto*: it is a fusion of the merely *de facto* with what would be otherwise merely logical subject, creating something assumed by a substantive subject as itself. The self has to have substantiality, specificity, content, in order to become an object of consciousness; without substantiality, the inner gaze of self-consciousness would pass straight through.[10]

The absolute iteration of something that is only relatively unchanged makes for the seeming paradox that the 'vertical' dimension of identity is not affected by even radical changes in the self: 'That I am this ...' is invulnerably iterated by RT even when, as in the very late stages of Alzheimer's disease, all who know me would be unanimous in asserting that 'RT is no longer himself'. While Mrs Tallis may assert that RT is 'No longer the man I married' or 'No longer the husband I have been married to for thirty years', RT is, so long as he is alive and aware, himself and absolutely so. He is no longer the person that Mrs T knew as her husband, but he is himself, and a person, whatever the solitary hell to which his cognitive collapse has confined him.[11]

The horizontal dimension of identity by contrast *is* relative. We could represent this contrast as follows:

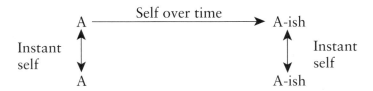

It is to the horizontal dimension that we must now turn.[12]

## 7.5 THE PERSISTENCE OF SELF: PERSONAL IDENTITY OVER TIME

The horizontal dimension of identity is the persistence over time of 'a something is a someone', 'a what that is a who': Raymond Tallis, who is in some vital respect the same at $t_2$ as he was at $t_1$. The questions that have occupied centre stage in much recent philosophical discussion of personal identity are these:

a) What kind of entity must persist in order to underpin the enduring self?
b) How true does this entity have to remain to itself in order to count as persisting sufficiently to deliver enduring identity?

Or:

a) In what does the endurance of the self subsist?
b) How much change can be tolerated in this substrate before it is declared that identity has been lost or changed?

Although we have argued that the horizontal dimension, endurance over time, is a secondary manifestation of identity, with the instantaneous assumption of I-hood being primary, these questions are of immense importance; for the enduring self lies at the heart of what we feel ourselves to be and is a necessary prerequisite of planning for the future, taking responsibility for the past and being an ethical and directed human being. While instantaneous identity is retained even in delirium – when one thing follows another in rapid and bewildering succession and life is a multi-coloured blizzard of disconnected experiences – much (but not all) of what constitutes substantive person-hood is nearly lost.

The immemorial answers to the question of what it is that, by persisting, underwrites or constitutes enduring personal identity are either

a) an immaterial substance such as the mind or the soul; or
b) a material entity such as the human body or (more recently) the human brain.

Souls have largely disappeared from the philosophical discussion of identity, mainly because they have come to seem too deeply implicated in a religious framework which it was impossible to redeem from thickets of confusion. To accept the notion of a soul was to take on board too many other assumptions about the nature of man, his origin, his destination and his place in the universe. Souls also provide very unsatisfactory answers to what are increasingly regarded as essentially empirical questions about the self – or questions about an empirical self.

David Hume's report of his failure to discover any distinctive intro-spectable thing corresponding to his self has driven much subsequent discussion:

There are some philosophers who imagine we are every moment intimately conscious of what we call our *self*; that we feel its existence and its continuance in existence; and are certain, beyond the evidence of a demonstration, both of its perfect identity and simplicity ...

Unluckily all these positive assertions are contrary to that very experience which is pleaded for them ... For my part, when I enter most intimately into what I call *myself*, I always stumble on some particular perception or other, of heat or cold, light or shade, love or hatred, pain or pleasure. I never can catch *myself* at any time without a perception, and never can observe anything but a perception.[13]

Since, at any rate, the soul was unchanging as well as immortal, and since it entered the body when the latter was still *in utero*, it was difficult to see how it could become the basis of something so manifestly changing (as well as in some respects unchanging) as a human self – at least as it was discovered to introspection. Souls do not reflect the '-ish' in the horizontal dimension ('A = A-ish') of identity. If the soul still has a place in the discussion of the enduring self, it is in the guise of a logical subject, the 'I think that accompanies all my perceptions', 'the transcendental ego', etc. In short, it can retain its place only by shedding (specific) content.[14]

As for the body, we have seen that it does not of itself provide the ownership, the sense of me-here, that lies at the heart of personal identity. Or not, at least, if it is viewed as a third-person material, organic object. This is not, of course, the whole story of the body. Moreover, the body is central to the identity we have for others, to *their* sense of our enduring identity, and consequently to that part of our own sense of our enduring identity that we derive from others' awareness of ourselves. The role of the body in 'tagging' experiences and connecting them with self-consciousness goes very deep indeed. Self-consciousness is inseparable from the notion of one's self as an object in the 'weighty' sense – that is to say, as capable of being both perceived and existing unperceived. This object, since it is something that one is aware of as one's self, must at the very least be a sentient being, in other words, a living organism. The centrality of bodily existence to self-consciousness, therefore, is established.

For the present, however, we shall focus on an idea that has dominated theories of personal identity since it was first put forward by John Locke. This inner aspect theory sets aside both enduring immaterial beings such as souls and enduring material things such as bodies in favour of psychological continuity through memory. As a basis for the persistence of the self over time, memory seems a kind of halfway house between an immaterial soul and a material body. (Indeed, for mind-brain theorists, it combines the two: psychological continuity is embedded in the enduring characteristics of the configuration and activity of the brain.) It is attractive for another reason: memory is both a heaped-up treasure trove which may provide evidence to others that a person is the same person and an internal link that reveals the enduring sameness over time to the person herself. It seems to be part of the experience of continuing identity and that by which it is demonstrated: memory is both constitutive and epistemic.

### 7.6 ENDURING IDENTITY OVER TIME: INNER-ASPECT THEORIES

While the quasi-tautology of the instantaneous self is absolute (analogous to 'A = A'), the persistence of identity over time is relative: it has the form 'A = A-ish'. The scope or laxity permitted by the '-ish' will depend on what counts as a significant difference. Some '-ish' is essential, if only because the world(s) that selves inhabit (and create) change(s) with time. What is more, selves are continuously developing. Learning and the acquisition of skills are changes in one's self; indeed, to experience anything is to be changed in some degree. The self over time cannot be absolutely self-same over time: life itself subsists in change; to live is to be changed. Consequently, A and A-ish (e.g. RT at time $t_1$ and RT at time $t_2$) can never be objectively identical even when they are separated by small intervals of time. Given that change reaches to the heart of the self, there must be tolerance of change and a theory of the self based on psychological continuity across – on memory – is therefore intuitively very appealing. The persisting self must be forged out of those 'fugitive impressions' that Hume identified as the only things he could find when he looked for his self. Fugitive impressions are caged by being converted into memories. Memories endure: they can be accessed, and be influential, long after the experiences that gave rise to them took place. Because they endure, they also add up: there is at any given time a large corpus of memories that is relatively little changed by the new experiences enriching their stock or by the loss of old memories which have decayed through time. While old memories will be lost and new memories laid down, there will, at any given moment, be a huge overlap between its body of memory and that of the previous moment – or day – or year – sufficient to ensure that RT at $t_1$ and RT-ish at $t_2$ will both count, and be counted, as RT. The overlap, moreover, is greater if memory is not construed too narrowly. It should include not only episodic memory of events in one's life, or declarative memory (such as of facts one can recite), but also the memory implicit in completed learning which may be present in skills, expectations, daily routines one has got used to, responsibilities and duties one assumes, habits and character traits. In the end, however, it is authenticated episodic memory that forms the bedrock of personal identity. (Of this, more presently.)

To put it another way: there is a large 'deposit account' of past experience that is proportionately little changed by moment-to-moment transactions in the 'current account' of experience. The small change of moment-to-moment experiences, and the moment-to-moment changes that occur in the self, are as it were cancelled by the relative stability of the accumulated heap of the personal past available in memory.

The overlap between the corpora of memory at successive times is the link between what it is to be myself at any given time and what it is to be the same self over time; between the Existential Intuition 'That I am this (here, now)' and the fact of my being a more-or-less unchanging self which is evident to different degrees to others and to myself. The slippage – the difference between mere overlap on the one hand, and on the other stasis or absolute or precision iteration – marks the difference between the I that changes and the unchanging fact that 'I am this …'.

The heap of memories does, however, change and the question then arises as to how much change should be tolerated before the self should be considered to have changed so radically as effectively to have passed out of existence – at least as *that* self. This has been the focus of much of the recent discussion of theories of identity based upon the psychological continuity.[15] Philosophers investigating the notion of personal identity within the framework of Locke's suggestion that personal identity inheres in psychological continuity over time as guaranteed by memory have encountered two problems. The first is that there is very little immediate recall of the remote past. The direct memory connections between me now and my childhood are few and far between: an atoll of recollection in an ocean of oblivion. And yet neither I nor anyone else doubts that I am the same person as the RT of 10, 20, 30, 40 or 50 years ago. I am (to highlight the forensic concern that prompted Locke's inquiries into selfhood in the first place) still responsible for his (my, earlier) sins; and I still have right to ownership of the books he bought then and have not sold on. My friends, so long as I have not fallen out with them, claim me as their friend. And so on.

It has been argued that the lack of direct continuity is made up for by indirect continuity through the overlap of (rather shorter) direct memory chains. There is a massive overlap between today's memories and those I had yesterday; and between the latter and those I had the day before yesterday; and so on. The thread that runs through the entirety of my life is made up of overlapping strands. The problem then arises of determining *how much* overlap, and over what period of time, is necessary to ensure the requisite amount of continuity.

The second problem is that of finding a way of independently checking that the memories recalled at time $t_2$ are (even roughly) the same as those recalled at time $t_1$. If false memories had entered his archive between $t_1$ and $t_2$, RT might believe that he was the same person at both times, when he might in fact have had a totally different psychological composition at $t_1$ compared with $t_2$. The only way to differentiate between true and false memories would be to establish an audit trail all the way from the present to the experiences that gave rise to the memories: true memories are those that are rooted in the singular experiences they purport to be memories of.

One of the most celebrated recent discussions of these problems is in Derek Parfit's brilliant *Reasons and Persons*.[16] Parfit distinguishes between 'psychological connectedness' ('the holding of particular direct psychological connections') and 'psychological continuity' ('the holding of overlapping chains of *strong* connectedness'). He argues that, for connectedness to do the job of continuity, there have to be enough direct psychological connections between one day and the next: he chooses the entirely arbitrary figure of 50 per cent as the criterion for the requisite *strong* connectedness. Although Parfit's ultimate aim is to attack neo-Lockean attempts to found identity over time on psychological continuity, it is still worth pointing out a profound problem with this attempt to strengthen Locke's theory. The memories that overlap are only potential memories. Unlike Jorge Luis Borges' famous character 'Funes the Memorius', I do not spend the entirety of my life in almost total recall of all my life. I do not, for example, pass Day n + 1 recalling the experiences of Day n. Indeed, very few of my experiences will actually be recalled: the things I do remember will probably be less than a millionth of 1 per cent of the things I could (with effort) remember if I chose to do that. (The reader doesn't have to be told that the figure is plucked out of the air!) Just how few of our possible memories we do remember is brought home to us when we are reminded at random of an occasion that took place many years ago. We find, if the memory is there at all, that the prompt will enable us to recall a myriad of details – how the sun looked, what X said, what the leaves sounded like, how I felt, etc. – that we do not bother to remember normally. Just how much of Parfit's 'strong connectedness' can be left to an overlap of memories that one does *not* stop to remember – to potential memories that remain potential – is far from irrelevant. This will be a major source of variation of the memory-contents each day. Day n + 1 may remember a totally different, very small sub-set of the experiences of Day n – 1 and its predecessors than Day n will: different sets of memories will be dormant and different ones will be awoken as we move from Day n to Day n + 1; or from Moment n to Moment n + 1. The 50 per cent overlap rule, therefore, will hardly apply to actual memories; only to possible memories. Even then, different memories will be possible on different days: the company we are in, the moods we are feeling, the jobs we have to do, the prompts we encounter, will differ massively from day to day.

In short, although the balance of possible memories carried over from day to day is only slowly changing, only a minute (and wildly varying) part of this balance is activated in transactions and it will be a different minute part from day to day.[17] The truth is, most days are recalled from the viewpoint of their successors as at best a haze of 'I was there' (or of an 'I was') enveloping particular episodic memories. It is (to anticipate the point to be made by Bishop Butler and which we shall discuss presently) this haze – combined with a more elusive sense of 'How I came to be this', 'How I came to be here', 'How I came to this pass' – that makes the memories relevant to, supportive of, the sense of one's continuing identity, which is (as we shall see) something like a principle of felt coherence.

Let us, however, pretend that Parfit's notion of strong connectedness is unproblematic and that the strengthened version of Locke's idea that he creates in order to attack, is valid. In addressing the question of 'how much overlap' – a question that Hume considered a grammatical rather than a philosophical one because he believed the unified self to be a 'a fiction' (see note 15) – Parfit builds on the thought experiments suggested by writers such as Bernard Williams. He imagines a mad brain surgeon who carries out what is effectively a functional brain transplant, by operating switches that incapacitate those neurones that house my memories, so that I become amnesiac, and others that will implant Napoleon's memories in my brain. Parfit imagines that he does not do this all at once but gradually, neurone by neurone. It is assumed that the neurones that are being put out of action carry RT's memories and the neurones replacing them carry other memories – for example, those belonging to Napoleon. At what point in this process does RT cease to be RT and become Napoleon? What proportion of his memories has to be deleted in order for him to have lost his original identity and gained a new one?

Parfit points out that there is no principled answer to this; just as there is no principled answer to the Sorites Problem or the Paradox of the Heap. There are, as philosophers frequently say, *no facts of the case*; for what is judged to be the case is not a matter of fact but of definition or stipulation. If we claim that the removal of a single grain cannot change a heap of sand into something that is not a heap, it would seem that the repeated removal of a single grain cannot either.

> Our claim forces us to admit that, after every change, we still have a heap, even when the number of grains becomes three, two and one. But we know that we have reached a false conclusion. One grain is not a heap.[18]

The original proposal that strong connectedness requires the handing over of more than 50 per cent of memories from day to day (which, incidentally, could lead to only 1 in $2^{364}$ memories being retained by the end of a year – so much for *strong* connectedness) looks pretty arbitrary. (It also makes time the maddest of the mad brain surgeons.) Analogously, there is no reason why we should take 50 per cent loss of neurones corresponding to loss of 50 per cent memories as the point at which identities change. To say that I am RT when I have 51 per cent of my memories (and habits and traits) and 49 per cent of Napoleon's and Napoleon when I have only 49 per cent of my memories is patently arbitrary and, indeed, absurd. If persistence truly is graded, then one cannot flip from one identity to another at the moment the removal of a single memory takes one past some arbitrary proportion of preserved memories.[19] If, on the other hand, one denied that there was such a point, then presumably one could have all of one's neurones/memories replaced by another's and still remain oneself – which would hardly be consistent with the psychological connectedness theory of personal identity.

This leads Parfit to conclude that personal identity isn't something you either have or do not have. It is rather like baldness. When I had a full head of hair I was obviously not bald. Now that I have a shiny pate, I manifestly am bald. The transition from one state to the other took place hair by hair but it does not make sense to say that I became bald at a particular time or that the removal of one particular hair marked the transition from hairiness to baldness. The judgement that someone is bald is somewhat arbitrary within a broad range of hair loss. It is therefore not entirely intrinsic to the head in question. By analogy, the psychological connectedness hypothesis, if accepted (and Parfit seems to accept it as the best account of the, for him doomed, notion of personal identity), suggests that personal identity is not intrinsic: its presence or absence lies in a judgement outside of oneself.[20]

Parfit derives great comfort from this. We should not fear death because this implies an over-attachment to an identity that is not something real in itself. 'The word "I",' he says, 'can be used to imply the greatest degree of psychological connectedness'. It does not refer to an absolute identity: 'what matters in the continued existence of a person are for most part, relations of degree'. The Sorites Paradox, which shows that there is no definite point at which the removal of memories would result in the removal of my identity, liberates us from our attachment to a person-centred morality and our person-centred notion of our self-interest which fosters a narrow egocentricity. If we can be weaned off the idea of a continuing personal identity, we should be more inclined to espouse a rational altruism, an impersonal morality, that takes no account of particular persons and is mindful only of the whole. The self-interest that cares for its own future or that fears death thus has no grounds.

There are two possible reasons why we may not be required to draw this mad conclusion which, if it were valid, would be wonderful. First (and this may not be decisive), the thought experiment is flawed. It assumes that memories are atomic, like the grains in a heap of sand or the hairs that used to adorn my head. In fact, they are nothing of the kind. Even a seemingly isolated episodic memory is necessarily embedded in a very complex framework with respect to which it makes sense: it belongs to a world. (Merleau-Ponty made the same point with respect to so-called individual perceptions and atomic sensations.) My memory of X's smile, for example, may not be explicitly clothed in the life I was living when I experienced her smile, but it will be imbued with the world to which it belongs: myself at a certain time of life, a particular place, a particular narrative to which my encounters with her belong. Memories are enworlded, existing as only parts of a nexus of meaning. Likewise (as we shall presently discuss) the sense of being-here-now is inseparable from a sense of how-I-came-to-be-this-and-here-and-now.

Second (and more radically), a theory of personal identity grounded in psychological connectedness focuses on the horizontal dimension of identity at the expense of the vertical dimension and consequently the moment-to-moment reality of being a human being. Personal identity goes deeper than any objective or observable (or even recallable) facts about me – including the facts about the retention of memories – because this identity is presupposed in every single one of the experiences, memories and thoughts that comprise the inner truths about me and, for example, my connectedness or disconnectedness. 'That I am this thing' is more primordial than 'That I am *still* this thing' or 'That I am the (same) thing that I was then'. The sense of personal identity *is* intrinsic to the person in question, irrespective of whether the judgement that it is conserved over time is an external and arbitrary one. What Parfit should have concluded from his thought experiment was not that the notion of a personal self enduring over time is false or that identity is unimportant, but that it cannot be *derived* or be dependent on support from *evidence* and its importance cannot be justified in this way – or at all.

This conclusion may seem rather harsh, not only to Parfit, but also to psychological continuity theories based on memory. Let us therefore examine another serious problem with such theories: that of authenticating memories. If my remembering some experience is going to be invoked in support of the belief that I am the same person who had the experience, then it is important that the memory in question should truly be a memory of that experience. It is no good if I have also to rely on my memory to reassure me that I really did experience that experience. False memories are well attested to: in ordinary life people can sincerely 'remember' things that never happened. This is not merely confined to distressed or psychologically disturbed individuals in situations of heightened suggestibility, such as are found in psychotherapy. A recent study[21] has demonstrated how easy it is to implant fabricated memories in normal subjects told about non-existent events from their childhood (supposedly derived from parental accounts) using guided imagery and repeated retrieval.

The subset of memories most directly related to the explicit sense of personal identity are 'episodic memories'. The notion of episodic memory is a complex one. It incorporates in the conscious act of remembering personal experiences, an aspect of memory that is most closely related to the ability to travel mentally in time. It is 'the kind of memory that renders possible conscious recollection of personal happenings and events from one's personal past and mental projections of anticipated events into one's subjective future'.[22]

In a true episodic memory, one remembers not just, say, a fact but also the particular episode in which the knowledge was gained: one remembers learning it.

Much remembering is not truly episodic in this sense. I may learn a list of words and then, at some future time, be able to say which of these words is present in a new list. I may be able to achieve this not by explicitly recalling the act of learning the first list but by some other means – for example, word recognition through semantic memory. Subjects are able to 'know' that some words have occurred in the list even if they are unable to have conscious recollection of having seen the word in the list. More generally, we can know about a past event without mentally travelling back to re-experience the retrieved event. Even patients with dense amnesia, who cannot recall learning episodes and in that sense lack functioning episodic memory, can nevertheless recall words from previously studied lists in response to relevant cues. Episodic memory, unlike the memory for facts (even facts about one's self), is intrinsically token and has a token referent. Factual memory may be token or type; for example, type as the referent of a written down fact and token in the act of remembering.

William James emphasised the distinctive character of episodic memory, describing it as

> a type of awareness experienced when one thinks back to a specific moment in one's personal past and consciously recollects some prior episode or state *as it was previously experienced.* (emphasis mine).[23]

It is, he said, 'like a direct feeling; its object is suffused with a warmth and intimacy to which no object of mere conception ever attains'. It is this type of awareness, rather than the *content* of the material – auto-biographical or non-autobiographical – that distinguishes authentic episodic memory.[24]

Episodic memory, based on directly recalled experiences – active remembrance, knowledge that can recollect the occasion when it was acquired, recollection imbued with the sense that I really was there then – seems, if there is such a thing, to be gold standard material for psychological connectedness and the inner aspect of personal identity. Unfortunately, even if one set aside the (damaging) fact that episodic memory is patchy and haphazard, personal identity founded on it seems to be built on sand.

Let us first revisit the considerations that led Parfit to substitute psychological continuity ('the holding of overlapping chains of *strong* connectedness') for the more demanding psychological connectedness ('the holding of particular direct psychological connections'). Identity is supposed to reach back to the beginning of one's existence – to the start of one's self – but episodic memory does not do so. We remember very little of our early life and yet we remain in some sense responsible for what we did then. If I committed a crime at the age of ten, I am identical with the person who committed that crime.[25] This continuing responsibility is the reciprocal or obverse of the rights we carry with us through our lives; for example, the right to have my achievements recognised or my ownership of property accepted. If at the age of ten I invest money in shares which grow in value over the years, I am entitled to cash them to boost my pension at the age of 65 even though, without the documentation, I should not be able to remember having made the investment. The fact that I have changed 'out of all recognition' since then would not release the institution holding the shares from their obligations to me, so long as the audit trail linking my purchase with the present is in place.

My continuing identity does not, however, reside solely in objective documentation. It must have a subjective component. On this, all parties are agreed. Even so, as Parfit has emphasised, the almost complete failure of memory to reach from one end of one's life to the other does not undermine the psychological theory of identity, so long as one allows continuity to be replaced by connectedness. While the memories of an old person may reach only to a limited extent into childhood – and many of those memories will, through repeated re-tellings, have lost their character of being genuine episodic memories – there may be indirect continuity. This enables Parfit to deal, on Locke's behalf, with Reid's famous example of the aged general, though Parfit uses this to strengthen psychological connectedness theories only prior to moving in for the kill.

Against Locke's claim that 'whoever has consciousness of present and past actions is the same person to whom they belong' Reid cites the example of the aged general who could remember the young officer he had once been who had shown bravery in battle. The general and the young officer therefore showed the necessary psychological connected-ness to count as the same person. The young officer could remember being the boy who had once been flogged for stealing apples from an orchard. The young officer and the boy were, therefore, also the same person. The general could not, however, remember the boy who had been flogged for raiding an orchard. There was a worrying lack of transitivity between the identity the general had at different stages of his life: $A_3$ remembers $A_2$ and $A_2$ remembers $A_1$ but $A_3$ does not remember $A_1$. Of course, the general may have knowledge of what had happened to the boy he once was: someone may have reminded him, or he may even have recorded it in memoirs compiled earlier in life. But this knowledge would not count as genuine remembrance in William James's sense and would not truly amount to a restoration of psychological connectedness in an intuitively satisfying sense. Since general and boy were not directly psychologically connected, they were not the same person. There was therefore a paradox:

|  |  |  |
|---|---|---|
| Elderly General | = | Brave Young Officer |
| Brave Young Officer | = | Flogged Boy |
| Therefore, Elderly General | = | Flogged Boy |

But the lack of direct psychological connectedness – of an unbroken thread of memory – between the Elderly General and the Flogged Boy proved that

Elderly General    ≠    Flogged Boy

How can one reconcile these contradictory conclusions?

This is where 'the overlapping chains of memory' come to the rescue. The requisite continuity is not of a single block of memories enduring throughout one's life but of overlapping threads:

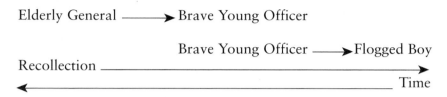

This does not, however, permit us to dodge the problem already noted of determining how much overlap there needs to be from moment to moment, or from epoch to epoch, for psychological connectedness sufficient to maintain personal identity and for the same answer to be given to the question 'Who am I?' when it is asked at different times of one's life. There is no principled answer to this question and yet it is not empty; not, at any rate, if we lay great store by the notion of enduring personal identity *and* believe that it inheres in psychological connectedness through memory. Hume's view that the question of whether identity is or is not preserved is a grammatical rather than a philosophical problem because persistent identity based on unchangingness (or on something remaining unchanged) depends on definitions seems to apply also to the overlap theory.

Reid's paradox of the elderly general is particularly illuminating because, by default, it highlights the centrality of episodic memory to the intuitive attractiveness of psychological connectedness as the backbone of identity and the guarantor of continuity of identity over time. Nothing less will do. Comparatively 'third-person' forms of memory – memories not infused by a sense of remembering – are unsatisfactory. Being reminded of the facts of my boyhood by reading the magistrates' records of my theft of apples would not restore it to my personal identity, which certainly as regards the aspect we are exploring at present (and as Bishop Butler pointed out) is essentially a *sense* of personal identity. It is relevant here to examine the distinctive character of episodic memory from this point of view.

According to Mark Wheeler and colleagues – echoing Bishop Butler – fully developed episodic memories *presuppose* the sense of self. It is

> only through the sophisticated representation of self can an individual autonoetically recollect personal events from the past and mentally project one's existence into the subjective future. ('Towards a Theory of Episodic Memory', p. 334)

The concept of 'autonoetic consciousness' is complex: it is 'the capacity that allows adult humans to mentally represent and to become aware of their protracted existence across subjective time'.[26] Autonoetic consciousness is contrasted with noetic consciousness, 'which is experienced when one thinks objectively about something one knows'. (One can have a noetic consciousness even of autobiographical facts, as when in late life one encounters such facts in a memoir one composed before one had forgotten them, consider the elderly general reading a memoir he wrote many years before about his boyhood.)

If the relationship between autonoetic consciousness and episodic memory seems circular, this is not accidental. The circle is not vicious but virtuous: autonoetic consciousness and episodic memory 'ratchet one another up', or co-evolve, once the process has been set in motion. True episodic memory of a fact is, as we have noted, associated with a recollection of the source of the knowledge of the fact and of the occasion in which one learnt it. The extraneous details of the episode of learning even about third-person things – the teacher's facial expression when you learned about Boyle's law, the evening light when you discovered that 'To be or not to be' was a quotation from *Hamlet*, etc. – makes the episode contribute to the sense of 'I was there': '*I* was there' plus 'I was *there*'. Recollection of the source of knowledge and the link between retrieved knowledge and a subjectively experienced episode are two aspects of the connection between episodic memory and autonoetic consciousness.

The sense that a particular memory is an authentic episodic memory – that it is the memory of something that *I* experienced – and the objective fact that I did experience the event in question are separable, as the tragedies brought about by the appalling irresponsibilities of recovered memory therapists have dramatically illustrated. Not only can things that happened but were not directly experienced – only accessed through factual reports – seem to have been directly experienced; but so too can things that never happened, as was demonstrated by the studies of Porter et al., alluded to earlier. The vividness of the seeming episodic memory is no proof of its authenticity. It is, of course, possible to find objective evidence that an individual really was present at the occasion she remembers vividly. For example, a photograph may show her 'actually' there at the dinner party she recalls so clearly. But this is not reassuring; for it may not necessarily be an example of a link between objective autobiographical fact and subjective memory. We often know ourselves to have been at occasions about which we have much factual information, but no direct recollection. One of my favourite childhood photographs is of our family posed in the sunshine at Land's End. It includes me, in short trousers, smiling at the camera. I remember nothing of the occasion, nor even of the day it was taken. Even more disturbingly, we may develop 'vivid' memories of occasions we have been told about, even though we do not directly recall them. Piaget tells a famous story of his own very vivid first memory. It was when he was out with his nursemaid in his pram in the park and she was attacked. He could recall the great size of the attacker (as he would seem to a small child) and the nursemaid's terror and bravery at fighting him off. Towards the end of her life, his nursemaid confessed that she had invented the event because, having fallen into conversation with her boyfriend in the park, she had lost track of the time and was in danger of being scolded for being late.

The dissociation between the kind of memory – episodic memory – that is central to my sense of continuing identity and actual past experience and the irrelevance of objective data for authentication shows the fundamental weakness of a notion of identity based on psychological connectedness secured through memory. The authentication of episodic memories so that they qualify to contribute to personal identity over time can be carried out only by me and no objective data can assist: differentiating between mere (but accurate) recollection of a real event infused with quasi-remembrance and accurate recollection of a real event infused with true remembrance is ultimately an internal matter. I do not, however, have the means within me finally to distinguish between true and false episodic memories. It is an objective matter of fact (about which I may be mistaken) that I really did experience such and such an event; it is a subjective matter that the memory of such an event is associated with James's feeling of remembrance (of something that happened to me). Thus I cannot settle the matter conclusively from 'within'; nor can I settle the matter from 'without'.

The very sense of self with which episodic memory is imbued *presupposes* autonoetic consciousness, while autonoetic consciousness seems to have to be built up out of – or at least endorsed by – episodic memories. Wheeler et al. suggest that the relationship between autonoetic consciousness and episodic memory may be as much a matter of definition as of empirical facts: episodic memory is defined in terms of its dependence on autonoetic awareness. They also note, however, that the development of episodic memory 'parallels' the development of autonoetic consciousness, as if they were mutually dependent. In connection with this, they argue that amnesia for infant experiences is due to the fact that, while infants certainly remember and learn, their experiences are not episodically remembered in later life because there is no autonoetic awareness in early childhood:

they cannot travel mentally back in time to recollect happenings from the first few years of life as personally experienced events because in one sense the events were never personally experienced. (p. 346)

To anticipate a distinction that will be of great importance in Volume 3, infant experiences are closer to the pre-indexical awareness of animals than to the fully indexicalised, subject-object awareness of developed humans.[27] For the present, we note – *and this is absolutely central to our argument* – that experiences that lead to memories cannot contribute to a sense of enduring self unless they are experienced by selves that are experiencing themselves as selves. 'That I was there ...', 'That this happened to me ...', 'That I extend in time from then when those events happened to me to now when I am recalling them ...' all depend on my feeling 'That I am experiencing this ...': in short, on an experience being imbued with the Existential Intuition in the form 'That *I* am experiencing this ...'

The continuity of memories would provide the requisite psychological continuity only if the memories carry the necessary charge of 'remembrance', of being personally experienced – so that I (now) am/was the I (then) who had that experience which is now a memory – as well as *in fact* being personally experienced, or experienced by the aware creature that goes by the name of Raymond Tallis.[28] That is why personal identity cannot be secured merely by the volume or bulk or proportion of preserved memory; why the issue of 'how much' overlapping there is between the actual or potential memories of one moment and the next is irrelevant; and why the Sorites Paradox does not deliver any kind of blow to the notion of personal identity, since the latter does not depend on quantity of memory or other psychological contents imagined in the absence of a presupposed 'instantaneous' or 'vertical' sense of personal identity. Even *total* preservation of objective semantic memory (for autobiographical and non-autobiographical facts) – along with the procedural memory embedded in skills and the implicit memory implicit in habits, attitudes, orientation in the widest sense, broad or general expectations, character traits – would not deliver continuing personal identity without episodic memory infused with and based on experiences presupposing personal identity.[29]

It was Bishop Butler who pointed out in *The Analogy of Religion* that personal identity is 'consciousness of personal identity'. He described Locke's view that personal identity resides in continuity of memory as a 'wonderful mistake' since

It is self-evident that consciousness of personal identity presupposes, and therefore cannot constitute personal identity, any more than knowledge in any other case, can constitute truth, which it presupposes.[30]

My past memories cannot prove that I who remember and the recipient of the experiences that I remember are the same person unless a) both are taken to be persons; and b) the memories that link me with the experiences of an earlier event and those experiences themselves are taken to have been had by the same person. The central intuition that those experiences which I remember are 'mine' depends on my faith in my memories to differentiate between what is/was not and what is/was mine; or to sort out from within themselves which are, and which are not, authentic. That these memories are *mine*, that they faithfully report certain experiences, and that those experiences were also *mine*, would have to be established through memory according to Locke's theory; and yet for those memories to be able to establish these things, the latter would have to be presupposed. Without such presuppositions, not only would we be unable to trust memory to tell us what is us and what is not us; there would be nothing for trust to get a handle on. The distinction would not make any kind of sense.

Without the continuing presence of the Existential Intuition, we could indeed do what Parfit (for honourable reasons) aims to do: namely, 'describe our lives in an *impersonal* way'.[31] But our lives, unlike those of animals, are emphatically not impersonal. Any line of reasoning that leads to an impersonal account of persons must be pointing in the wrong direction. While Parfit correctly concludes that psychological connectedness cannot deliver unity of personhood over time, or anything corresponding to personal identity, he is mistaken in concluding from this that enduring personal identity – such that it makes sense to have a special concern for our own future – is simply a stubborn myth that happens to command universal belief. If Parfit's identityless account of humans were true, it would be difficult to find a basis for the sense of responsibility – both for particular actions done and in the more general sense of having inescapable responsibilities – for one's job, for one's dependants, to keep engagements, etc.).[32] As Reid pointed out, it lies at the heart of morality, of the sense of duty, of enduring relationships, of citizenship – of pretty well all that matters in human life. Free-floating, unowned consciousness is unlikely to fill the hole left by the departure of personal identity.

The fundamental problem with theories of personal identity based on psychological connectedness – 'inner aspect' theories – is that they are circular. This may be a particular problem where psychological connectedness is inscribed in memory, but there are very good reasons, as Hume pointed out, for giving memory a central role:

> As memory alone acquaints us with the continuance and extent of this succession of perceptions it is to be considered, upon that account chiefly, as the source of personal identity.[33]

It implants solidity in what would otherwise be an endless torrent of what Hume characterised as 'fugitive impressions'. The sum total of experiences at time $t_1$ is not very different from the sum total of experiences at time $t_2$, if $t_1$ and $t_2$ are reasonably close. For Hume, of course, this solidity was fictitious. Personal identity is a fiction, as is the continuing identity of anything. Memory, he says, 'not only discovers the identity, but also contributes to its production, by producing the relation of resemblance among the perceptions' (p. 236).[34]

The Sorites Paradox invoked by Parfit might be less damaging to a concept of personal identity based on memory if one could accept that identity over time might be a matter of degree – that 'I' could be more or less preserved. This option was (correctly) rejected by Reid, for whom identity was either absolute or not at all. While he shared Hume's view that the identity of an *object* was a grammatical fiction and its preservation a matter of stipulation, he disagreed strongly with Hume on personal identity – which was for him the only true or intrinsic form of identity. In a famous passage, Reid contrasts personal identity with the identity of material things such as trees and ships:

> The identity of ships and trees is not perfect identity; it is rather something which, for the convenience of speech, we call identity. It admits of a great change of the subject, providing the change is gradual; sometimes, even of a total change. And the changes which in common language are made consistent with identity differ from those that are thought to destroy it, not in kind, but in number and degree. *Identity* has no fixed nature when applied to bodies; and questions about the identity of a body are very often questions about words. But identity when applied to persons, has no ambiguity, and admits not of degrees, or of more or less. It is the foundation of all rights and obligations, and of all accountableness; and the notion of it is fixed and precise.[35]

The assertion that 'identity, when applied to persons, has no ambiguity, and admits not of degrees, of more or less', allied to the claim that the concept of identity is properly applicable only to persons, captures a fundamental truth about instantaneous identity – that it is absolute – and the priority instantaneous has over enduring identity. 'That I am this …' admits of no degrees. This corresponds to our earlier expressed view that there is no identity without self-identification or, more precisely, 'self-entification'. Reid goes astray, however, in extending the absoluteness of the vertical dimension to the horizontal dimension of identity.[36] He does not allow degrees of fidelity to oneself over time; and this is the force of his 'aged general' argument against Lockean accounts of the self, which we discussed earlier. A persistent overlapping of memories from one end of one's life to the other is, for him, an unsatisfactory substitute for continuity of memories, even if there were such a thing as a self-validating memory; it is yet another dimension of relativity introduced into the notion of personal identity. Such laxness was unacceptable to Reid because true persistence of self for him is the rock on which rights and obligations, morality itself, are founded.

What we may take from Reid is the argument that, if we rely on memory as the basis of personal identity, we arrive at a notion of personal identity that is at odds with the sense of self we all enjoy and on which human society is built. Others who have a more liberal interpretation of identity over time and are still inclined to appeal to continuous overlapping partial recall of a past that is one's own past run into the problem of finding an external validation for memories to ensure that they are truly memories – that are truly connected with the personal experiences they are memories of.

While, for the reasons we have given, memory cannot of itself provide a basis for the sense of personal identity, it would be absurd to dismiss the central role of memory in specifying the content of our sense of identity, in our sense of who we are. We need memory to give temporal depth to the 'I', to make it more than a standing dot of iteration. If memory is to provide extendedness over time in this way, we need to find a path to an audit trail not dependent on memory or the sense of self, linking today's episodic memories with past experiences so that true memories can be distinguished from false ones. For this we need to move outside of the psyche. Enter (or re-enter) the body.[37]

## 7.7 ENDURING IDENTITY OVER TIME: OUTER-ASPECT THEORIES

Our present concern is not with what makes an individual a specific 'I' at any given time but with what makes her be, or count as, the same 'I' over time. The question arises at least in part because living is changing. What kinds of changes are permitted without change or (much the same thing) loss of identity? What Hume called 'sympathetic change' is one – as when part of a ship is replaced. Another is gradual change. If change is both sympathetic and gradual, there is an inclination to conclude that token or numerical (as well as type) identity has been conserved. There is a third criterion: one in which the entity in question can be continuously tracked. These clearly apply to any physical object where (to put it perhaps a little tendentiously), there is always a potential 'identity audit trail' set out in space-time.

These are the reasons why the body seems attractive as the place in which to find the basis of continuing personal identity, leaving aside the obvious biological ones and any bio-genetic account of the origin of selfhood. For a start, unlike memories, the body does reach to both ends of one's life: the body with which one is born is the body one takes to the grave. Of course, there are changes en route; so radical that one could not confidently pick oneself out of a group of babies on the basis of physical appearance alone. Even in the relatively stable period between growth and senescence the body is always changing: its entire contents we are told are replaced every seven years. There is, however, a relative persistence of form and where the form changes, there is continuity between its phases: it is possible therefore to trace a continuous link between all the stages of my body. The changes are, moreover, usually gradual: there is enough preserved unchanged from year to year to sustain the sense of continuity. I see the same body day in day out, year in year out, because the changes are largely imperceptible and objectively gradual: most of the matter of last year's body and its organisation is present in this year's body. Moreover, there are sufficient people around me who see me at close enough intervals of time to be able to recognise me, as well as to track my continuity. Their reliable immediate recognition of me on the basis of my bodily presence reinforces my sense of unchanged numerical identity. These others, moreover, on seeing my body, address me by the name to which – directly and indirectly, inwardly and outwardly, via memory, habit and documentation – so much of my life is attached. Underpinning all this is the spatio-temporal continuity that links one moment with the next: my body passes smoothly from moment to moment and the most impressive aspect of this smoothness is the continuity of the lines it traces in space throughout my life. Its four-dimensional world-line is undashed.

These are the superficial reasons for looking to the body for external validation of continuing personal identity. There are, however, deeper attractions to notion of the body as the guarantor and marker of continuing identity. Our discussion of these attractions will take us back to the arguments advanced in Chapter 4. There, it will be recalled, we examined the case advanced by Strawson and refined by Cassam for the necessary embodiment of the 'I'. The argument was based on the necessary connection between self-consciousness and awareness of self as a physical object. A self-conscious subject must not only be able to self-ascribe her representations but also 'must be capable of consciousness of her own numerical identity as the subject of diverse representations'.[38] Intuitive awareness of oneself as a physical object is a necessary condition of self-consciousness, and of consciousness of self-identity because it is physical objects alone that can provide the basis for numerical identity. One could not enjoy self-identity without having some means of discriminating oneself from the world:

> to have a sense of oneself as determinately shaped is ... to have a concrete sense of where one ends and where the rest of the world begins. Awareness of the subject of one's experiences as something with a determinate shape, as well as solidity and location, is a necessary condition of consciousness of self-identity because it is in being aware of one's spatial properties that one satisfies the discrimination requirements on self-reference. (p. 142)

This thought is ultimately rooted in the Strawsonian intuition that the only identifiable (or re-indentifiable particulars) are material objects.

This, then, is a (greatly impoverished) re-run of Cassam's rich argument (discussed in Chapter 4) for holding that self-consciousness requires one to intuit oneself as being a corporeal object among corporeal objects. Personal identity requires that one should feel oneself to be 'shaped, solid and located'. No body-object, no self-consciousness; no body-object, no identity; no body, nobody. (The echoes of the mantra of Chapter 5 'no body, no here' are deliberate.)

The link between the body and identity at a particular instant is the Existential Intuition, 'That I am this ...' where the 'this' in question is in some sense (not specified in Cassam's arguments and shown to be rather unclear in our previous discussion) the body attached to our name. Without such a basis for identity at a particular time, we cannot found identity over time. We run the danger, in short, of ending up in Parfit's world of human lives consisting of unattached, impersonal reels of consciousness. Can the body, however, provide us with more than this: can it provide the link between the instantaneous 'I' and the enduring identity of Raymond Tallis? Supposing (as we shall suppose) that, while memory cannot of itself establish personal identity (because the sense that the memories had by me are *my* memories presupposes personal identity), memory gives temporal depth to an instantaneous identity established through the Existential Intuition, where would the body as it were fit in? What does the body bring (apart from experiences to have memories of)? I want to suggest that it brings the ultimate basis of authentication of memory through the Existential Intuition. The latter, as we have argued, is self-affirming. There is a core of subject-truth, captured by 'That I am this ...' where 'this' is, at least in part, a subjective state of the body engaged in some activity. The Intuition not only informs experience – making these experiences 'mine' – but also forms the seed of an identity that can then acquire temporal depth, acquire a horizontal dimension of endurance over time. The body, necessarily linked with immediate self-consciousness, and the explicit bearer of those experiences which will become the authentic episodic memories that carry the extended sense of self, can provide the basis for authentication of those memories. By this means it can make possible an identity-over-time that is not founded on a circular audit trail but, in the final analysis, on a self-affirming intuition of first-person being. Let us examine these suppositions.

The most intractable obstacle to finding a robust basis for enduring personal identity in psychological connectedness through memory when the latter is envisaged as effectively disconnected from the body is that of differentiating true from false episodic memories; of separating apparent memories of experiences I imagine I have had from memories of experiences I truly have had. Whereas the former are as much part of me-now as the latter and may carry as potent a charge of 'remembrance', only true memories underpin my identity over time. In separating true from false episodic memories, we may adopt two possible auditing tactics.

The first attempts to trace the connection between the memory and the apparent original experience. The second establishes the validity of the experience – establishes, that is to say, that it really was an experience rather than, say, an hallucination at the time or subsequently – on the basis of powerful circumstantial evidence. The body seems to be able to provide support (or the idea of the body provides the conceptual framework) for both kinds of audit – especially, but not necessarily, if one has a physicalist account of mental contents such as memory.[39]

Let us consider the first kind of audit: establishing a causal chain linking the experience E that took place at time $t_1$ with the memory M of E at subsequent times $t_2$ and $t_3$. According to standard physicalist theories of consciousness, memory is secured by the persistence in the brain of patterns of activity in particular sets of neurones (let us call it A). The memory is authentic if A was ignited, when E was had at time $t_1$, by the events E was an experience of. This latter rider is required in order to exclude cases in which A arises spontaneously at any time after $t_1$ (as in, for example, temporal lobe epilepsy associated with dysmnestic phenomena) in which case the 'memory' would not be a memory at all. Likewise, if A was ignited as a result of current attempts to remember or if – perhaps under the influence of a persuasive recovered memory therapist – a slightly different activity B was changed into something like A.

The persistence of A in the brain, which makes it possible to have a memory M of E, is a necessary but not a sufficient warrant of authenticity: A has, in addition, to be an effect caused by the events experienced at time $t_1$. And here the body provides not only a putative physical basis for the memory, but also a visible way of authenticating it. This is connected with the body's special role in enabling that one not only has experiences, but has one set of experiences rather than another. As Strawson put it, in the passage we quoted in Chapter 6:

> for each person there is one body which occupies a certain *causal* position in relation to that person's perceptual experience, a causal position which in various ways is unique in relation to each of the various kinds of perceptual experience he has ...[40]

Bodily identity and 'inner' or personal identity secured through memories of actual experiences made possible by the body merge in the necessary causal relationships between the body and the experiences that are possible for the embodied person. This is another aspect of the necessary link between being embodied and being (in a particular) here.

This may still take rather too much on trust. It would not, anyway, satisfy a sceptic who argued that the seemingly unbroken causal chain linking the memory M, the body-based sense experience E and the events causing the experience could be simulated by a backward reference of pseudo-memories created by current neural activity corresponding to A. A produced in this way would feel like a true memory M of experience E. Something more is needed before the causal relationship between experiences and the body can fully authenticate memories and separate true from false episodic memories.

This, the second audit strategy, was first suggested by Descartes at the end of his *Meditations on First Philosophy*:

> And I ought to set aside all the doubts of these past days as hyperbolical and ridiculous, particularly that very common uncertainty respecting sleep, which I could not distinguish from the waking state; for at present I find a very notable difference between the two, inasmuch as our memory can never connect our dreams one with the other, or with the whole course of our lives, as it unites events which happen to us while we are awake ...when I perceive things as to which I know distinctly both the place from which they proceed, and that in which they are, and the time at which they appeared to me; and when, without any interruptions, I can connect the perceptions which I have of them with the whole course of my life, I am perfectly assured that these perceptions occur while I am waking and not during sleep. And I ought in no wise to doubt the truth of such

matters if, after having called up all my senses, my memory, and my understanding, to examine them, nothing is brought to evidence by any one of them which is repugnant to what is set forth by the others.[41]

The principle invoked here is that of coherence, consistency at a deep level: waking experiences and the memories associated with and enjoyed during wakefulness hang together. In sleep, incoherence, inconsistency is the order of the day. Sleep is governed by the Law of the Included Muddle.

We have to be cautious, of course, in invoking the principle of coherence of memories and perceptions with other memories and perceptions as evidence that they are of things that truly happened. Plausible untruths are plausible precisely because they hang together – either with other plausible untruths or with things that are true. False memories uncovered during recovered memory therapy illustrate this rather dramatically. There has to be something, if not outside the magic circle of mutual confirmation, at least ensuring that that circle is deeply rooted in the very structure of experience. And this, again, is where the body comes to the rescue.

When, in a court of law, the barrister for the defence is trying to prove that his client could not possibly have committed the crime, he invokes the fact that the client was a long way from the scene of the crime when the latter took place. This evidence goes beyond the client's testimony to the effect that he was in another country: it includes corroboration from other, presumed to be truthful, witnesses, who are able to confirm that they saw the defendant at the place he claimed to be and at the relevant time. The force of the alibi resides in the fact that, being embodied, the defendant could not have been in two places separated by 1,000 miles at the same time. Likewise, he could not have skipped from one to the other in a very short period of time. Teleporters, while commonplace in the philosophical discussion of personal identity, are not seen elsewhere. Getting from one country to another takes time. The prosecution's position that the defendant carried out the crime with which he is charged is therefore inconsistent with the direct, corroborated evidence that he was elsewhere. The impossibility of being in two places at once, the necessity to be in the place where the crime occurred (England) in order to carry it out, the evidence that he was in another country (Spain) when the crime took place and the limits on the speed at which he could have transferred from Spain, where he was seen at 21:00 hours, to England, where the crime took place at 21:10, which meant that he could not have got from the one to the other in time to do the crime, are all consequences of embodiment.

Embodiment imposes spatio-temporal constraints on the body, on visibility and on action, which are fundamental to the difference between a coherent and an incoherent sequence of events, between (true, waking) perceptions which can be 'connected with the whole course of my life' and (false, dream) perceptions which cannot. It provides the basis, at least in theory, for distinguishing false from real memories. It is precisely because recovered memories are given without context, that they are uprooted from 'the whole course', that they are not assigned precise dates and times and precise locations (other than childhood or the remote past), that they are so difficult to refute. They are typically uncorroborated; but because they are cannot be corroborated this is not regarded by some as damaging to their status as testimony.

A true memory is of an experience you were literally in a position to have. Ideally, the audit trail should track the body's movements from the present where memory M is being remembered backwards to its location when the experience E on which the memory was based was experienced. In practice, that is never possible: we cannot recall all the tracks of our body over the earth. There are, however, what Peacocke (cited in Cassam, *Self and World*, p. 39) calls *intertemporal restrictions* on self-location. They in turn are based on broadly defined sequences of possible movement of the body: I cannot be in Spain at 9 am and doing a ward round in Salford five minutes later (not, at least, without remembering an intervening experience of some new form of magical transport of my body). The fundamental notion is that places where experiences are had have to be connected – the body moves continuously through space – and there are constraints on the rate of passage between them. This unexceptionable notion, however, depends on the assumption that experiences have to be had in certain places: you have to be located in a certain place in order to have a certain experience. This assumption in turn is inextricably associated with the notion that experiences are the result of interactions between the body and the place in which it is located; or between a body located at a certain place and the objects surrounding it at that place. The two linked notions – the embodiment of the experiencing subject and causal interactions with the body making the experiences possible – underpin the idea of an actual, singular, experience subsequently echoed in a valid episodic memory.

Even where the individual audit trail is (as it usually is) incomplete, Descartes' principle of overall coherence between true, waking experiences, as opposed to false, dreaming ones, still serves to differentiate real from false memories – particularly as the coherence extends beyond the individual to other individuals via their testimony, corroboration and non-corroboration. I may dream that I am skiing in the Alps when I am actually nodding off in a lecture. That this is a dream is demonstrated not only by the failure of subsequent, and the memory of preceding, experiences to cohere with the dream, but also by the failure of others to corroborate my dream-memory of having been in the Alps. It fails both internal and external audit. The testimony of others is especially relevant here: they are able to testify because they have direct (as well as indirect) knowledge of my likely experiences because they are co-located with me. Those sitting next to me in the lecture are party to similar experiences as I would be having were I awake because of their being similarly located. It is well known that a lecturer is someone who talks in other people's sleep and each sleeper will be dreaming differently. In contrast, each member of the audience will have similar wakefulness: while I dream that I am skiing in the Alps, you dream that you are sunbathing in Spain, and he imagines he is walking with the children; but we all wake in a lecture. We have separate trails leading to and from the lecture but we have a common scene in which we participate when we are seated in the lecture theatre. Our adjacent bodies underpin a co-location in which we are exposed to a common set of potential experiences. As Heracleitus said, 'the waking share a common cosmos, each sleeps alone'. In this case: the waking share a common lecture, each dreams his own dream.

The case for the role of the body in providing an external criterion for authentication of the memories (and indeed the experiences), on which the sense of continuing identity over time might be founded, appears persuasive. The body seems in addition to provide a more direct basis for continuing identity over time directly through its public aspect – available to myself as well as others. Its relative sameness from day-to-day is an outward and visible sign (or claim, or earnest) of my inner stability; of the sameness, or unchanging token identity, or oneness, of the 'I' that is embodied in it. Even its gradual changes with age seem like a deposit account of accumulated me, set out in space, complementing the current account of me unfolding in time in the body's present activities:

Thus is his cheek the map of days outworn.

As the tag and anchor of (stable) personal identity it still scores highly because, even where there are sudden changes, as after an accident, it still retains spatio-temporal continuity through a public world-line. There are no jumps. Since, moreover, it presents an outward and visible mark of my continuing identity and since it is visible to others, my own sense of my continuity and stability is reinforced by others' assumption of myself as the same person, operating of course under the same name that itself tags my token identity and affirms my singular continuation. The body, in short, is the seat of others' sense of my identity which, internalised, may be the most potent contribution to my secure sense of 'being the same me' over time, in the face of a flux of current feelings and experiences. Others' relatively stable expectations (and, corresponding to this, relatively stable behaviour to myself, and relatively stable expectations of my behaviour) are themselves immensely stabilising, sometimes almost imprisoningly so. I sometimes feel set in aspic in the collective gaze of the Other that thinks it know me through and through – is both knowledgeable and knowing – and is liable to treat change as instability and even development as deviation out of character.[42]

Before we get too used to patting the body on its head for solving our problems of identity, it is important to remember the unfinished business. Yes, we agree, for the reasons given by Cassam, that the very idea of self-consciousness seems inseparable from consciousness of something 'shaped, solid and located' – in short, from something like the human body. As Cassam puts it, 'introspective awareness of one's thinking, experiencing self as a physical object among physical objects, is a *necessary* condition of self-consciousness' (p. 3); and a physical object is, as he repeatedly emphasises, something 'shaped, located and solid'. Only a material object like a body has a fully developed token identity that can be highlighted through repeated identification and give rise to the sense of personal identity. And this has proved very handy for our developing a non-puzzling notion of identity-over-time in which bodily stability and accumulative memory both play their part, bringing in the body does import problems of its own. Some of these we have already touched on.

First, there is the problematic fact that the body, *qua* material object, or biological specimen, has nothing in it that corresponds to the experiences of it that I have, the experiences that make it my body, and, beyond this, make me be, to some extent, that body. Second (and connected with this) is the uncertainty as to how much of the body I am and how much of my body is me. The Strawsonian and post-Strawsonian object to which the self-ascriptions of self-consciousness are ascribed is a featureless unity. The body of the embodied subject, by contrast, is quite different, as we discussed in Chapter 6. There is hardly anything of my body with which I am entirely identified but little of my body with which I am not, either explicitly (foreground) or implicitly (background), to some degree identified at *some* time or other. How is such a body requisitioned by a self as its instrument and oriel? How do the elements cohere? If the body is that in virtue of which we are self-conscious, how do we square its endless fluctuations, its spontaneous and induced instabilities, with the notion of a persisting self? How do we fit the thoughts that occupy our days and seem to belong to the inner pentralium of the self within the framework of the phenomenal body? While we may agree with Cassam that 'a subject who is capable of consciousness of her own identity must in general be presented to herself as a physical object and must at least think of herself as spatio-temporally located' (p. 153), we shall still find it difficult to know exactly how to connect the spatio-temporally located physical object that is the body with the complex, structured experiencings that add up to a self.

For we are not invoking the body here as a mere 'tag' for the self, a way of holding together the otherwise ownerless and scarcely cohering experiences of which it may or may not be composed. Cassam's invocation of the body is in support of 'a materialist account of self-consciousness rather than a materialist account of the self' (p. 7). While I would not wish to succumb to the charms of neurophilosophy and identify the self with the brain, or even with the body, I still believe that the role of the body in personal identity goes deeper than this. The body is not merely the bearer of identity; it is the very tissue of it. The body is deeply implicated in every aspect of the self, including (causally) the nature of the experiences it has and its integrated sense of itself and of its being itself here and now. To vary our mantra: no body no here, no now, no self.

Cassam also touches on, though he does not resolve, a circularity that remains in the audit trail even when we invoke the body to help us to differentiate false from true memories. This is a circularity we noted in relation to the establishment of 'here'. For Cassam it is connected with self-location and the fact that 'just as one might argue from where one is to what one is perceiving, so one might also infer one's location from what one takes oneself to be perceiving' (p. 38). We may use landmarks to determine our location and infer the identity of landmarks from where we assumed ourselves to be located. 'What these things here are' and 'Where I am' seem to be *interdependent*, as does 'What here this is' and 'What it is that is here'. (The conclusion of Chapter 6 could have been 'Here is where my body – inexplicably – inheres'.)

At a superficial level – at a level of factual knowledge rather than of primordial existence – the problem of self-location does not seem to arise if the landmarks are unique. To use Gareth Evans' example (cited by Cassam), there is only one Marble Arch and it is in London; here is Marble Arch; so here must be London. The trouble is that landmarks tend not to be unique and there are no landmarks that are, as it were, necessarily or logically, rather than merely contingently, unique. There is no reason why there shouldn't be a replica of Marble Arch in Dallas. What will not be replicated in Dallas will be the surroundings. Even if a billionaire were able to recreate Marble-Arch-plus-its-distinctive-London-surroundings, the re-creation would be of only a small part of London. Eventually, I would leave the replica London and re-enter first-order Dallas and this would constitute the majority of the territory I wander round. Moreover, there would be the inter-temporal restrictions on self-location referred to earlier, which lead me to expect that I shall encounter adjacent places in roughly adjacent times. I may be able to flip from a picture of London to actual Dallas but not from London to Dallas in a few seconds. Replicas of Marble Arch will always be served up in a context that tells me whether I am in fact in London or Dallas.

The invocation of context to enable us to resolve the problem of duplicates echoes aspects of Descartes' argument referred to earlier when, at the end of his *Meditations*, he packs up his spell-book and tells the Evil Demon to go to the Devil. In both cases, the circularity issue seems to be addressed only at a superficial level; for it presupposes that a nexus of 'heres' will have been established and that these will provide any additional criteria I may need in order to know where I 'really' am. It assumes, that is to say, a huge amount of background knowledge of the world and a large capacity for recalling my own movements. In order not to be fooled when I enter the Marble Arch-and-surroundings mock-up in Dallas, I need to retain not only objective knowledge about the respective locations of London and Dallas, but also memories about my own tracks over the last few hours. This assumes that I can link my present experiences with my memories – including memories of facts – and the latter with the experiences that will authenticate them. Authentication in turn requires self-location with respect to the experiences on which the authenticity of the memories is based. The self-location with respect to those memories, however, presupposes authentication. Thus the circularity.

Now it might be argued that the circle is not vicious because it is a small circle located in a much larger, non-circular context. Any given moment of self-location reposes on a body of coherent experience out of which emerge not only specific acts of locating but general principles (spatial continuity, limited speed of travel) and factual knowledge (e.g. Dallas is many thousands of miles from London). This, however, will not deliver what is required at the level at which we are thinking; for establishing this body of knowledge rather assumes what we are trying to derive. As Evans points out:

self-location cannot be in general a momentary thing. For ... self-location depends crucially upon the axiom that the subject moves continuously through space; and that axiom can be brought to bear upon particular questions of location only if the subject has the capacity to retain information about his previous perceptions and to use the information in making judgements about his past, and thereby his present, position. (in Cassam, *Self and World*, p. 39)

All of which presupposes a self justifiably confident in ascribing memories, perceptions, etc. to itself!

This disappointing outcome is not surprising because the body as the ultimate authenticator of memories, being the guarantor that they are based on perceptions, has at once to establish where it is through the things that surround it and to establish what things are that surround it through a knowledge of where it is. All the body can do is to establish 'here' (although how it does that we do not know) and not the objective location – the 'where' – of 'here'. How we get from the deictic location 'here' to an objective location that is both unique and non-indexical, is not clear.

We shall revisit this in Volume 3 when we examine the passage from sentience, via perception, to 'deindexicalised' awareness, or (factual) knowledge. For the present it is perhaps reasonable to settle for the assumption that the 'here' built into bodily self-awareness, and the 'where', the orientation, that comes with this are sufficient for most purposes most of the time. After all 'here' is primarily lived and lived here is not read from a map that has to have built-in safeguards against confusion from duplicate entities. By the time we get to living in places where orientation requires deindexicalised knowledge, systems of tagging will have been established that will not be liable to lead to persistent or routine confusion. In short, by the time human beings have started to live in cities, they will be able to devise a proper scheme of street-naming and house-numbering and, in general, place-marking. This does not have to be built into the 'hereness' of the Existential Intuition.

### 7.8 THE UNTHINKABILITY OF PARFIT'S (AND OTHERS') THOUGHT EXPERIMENTS

One problem that the necessary link between self-consciousness and embodiment does not have to deal with is the argument that there is no necessary link between the self and a *particular* body. This (pseudo-) problem has been expressed by Swinburne as follows:

Since the body which is presently yours (together with the associated apparent memories) could have been mine (logic and even natural laws allow), that shows that none of the matter of which my body is presently made (nor the apparent memories) is essential to my being the person I am. That must be determined by something else.[43]

This worry is, I believe, based on a confusion between token and type identities. It is certainly true that the general kind of person I am need not be linked with the kind of matter of which my body is made. It is not, however, true that the actual person I am could have been linked with another body than the one that I have. The Existential Intuition that lies at the root of personal identity could not arise in the wrong body. 'That I am this ...' could not have, as it were, the wrong reference or indeed any other referent than the body that 'I' live. My body and 'I' are indissoluble not only as a matter of empirical fact but also logically. My 'I' begins as my body's awakening to itself. Body and 'I' do not come from separate places and are brought together by some kind of ontological dating agency. It is easy to see why Swinburne thinks otherwise: as a Christian philosopher he is committed to the notion of an eternal soul entering a transient body.

Identity, even beyond the primordial form it takes in the Existential Intuition, is also not merely contingently related to my body and its history. The actual matter of which my body is made – matter occurring in a particular place and enduring over particular times, the token specimen of matter – is connected with the actual experiences and these in turn build up the valid memories that make up my enduring self. My memories, if they are to be valid, must be based in experiences and these require a particular body with a particular history of being in certain places in certain times. While the history of my self and of my body might have been different – the body could have turned left in front of a bus rather than right on to the safety of the pavement and I would have had a totally different set of experiences and a different self – the two are conjoined. The one non-contingent fact about me is that I am born in this body.

This should make us think again about the mad brain surgeon and other thought experiments that have so excited philosophers over the last thirty or more years. Perhaps they are logically flawed; perhaps there is no non-contradictory way of describing them. The suggestion that a neurosurgeon might be able to implant, say, Napoleon's memories in my body so that I should then become Napoleon is not as clear as it may appear at first sight. Even if we take the 50 per cent point as that at which Napoleon gets the upper hand, it is still arguable that beyond this point it is still me – because it is still the body of RT – who happens to be possessed of Napoleon's memory, rather as in a form of non-convulsive status epilepticus, or a protracted delusional state. In other words, it is just as arguable that I remain RT, infected by Napoleon's memories, as that I have become Napoleon; and that my brain or body has become possessed by Napoleon's memories rather than that my body has been handed over to Napoleon and it, and I, have become Napoleon.

There is no intrinsic fact of the matter. It depends entirely on how what has happened is described. This in turn depends on the viewpoint from which the process is imagined. If it is imagined from a viewpoint that encompasses all of my life, then it could be described as the transition to a phase in Raymond Tallis's life in which he developed the delusion that he was Napoleon and even acquired Napoleon's capabilities. He could not, however, have acquired Napoleon's past. He could not, retrospectively, for example have brought about, through his reckless adventures in Russia, the destruction of the *Grande Armée*, not the least because Raymond Tallis was not born in 1812. If you describe the transition from the viewpoint of the post-operative phase of Raymond Tallis's life, then you cannot allow the existence of the experience, the phase that was Raymond Tallis, into consideration, because that was pre-operative. The thought experiment, in other words, is flawed because it cannot be described in a consistent way and hence cannot in fact be thought: it is actually nonsensical. You can't both take a viewpoint from both sides of the operation, before and after, *and* take a stand when you describe what happens from one side or another. Or you could not if the thought experiment described how things really are – for there would be no outside from which to see both insides at once. The claim that Raymond Tallis has become Napoleon requires an outside from which to view both insides. Such an outside implies that there is a basis for personal identity beyond memory and psychological connectedness through a stable mass of memories. To put it another way, the remembered events at the time and place when they took place could not be part of Raymond Tallis's body. They are not therefore part of Raymond Tallis – not even of a new, Napoleonised, phase of Raymond Tallis.

This untenable occupation of two incompatible standpoints when thinking about the thought experiment is not a new phenomenon in philosophy. Everyone knows the famous anecdote about Lao Tse. He is said to have claimed that he once had a dream that he was a butterfly and further claimed that he now does not know whether he is a man who once dreamed that he was a butterfly or a butterfly who is dreaming he is a man. To this we ask, who is it that is uncertain? From what standpoint is the uncertainty being entertained? It would seem that we have to imagine either a third party attached to, or transcending, two manifestations – butterfly and man – and wondering which one he is; or imagine he is the one or the other. There is no basis for the third-party notion, for there is no locus for such a party. (A rigid designator that was stable across the two designations butterfly and man would have nothing to designate other than a free-floating, type-wondering, which had no numerical identity.) We are therefore left to choose between the butterfly and the philosopher as the locus of the wondering. There seems to be no contest. The story, after all, started with the assumption that Lao Tse is a philosopher. Such a creature seems more likely to deal in wondering and riddles than a butterfly. Given also that the story is set in the distant past, we must assume a huge amount of our world is in place to sustain the notion of a philosopher who lived many hundreds of years ago. This is a world in which philosophers do and butterflies do not have identity crises. In short, we cannot entertain this story fully without removing the standpoint from which such a story could be entertained. The same is true of the mad brain surgeon thought experiment: it is unintelligible and, though it can be thought about, it cannot, strictly, be thought.

The notion of replacement of memories one by one is also flawed. We have already pointed out that memories are not atoms but belong to, and are inseparable from, worlds. If I were to accept one (token) Napoleon memory, I would have to accept the lot, for they are all linked. This is connected with the link between memories and the history of the body and the fact that the body – the token body that is Raymond Tallis's body – is obliged to be spatio-temporally continuous. One consequence of this, which we have already noted, is *intertemporal restrictions* on self-location. Memories of successive experiences cannot be of London 2004 and of Moscow 1812 without some plausible account of the transition from one to the other. No such plausible accounts are forthcoming. As Cassam (p. 39, quoting Christopher Peacocke) emphasises, 'the spatial scheme constrains the possible sequences of experiences it explains to those corresponding to *paths* through space'. Sequences of perceptions – and hence the sequence of valid memories – are related to sequences of spatio-temporally *adjacent* places. While the audit trail between memories and the experiences on which they are based, and so on – the connections between memories – can rarely be completed, the general principles inform all our understanding of probability, indeed possibility, that enables us to separate true memories from false ones – as Descartes pointed out.

These spatio-temporal constraints provide the skeletal basis of the holistic interconnectivity between my memories; for higher-level facts such as that my memory of your smile does not make sense in isolation from my memory of you, of our life together, of a certain period of my life, of large lumps of the world I live in, etc. And there is a holism that connects the history of my body together and connects this in turn with the holistically coherent history of myself – the place and time in which my body lives and the places and times in which I live and become, and act out, myself are not separable.

Just how complex the restrictions arising out of the interconnectedness of one's life and how densely interlocking valid memories are may be demonstrated by a simple example. If, for example, I remember leaving my coat at work yesterday, on top of the papers that I had rushed to my office to work on, and then find when I go to work that my coat is, indeed, there and carelessly thrown on top of those papers (a marker of the great haste I also recall), then the truth of a nexus of memories is upheld. The practical logic of everyday events upwardly adjusts the probability of a vast number of recalled facts about myself, radiating from the single validated memory: not only that I, indeed, left my coat at work, but also that I was working on certain papers yesterday, that I was at work yesterday, that my place of work is such-and-such, that I can reach it by such-and-such a route, that I have a job that involves working on certain papers in such-and-such an office. In short, the confirmation of a certain factual memory sends out ripples of validation through an entire network of linked facts. This wider validation is not merely a matter of coherence at a particular dubious level; for the bloc of memories (or potential memories) that is upheld is not directly coherent in the remembered world out there.

We overlook this (deep, wall-to-wall) holism if we forget that the memories that underpin identity are episodic memories of essentially token events and imagine that they are semantic or factual memories, which can be served up in any order and gathered together in all sorts of ways: encyclopaedias, dictionaries, forgetful schoolchildren. I suspect that this confusion accounts for much of the conceptual plausibility of thought experiments. You can infuse into me, as token experiences of memory-types, the facts about Napoleon's invasion of Russia but not his token-experiences of the invasion or the episodic memories in so far as they are connected with the (unrepeatable and hence inaccessible) token-experiences. The fact that I may occasionally have remembrance-loaded episodic memories of events I never actually experienced should not be over-interpreted. It should place us on our guard against purely intra-psychological guarantees of the truth of our memories. We need the body, acting under all sorts of constraints, to create an independent audit trail. But it is precisely the relationship to the body (and the rooting of identity in the Existential Intuition) that means that holistic coherence is not only required but is the norm. Even people subjected to delusions have for the most part a consciousness that is not made up of delusions. The man who thinks he is Napoleon (without the help of a mad brain surgeon) would have to get the overwhelming majority of things in, and about, his life right to survive sufficiently to imagine he is Napoleon. A few false memories do not imply that it is possible to make a whole person out of errors, even less if those erroneous memories are instilled piecemeal. The body that provides the basis for distinguishing between false and true episodic memories also maintains the distinction between token-memories of event-types and token memories of actual occurrent events.

Contrary to Swinburne's assertion, then, natural law does *not* allow me to be separated from my body, my memories to be dissociated from my body, or you or your memories to swap bodies with mine. Moreover, the notion that your memories might be associated with my body seems a *logical* possibility, rather than a contradiction, only so long as the criterion of a true memory is forgotten; that is to say, the connection between such a memory and an experience; and consequently between such a memory and a particular location of a particular body in space-time. While type-memories (for example, remembered facts) might theoretically be linked to any instances of bodies with certain general characteristics – characteristics that your body and mine share – essentially token memories are linked with token bodies with singular histories; in particular, with unique paths through space-time. There cannot be two token bodies occupying the same paths through space-time. My token memories and myself, therefore, could not be associated with your body because your body could not occupy the same space-time path as my body.

It might be argued that I am accepting the notion of a 'token memory' too uncritically and assuming that memories are unique, singular, non-duplicable. Against this, someone might say there is no logical reason why there should not be two memories $M_1$ and $M_2$ which had identical characteristics. Crucially, they would both be complete in the sense of being about particulars fully specified, and have no feature-places unsaturated: each would be about a particular event taking place at a particular point in space-time. The one remembered by me (who was there at the putative location of the event) would be true and the one remembered by you (who had not been present at the event) would be false. From which it would follow that your body could have a sequence of token memories identical to the sequence of token memories associated with my body and, although the memories associated with one of our bodies (yours) would be false, this would not undermine the general point that our bodies could be logically disconnected from whatever it is that makes up our person, so that my body could be yours, and vice versa. If all the memories were transferred – or replicated – then Descartes' test of incoherence, demonstrating the transferred memories, or the copied memories, to be false, would not help. Totally coherent false memories are indistinguishable from true ones.

The cost of sustaining this thought experiment is unacceptably high. It requires that we do not fully take on board the implications of the holism of memories so that, for example, we underplay the importance of the connection between our memories and the space-time paths of the (token) bodies we have. If we do underplay it, then indeed we have no means of distinguishing true from false memories; more than that, the distinction is utterly meaningless. If, on the other hand, we insist on the importance of the connection between the space-time path of the (token) body – unique to that body – and experiences that underpin true memories, then we must reject the notion that your body could house my memories and my body house yours. The connections between particular bodies and particular persons ceases to be accidental. And this is, of course, the case. The person I am – and, even more, the memories I have – depends on the experiences I have had. These are inseparable from the necessarily unique space-time paths of the token body that is mine. The idea that my memories could just as well be associated with your body as with mine seems plausible only if we are talking about types of memory as opposed to token memories. My memory of 'a cat' could be had by you; you, too, after all, have memories of cats. My memory of the cat Felix, seen from a particular angle at a particular time, could not have been had by you, as you could not have the same actual experience, if only because your body could not have occupied the same point in space-time as me. One body pushes another out of the way. *A fortiori*, the sum total of such token memories – or memories with token contents – most certainly could not. It requires a particular body, with the characteristics of my body, with the moment-to-moment sensory attunement of my body occupying the space-time path of my body – a space-time path that began with the fertilisation of a particular ovum by a particular sperm. It requires, in short, my body. No other body will do.

In developing our case against Swinburne's notion of swappable bodies we have not relied on the bio-genetic account of the Existential Intuition. Such an account would certainly rule out body-swapping, for the 'I' is the appropriation of a particular aware organism by itself as its self. It reveals what lies at the heart of identity, and what ultimately provides the only criterion to differentiate true memories from false ones. What gives identity temporal extension and stability – so that it counts as the same across changes – is the notion that 'I am this thing', in particular, that 'I am this body'. It is this that forbids the notion that any other body could have had my memories and experiences. The feeling that 'personal identity is something ultimate, unanalysable in terms of such observable and experienceable phenomena as bodily continuity and continuity of memory' (Swinburne, *Personal Identity*, p. 26) is both valid and incomplete: it captures an essential aspect of personal identity, but overlooks other aspects. The observable and experienceable phenomena are not in themselves sufficient to found identity, but are required to give its endurance over time some kind of content. Instantaneous identity requires the Existential Intuition, which both transforms the living organism into an individual with an identity and weaves that identity into particular (real, actual) experiences. Enduring identity requires that those experiences should be connected over time, via memory authenticated by its connections with experiences that are the experiences of a particular body.[44] The objective fact of my intimate relationship to a particular body is not merely contingently connected with my identity; but at the same time, objective facts – continuity of body and overlap and connectedness of memory – alone do not make for personal identity. They have to be 'appropriated', through the Existential Intuition that assumes the body as that which I am.

Both the vertical and horizontal dimensions of the self, therefore, are necessary to establish what we regard as 'personal identity'; and the vertical dimension has priority. Without the Existential Intuition, the continuity of the body is merely resistance of a physical body to change, mere inertia, and the continuity, connectedness or overlapping of memories, in the absence of criteria to separate true from false memories, would take us no further than the pell-mell of impressions that Hume 'stumbled' on when he entered 'most intimately' into what I call *myself*. The horizontal dimension of identity would not, of itself, count as a dimension of identity at all without the standing iteration of the vertical dimension, the 'am' that permeates the aware, engaged body. Let us now return to that vertical dimension – relatively neglected in much debate on identity and the self – and ask ourselves whether it is truly vertical. Or whether, indeed, it can be truly separated from the horizontal dimension of identity extended over time.

## 7.9 THE DIAGONAL SELF

In the first instance, that which is appropriated as self, as me, is my body. The body's spatio-temporal continuity, and the audit trail that its necessarily continuous world-line thus provides, enable memories (which, unlike experiences, can occur in any order and at any time: recollection is a randomly pointed torch in a dark cellar) to be authenticated. It is through the body that memories are both immediately and subsequently linked with experiences and are tethered to the explicit here-now that the body, through the Existential Intuition, makes available. The self-apprehended body is the ultimate anchor of the self-consciousness that lies at the heart of personal identity and validates the remembrance that pervades episodic memory.

So much for the story so far. It is now time to strike a jarring note: the so-called 'vertical' and 'horizontal' dimensions of personal identity are abstractions that cannot exist independently of one another. This, after all, was why Lockean accounts of personal identity failed: they tried to establish identity-over-time without considering identity-at-a-given time. There are, what is more, several reasons for being uncomfortable in particular with the notions of the vertical dimension of identity and of an Existential Intuition in which the self is instantaneously asserted. Indeed, the present author is aware that he may be the only person to think that these notions have anything to commend them. There is the question of whether the vertical dimension of the self is truly vertical and, closely connected with this, whether there is anything corresponding to the 'instantaneous' self. And there is an undeniable opacity in the concept of an Existential Intuition, which links the contents of the instantaneous self to itself. (Ultimately, it is a phrase whose sense has to be ignited by the reader's own intuitions.) We shall examine these reasons for discomfort separately, though they are deeply connected.

The instantaneous or vertical dimension adds the 'id' to the 'entity' to create the 'id-entity': the Existential Intuition is an *iteration* (which is not, of course, in any sense a duplication); a 'standing' iteration. The horizontal dimension – the objective persistence of something (a body, a set of character traits, a collections of habits, an ability to recall certain events) – contributes the 'entity'. While there is no identity without an enduring something, a continuant, to which it might be attached, there equally is no identity without an 'id' to do the attaching; there is no enduring self without an instantaneous self. The question this will then provoke is 'How instantaneous is the instantaneous self?' More radically, we might ask: Is it valid to separate the experienced identity of the moment from experienced identity over time? Does this separation even have the validity of the avowedly artificial separation of the vertical and horizontal components of motion in the analysis of the parabolic path taken by a projectile? More particularly, can the self ever be a matter of an instant? Can it ever be confined to the instant?

The answer to both these cases must be 'No'. The sense of who I am – beyond the most primitive level of bodily awareness – is woven out of *meanings* and must consequently reach into the past where those meanings were established and the future whose key they hold is. If it is necessary to view perception and memory holistically, it is even more necessary to view the self and personal identity holistically. To put this another way, the self relates to a world that has temporal depth: it is rooted in the past and is open to the future. In order for the self to make any kind of sense of itself, for self-presence to be meaningful, it has to be impregnated by the past and pregnant with the future. If 'I' is ever going to be more than an extensionless point, its instants need to reach beyond the instant; at the coarsest level, 'I' requires an historical context, a temporal depth, for it to be contentful, or for its contents to signify. (It is not too much of an exaggeration to state that I am who I remember I am and who has such and such a future is shaped by the who I recall myself being. The who is a who that remembers a who.) There is, in brief, no pure instant of RT because every instant is an instant of a self-world and so reaches out in space and time: each supposed instant is world-steeped; synchro-diachronically flooded.

Identity, in other words, cannot be established solely on the basis of a self-apprehended body that exists in space and has little temporal depth – any more than it could be established on the basis of memories that are set out in time but have no spatial extensity. 'Here', for example, is imbued with the 'theres' that I have come from and am going to. While 'here' is a spatial counter-point to theres, it is a way-station temporally between theres. The sense of 'What I am here' is informed by the sense of 'What I am at' and 'How I got here' and 'Where I am going to' – all in the broadest sense. The Existential Intuition grows beyond the bounds of the body in the narrow sense into a world that corresponds to a self. The iteration of the self-apprehended body plants the flag in the sensory field and, from this, self and world grow interactively. This would not be possible if it were a succession of isolated instants.

There is, of course, nothing original about these observations. Bergson famously remarked that 'every instant has a thousand memories'.[45] Indeed, some may think that it is only the present writer who has to be reminded of them. We need to consider, however, what implication they have for the notion that without the instantaneous sense of self, asserted as it were from within, there is no basis for continuity of personal identity. What does it signify if the 'I' is 'temporally smeared'? Nothing damaging, I believe, for the notion that we have to consider two dimensions of the instantaneous self. For while the self that is experienced instantaneously is spread over many moments, the instants of its assertion are objectively moments of time. Indeed, the spread-out-ness (or, to use Heidegger's phrase, about the temporalisation of *Dasein*, the 'stretched out stretching itself along'), is essential if the instants of the self are going to cohere into an enduring self and personal identity. Smearing ensures that the self is not a mere succession of separate self-moments, a Humean parade of fugitive impressions, a bundle or collection of different perceptions without anything to bundle or collect them together, a mere aggregate of disaggregated self-instants. This requires us to admit an added complexity to the relationship between the objective entities that underpin the self and the instantaneous assertion of the self; between the Existential Intuition and the 'this' that is 'am-ed' in it.

Let us begin with the Existential Intuition:

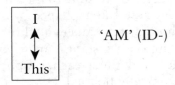

This is affirmed at each instant in the life of the subject:

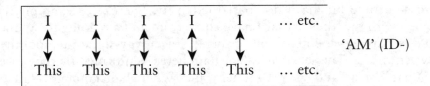

The id- in identity is linked to something that endures. This is variously seen as something purely externally enduring, such as a body that changes slowly enough to be regarded as the same body; as something internal, such as a relatively stable corpus of episodic memories infused with the feeling of remembrance; or as something that has both internal and external faces, such as habits, traits, evidence of things learned, character, continued assumption of duties and responsibilities. Most probably, it is a combination all of these things: a remembered, remembering, experienced, experiencing body. This provides the -entity' in identity:

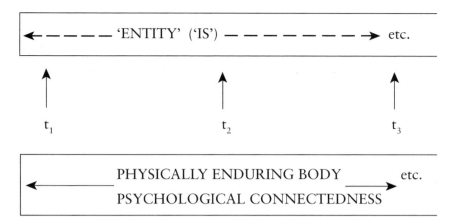

The (notional) successive momentary I's are rooted in past and present. They participate in a temporal smearing, corresponding to a notional diagonal dimension, as well as a vertical dimension capturing the Existential Intuition:

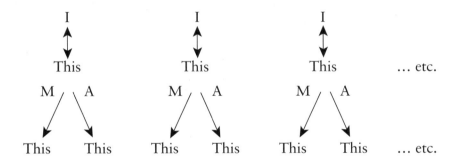

M = memory; A = anticipation.

The continuity of the entity that I am (my body) is located in objective or public time, while the temporality of the instantaneous I is located in subjective, private or indexical time:

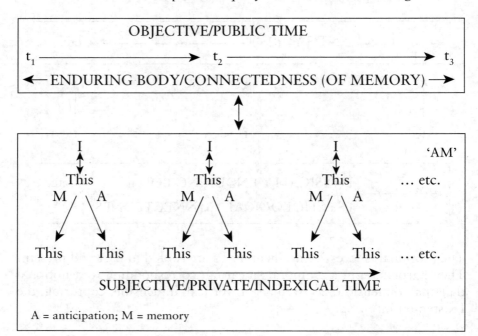

And so the entire picture of 'id'-entity emerges:

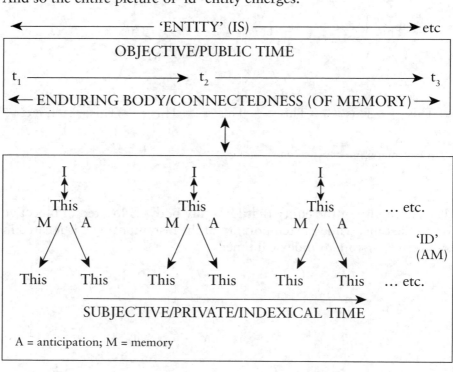

This picture identifies three dimensions of personal identity: the vertical Existential Intuition; the horizontal enduring entity – for example, a persisting (remembered-remembering, experienced-experiencing) body which the Intuition apprehends as 'myself' and which exists in objective, physical time; and the diagonal dimension which carries the link between the instantaneous self and the personal past(s) and future(s) to which it relates. The schema leaves many things unexplained; most notably the relationship between the private or indexical dimension of time in which the instantaneous self is 'smeared' so that is connects with itself over time and the objective time which corresponds to the (public) continuation of the enduring self.

The relationship is certain to be complex, not the least because tenses do not exist in objective time and yet they are central to temporal self-location and the 'smearing' of the instantaneous self. More puzzling still is the origin of the simultaneities that lie at the heart of subjective time and which, none the less, after Albert Einstein and Hermann Minkowski, we know do not exist in the spatio-temporal manifold into which objective time is assimilated. In short, we do not know how subjective time is 'inserted' into objective time.[46] It is a reasonable conjecture that the indexicalisation of time, like that of space, is connected with the apprehension of the engaged body in the Existential Intuition – and that both are essential precursors to the discovery of the deindexicalised, objective time of physics – but beyond that all seems deeply muddled.

### 7.10 BEING (OR NOT BEING) ONESELF

There is another equally insoluble problem; namely that of the *scope* of the Existential Intuition that we have expressed as 'I am this', 'That I am this', 'That I am this (thing, entity)', etc. We have at various points in this book considered the referent of 'this'. When we try to flesh out

'That I am this'

we always run into difficulties. While it is a matter of grammar that 'I' is whoever says they are 'I', grammar (and logic) cannot extend very far into 'I am this' once 'this' starts taking substance on board, when, for example, 'this' tries to import into itself the body, or parts of it. The fact that the instantaneous self is a blob or a smear rather than an extension-less point, that it has material substance in the form of the body that it is given in some sense to be, places our interpretation on the borderland between matters of logic and matters of substance. We do not yet have the Existential Grammar we postulated in Chapter 2 to deal with this.

We are simply unable to define the legitimate scope of the 'quasi-instantaneous' I, of the carnal assumption of self.

It is tempting to try to borrow the boundaries of the body for the limits of what can be immediately assumed as one's self. But this invites the absurd conclusion that the Existential Intuition should be limited by the skin, suggesting an egregious branch of logic: epitheliology. Besides, it would require us to place biological constraints on an assumption whose origins biology may explain but whose subsequent manifestations go beyond biology. The self is neither confined to the body nor is it universal throughout the body, especially the body as revealed not in immediate awareness but indirectly through perception or even more indirectly through knowledge. I am (live, be) only rarely the tips of my ears and never my serum potassium. It is also tempting to borrow the boundary between matters of knowledge and of immediate experience: we can be (I can 'am') what we directly experience, but not what we merely know or think we know. This is quite unhelpful because, as we discovered, the boundary between awareness by direct acquaintance and awareness by discovery or by description are perforated: what I exist, for example, does not confine itself to what I can experience or exclude itself from what I merely know. This is the case not simply because less than the totality of what I can directly experience is available to me as part of myself at any one time, but also because what I know is part of what I am – it contributes enormously to the shape of the world which my self has as its cognate object. What is more, as we have repeatedly noted, the line between indubitable (and unfalsifiable) immediate experience and falsifiable contents of consciousness is neither straight nor continuous. At the level of the Existential Intuition this simple distinction does not operate if only because, as we shall discuss in Volume 3, the world of knowledge and of truth and falsehood is a late consequence of the Intuition. There is also the difficulty that my experiencing something – even as intimate as a part of my body – is not the same as my knowing it. Or rather, there is a gap between my experience of parts of my body, on the basis of which I am assume them as myself, and the objective properties of those parts. It is possible to have an experience of a thing and not to experience that thing.

The only way of guaranteeing that the 'am' that connects 'I' and 'this' in 'That I am this …' never imported something into the right-hand side of the equation which was not present on the left would be for 'I' to be extensionless. If it were extensionless, however, the transformation of 'something' into 'I' would be a non-act and the 'I' would be empty. The continuous self-stipulation that is the Existential Intuition would stipulate nothing. This was perhaps the essential insight of phenomenologists, such Heidegger and Sartre, for whom the self – *Da-sein* for Heidegger, the *pour-soi* for Sartre – lives in a permanent state of non-self-coincidence: it doesn't quite manage to be, or catch up with, or be coterminous with, any 'this' it assumed as itself. Unfortunately, this made it a nothing – or, in Sartre's case, nothingness – with the 'ness' only making things worse by removing nothing from individuals and making it a category of sorts, like 'being', or a substanceless substance.

The idea of the diagonal dimension of personal identity is possibly a compromise between two versions of the self that fail in different ways: a point-identity that fails to unfold; and objective bases – the body, a corpus of memory – that fails to enter fully into the instantaneous self and to link the 'I' with an enduring or substantive self. This latter failure manifests as our inability wholly to be the objective things by which we are recognised and identified: there is a lack of congruity between that by virtue of which we are familiar to ourselves and to others (whose familiarity we experience as in part an aspect of the familiarity of ourselves), that by which we continue to be identified by others, and that which is gathered up in the continuing act of assumption in the Existential Intuition of the self. There is a failure to *be* our identity. This has many uncomfortable consequences, some of which are worth exploring.

First of all, there a discrepancy between the unchanging and absolute identity of the instantaneous self with itself – the eternally reiterated 'I am' – and the gradually changing visible identity of the enduring public person. This discrepancy only rarely leads to an internal shearing force, not only because change is imperceptible, but because 'That I am this' is the presupposition of every moment of our lives and any sense of our having changed belongs to the rare periods of reflection rather than the much longer periods of 'absorbed coping'. So even when, after many years, someone whom I knew very well does not recognise me, I do not feel that I have *essentially* changed. There is also an element of rationalisation: RT notes that the young medical student and the middle-aged professor both go under the name RT, but he believes RT is essentially unchanged because RT is fundamentally the same person who has simply gained more experience of the world. The present-day professor is as much an expression of the 'I' who is 'I' as was the medical student. The assertion by an octagenerian that 'Inside I feel I am just the same person as I was when I was 20' may be a cliché but it captures a fundamental truth. There is something unchanging at the heart of the subject-truth that is the Existential Intuition. Wherever we go in life, whatever course we take, we always take ourselves with us; this self is not objectively the same. But from the self's point of view (which is both privileged and underprivileged), whatever transformations my self undergoes, it is always the same self because it is always 'my self'. The iteration is unchanged. The Existential argument goes as follows:

I (at $t_1$) am this ———→ I (at $t_2$) am this-ish
I = I
Therefore This = This-ish

I do not change, though the body that I live, and the life that I suffer and the way I think about myself are constantly changing. Just as I am the same I when I am thinking, glowing with sunburn, frightened of dying, ashamed; I am also the same I when I am 80 as when I am 20, whatever others may think and say and I aver. My body may change, but I do not: after all, my body, considered separate from me, has no identity.

The problems we noted in Chapter 6 of the bodily contribution to identity – which are in part a problem of trying to reconnect knowledge with immediate experience (or objects of knowledge such as my limb when I catch sight of it, or my bone marrow when I read about it, with my lived self) – get even more complex when we take into account the temporal 'diagonality' of the instantaneous self which is not truly instantaneous but is temporally smeared, invested in things haloed with meanings derived from past experience and reaching into an indeterminate future. Not only do we have a bewildering variety of present bodies, but also an indefinite number of past selves, of instantaneously felt I's and summed Raymond Tallis's. These all haunt the diagonal Intuition; and yet we seem from moment to moment to be unified: 'I am this …'. The *de facto* unity of the body cannot solve this for us; leaving aside the earlier mentioned fallacies of epitheliology, which tried to use the skin to limit the scope of the Existential Intuition, we see from the complexities of embodiment uncovered in the previous chapters that the unity of the body is simply not available as a given to which the self can help itself; indeed, the multitude of bodily schemata and phenomenal bodies quarried by the living creature out of the objective body proves that if appropriating one's body as one's self were a project, it would be in deep trouble.

The indubitable attractiveness of the body as a basis for self-identity is nevertheless real, and it is in part due to the fact that it is the basis for the identification of oneself by others; that it is a point of attachment for others' stable expectations of oneself and for all the habits, roles, positions that make one seem to be a rather more stable thing than the events of one's life might lead one to expect. The body can acquire a carapace of civic being that is a sight less evanescent than the states of my body or the schemata that I assume out of it. There would be no Professor Tallis without Raymond Tallis's body; but Professor Tallis holds the various states of Ryamond Tallis's body together over time in the way that those states could not cohere of themselves.

This is the key to the 'diagonal dimension': that which is instantaneously available is something which gathers up a prolonged stasis. The gaze of others – which at the very least confers a seamless unity on our body and a relative unchangingness – makes temporal depths available to us in an instant. The gaze in which you figure as Professor Tallis imports enduring identity into the moments of the self. Even so, it is important to keep separate the sense of our own instantaneous identity, from others' sense of our continuing identity and the objective reality of the continuing identity of something such as the body by which we are tagged. Being tagged is not the same as assuming, having or being, an identity. I do not find out who I am by identifying which body is mine by, say, consulting a ticket on my wrist.

At any rate, when we try to determine the contribution of the body to the *scope* of the instantaneous self (without the body there would be no self), we run into all sorts of difficulties. Worse still, it is never entirely clear whether our uncertainties are definitional or due to lack of psychological knowledge. Shall we include all the sensations served up by my body (the instantaneous lived body)? Shall we add in the sensations served up to my body? How far shall we go beyond the body? Shall we spread the scope of the Intuition into the objects that surround the body; into the thoughts and memories of the moment; into the wide, nebulous preoccupations that pervade every moment and the complex framework from which they derive their significance? The truth is that, once the Existential Intuition exceeds – as it must exceed – an extensionless point, it becomes difficult to think of a principled way of delimiting its scope. One thing is certain: invoking the body does not give us all the answers we need.

Ordinary tautologies allow no slippage: it is not a question of a 'good enough' fit or a rough fit: there is no tolerance. The Existential Intuition is an ever-changing assumption and successive assumptions – that 'I am this$_1$' and that 'I am this$_2$' – are not easily separated. What makes the body my body, or me, in the way that a chimp's body is not 'mine' or 'me' for the chimp, may have a biological explanation. But the mode in which we humans now possess our bodies, and the identities to which they contributed, cannot be captured biologically. And yet we need the living body, or something like it, to make the subject more than a mere point of consciousness and to give the Existential Intuition actual content – a definite content and a limited scope. And that's about all we can safely say.

## 7.11 CONCLUDING REFLECTIONS: IDENTITY, 'AM', 'IS'
### AND THE BODY

Our inquiry into the relationship between the body, memory, the instantaneous self and the enduring self have brought no solutions, but have, I hope, highlighted and perhaps even clarified some of the problems – and placed the curious nature of the personal identity in plainer light. The fundamental intuitions behind this chapter are close to those that moved Reid to write as he did in the passage quoted earlier; namely, that material objects do not truly have identity in the way that human beings have. '*Identity*,' he argues,

> has no fixed nature when applied to bodies; and questions about the identity of a body are very often questions about words. But identity when applied to persons, has no ambiguity, and admits not of degrees, or of more or less.

Identity in this true sense cuts beneath the type identity of material objects – and arguments about whether a particular object should still count as a horse, or when a pile of sand being diminished grain by grain should cease to qualify as 'a heap'. It also cuts beneath the token identity of material particulars – and arguments about whether this tree which has grown from a seed is still the same thing as the seed; or (to give an example nearer home) whether my 57-year-old body is the same thing as the three-month foetus which would shortly be christened 'Raymond Tallis'. Intrinsic, as opposed to conferred identity, personal identity is not a matter of degree, or of stipulation that allows some degrees of change and not others. Identity truly understood is self-stipulating and absolute. Or, rather, it is absolute because it is self-stipulating.

Personal identity may (somewhat riskily) be described as 'an existed tautology': I am what I am that I am, where the second 'am' is meant in a rather unorthodox active, quasi-transitive sense: 'am-ing'. No external criterion is needed to help me identify the self that I am and no external criterion could be invoked to override my sense of my continuing self and to prove that I no longer exist, that my self has ceased to be.

These statements need to be interpreted carefully. Because the Existential Intuition is not empty, there are constraints on self-stipulating identity. First, 'am-ing' is not the same as 'saying'. 'I am what I am that I am' does not, therefore, translate into 'I am what I say I am'. While 'A am A' has more latitude than 'A is A', this applies only at the level of particulars, indeed singulars. I cannot stipulate myself to be an entity of a particular kind, partly because I am not an entity in the requisite sense, but more importantly because I am not an entity of a general kind. I am not a god simply because I feel I am a god. Nor am I an entity of the kind picked out by a singular referring expression. I am not Napoleon simply because I believe that 'I am Napoleon' – or only in a very modified sense that takes away the substantive content of my claim. Nor is it sufficient that I feel that 'I am Raymond Tallis' for me to be the person thus christened. The Existential Intuition does not license me to help myself to the characteristics of a type of entity or of singular entities picked out by referring expressions. Except in a very special sense we have tried to define, the Existential Intuition cannot cross the gap between language and what is the case. Though when cast in the form of a proposition, it lies between language and what is the case (which is why, in that form, it is seen to have unique properties, captured by an existential grammar), it cannot make anything be which does not exist. It has the power only to make that which I am already be me explicitly.

Second, precisely because the Existential Intuition is not simply a general form but does have specific content, it has to be attached to an enduring particular. This link was encapsulated by Reid:

> my personal identity ... implies the continued existence of that indivisible thing that I call myself. Whatever this self may be, it is something which thinks, and deliberates, and resolves, and acts, and suffers. I am not action, I am not feeling; I am something that thinks and acts and feels.[47]

The question then arises as to the nature of the something that 'thinks and acts and feels'. And therein lies considerable difficulty. We might have hedged our bets by leaving the translation of the Existential Intuition as 'I am this'. By this means, we would restrict its content to a link between two indexicals – the first-person pronoun and a demonstrative. This is unattractive for two reasons: a) it denies the self any contents, when selves manifestly have contents beyond mere thisness, or abstract deixis; and b) it erases the distinctive feature of the Existential Intuition, namely that it is asserted and lived – asserted through being lived. 'Am' goes beyond mere equivalence. It is about lived being. Reid's essential point is the Heideggerian one that all true identity is existed identity.

First-person being, personal identity, lies on the cusp between equivalence across a difference and immersion; between the identification with something other than one's self and the tautologous coincidence of a thing with itself. This ontological mezzanine position is captured in, for example, the term 'embodiment'. If Raymond Tallis was Raymond

Tallis's body in the way that a pebble is a pebble, we wouldn't speak of 'Raymond Tallis's body' or of Raymond Tallis being 'embodied'. Conversely, we don't say of a pebble that it is 'empebbled'. Being embodied (as we discovered in Chapter 6) means that we are both more, and less, than our bodies. There is a distance between us and our bodies across which our selves are *em*bodied (and our bodies are haunted by selves). It is this ever less complete identification with the body that makes possible true identity in Reid's sense and the various 'identifications-with' that ultimately reach far beyond the body, as when I feel myself to be 'a nice bloke', 'a doctor' 'a true-born Frenchman', or whatever. The gap opens up questions and a quest. When the who awakens in the body, the what of the body does not answer the question, also awoken, 'What am I?' Such questions cannot haunt, nor turn into a life-long quest for, non-human living creatures. They *are* bodies in a third-person sense. The questions grow in the gap signified by the 'em-' in 'embodied',

Without the body, there can be no basis for continuity, substantiality or even individuation of the self. The body is that in virtue of which the 'this' that I am acquires singularity; or the means by which self-consciousness has a substrate to get a grip on. Asserting this will seem rather odd if one adopts a biogenetic approach to the Existential Intuition. It makes sense only if one starts from, say, Descartes' imaginary metaphysical prison, in which a thinking 'I' is alone with her thoughts. By the same token, it would be absurd to think of the body as simply an answer to a philosophical problem and acting as a 'tag' for our identity, or as the bearer of it. The Cartesian starting point (which is close to that of Hume and Kant) could lead you to ask all sorts of odd questions; for example: 'Why should the subject be required to throw in its lot with something (the body) that requires dinner in order that it should acquire and retain its particular identity?' This kind of question makes sense only if one begins with the subject in a transcendental realm as opposed to awakening in the body.

The body links 'inner' and 'outer' aspects of identity. The outer aspect is rooted in the fact that the body (unlike, say, my memories) is visible to others and is relatively unchanged over a long time. It can be identified and re-identified. The inner aspect of identity is satisfied by the fact that my body is largely what I live and hence 'am'. The problem is that, for others as for myself, the visible body, the one we shake hands with, is not identical with my identity: my identity includes my behaviour, my corpus of knowledge, my memories, the institutions I identify with, and so on. For others, at any rate, my body may usually reliably lead them to identify myself but may not deliver the self that they expect. I might have a relatively unchanged body and yet, due to brain injury, have lost my memory and all those things – job, relations with others, interests, passions, sense of being located in a framework of past and future – that define (and indeed constitute) my *personal* identity. The argument might then move on to revolve around the criteria for defining 'the same body' or 'a relatively unchanged body' – precisely the problem that Reid encountered and caused him to withhold the notion of 'identity' from material objects. The danger here is of a circularity; namely that we shall regard a body as the same or as unchanged so long as it functions in such a way as to sustain unaltered those things that count in defining personal identity. The radical suggestion that so long as the body exists, then identity is preserved would force one to conclude that even a corpse was 'selved'. The body, at the very least, has to be alive and self-conscious.

Although what I am – for myself and for others – is to a degree dissociated from my body, there is no way we could arrive at anything like personal identity without the body: this is where it begins and this is where it has its deepest roots. Personal identity and the sense of self could not be elaborated in some disembodied state. What is more, only *human* bodies have the complex elaborated selves, the explicit sense of self, that we see expressed in the everyday lives of people. There must, therefore, be something special about such bodies that permit the emergence of selfness of this kind. While there can be no credible metaphysical requirement that the Existential Intuition requires creatures with toenails, at least some of our bodily design features – beyond life-supporting characteristics – must be necessary for it to wake up – and we attempted to identify these in the earlier chapter. While the distinctive biology of the human body may not fully explain the emergence of the kind of subject that we are, it does seem to make sense of why it is in such a body that the developed subject uniquely emerges; why human beings, unlike any other living or non-living entity, have identity.

### NOTES

1. P. F. Strawson, *Entity and Identity and Other Essays* (Oxford: Oxford University Press, 1997), pp. 3–4. Strawson, in the title essay of this collection, argues for the restriction of a 'criterion of identity' to those rather special cases (such as the direction of straight lines and numbers of members of sets) 'in which the supposed criteria can be precisely and strictly stated in a clearly applicable form' (p. 2). In the case of ordinary substantial individuals – such as dogs or men – we should refrain from using this phrase and speak only of a *principle* of identity. In the Introduction to the collection, he recants.
2. Ibid., p. 3.

3. Assuming that is that it amounts to more than the tautologous assertion that general meanings of words capture, without further ado, the general meanings they have.
4. For Fichte, the essence of selfhood was in an active positing of its own self-identity. Self-consciousness is an auto-productive activity – a fact-act.
5. Richard Swinburne, in Sydney Shoemaker and Richard Swinburne, *Personal Identity. Great Debates in Philosophy* (Oxford: Blackwell, 1984), p. 3.
6. *The Cambridge Dictionary of Philosophy* (Cambridge: Cambridge University Press, 1995), p. 574. Interestingly, though, he also says that 'asking what the identity of persons consists in is just a way of asking what sorts of things persons are'.
7. Rudiger Safranski's account (in *Martin Heidegger: Between Good and Evil*, transl. Ewald Osers, Cambridge, MA: Harvard University Press, 1998) of Heidegger's notion of 'existence' provides a helpful gloss on the distinction being made here: 'by existing we are not merely present, but we must exist ourselves; we not only live, but we must "lead" our life. Existence is a mode of Being, more precisely: the "Being accessible to itself" ... Existence is something that is, something that, other than stones, plants, or animals, stands in a self-relationship. It not only "is", it also becomes aware that it is "here" ... Existing, therefore, is not a being-present but an implementation, a movement' (p. 124).
8. It is this above all that justifies our treating patients with end-stage Alzheimer's disease as persons and not as animals. Almost to the very end, the intuition 'I am this ...' persists despite the erosion of memory and other mental faculties, of a sense of future, of responsible, caring human behaviour. While Mrs Tallis may correctly say of Raymond Tallis (RT) that 'he is no longer the person I married', that he is a greatly diminished person, it would not be correct to say 'He is no longer a person'. One thing is certain: others will notice that RT has changed or that 'the old RT is no longer' before RT does; for RT is always himself for himself. Even when he catches himself doing something he would once have deeply disapproved of or when he sees his aged face in the mirror, he will still be inclined to feel that he is still himself 'inside' – or 'deep inside'. The grey-haired man who looks at him out of a mirror seems as remote from him as the raw, long-haired youth he sees in photographs of himself as a student who would not have recognised this grey-haired man. A middle-aged man is his own remote descendant, living in a world his earlier selves would not recognise. Parfit would argue that it follows from this that the futures that we dimly intuit or actively work for house our absences, and we should worry no more about our 'own' futures than those of anyone else.
9. The Kantian subject has difficulty being anything substantive principally because it has been called into existence as a principle of coherence to deal with Hume's problems of trying to find something to bind sensations; as something, one might uncharitably conclude, invented to get Kant out of a hole.
10. Other selves, of course, contribute to self-consciousness: it is the gaze of others that gives the self at a certain level its greatest charge of substance. We feel our selves in their most curdled or solid state when our self-consciousness is infused with others' consciousness of ourselves. The initial assumption of the self, however, always comes first. Without that assumption, there would be no self to curdle in another's awareness. The Cartesian 'I' which, like the Kantian subject bears the marks of its origin, is alone and self-transparent. It is the product of a methodological solipsism in which each is absolutely alone, living inside the possibility that everything is 'my' dream. Others' selves that add density to our own have themselves, of course, to have substantiality; and this requires them to be perceivable by us.

11. It might be argued that I am here merely offering a definition of 'person' – any human in which the Existential Intuition is still active – which could be challenged. Locke famously located the distinction between the person and the 'man' – a biological member of the human species – at a different point. For him a person had to have both the bodily continuity of a man (be a continuous spatio-temporal organism of the correct species) and psychological continuity through memory. This is true; but there is no definite point at which the shrinkage of self is such that one is justified in refusing ascription of personhood.

12. The separation of the vertical and horizontal dimensions of the self is not, of course, absolute. It is an artefact of analysis. I shall return to this in due course.

13. David Hume, *A Treatise of Human Nature* (New York: Doubleday, 1961), Part IV, section 6, p. 228.

14. One might imagine that the contrast between the vertical and horizontal dimensions of the self could be mapped on to the contrast between the transcendental self or ego (or the logical subject) and the empirical self. This mapping does not work, however, because the vertical self, unlike the transcendental ego or the logical subject, is contaminated with empirical substance: the body, etc. as mediated through sensations. It is particularised by that which is intuited through it.

15. As Hume pointed out, the sameness that is supposed to underpin identity is an artefact – 'all objects, to which we ascribe identity, without observing their invariableness and uninterruptedness, are such as consist of a succession of related objects' (*Treatise*, p. 231). So-called stable, single objects are really a succession of slightly different objects and what determines whether we call them different objects or the same objects is the proportionate size of the differences. A mountain may be added to a planet without altering the claim of the planet to be the same planet whereas a change of a very few inches would destroy the identity of some bodies. Identity may survive massive, even total, change of substance, so long as it occurs gradually or there is retained 'sympathy of parts to a common end' as in the case of a ship repeatedly refitted until all its material has been changed. In a rather startlingly modern turn of phrase, Hume argues that 'all the nice and subtle questions concerning personal identity can never be possibly decided, and are to be regarded rather as grammatical than as philosophical difficulties … All the disputes concerning the identity of connected parts are merely verbal, except insofar as the relation of parts gives rise to some fiction or imaginary principle' (ibid., p. 237). Our argument here is that this is true of the identity of material objects and (for example) institutions but not of humans. We shall argue, along with Reid, that only human persons have identities in the non-grammatical or fictional sense.

16. Derek Parfit, *Reasons and Persons* (Oxford: Clarendon Press, 1987).

17. The fact that this is overlooked, or not accorded much significance, reveals something about how neo-Lockeans think about the self: that it can be left to look after itself and that it is not primarily conscious; that it can be something largely deposited in an archive. But, as Bishop Butler pointed out, identity cannot be separated from consciousness of identity: it cannot all be tidied away into presupposition. The sense of my connectedness, inseparable from the feeling that I am coherent, cannot be deposited in objective reality but has to be realised in subjective awareness.

18. Parfit, *Reasons and Persons*, p. 232.

19. Not the least because it would reduce the difference between RT and Napoleon to one memory.

20. See also Derek Parfit, 'Personal Identity', *Philosophical Review* (1971); reprinted in Jonathan Glover, *The Philosophy of Mind*. Oxford Readings in Philosophy (Oxford: Oxford University Press, 1976).

21. Stephen Porter, John C. Yuille and Darrin R. Lehman, 'The Nature of Real, Implanted, and Fabricated Memories for Emotional Childhood Events: Implications for the Recovered Memory Debate', *Law and Human Behaviour* 23(5) (1999): 517–37.

22. See Mark A. Wheeler, Donald T. Stuss and Endel Tulving, 'Towards a Theory of Episodic Memory: The Frontal Lobes and Autonoetic Consciousness', *Psychological Bulletin* 121 (1991): 331–54, on which the present discussion has been heavily reliant.

23. Quoted in ibid., p. 333.

24. There is, of course, some connection with content: there are certain things that I could know only if I truly was 'there', certain details that must surely be available only to one who remembers on the basis of a remembered experience. This connection is not absolute: it may be strong enough to count as circumstantial evidence in court. But it does not cut much ice in the present context, as we shall see.

25. It was forensic considerations that led Locke to propose psychological continuity theories in the first place. One could not be held responsible for a crime one does not remember carrying out. More radically he argued, someone cannot have actually committed a crime in the past unless he now remembers doing it. This argument has a particularly sinister resonance when aged war criminals cannot be brought to justice because they have forgotten their wickedness. The perpetrator who forgets is separated from his crime.

26. Autonoetic consciousness is about the future as well as the past. The relevance of this to the relationship between the self and agency will become apparent in the next chapter.

27. In this context, it is interesting to quote Wheeler et al., who remind us that 'only humans, among primates, appear to have a reflective consciousness of the self as an entity across time'. It is only humans who have the self as something that grows and fattens as a something in its own right.

28. It would be possible to spend a lot of time teasing out this 'in fact'. A true memory is obviously one that is causally connected with – or occasioned by – the event of which it is a memory, of the event that gave rise to the experience. As several writers have argued, it is not enough to trace causal connections: they have to be of the right kind. It might be possible for the event I 'remember' to have triggered off an electrode implanted in my brain so that I had an experience corresponding to the experience of the event. But my memory of that 'experience' would not be a true memory; it would be only a quasi-memory. Just how interesting I find this argument may be judged from the fact that I have confined it to a note.

29. In other words, no amount of piling up evidence to support the notion that I really did have those experiences that I remember having would authenticate memories at a necessary level. The fact that I can speak fluent French is potent evidence that I have had much experience of listening to, learning, practising French phrases; but this does not prove that a particular recollection – say, of my teacher's face when she taught me about the use of the imperfect tense – is not a fabrication.

30. Bishop Butler, *The Analogy of Religion*, First Appendix (1739), in J. Perry (ed.), *Personal Identity* (Berkeley: University of California Press, 1975).

31. Parfit, *Reasons and Persons*, p. 217.

32. The connection between identity and responsibility is profound: it reaches to the roots of the relationship between agency and the self, as we shall discuss in the next chapter.
33. Hume, *Treatise*, p. 237.
34. The less sceptical claim, 'that memory does not so much *produce* as *discover* personal identity', does seem to follow from the fact that we ascribe to ourselves things that we have forgotten. I cannot, for example, remember all the steps that led up to my becoming what I am now but it would 'overturn all the most established notions of personal identity' (Hume, *Treatise*, p. 237), if I were to deny that these steps belonged to my present self. We 'extend our identity beyond our memory' and it is 'incumbent on those who affirm that memory produces entirely our personal identity, to give a reason why we can thus extend our identity' (ibid.).
35. Thomas Reid, quoted in Parfit, *Reasons and Persons*, p. 323. We could capture Reid's fundamental doubt about the continuing identity of material objects which inevitably change with time: the names change more slowly than the named. This is partly a matter of the limits of perception and partly a matter of convention, itself in part rooted in the exigencies of practice and partly in the stabilities of language. Our agonising over whether or not something counts as having the same numerical or the same type identity is a response to a sense of semantic shear between a stable name and a changing description. For Reid, the notion of the identity of material objects is stolen from that of persons. It is borrowed or conferred. This is evident not only from the fact that a *decision* has to be made as to whether or not a given material object is or is not the same (type or token), but also from the fact that objectively continuing unchanged is not sufficient to make for identity. The latter requires a conscious being to visit object O at time $t_1$ and to revisit it at time $t_2$ and judge that it has not changed. This, in turn, depends upon picking out object O as a single thing to which criteria of 'no change' or 'sufficient change to judge as no longer being the same object or no longer existing' can be applied. While relatively unchanged continuation is the truth condition of identity assertions, the judgement of a conscious being (that 'This is O' and 'O has not changed') is an existence condition of identity.
36. Parfit makes the opposite mistake. He correctly concludes from the Sorites Paradox and other arguments that our continued existence is not something that must be determinate and all-or-nothing. He incorrectly concludes from this that our existence at any given moment is also indeterminate, non-absolute, 'admitting of degrees'. This in turn leads to his incorrect conclusion that identity is indeterminate and the self a fiction. This is the result of failing to separate the vertical and horizontal dimensions of the self; or of identifying the subject of experience with the enduring self.
37. It is arguable that psychological connectedness theories are bodily theories of a kind if one assumes (as Parfit does) that memories are inscribed in neuronal activity. This is irrelevant if we are concerned with the contrast between 'inner aspect' theories of identity (where identity is, as it were curated, by the one who is identified) and outer aspect theories where identity is at least in part in the keeping of others. Bernard Williams was a particularly powerful advocate of bodily continuity as the basis for continuing personal identity over time.
38. Quassim Cassam, *Self and World* (Oxford: Oxford University Press, 1998), p. 26.
39. One may believe, as I do, that body/brain/neural activity is only a necessary but not a sufficient condition of experience and still find the body capable of providing

the substrate for the necessary audit trails.

40. P. F. Strawson, *Individuals* (London: Methuen, 1957), p. 92.
41. *Meditations*, p. 199.
42. We have moved to the higher reaches of the self. Here, there may be more than one identity per individual person. My *persona* at work, at play, with my children, with my wife, with a chance-met stranger on a train, on the podium, by a patient's bedside, will all be significantly different. People are often intrigued, surprised, even disoriented, seeing someone they know well acting in a setting quite different from that in which they have got to know them. This is not, of course, sinister; although the different roles one has in life (and in life between formal roles) demand different actors, this is not a question of the self splitting into crowds of separate selves. The personae are in communication with, in continuity, with one another. Children who are not used to this often find it very difficult to deal with their parents when they are with their peers. The thought of one's mother suddenly appearing in the playground without warning is enough to put any seven-year-old into an identity crisis.
43. Shoemaker and Swinburne, *Personal Identity*, p. 26.
44. The most intimate connection between the truth of memory and the reality of experience is captured in the equivalence between 'I really was there' and 'I really am here'.
45. Or, as it was put beautifully by the Italian poet Ungaretti: 'M'illumino / D'immenso.' Dilthey emphasised how the present was infused with the past and future. Husserl too pointed out that seemingly punctate time did not consist of a succession of discrete 'nows': the present retained the past (like a comet its tail) and protended into the future. This deep connectedness of the moments of experienced time was expressed most profoundly by Heidegger. Care, which is constitutive of *Da-sein*, and which is lived temporality, is 'being-ahead-of-oneself-already-being-in (a world) as being-together-with (innerworldly beings encountered)' (*Being and Time*, p. 292). This is bewilderingly dense but it underlines how care encompasses all three aspects of time: the future (being-ahead-of-oneself), the present (being-together-with innerworldly beings) and the past (already-being-in-the-world). Care lies at the heart of temporality and temporality is the essence of *Da-sein* and its world. *Da-sein*, he argues, 'does not exist as the sum of momentary realities ... *Da-sein* does not first fill up an objectively present path or stretch "of life" through the phases of its momentary realities, but stretches *itself* along in such a way that its own being is constituted beforehand as this stretching along ... In the unity of thrownness and the fleeting or else anticipatory being-toward-death, birth and death "are connected" in the way appropriate to Da-sein. As care, *Da-sein is* the "Between"' (*Being and Time*, p. 343). Leaving aside the highly personalised terminology, Heidegger's point is surely well made. *Da-sein* is not a succession of 'moments' or 'instants' of itself, in the way that an object seen objectively may be regarded as being. Its moments are interpenetrated: the *occurrence* of *Da-sein* is a 'stretched out stretching itself along' (ibid., p. 344).
46. See Raymond Tallis, *A Conversation with Martin Heidegger* (London: Palgrave, 2002) for a discussion of the problems that result when human temporality is given priority over physical time, as is the case in *Being and Time*.
47. Quoted in Parfit, *Reasons and Persons*, p. 223.

# CHAPTER 8

# Agency and First-Person Being

If all movement is always interconnected, the new arising from the old in a determinate order – if the atoms never swerve so as to originate some new movement that will snap the bonds of fate, the everlasting sequence of cause and effect, what is the source of the free will possessed by living things throughout the earth?

Lucretius, De Rerum Natura

Freedom is the first blessing of our nature.

Gibbon[1]

## 8.1 INTRODUCTION

Our focus so far has been on a rather passive 'I', the child (in the first instance) of the discovery by the engaged, aware body of itself *as* itself. Inasmuch as it is not the outcome of events outside the charmed circle of self-discovery, it is not a mere product; even less a mere by-product. Nevertheless, the Existential Intuition apparently results in little more than narcissistic 'I-ing' that would cut no ice in the tough world the body inhabits. There is nothing to suggest that the elevation of the animal body from third-person organic existence to first-person would deflect the organism from its preordained fate and play an active part in shaping the history of that body, even less in directing it. The biological roots of the Existential Intuition seem only to emphasise the likely impotence of personhood controlling the impersonal organism in which it pitches its tents.

Building on the arguments set out in the first volume of this trilogy, and briefly rehearsed in Chapter 1, I shall argue for a central role of the Intuition in establishing the freedom humans uniquely enjoy. By providing a naturalistic explanation of this key to the distances that humans have placed between themselves and the natural world, I shall make it more difficult to deny human freedom on the grounds of its theoretical impossibility. I will advance the hypothesis that human freedom, if it was at first an illusion, has been a progressively self-fulfilling or reality-producing one.

## 8.2 THE ENCROACHMENT OF DETERMINISM

It is often remarked of human freedom that all experience is in favour of it and all arguments are against it. The 'all' in each case is somewhat exaggerated. Some behaviour – for example, that of brainwashed individuals who find themselves doing things at odds with their usual beliefs, or of people in the grip of complex partial seizures acting out automatisms – seem unfree even to the behaver, at least in retrospect. These unusual experiences undermine confidence in our freedom in more normal circumstances. And a few arguments – such as those associated with the Existentialist – have been deployed to support the notion of an inescapable, if situation-dependent, freedom. Nevertheless, there is a tension between our subjective feeling (and all-pervasive assumption) that we are free and an objective view which makes that freedom incomprehensible. Nowhere has this tension been set out more clearly, and more poignantly, than in Thomas Nagel's *The View from Nowhere*.[2]

While it remains impossible sincerely to 'un-feel' human freedom, it is getting easier to 'unthink' it. The more we appear to be part of the natural (biological, material) world, freedom becomes increasingly incomprehensible and our belief in it more difficult to defend. The supernatural account of human beings as exceptional creatures uniquely made in the image of God provided a framework in which humans could be granted at least a margin of freedom.[3] The displacement of theology, which granted us a privileged place in the universe, by science, which denies any species a privileged place, makes it difficult to find a basis for a uniquely developed human freedom. If human beings are not exceptional creatures, then it cannot be true that they can exercise exceptional freedom. Recent advances in bioscience, by extending our knowledge of the role of unchosen mechanisms in voluntary activity, would seem to drive a stake through the very heart of human willing.

The erosion of the supernatural, or extra-natural, basis for human freedom by the elaboration of an evermore precise and comprehensive naturalistic account of human beings had several distinct components. The first was the discrediting of vitalism. The vitalist doctrine held that living organisms were fundamentally different from non-living entities – either because they contained non-physical elements or because they were governed by laws different from those that regulated non-living things. The breakdown of the distinction between living and non-living entities may seem less important for the present discussion, given that it was in part a reaction against the Cartesian notion of animals as machines which emphasised the distance between thinking humans and animal automata. Vitalism, it might therefore be argued, *narrowed* the gap between humans and other animals, making humans *less* rather than more exceptional. Even so, the abolition of the barrier between living and non-living creatures in the context of post-Enlightenment materialist thought reinforced the idea that living creatures were merely samples of the material world. When (as happened subsequently) the barrier between humans and other animals was broken down, humans too became part of the material universe, instead of being inhabitants of a relatively privileged enclave of living creatures. The emergence of biochemistry, a key consequence of anti-vitalism, not only made the techniques of chemists part of biological science, but eventually subordinated biology to chemistry, a trend that reached its fulfilment in the currently dominant belief that the fundamental truths about living organisms are those revealed by molecular biology.

The second component was the rise and rise of Darwinism. Darwinism apparently closed up the distances between humans and non-human living creatures. After Darwin, we are expected to accept that there is nothing especially special about humans, given that they are products of the same processes as those that have generated monkeys, scorpions and bacteria. The Darwinian account of Man's place in nature was reinforced by the neo-Darwinian synthesis of genetics, molecular biology and evolutionary theory. This placed great emphasis on the close genetic affiliation between humans and other beasts, reflected in the much quoted fact that humans share 98 per cent of their DNA with other primates. The implication is that, if there really is a difference between humankind and the beasts, it is marginal – perhaps 2 per cent.[4]

The third component has been the tearing down of the barrier between the human body and the human mind, supposedly on the basis of neuroscientific observations that (it is claimed) show that brain activity and mental phenomena are identical; or, at the very least, that how we think, feel, remember (and so act) is determined by brain activity and shaped by biophysical mechanisms that differ not at all from those that may be observed in other animals, or indeed elsewhere in the material world.

While vitalism seems indefensible, the other two assumptions – that genetic similarity invalidates belief in fundamental differences between humans and other beasts and that human minds are identical with the activity of human brains – are deeply questionable.[5] Nevertheless, these changes in the way the human body and the human mind are understood has made our unique freedom difficult to explain; and for many thinkers this means that it is implausible. It is as if the bioscience of the last two centuries has revealed an ever more intimate insertion of the material world, governed by physical laws, into human behaviour. Even if human behaviour is not yet fully assimilated to natural processes such as the growth of crystals or the tropisms of plants, it is not all that different (so the argument goes) from the behaviour of other creatures, and certainly not from that of the higher primates: they fall under the same genetically, neurohumorally, etc. mediated laws of physics. How, after all, can humans be more free than monkeys if they are, on objective scrutiny, in respect of the things that seem to matter for freedom, materially so little different from monkeys? Surely the difference between instinct-driven, largely involuntary, animal behaviour and reason-led, chosen human behaviour is an illusion. Both are expressions, in the last analysis, of the laws of physics.

The denial of the seemingly profound differences between human and animal behaviour has been a key element in thinking about humans over the last couple of centuries.[6] One of its most recent and extreme manifestations is evolutionary psychology which has been widely influential both within and beyond academe. For evolutionary psychologists, individual behaviour and even social institutions are expressions of genes that exist because of their superior adaptive value, the vast majority of which are common to humans and higher primates. The implicit, largely unconscious, principles that inform gene-determined human behaviour are rooted in their survival value; and the entity whose survival is served is not the conscious organism but the genome itself.[7] As Richard Dawkins put it, 'we are survival machines, robot vehicles blindly programmed to preserve the selfish molecules known as genes'.[8] The real reasons for our actions are beyond our ken and for this reasons are not truly voluntary.

The plausibility of evolutionary psychology, which almost completely eliminates the gap between humankind and the rest of animalkind, has been heavily dependent on two strategies: re-describing human behaviour in terms of animal behaviour; and anthropomorphising animal behaviour. Darwinism has given place to a pathological variant: Darwinosis. These strategies are seen to be implausible once they are exposed to daylight.[9] Nevertheless, given the overwhelming evidence for the Darwinian – or Darwinotic – belief that humanity emerged from animality, anyone who maintains that humans are different from animals in respect of something as utterly fundamental as freedom of action has a lot of explaining to do. Human freedom seems particularly difficult to account for in the light of the following facts: all animal bodies are part of the natural world; human bodies (and their brains) are in many respects very close to other animal bodies (and their brains); one part of the human body (the brain) has a key role in seemingly deliberate action.

In the absence of a satisfactory account of human freedom, it will (not unreasonably) be argued that there is no basis for believing in it; humans are no more free than other living creatures; and, in view of what bioscience has taught us about the physico-chemical basis of living creatures, they are no more free than other entities in the material world such as falling pebbles and running water. The further argument that our belief that we are free is an *adaptive illusion* – it must be good for morale to believe that one has brought about (and so has control over) some of the things that befall one and hence of survival value, even if it isn't true – seems compelling. With the gap between humans and other animals narrowed, and the identification of the human mind with the functioning of the brain, the fundamental difference between human actions and other events in the material world – between deliberately chosen, reason-led, behaviour and materially caused material effects – seems to have been illusory. The impersonal, unbreakable laws of the physical world encroach on, engulf and digest humanity.

One could be forgiven therefore for thinking, like the pre-eminent neurophysiologist Colin Blakemore, that human beings are sites, like any other, where the laws of nature operate, places through which pass the causal chains that originate outside of us:

> The human brain is a machine which alone accounts for all our actions, our most private thoughts, our beliefs. It creates the state of consciousness and the sense of self. It makes the mind ... To choose a spouse, a job, a religious creed – or even to choose to rob a bank – is the peak of a causal chain that runs back to the origin of life and down to the nature of atoms and molecules ...We feel ourselves usually to be in control of our actions, but that feeling is itself a product of our brain, whose machinery has been designed, on the basis of its functional utility, by means of natural selection ...All our actions are products of the activity of our brains. [It] makes no sense (in scientific terms) to try to distinguish sharply between acts that result from conscious attention and those that result from our reflexes or are caused by disease or damage to the brain.[10]

Given that humans are so utterly embedded in non-human (or not specifically human) material universe whose unfolding is regulated by natural laws which are, if correctly described, unbreakable almost by definition,[11] freedom, if it does exist, is impossible. Something, it seems, has to give: human freedom or the law-like universe of science.

I will argue that it is possible to accept all that recent bioscience has really demonstrated (as opposed to what scientism merely *claims*[12]) about the closeness of the relationship between humans and beasts and living and non-living matter without having to believe that the remarkable and unique margin of freedom we humans presently enjoy is an illusion.[13] I will offer an account of human freedom that is compatible with our biological origins and with the nature of our bodies as organisms. In a nutshell, freedom is possible because we are distanced from our biological status by the Existential Intuition. This, as we have earlier discussed, itself has a biological explanation, so the escape of human beings from biological constraint – and from being mere way-stations in a causal nexus – was contrived by biological means. The margin of freedom made available to individual humans by the awakening of subject-object, user-used distances within the organism, is vastly augmented by what is, effectively, a pooling or collectivisation of such distances. With succeeding generations of humans, the pool becomes wider and deeper and the distances between humans and the natural world become greater and ever more complex. Self-awareness is elaborated into selves addressed to, and interacting with, a world that is increasingly the product of previous self-awarenesses, that are in turn internalised in selves.

The discussion of the elaboration of selves and worlds will largely be deferred until the next volume. For the present the focus will be on the fundamental process by which the seed of freedom is planted in the human body and grows in the human species. There are two key elements to the explanation offered here of human freedom:

a) There is an inseparable link between the Existential Intuition and the intuition of agency – 'That I am this ...' and 'That I am doing these events' are a twin birth.[14]
b) At every stage in its evolution and growth, the sense of freedom is in part illusory and, as such, is a self-fulfilling illusion.

It is an important feature of my hypothesis that human freedom did not come all at once: it has grown collectively over many hundreds of thousands of years and it has grown in parallel with the elaboration of millions of human selves and the collective world to which they contribute and upon which they draw.[15]

Several points should be made at the outset. First, as I have already remarked, there is nothing original in my identifying the human hand as the key to the differences between mankind and the rest of animalkind:

Anaximander, Immanuel Kant, Erasmus Darwin and the great anatomist Frederic Wood Jones, to name just a few, have been here before
me. What is original – especially in the intellectual context just
described, where 'biologisation' of humans is taken to demonstrate their
lack of freedom – is the invocation of the biology of the hand to explain,
rather than to explain away, the profound differences between man and
beasts. I offer biology in support of a philosophical distinction between
(comparatively) free humans and unfree beasts and not, as seems
fashionable at present, as a way of eliminating it. Second, the link
between the hand and human freedom is offered as an *hypothesis*. More
than any other part of the present volume, it makes empirical claims
that could do with more empirical support than I can provide. (Though
there are some interesting clues from, of all places, neuroscience, which
we shall allude to.) If most of the verbs in this chapter are cast in the
indicative rather than the subjunctive mood, this is purely for reasons of
stylistic felicity. Continuous tentativeness makes wearisome reading.
Some key ideas are offered up for critical inspection. This is connected
with a third and final preliminary point. There are several components
of the argument that are even less clearly worked out than those in
previous chapters and certainly less clear than they should be. These
mark those places where much more work needs to be done. Until that
work is done, the re-casting of mankind as 'handkind' – and the link
between having a full-blown hand and the emergence of humans as self-
conscious agents – remains not only an untested hypothesis but also an
incompletely formulated one.

### 8.3 THE EXISTENTIAL INTUITION AND THE AGENTIVE SELF

The version of human freedom that I wish to defend incorporates not
merely freedom of action – the freedom to do what one wills at least at
some time – but also freedom of the will – the freedom at times to
choose one's willings. This conception of freedom seems most directly
incompatible with both physical and psychosocial determinism. This
conception is articulated in Robert Kane's wonderfully clear and
comprehensive *The Significance of Free Will*. According to Kane,

> *Free will ... is the power of agents to be the ultimate creators (or
> originators) and sustainers of their own ends and purposes.* This notion
> should be distinguished from free action, and not simply because free will
> is a power. To act freely is to be unhindered in the pursuit of your
> purposes (which are usually expressed by intentions); to will freely, in this
> traditional sense, is to be the ultimate creator of your own purposes.[16]

Crucially, an individual enjoying freedom of the will should be in a position to bring about events that would not have otherwise occurred. This is incompatible with determinism, which, as Kane says, does not allow for 'the power to do otherwise' (p. 44). Truly free agents must generate alternative possibilities which can be selected or chosen between. The challenge, therefore, is that of explaining how human beings – who are seemingly immersed in, or part of, or dissolved in, the natural world – can invoke and actualise such possibilities, and so act on the natural world at least in part *as if from outside of it*.[17]

In trying to make human freedom believable, then, we have to answer two distinct questions: a) How did humans come to be the *origin* of their own actions in the way that, say, chimpanzees are not? b) How did they import so many alternative possibilities into a material universe of which they are a part, and whose unbroken regularities seem to add up to a Laplacean machine that does not allow for alternative possibilities? These two questions converge in a third: c) How do humans come to be more than mere conduits for the causal processes that operate in the material world, so that they are able to act in accordance with, or under the influence of, reasons, beliefs, formulated intentions, that do not seem to figure in the lives of other creatures?

Any account of human freedom and of our collective (if partial) escape from biology must, self-evidently, begin with biology. The links between possession of a full-blown hand and the awakening of the human subject in the animal organism have already been set out *in extenso* in Volume 1 and more succinctly in Chapter 1 of the present volume. Our present task is to examine the connection, prefigured in the Existential Intuition, between selfhood and agency. Even so, a brief reprise of the elements of the bio-genetic account of first-person being seems in order here.

The hand, it will be recalled, has a particular status, unique in the animal kingdom: 'meta-fingering' and 'constrained manipulative indeterminacy' (which we shall shortly revisit) makes the hand a *proto-tool* – something the organism consciously *uses*. The tool-like status of the hand in its turn instrumentalises the human organism as a whole and it is this that ignites the sense of agency, and indeed subjectivity, within it. Once the threshold of bodily self-consciousness was crossed, a feed-forward mechanism, with increasing elaboration of self-consciousness and agency, began. This would soon be driven largely by secondary consequences of the possession of a proto-tool, most importantly the spread of the sense of 'toolness' beyond the hand and the body: the tool-like hand inspires extra-corporeal hand-extending tools. Although non-human animals also seem to use tools, their low-ceilinged, stereotyped forays into apparent tool-use are not rooted in an instrumentalised awareness of their own bodies. Compared with us, chimps are chumps: the acme of animal 'tool-use' – the use of a stone to crack a nut – takes a chimp five years to learn.[18] It is doubtful therefore whether it is truly analogous to human tool-use. Tool-use not only extends actual agency, but also extends awareness of it and with this, the *aura of possibility* that, for an emergent agent, surrounds actuality.

An explicit extra-corporeal tool, moreover, has many important incidental properties: it places an arrested image of agency, and of highly generalised human intentions, even of needs and the path to their satisfaction, outside of the body. As such it makes these things publicly visible. This opens up an increasing collectivisation of the consciousness of individual members of the human species. This sharing opens the path to the socialised (and eventually factual) knowledge, which only humans enjoy, from the sentience to which other animals are confined: it makes possible a pooling of solitary animal needs into those explicit scarcities that human collectives address.

The central role of (hand-inspired) tools in facilitating distinctively human forms of socialisation – mediated through artefacts which externalise agency, needs and intentions – has been attested to by many palaeoanthropologists. Furthermore, as was argued in Volume 1, hand-triggered use of tools – abstract and in some sense arbitrary signs whose use involves skills and mobilises areas of the brain, overlapping with those ultimately involved in speech – is the precursor of human language. All these converging and synergistic developments – instrumentalisation of the hominid body, the use of tools, collectivisation of consciousness, and ultimately language – would subsequently both drive and be driven by increased complexity of the human brain. The collective awakening of humanity out of organic sleep was gradual. Progress was slow at first (over a million years separate the pebble-chopper from the hand-axe) and took millions of years to reach its present dizzying rate.

In Volume 3 we shall discuss other long-range consequences of the hand-inspired Existential Intuition: the progressive differentiation of subject and object, the elaboration of the self and its world, the unique role of reason in human activity, and most fundamentally the emergence of the propositional awareness, with the separation of appearance and reality, actuality and possibility, and factual knowledge and directed inquiry, as its manifestations. For present purposes, I shall focus on one aspect of the transformed relationship to one's own body that arises out of having a hand: the differentiation of one's body into the parts that one uses and the parts that one is; the differentiation, in short, into user and used. The awakening of the human agent in the animal organism ultimately derives from this. Our ability deliberately or genuinely to *utilise* our body makes of it, or oneself, a point of true origin, a new beginning in the universe. Bodily self-utilisation trans- forms hominids' sites of organic events into actors who to some extent shape their own destinies and lead, rather than merely live, their own lives.

To appreciate the connection between the hand and agency, it will help to think of the hand as a seat of choice. There is a wide variety of available strategies for successful manipulation in any particular situation; however, there is constraint on the range of grips that might be of practical use – hence the phrase 'constrained manipulative indeterminacy'. The constraint is exerted by an inchaote sense of purpose: indeterminacy is within the bounds of meaningfulness. (This is sharply different from the quantum indeterminacy which some have appealed to as an escape from the straitjacket of causal determinism.[19]) Manual choosing, moreover, takes place in a context of an especially intimate interaction with the manipulated object, underscored by constant direct sensory feedback about the position of our hands, their relationship to the object of interest and the progress of whatever operation is being performed, through skin sensation, limb propriocep- tion and vision. It is shaped by the purpose of the manipulation of the properties of the manipulandum. This is central to the very special relationship we have with our hands when they are engaged in manipu- lative activity. Because the hand is importantly in relation to itself throughout manipulation – through opposability and the mutual touching of the tips of the fingers – it imports a high-level bodily awareness. As we argued in section 1.2 and in more detail in Volume 1, this unique level of self-addressing explains the key role of the hand in awakening the seeds of selfhood and agency; why the seeming freedom of movement of other bodily parts has not delivered these things; why it is *manipulation* that has awoken the intuition that, among the flow of events, there are some that I *do*.

The combination of second-order fingering and constrained manipu- lative indeterminacy makes the hand the agent of our unique transition from purposeful activity (in which all living creatures engage) to explicitly purposive activity, with a consequent gradual displacement of instinctive behaviour, tropisms and automatic responses to stimuli, by deliberate activity. Even though voluntary actions must still be fashioned out of, or built on, biological mechanisms, there is an increasing contrast between the stereotyped mechanisms that make human actions possible and the non-stereotyped nature of those actions. Stereotyped mechanisms are deployed to non-stereotyped manipulations: proto-acts.

To recap: I feel myself to be an agent – as one who *does* – because the inchoate sense of my hand as a tool awakens a more general instrumentalised relationship to my own body. The dialectic does not stop there: the hand itself then becomes more explicitly the agent of a body that wills events – or rather of an embodied individual who wills events or outcomes:

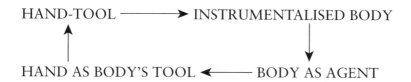

HAND-TOOL ⟶ INSTRUMENTALISED BODY

HAND AS BODY'S TOOL ⟵ BODY AS AGENT

The Existential Intuition – 'That I am [this] …' – delivered by the hand-tool has two aspects: consciousness of self in the form of bodily self-awareness, or awareness of the behaviourally engaged body; and the sense of this embodied self as an agent. These are inextricably linked. 'That I *am* this' and 'That *I* am *doing* these happenings' (or 'These happenings are my *doings*') are in their least developed form like the recto and verso of a sheet of paper. It is only subsequently that selfhood and agency differentiate, so that it then makes sense to link together, as if they were separable, the self and its actions, and to attribute the latter to the former. (Kant, of course, acknowledged the close link between selfhood and agency, in his link between personhood and autonomy.)

We may imagine that the initial intuition delivered to early 'Handyman' would be of the engaged organism (its body) interacting with its environment in a way that objectively (to the eye of the biologist who later emerged) has purpose – for example, serving a need (and experienced as a directed appetite such as hunger for a particular edible item) – though not explicitly purposive, in the sense of being driven and informed by, and addressed towards achieving, a goal that is explicit to the organism and conceived in more or less general terms. (Hungers, unlike reasons, do not have to be formulated, assented to, understood or even intuited, to shape behaviour.) The primitive self-consciousness of that early hominid could be captured by 'am' where the scope of 'am' is of that part of the body as it is experienced as engaged in the purposive behaviour; or the body in so far as it is thus engagedly experienced and experientially engaged. 'I am' would, as we have said, *suffuse* the engaged body, like a blush. It is an assumption of a fleshly being engaged with the material world by the same fleshly being engaged with the material world. It is the engaged organism assuming itself as itself.

As such it cannot be in error. To reiterate the argument of earlier chapters, the Existential Intuition is a subject truth that is not conditional on third-person objective facts about the material world. I can hardly be mistaken that I am this engaged body. I may be mistaken over certain details – for example, I may feel a limb that is not there (as when an amputee suffers from phantom limb pains) and feel that that limb is part of me. But I cannot be mistaken that it is I who am struggling, say, to manipulate a particular object. 'Am' is irrefutable precisely because it is global or diffuse: self-consciousness overarches specific contents of consciousness. It makes no particular claims about the referents of particular elements of my experience of myself or of the world. The Existential Intuition is invulnerable because it is not (for example) a matted block of propositions or implicit assertions.

Even so, talk of invulnerability may ring alarm bells. The assertion that I cannot be mistaken that it is *I* who am struggling to *do* something may suggest an attempt to sneak into the scope of irrefutable self-consciousness something objectively or factually true – that the events in question are actions rather than mere happenings. After all, one may dream that one is doing all sorts of things (running away, fighting, sitting an exam) while one is passively asleep in bed.

We may bypass this objection by remembering our biological starting point: a creature – an early hominid (or a developing infant) – which gradually assumes its body as its own. This assumption is an act of appropriation of its body as itself. It is not merely 'a statement to that effect' but an enactment of it; or more precisely a 'dawning to that which one is'. The sense of 'am' that suffuses the needing, appetitive, engaged body is not a random alighting on a thing which one then chooses to be; nor is it a discovery that one is this thing (rather than any other), an act of identification of which bit of the world is oneself, a discovery, which could in theory prove to be mistaken. Most to the point, it is an *engaged*, aware body assuming itself as itself. It is difficult to see how this assumption could be open to correction.[20]

Self-consciousness, the assumption of the active body as 'I', and the inchoate sense of agency, are it seems reasonable to conjecture, fused in the most primitive stages of (distinctively) human consciousness. The sense of one's body as a tool and as one's own (or as one's self; or 'what I am') are conjoint twins of the self-addressing, self-interacting, versatile hand, which awakens both the sense of agency and the subject-object divide in accordance with which one's body is possessed as one's own. The essence of agency is an identity between 'am' and certain events; or the inclusion of certain events within the scope of 'am' that goes beyond the inclusion implicit in the fact that they are suffered.

Although agency and embodied selfness are, at least initially, inseparable, the discussion so far has established only that the sense of 'am' (with its uncertain scope) is incorrigible. The extent to which this is true of the sense of 'do' – *once 'am' and 'do' differentiate* – remains unclear. Even if I could not possibly be mistaken that I 'am' this – whatever 'this' is – I could surely be illuded as to the feeling that I 'do' this [event]. Is it not possible that these events seemingly brought about by me are in fact mere physical happenings rather than the actions of myself as agent? I want to suggest that the progression of humans to their comparative and genuine freedom – their progressive liberation from the fettered state of the organism – has resulted from a gradual extension of the scope of 'am' identity to enclose events that then become actions: a process of 'catching up' with a putative agency. The attribution of agency extends beyond the 'am' at any given stage and drives an expansion of 'am' so that the self-attribution of agency and responsibility, which is in part illusory, becomes subsequently true.

In parallel with this, there is a differentiation and stratification and folding of the Existential Intuition of the agentive-self, which is initially the active body suffused with 'am', into:

a) a complex, layered self extended in time (corresponding to the person with an elaborated identity); and
b) an agent with ever more complex drivers to action (reason-mediated rather than directly need- or appetite-driven) and ever more complex actions (with many intermediate steps, many increasingly abstract frameworks making sense of, and occasioning, the intermediate steps).

### 8.4 THE AM-GROUND OF AGENCY: 'I' AS ORIGIN

How does this relationship between an expanding 'am' and a seeming expanding scope of agency really work? How does it get round the most puzzling requirement for free will, namely that agents should '*be the ultimate creators (or originators) and sustainers of their own ends and purposes*'? How can any entity be the *origin* of anything? A living entity such as a human organism is surely a local nexus of causes and effects in a limitless nexus of causes and effects. Anything that happens in that organism – including the actions it undertakes, the willings that drive those actions, and the experiences and the motives, instincts and needs that underpin those willings – must owe its origin to something outside of itself, ultimately to the first events in the universe. Isn't my seemingly voluntary action of raising my arm to demonstrate the reality of my freedom traceable to me-shaping events that have an unbreakable causal ancestry that extends beyond my ken and indeed my life and that of the species to which I belong? Is it not obvious that our bodies – the thing we humans can most claim to be – are mere conduits for extra-corporeal causal chains? How, then, can it be that (to use Aristotle's term) we are, or have within us, 'the 'origin' *arche* of the action', as a result of which the action is *our* action? How can such an *origin* be pitched in the material universe of which we are a part?

I want to argue that the Existential Intuition is precisely that which creates the *point of origin*: with the Existential Intuition we have *a new point of departure*, in an otherwise boundless material universe of causes leading in all spatio-temporal directions, connecting the Big Bang with the Big Crunch. 'That I am this ...' plants the flag of 'here' and 'now' and makes our bodies a new point of origin in virtue of which humans are the true 'arche' of those events we believe to be our freely chosen actions.

This central role of the Existential Intuition may be illustrated diagrammatically (see opposite). Let us concede that the material universe is a boundless nexus, tangled or matted block of causal chains, some of which pass into and out of human organisms. The nexus of effects (E) which in turn become causes (C), which are labelled 'E/C's, enters a zone in which some of them are assumed (in both the senses of the word we have noted) under 'am' as the self of the organism: the realm within the engaged organism of which the Existential Intuition (which cannot be mistaken) intuits, asserts, and *exists* 'That I am this'. The assumption 'That I am this ...' is the assumption of an engaged organism – perhaps revealed as a cluster of events – as one's self; the assumption by the engaged organism of itself. The Intuition encompasses an area, within the engaged aware organism, where some things (events involving limbs, etc.) are assumed by and as one's self: 'I am this ...' (collection of body parts, flurry of events, body parts revealed through events in which they are engaged). It is this assumption – marking the emergence 'am' into a world of 'is' – which turns certain events into actions by incorporating them into the 'I' – which is a new place of departure or origin in the universe. 'Am', in its primordial form the assumption of happenings in a body that is assumed as one's own body, provides the new beginning that makes the (selved-)body a point of origin, in a boundless causal nexus. This is how free will arises and humans start to become free: a self can 'own' events involving his/her body and hence 'own up to' them as his/her actions.

*How Humans Became Points of Origin in a Boundless Universe*

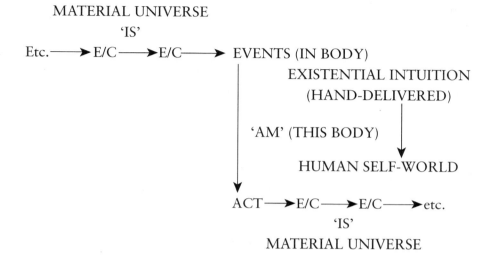

NOTES

1. 'E/C' = 'EFFECT/CAUSE' – i.e. an effect that then becomes a cause.
2. The point-intuition 'AM', 'THAT I AM [THIS]' is unpacked over human history (several million years) to a (collective/individual) self addressing to a (collective/individual) world.
3. It follows from this that humanity did not become free all at once. It became increasingly free as the interaction between the organism and the environment became displaced by the interaction between selves and human worlds.


If the assumption that makes the engaged human body a place of origin seems circular, this is exactly as it should be, for 'am' identity – unlike 'is' identity – is not an external equation between one object or set of events and another but between an object engaged in events and itself. As we saw in Chapter 7, the complement of the assumption (whatever corresponds to the demonstrative 'this' that 'I' 'am') is not arbitrarily chosen – as if events were picked out at random. 'I', 'personhood', 'am' cannot alight on anything – a stone, a tree – or any events – and take responsibility for them. 'I' must arise in a conscious creature verging on self-consciousness. Even at the pre-human level animals suffer their bodies and engage the world in and through them, though not in the instrumental way humans do. The emergent human agent is built on, or out of, the biological material of the appetitive, active, animal. The springboard of the human self is the suffering, needing animal and the events that are apt to be appropriated as actions are those that are relevant to meeting those needs, and addressing that suffering. (The *springboard*, be it noted: we humans left the springboard about six million years ago – the events that are now manifest as voluntary actions are only indirectly related to basic needs we share with animals. To vary the metaphor, trying to find what it is or means to be a human being by looking at the lives animals, even our nearest kin, is like looking for a self-fuelling rocket on the launch pad which it left several million years ago.) It is the engaged organism that the human primordially 'ams'. The initial locus for the cluster of events that 'I am', where some events are assumed as *my actions*, is the body that is assumed as 'me' – roughly what Merleau-Ponty called *le corps propre*, rather than the objective body as revealed to the anatomist or physio-logist – though the field of 'am' subsequently extends beyond the body.

Surely, it might still be argued, it is possible that the assumption that I am *responsible* for this thing, this engaged organism, or for some of the events with it, such as my arm moving, might yet be illusory. Is it not possible that, for all that the Existential Intuition may result in the human organism's feeling responsible for some of the events that flow from it, this may be a mistake? Might we not be justified in saying of our actions what Oedipus said of his misdeeds: 'I suffered these deeds more than I enacted them'? Did we not earlier give some examples of actions for which I seemed responsible but which ultimately proved to be 'implanted' in me? Well, while we may be mistaken about our role in individual events that seem to be our actions, it does not seem possible in relation to our entire lifetime's career of actions; indeed, explicitly suffering events as our own and hence as deeds, as Oedipus did, mark the point of transition from being a mere patient or locus of events to being an agent. The key thought here – and it can be used against psychological determinism (as we shall do in Volume 3) as well as physical determinism – is that the originating Existential Intuition is the point at which self and agency cannot be separated: where there is an 'am' there must fall within its scope events which are mine. Energised by my appetites, they are not merely events that befall me. The wider the scope of 'am', the wider the scope of the events that are 'mine'. There are more places to which we may trace actions as a source in ourselves. More generally, it would not make sense to separate ourselves from all those events that we currently call 'our actions', since that which is engaged in them *is what we are*. At the point of convergence of 'am' and the actions, 'This happens' cannot be intelligibly separated from 'I do'; or the events from the doing self. Those events we are, which are assumed in the self, are free. And while I may be mistaken as to the interpretation and nature of *some* aspects of what is assumed in the

Existential Intuition, I cannot be mistaken as to all its contents. My sense that certain events are part of me as actions can no more be entirely mistaken than can my sense of self be a lifelong error.

Which is not to say that we do not make errors in attributing events to ourselves as actions we have originated. Indeed, the erroneous assumption of responsibility – or the extension of the scope of responsibility beyond the borders of am – is actually important for the progressive extension of human freedom. The scope of such events assumed as actions (and hence of our freedom) expands as the territory of the self – interacting with an expanding, humanly created, as opposed to a natural, world – expands, as it has done over the history (and pre-history) of humanity and does in the developmental history of individual humans. The expanded scope of 'am' and of the agent-self is particularly evident in the complex reason-driven actions of (perfectly ordinary) everyday life. The boundaries of the Existential Intuition define a realm within which I am the origins of acts because certain events are inseparable from what 'I am'. The irrefutable Existential Intuition makes it valid to separate actions that seem to be mine from events that seem not to be mine – to be involuntary, to be mere events that happen to have my body as their locus. This is the key to evading not only physical but also psychosocial determinism.[21]

Let us scrutinise this basis for the seemingly very real differentiation between events in, say, my body that are not my actions – such as my arm twitching – and those that are – such as reaching for a cup or my lifting up my arm to demonstrate the freedom of my will in the course of a philosophical argument. The difference lies in the *frame of reference* that accounts for the fact that the event occurs at a particular time. The twitching of the arm has only a material basis – the nervous system firing spontaneously – and no frame of reference. Reaching for the cup has as its frame of reference a particular purpose that I have: at the very least, it requires an appetite or a habit and a (very complex) sense that acting on it is permitted and appropriate. Lifting my arm in the course of a philosophical argument has as its frame of reference not only a particular purpose, but my longstanding engagement with a complex philosophical literature about the freedom of the will.

These frames of reference – which have become ever more complex in the cultural evolution of humanity and in the development of individual human beings – are not merely external to my action in the way that a frame encloses a picture: they are *part of me* inasmuch as they have been internalised and 'motivate' the action. They belong to the realm of 'am'. The wider, or more complex and more abstract, the frame of reference, the greater the distance between bodily events that originate with me and are genuine actions, and those that are not and cannot be thought of as genuine actions. We may generalise this to say that an action is free, and its being willed is itself free, in proportion as it engages more and more of a personal self, ever richer and more abstract frames of reference, and its occurrence is less amenable to explanation in terms of the immediate causal neighbourhood of the here-and-now body. The beyond-the-body frame of reference of truly free actions signifies the extent to which they are not explained by, or explicable in terms of, the physiological or other properties of the biological organism. The framework is the 'am-ground' or 'am-soil' out of which the action grows.

This is connected with our intuition that an action is more of a human, free action the more it is driven by *reasons*. Reasons have two important, connected features: they are general and they are abstract. Generality and abstraction are aspects of *possibilities* which, strictly, do not exist in the material world, rather than actualities which do. Possibilities exist only for higher-order consciousness; for first-person beings. They are rooted in selves. 'Doing things for reasons' – which may be explicit or recoverable in response to challenge – separates humans by an ever-widening gulf from the animal kingdom. (Of this, more in Volume 3.)

The ever-extending freedom of human actions – in the history of emergent humanity and in the history of a developing individual – is marked by their tapping into a greater and greater part of an individual's biography – corresponding, or addressed, to proliferating, layered and ever more remote frames of reference. These insulate those events that are actions from the uninflected causal pressures of the material world. As the human race gets older and ever more remote from the putative starting point at which hominids separated from pongids, the deposit account of 'am', which individuals may take 'off the shelf' as they acquire (in development) the shared world, gets richer and richer and the am-soil deeper.

The extent of these depths may be illustrated by a relatively ordinary action: my going to London for a meeting at the Royal College of Physicians. Each of the vast numbers of movements comprising my journey to London, my journeying within London, what I do when I get to my destination, and my return from London, makes sense only with respect to the overarching purpose (which may be very ill defined and is certainly highly abstract – e.g. 'improving Registrar training' or 'adding to the number of brownie points on my CV') of the meeting in London. The particular movements I make – turning the key in a door at a particular time, giving an instruction to the cab-driver, turning over the pages of documents I don't particularly want to read on the train, taking a particular route through the streets, hovering outside the building because I am early – are occasioned by this abstract overarching purpose which has tentacular roots into the cumulative subsoil of the self: they are requisitioned for, and would not have occurred without, such a purpose. The complex hierarchies of movement over several years requisitioned to subserve an ordinary activity such as 'Monroe-bagging' – climbing all the mountains over 3,000 feet in Scotland – are mind-boggling. The single goal may link the very elaborate movements associated with closing the door of my house – at the beginning of a journey to Scotland – in 1960 – to the equally complex movements associated with working late on a particular weekday in 2003 in order to clear the desk for a long weekend. Such a complex of events could not take place unless the individual not only wanted them to happen, but knew what he was doing: the actions require not only that he should have the appetite for them but also that he knew what (and that means why[22]) he was performing. Truly free acts are actions that would not have occurred without their being intelligible to the actor.

Bodily events that look like actions but are not rooted in this 'am' soil – seeming not to be locatable in the complex, multi-layered framework of my characteristic activities or, if complex, apparently occasioned by frameworks other than those that frame and enable the activities – are regarded as being 'out of character'. They arouse the suspicion of being involuntary – perhaps carried out under duress or manifesting pathology. I may be inclined to report the ballistic twitching of my arm, which is meaningless and lacks an am-framework, to my doctor but not my reaching for a glass, even though, when viewed from a purely physical or physiological point of view, they share many features. Drug-induced behaviour likewise lacks the frame of reference of myself, unless I am a regular drug-taker when my series of earlier, initially voluntary choices has by a succession of 'self-forming willings' (to use Robert Kane's concept) made drug-taking and its consequences part of a new self and as such rooted in 'am-soil' and part of my identity.[23]

An action, then, is phenomenologically – and genuinely – distinguished from an event that is merely the effect of a material cause in virtue of its drawing on a large quantity of 'accumulated' self. This distinction does not, however, of itself explain how an initial, arguably illusory, sense of agency became self-fulfilling. The explanation of the gradual validation of the illusion, or the gradual widening of the scope of the validity of the sense of agency, requires us to postulate a process driven – over the history and prehistory of humanity – by a narrow margin of difference between actual and assumed agency; whereby the scope of assumed agency slightly exceeds the scope of actual agency courtesy of a constantly over-reaching self. As a result the am-soil is extended and this forms the basis for a further extension of agency. The two as it were *ratchet each other up*. The sense of doing also reinforces the sense of self: 'I do' thickens and sustains the sense of 'I am'.

The basis for this progressive, and subsequently justified, over-reaching will be examined shortly. For the present, we may note that it depends on the involvement of a third party – or element – driving this virtuous spiral from outside. This third party is a specifically human, shared, *world* built up out of the socialisation of consciousness initially made possible by tools that a) are had in common, and b) symbolise shared needs and shared insights into providing for those needs. This human world becomes something to be taken 'off the shelf' in increasing quantities by selves, by consciousnesses, appearing later and later in pre-history and even more so when writing inaugurates the, comparatively so far very brief, written history of humanity. Actions become increasingly free – because they are constituted out of increasingly complex sequences of events that are increasingly me (or distinctively human) – as they grow out of an ever richer and deeper 'am-soil' itself increasingly represented in each of us as an inlet in the 'human-world-soil' created by the collaborative activity of many millions of selves. To pre-empt the suggestion that our apparent case for human freedom is merely a switch from physical to psycho-social determinism, it is important to point out that the world-soil is not tipped into us as soil into a skip, but is in part embraced by us and acts as the springboard of our individual freedom: it, too, is 'assumed'. We may think of the human world as a growing enclave within the material world; and of a self as a private inlet from that world – truly 'I', though its tissues are created by we. This is no more paradoxical than that the deepest roots of personal identity lie in our impersonal bodies.

Let us reiterate the key arguments or intuitions that we have mobilised so far against determinism:

a) That which I am is, in the first instance, the engaged body, participating in certain events.
b) This means that I am certain events: 'am' and 'activity' are inseparable.
c) As the scope of 'am' grows, so does agency. The widening scope that is assumed in the Existential Intuition is a parallel expansion of selfhood and agency.
d) As this scope grows, the extent to which what happens in my life – to which my life happens – is reduced and the extent to which *I lead my life* expands.

The worry and despair provoked by determinism are that it seems to demonstrate that what we seemingly do comes ultimately from outside of us. We are helpless, and the credit and blame we take for our actions are based on a groundless prejudice: we are no more responsible for what we do than we are for the laws of nature which the events we call our actions express. The fundamental intuition behind my argument – and which I believe to be unassailable – is that which I *am* cannot be regarded as either being outside of me or as an external influence upon me. Selfhood is the guarantor of agency, makes agency intelligible, because it is that in virtue of which the outside and the sway of external influence do not engulf our entire being. The foregoing account of the merging of agency and identity – 'where there is 'am-ing' there is genuine doing' – brings to an end an otherwise endless and vicious regress, according to which willing is itself the product of (external) causes that antecede will, and the willing of willing is likewise the product of preceding causes; and so on. This regress, which undermines free will, gives seeming credence not only to physical but also to psycho-social determinism. Against this, we note that the Existential Intuition marks a point at which regression ends: it establishes a 'here' at which 'the buck starts'.[24] Willing is consequently not reducible to the product of unwilled physical events (such as, for example, those that install certain activity patterns in the brain, as Kane has suggested); nor can it be reduced to the passive reflection of psycho-social influences. For there is a point at which those psycho-social influences, far from being external determinants, are *what I am* and do not, therefore, show my actions to be mere reactions, unconscious as to their origin, meaning and purpose, and consequently somehow outside of me. (It is in the spirit of this observation that we may describe education as 'due' influence, in contrast to the undue influence of threats, terror and brainwashing.[25])

The failure to note the central role of 'am' identity in the authentication of voluntary action sometimes results in absurd requirements being placed on actions before they are allowed to have been genuinely free. If the realm of 'am' – in which events are mine, and are me, and are therefore potentially free – is overlooked, then all actual events in which we are engaged are somehow 'outside' of us. The self becomes the product of external forces: one is a mere product and one's actions are the product of a product. The contradictions inherent in such a line of argument may be illustrated by the conclusion to which it leads: namely, that to be *anything in particular* is itself a limitation of one's freedom; for example, to be a five foot ten inch male living in 2004, as opposed to a four foot female, living in 1400, is a limitation because one has not chosen these facts about oneself. This line of thought ends up with the daft notion that, if one is going to be free, one should not start from anywhere at all: one should have no particular needs, no aspirations! In order for a creature to have freedom, it should have no origin, and no reason to be one thing rather than another, no particular derived characteristics, no context even. This requirement would empty freedom of purpose – for then there would be no reason to do one thing rather than another – and, indeed, of content. There would consequently be no *particular* way of being an agent or for an agent. She may as well be discarnate and enjoy the directionless nothingness that that state has to offer.[26]

If we are to avoid this absurdity, we must recognise that freedom that is meaningful must be exercised in a context; and to this extent must in some degree be constrained. At the very least one has to be something in order to be a free agent. More specifically, the constraints – the context, the antecedents (including 'being this thing that I am') – are essential enablers. What is required for freedom is not that the individual should be acting in a void, disconnected from the material, psychological and social world in which she is already *embarqué* (as Pascal put it), but only that she should *first-person-be* the creature that she is; not that she should have chosen everything that she is, but that she should have assumed some of what she is as herself, on the basis of which she can choose; that she should appropriate part of the world as herself; that her being should be lit up by the Existential Intuition; that she should enjoy first person being – 'am-ing'. By this means, she will be able to lead a life that is her life rather than be merely a living creature.

## 8.5 THE PARALLEL EXPANSION OF SELFHOOD AND AGENCY: THE SELF-FULFILLING ILLUSION

Our account of human freedom envisages a biological mechanism igniting a progressive escape from biological constraint. I have focused rather directly on the hand itself, but it is reasonable to suppose that, very early on in the process, other elements became important: the literal tools inspired by the proto-tool of the hand; the reorganisation and expansion of the brain driven by a dialectic between ever more complex uses of the hand and of hand-tool combinations; the progressive socialisation of consciousness; and, finally, language. There is no space to examine these developments here; they have been examined in Volume 1 and some will be revisited in Volume 3. Suffice to say that there are good reasons for seeing hand-inspired tools as being key to both the preparation of the executive functions of the brain necessary for the emergence of both symbolic systems (and, ultimately, language in the narrow sense) and of sociality underpinning cultural evolution.[27] More generally, the potentially evanescent self-awareness of the individual human primate will be stabilised by the other's awareness of herself. I want, however, to make one or two points about a putative mechanism by which human freedom might be gradually extended; in short, to deal with the 'self-fulfilling' illusion to which I referred at the outset.

It is necessary first to step back a little. Freedom of the will in the sense I have taken over from Robert Kane implies that we are not only the *arche* of our actions, but that those actions actually change what would have otherwise taken place. This implies, as has so often been said, that *we have a power to do otherwise*,[28] that we were not always destined to do what we actually do. This is the aspect of freedom most starkly inconsistent with determinism: determinism allows only one outcome once the material universe, equipped with laws and initial conditions, is set going. In practice, it looks as if we humans have collectively altered the course of nature in the way that no other species has. The changes we have brought about are qualitatively, as well as quantitatively, different from those wrought by trees, insects and primates: we have brought into being objects and states of affairs which would otherwise have never been seen. How is this possible? John Stuart Mill argued that the ability of humans to 'make a different kind of difference' was not incompatible with unbreakable laws of nature:

> Though we cannot emancipate ourselves from the laws of nature as a whole, we can escape from any particular law of nature if we are able to withdraw ourselves from the circumstances in which it acts.[29]

Agency conceived as the ability to choose between laws of nature (or, for pre-scientific humankind, between 'patterns of happening') – and so to be able to subordinate nature to non-natural ends, to ends that nature certainly did not 'have in view' – is clearly distinct from the idea of agency as a supernatural kind of cause.[30] First-person being is neither a cause nor an effect – agents are at the point of origin, but not special non-physical physical causes of their actions. Such a mode of being is that in virtue of which an agent engages with a world of cause and effect, at least in part from the outside, enabling her to pick and choose between existing causal chains to shape the material world in accordance with her will – her needs experienced as appetites, her appetites assumed as purposes, her purposes transformed into practical reasons. Agency is not to be understood as an esoteric kind of causation but as a *self-positioning* among causes; or (to vary a well-known account of causation) a way of privileging certain events as causes so that we may use them as handles to manipulate the world. In order to act freely, we do not have to be lawbreakers, only law-users.[31] In order that the agent should be able to *utilise* laws by choosing between them, she has in some sense to be outside of them. We shall return to this point presently, but first let us examine the notion of free will.

Free will has caused a lot of puzzlement because, when looked at from the standpoint of materialistic physics, it seems to require that matter should get a purchase on itself; or that a piece of matter (a human body or a human being) should get a purchase on other pieces of matter. We can now see that to put it this way is to make things too hard for ourselves by looking at free will from a third-person standpoint. First-person being makes true agency possible because it is an aware (material) body getting hold of itself. That 'getting hold of itself', in the form of the Existential Intuition, is given content and suborned to securing a particular direction of events not merely through the objective, physical situation of the body, but also through the needs – made conscious as appetites such as thirst and hunger – that accompany the human condition and are part of our biological heritage. Appetites are utterly transformed in humans, as are the actions pertinent to them,[32] but they still, as it were, provide the basis of the energy that as it were *fuels* willing. While willing is not (ultimately) divorced from our biological origins, neither are humans merely places where causes in the form of reactions, reflexes, instincts and tropisms operate. While the energy, the drive to behaviour, that comes from unconscious needs and conscious appetites is refracted through the complex lenses of what 'I am', this is not merely a matter of deflection to essentially similar goals (so that, for example, writing sonnets is simply a different way of sniffing the genitals of a potential mate). The physiological givens are transformed – humanised and personalised: the Existential Intuition transforms (impersonally suffered) 'thirst' into something which may be expressed as the equivalent to 'I want a drink'.[33] It is this 'I want' – which builds on animal appetite raised to self-consciousness – that is the beginning, the point of origin in the universe, that true willing requires. (The springboard of human freedom is constructed not only out of transformed animal needs but also of transformed animal capacities. Human willing would be unthinkable if, for example, animal precursors were like stones and trees in being unable to move independently – even though, unlike humans, they are not *self*-moved.)

The self-appropriated human body – whose awareness has been transformed and developed over perhaps a hundred thousand genera-tions of humans, has an agenda of need, and has its history which in part overlaps the history of the self – is the basis of a freedom that, while it ensures that we are not merely way-stations in causal chains that begin and end beyond us, also does not allow us a (meaningless) autonomy in a vacuum.[34] The effort associated with the pursuit of goals (which in the most primitive stages are not clearly differentiated from animal appetites) and the apprehension of the engaged body as oneself lie at the root of truly voluntary activity. The sense that 'I am doing this thing that is happening' clearly lies deeper than any specific sense of obligation: 'ought' implies 'can' and 'can' presupposes the possibility of doing. Agency first, then ethics.

Human freedom operates not only with what happens, but postulates what might happen and hence what might be made to happen. While the material universe of causation is one of actualities, the world of human agency is one of possibilities that actualities may realise or fulfil. As the human race develops over hundreds of thousands of years, and individual human beings develop in the first few years of their lives, these are more and more loosely scripted. This last observation links with the *gradualness* of the human acquisition of freedom we have already alluded to.

The scope of human freedom correlates with the progressive extension of the 'outside' from which individual human beings engage with the natural world. Actions are coupled to frameworks that extend far beyond themselves. Beyond the earliest stages of the awakening to agency, the freedom of a particular action is no longer something determined within it alone; and it is no longer encompassed by the Existential Intuition understood as a momentary intuition. It has a wider underpinning. Free actions draw on a ground created by previous (less completely free) actions. These actions will have built the frames of references, the horizons, the human worlds, in which the later, freer, actions are possible. In the millions of years since humans first woke to the intuition of self and agency, the 'script' of the life that is led (beyond a life that is merely lived) has become looser and looser. The am-soil of actions – and the collective world created out of human actions – becomes richer, deeper and more complex.

The loosest script available to an agent acting to realise possibilities takes the form of an explicit reason-shaped plan – such as the one examined earlier of going to London to a meeting of the Royal College of Physicians.[35] The loosening of the script corresponds to the enormous expansion of the 'outside' from which we can exercise our freedom, from small beginnings as a point-sized intuition of self and agency – or more precisely an inchoate flush of 'am' and 'doing' – rooted in comparatively isolated organisms to the many-layered selves and the complex worlds – of reasons, knowledge, institutions and technologies – to which the collective of humans individually and collectively now relate. The pooled agency of humans from which individuals draw their power is magnified by the hundreds of thousands of generations that have gone before us and the many millions of contemporaries who, directly or indirectly, work with us. The profound differences between animal and human behaviour – between organic events that are caused and human actions that, while utilising biological mechanisms, and often prompted (directly or more often indirectly) by biological needs, are occasioned by reasons – arise as a result of the Existential Intuition that gradually creates an am-soil which can be an evermore robust springboard, an ever firmer new point of departure in the universe. Past choosing and free action strengthen the springboard for future choosing. Increasingly, the creature that we are has been shaped by previous willings.

This is the answer to the puzzle created by Mill's account of human freedom changing the natural world. If freedom is not about breaking laws but about choosing between them to serve one's will, how is such choice possible? It would seem that, in order to 'cherry-pick' between them, one has in some sense to be coming on them from outside. The am-soil, growing out of the initial Existential Intuition, *constitutes that outside*: while it does not permit humans to be at odds with the laws of nature – how could they be? – it does create an extra-natural space from which humans are in a position to do what Francis Bacon (quoted by Mill) says we can do: 'obey nature in such a manner as to command it'.

The astounding elaboration of the ability of humans collectively and individually 'to make a difference', to make things happen, to lead their lives rather than merely live them, is a result of the progressive elaboration of that 'outside'. For individuals that outside-of-nature is the am-soil of selfhood; and for humanity as a whole it is the collectivised am-soil of human culture. (The interaction of self and culture – such that the selves that drive cultural growth are in large part internalisations of previous cultural growth – is self-evident; though it must be emphasised that the ultimate origin of actions still lies within individuals.) What, however, drives the growth of am-soil and the gradual extension of the scope and predominance of voluntary action in individual human lives and humanity as a whole? To understand this, we invoke the notion of the self-fulfilling illusion.

I want to argue as follows: even if the initial sense of agency, arising out of the Existential Intuition that assumes certain events as 'me', were at first almost entirely illusory, it has the capacity to become less and less illusory. To put this another way, if it were in part an illusion, its illusory part is reality-producing. The gap between the present scope of our agency and what we imagine to be the scope of our agency is closed and, following this, the postulation of agency of yet wider scope creates another gap, which is closed in its turn. Our freedom expands as a result of our imagining that are we are freer than we in fact are. This process goes back all the way to the first stirrings of the Existential Intuition when the human organism senses that it *does*, is the author of, some of what befalls it.

The self-fulfilling illusion of ever-extended agency is like hypochondria. One of Lichtenberg's aphorisms seems to me to me to be very much to the point here:

> My body is that part of the world which can be altered by my thoughts. Even imaginary illnesses can become real. In the rest of the world my hypotheses cannot disturb the order of things.[36]

The first sensation that makes me feel I am ill is over-interpreted and this produces bodily changes that lead to other sensations that confirm my belief that I am ill. Eventually, I become ill. We may think of the inchoate sense of 'am' and of the agentive self in the early hominids as the equivalent of that first over-interpreted sensation.[37]

We need now to look more closely at the actual mechanism whereby this illusion works to extend our freedom. To understand this, we need to step back a little and reconsider the significance of the handy tools that grew out of the tool-hand. Tools not only (directly and indirectly) mark the distance between the nature in which other animals are immersed and the culture that distances humans from nature, they also provide the basis for progressive extension of that distance. In virtue of what do they do this? The clue lies in part in an observation by Wolfgang Kohler, which we discussed in Volume 1. Human tool-use, he pointed out, is unlike animal tool-use, even the use of tools by our nearest animal kin. It is a *social* activity based on *complementary* relations between the hands, whereas chimpanzee tool-use is the incorporation of the objects into whole-body locomotive skills.[38]

That is to say, it differs not only in respect of being a genuine instrumental activity, based on the instrumentalisation of the body, but also in respect of being a *social* activity. The initial ('nuclear') society of tool-use may be the cluster of subjects and objects established by the tool-hand within the body – for example, the cooperative activity of the two hands engaged in complementary and alternating roles as lead and subordinate. But it soon extends beyond this. For a tool, to a human animal already imbued with an inchoate sense of agency, is a visible extra-corporeal embodiment of a (general) purpose. Unlike the hand, it is separated from the body and from an individual human consciousness. Tools, which are often owned in common, are the inscription of distinctively human meanings in public space.

It is reasonable, therefore, to conjecture that tools support a collectivisation of human consciousness: they are outward and visible signs of human agency. They are able to foster the development of a layered self out of the layered bodily self-awareness we discussed in Chapter 6, and ultimately the socialisation of the self and the creation of a coherent, intersubjective world which is the theatre of its activity. The human agency extended beyond the body by tool-use widens beyond the individual human body and reaches into a 'world'. This is something that is experienced in common and its components are not only experienced similarly by all (as is the case of individual but similarly constituted organisms experiencing a natural environment that environs them all) but is had *explicitly* in common: it is a fabric of shared and public meanings. Courtesy of the hand's tools, the inchoate selfhood of 'am' enters into dialogue with an emergent sense of the other and hence to the possibility of a socialised consciousness, of a self-consciousness connected with, and expanding into, a collective of self-consciousnesses. This, the passage to a full-blown self, is thus secured (at least in part) by the implicit pooling of awareness in shared tools, in collectively owned artefacts.

We may therefore imagine a feed-forward process as follows:

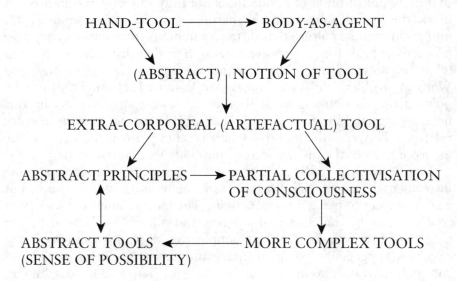

That is part of the story of the expansion of human freedom through the creation of an 'outside' that is outside of nature. Another driver to the unfolding of the self is a putative character of an agentive organism; namely, that *its reach consistently exceeds its grasp*. There is much trying and failing. This over-reach is imbued by a sense of possibility – of a goal that might be, but is not, achieved. At any given stage, the feeling of agency that exceeds actual agency; and there is an intuition of an 'am' which encompasses not only events that I (really) do, but also events that I might do. How do tools contribute to this sense of agency that is always slightly ahead of actuality?

There are two tool-based drivers to opening up and subsequently closing the gap between the scope of real and that of imagined agency. The first may be illustrated by the relative control of the proximal and distal ends of tools. The near end of a long stick used to achieve some purpose is controlled better than the far end. The stick both is (proximally) and is not (distally) an expression of one's agency. This defined gap gives agency a direction of travel, a place for the intuition of possibility to colonise. The second is the collective genius embodied in tools, the agency made available to individuals by the artefacts created by other individuals.[39] The collective other creates a collective space of possibility into which individual agency can expand, a human space outside of nature into which individual humans can grow. It is a space to which all contribute and make grow and which each generation inherits from its predecessor. The sense of possibility encouraging a reach that exceeds the grasp, the sense of the direction in which possibilities might be realised, clarified by the partly realised potential of the tool, and the 'off-the-shelf' technology already available at any given time from artefactual tools, thus work together to stimulate 'wishful thinking' and, by wishful acting, to close the gap between wishful thinking and the state of affairs it wishes to create.

Let us look a little closer at the role of the tool in inspiring the progressive enhancement of agency. The tool is set out in space as the bodily agent's external agent which keeps awake the sense of a permanent possibility of events that a) go beyond what is at present the case, and b) can be steered. The tool, in virtue of being a need-solution pair outside of the body, maintains the penumbra of possibility and at the same time guides over-reaching in fruitful directions.

We may think of this process as a means by which the 'am', which is immune from error and underpins the sense of 'do' – transforming 'it is happening' into 'I am doing' – borrows 'on account' a small notional or paper freedom which it does not yet have; delivers on that extended freedom; and so makes real the margin or penumbra of illusion around the real freedom it does have. By taking responsibility for things for which we are not yet strictly responsible, by extending our sense of what we might control, we eventually become able to control them and so become responsible for them. The implicit analogy is with someone who borrows money in order to invest and, having invested successfully, is enabled to pay back the original loan and invest further, and by this means builds up an extensive portfolio of stocks and shares. The reach exceeds the grasp; the grasp catches up; and from this position further reaching becomes possible; and so on *ad infinitum*. While the reach that exceeds the grasp is already active in the untooled upper limb hand, awoken from mere reaching to instrumentality, the tool italicises the sense of directed possibility that this awakens – literally and metaphorically pointing to what is possible, to a happening that is 'brought about'. Apparent tool-use in animals does not have this potential for expanding freedom because it is not based on an instrumentalised sense of the body and animal 'tools' are assimilated into a body schema: they do not arise out of a subject awoken in the organism.

The postulated sequence underlying progressive extension of freedom is that humans are led, by an intuition of control, of potency, of efficacy, that exceeds actual control, potency, efficacy, to directed experimentation which eventually actualises that control, potency, efficacy. This is possible because of the fundamental sense of agency that informs the human's relationship to its own body and the almost as fundamental intuition of the extension of agency (to actualise possibility) inspired by the example of extended agency seen in simple tool-use. This extended agency is both an extension of bodily agency and, given the nature of tools as extra-corporeal shared artefacts, and of agency beyond the body. The figure opposite summarises the hypothesis.

Even if the initial sense of agency, arising out of the Existential Intuition and the assumption of certain events as 'me' (or 'mine'), were at first almost entirely illusory, it has become less and less so. What is at each stage in part an illusion, is self-fulfilling at subsequent stages. While we may not be as free as we sometimes think we are, we are progressively more free than determinism would allow us to be or we are entitled to be at any preceding stage in our development. Several hundred thousands of years of human development have placed much clear blue water between human lives and the undeflected operation of the laws of nature.

Wishful thinking is a fundamental driver to the growth of agency: *some* wishes, at least, are horses.[40] Most, however, are not. 'The will to believe' has, at any given moment, a limited ability to extend individual or collective human agency beyond the mainland of the already achieved. Wanting, trying and belief are necessary to cross gaps between the already achieved and the achievable but not sufficient to cross large

*How Human Freedom Grew*

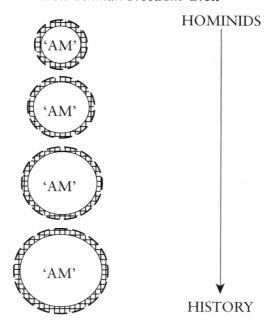

'AM' = Scope of agentive self
▦ = The scope of tool-inspired, tool-directed over-reaching of the agentive self

gaps. Gap-jumping may be very indirect. Wanting, trying and believing may enable me to jump an inch higher than before, but jumping a foot higher may involve more complex behaviour: repeated attempts, study, the help of a trainer, a reorganisation of my life to attend the gym. The passage from the human dream of flight to actual flight is yet more indirect. Individuals straining to be airborne is not enough. Some wishes are, well, horse manure.

Recent observations in neuroscience have thrown an interesting light on the role of illusion in extending the scope of agency. Many years ago, the neuro-anatomist Alf Brodal described his recovery from stroke. When his attempts to move his paralysed arm were assisted by the therapist, he had a real sense of *doing* the movement and this seemed to aid his recovery.[41] More recently, Ramachandran and colleagues have examined the illusion of voluntary movement and its impact on recovery from paralysis in more detail. In an earlier experiment,[42] they found that amputees with phantom limbs could experience movement of the phantom if, by mirrors, they were tricked into thinking that this was the limb that was moving. Interestingly, the neural activity associated with the illusion of movement was similar to that which is seen in people making real movements. (This fits with a growing literature that shows the overlap between the areas of the cerebral cortex that are activated in actual movements and those that are activated when someone simply observes a particular movement with the intention to imitate it.[43]) Most relevant to our present concern are their observations with patients who have paralysis on one side of the body after a stroke. If they are tricked, by means of mirrors, into believing that the movements they are making with their unaffected limbs are also causing their paralysed limbs to move, they will recover power more quickly.[44] Believing that one is 'doing' improves one's ability to do. The will to believe benefits from the prosthesis of illusion.

The significance of these neurological findings is uncertain; their philosophical significance even less clear. One should be cautious in invoking particular observations to support what is essentially a metaphysical position about the interaction between first-person and third-person (or no-person) being. As we shall discuss in Volume 3, the premature application of science, in particular neuroscience, to philosophical problems has been disastrous for clear thinking. Philosophy and science operate at different levels and this is as true of neuroscience as of any other science. Even so, it is difficult to resist thinking that these observations seem to support the notion that free action – and the growth of freedom (in an infant developing towards adulthood and in the human race as a whole) is based on something not too far off magic thinking. The greatest of all the magic thoughts – the profoundest, the most extensive, the most fertile – is the Existential Intuition 'That I am my body'. This has enabled the person to be cultivated, in a body that is largely impersonal and which, except in the general sense of making it possible for me to live, has for the most part hardly anything to do with my personal life.

I do not *do* my actions at the basic level; and yet I indubitably *do* them at the higher level. This is illustrated by an example we discussed in Volume 1 – executing a brilliant catch. For all sorts of reasons, it is evident that the immediate components of the catching are *done* by me. I do, however, voluntarily position myself in the field to be favourably located for catching. I voluntarily participated in the cricket match: I did not arrive at the ground as a result of a series of reflex twitches. Most important of all, my brilliant catch was the result of hours of training, which involved much deliberate activity: the hours in the nets, the reorganisation of my life in order to be able to attend practice matches, etc. While the reaching out for the ball had taken place before I had even thought of it, the fact that this could happen was the result of much deliberate doing on my part, such as swapping the on-call rota with a friend who, I believe, 'owed me one', so that I could get to the nets in time. In short, I was such an effective mechanism at that crucial moment in the match as a result of training.

We deploy our personal agency to be more effective impersonal mechanisms when the time comes. We could put this a little too strongly by saying that 'I did the training – organised my life and so on – so that *it* – my body – could catch the ball'. This is one of the most important consequences of our sense that we *are* our bodies; that I *am* this flesh. The magic thought that I *am* this flesh is even more effective when it is qualified by the sense that I am not it entirely. That my body is, for the most part, something that hasn't particularly got me, or my busy, important, life in mind enables me to subsume it more effectively to what I have in mind, and my busy, important life. The fact that, ultimately, we rely on bodily mechanisms for our free actions does not narrow the gap between reflexes and deliberate behaviour. There is a world of difference between the reflexes that save one from harm as one stumbles on the stair and the brilliant performance of Beethoven's Op. 111 piano sonata, which depends on physiological mechanisms but was made possible by years of concentrated study, commitment, organisation and reflection.

## 8.6 THE FIELD OF FREEDOM

The example of catching a ball – where we cannot make sense of what we do at that moment without looking widely beyond that moment – highlights something else. Much otherwise excellent debate about free will and freedom of action is distorted by a focus on particular dilemmas that ignores what one might call the field of freedom – the personalised ground of agency – that surrounds particular actions. Kane, for example, devotes much time to examples of individuals faced with a choice between two courses of action: a woman who has to decide whether to help save someone being mugged whom she passes on the way to an interview or arrive at the interview on time; and someone who has to choose between taking a holiday in one town or another. The exertion of free choice in the context of these dilemmas, he argues, requires the putative 'self-network' to assume one or other of its stable states, the one corresponding to one course of action, the other corresponding to another. Leaving aside the problems with the neuroscientific explanation of choice, approaching human freedom through isolated decisions is to miss the point that any given action is part of a complex tapestry of actions which we weave through our lives, lives to which we commit ourselves. Our lives are not a set of forking paths to be resolved by a series of discrete decisions: life is not a cascade of algorithms, and to lead one's life is not to algorithmise. Deliberateness (as we shall see when we discuss acting for reasons in Volume 3) is not punctate, a series of arias amid a recitative of automatic piloting.

Freedom is not exerted only with respect to difficult, or evenly balanced, decisions. The myth that it is lies behind the notion that freedom could only be expressed in certain 'extreme' situations (as the Existentialists believed) or in aleatory or gratuitous acts (preferably ones that would upset others' moral or merely probabilistic expectations). In short, freedom is to be found beyond the impossible choice between fighting for the resistance and looking after one's aged mother or in *The Vatican Cellars*. Freedom is in the pattern of deliberation that weaves the fabric of ordinary life; in, for example, the decision to eat a lot of fruit in order to secure a bowel action the following day; or to check the air pressure in the car tyres before a long journey. Our freedom runs through our lives like 'Brighton Rock' through Brighton rock. It is not – nor could it be – confined to a few blessed moments, a few set-piece episodes, the resolution of dilemmas, such as many writers have focused upon. We should not even focus on such episodes to make the freedom that pervades our lives, the self-expression that is ubiquitous in our actions, more *visible* because doing so distorts our idea of what freedom is.[45]

There is no such thing as an isolated act of free will, because no such act would make sense in isolation. The brilliant catch is rooted in many thousands of chosen actions, all subordinated to the chosen state of being a better mechanism. The isolation of actions from the world to which they belong is the essential fallacy in thinking of an agent as a cause, or as a source of causes; for causes are, by definition, isolated: they are picked out from the nexus of processes, albeit as linked to antecedent causes and descendent effects. The immediate reason for which I do something reaches past itself into an entire context of meaning, purpose and decision-making but it does not in doing so reach into a material world of causes in which reason is situated, as an effect or a product. An isolated act of free will, attached to an isolated cause (of an agent or otherwise), is as meaningless as an isolated perception lifted from a perceptual field.

We may think of actions as part of the foliage of a tree which grew from a seed, although in this case the seed is the Existential Intuition. To look for the causal ancestry of a particular leaf is like looking for the particular sunbeam that went into making a particular part of a cucumber; to bark up the wrong place. The freedom of an action is owing to the personal context – the am-soil – that creates the range of possibilities and it can be understood only as part of a *tapestry* of free actions. To develop Wittgenstein's observation that the essence of free will lies in the difference between 'I raise my arm' and 'My arm goes up', the difference is one of the contexts – between that of a myoclonic jerk and that of my decision to raise my arm for a particular purpose that makes sense only as part of a wider field of purposes. Self-conscious agency is situated in an almost limitless field of deliberation and explicit purpose.

In many ways, dichotomising freedom as the ability to choose between alternatives is making it much more primitive than it is. It reduces the situation of the self-directing human to that of an animal deciding whether to go to the right or to the left. The focus on choice between alternatives overlooks the complex expression of freedom that is implicit in the processes leading up to a dichotomous choice, it looks past all the long loops encircling large segments of self-world that provide the chosen context of the dilemma. Settling the range of options to be chosen from is as much an expression of freedom as is making a choice between them. And, as we shall see in Volume 3, it is present also in the millions of components of which a higher-order action such as 'fighting for the resistance' or 'looking after one's mother' is composed. As I develop as a person, I become a widening source of control of wider and wider reaches of my life. And this is true of the human race as a whole, as it has developed since hominids parted company from pongids.

## 8.7 CONCLUSION

My hypothesis about the origin of uniquely human freedom links self-awareness, identity and true agency in the 'am-ing' of first-person being. By connecting these consequences of the Existential Intuition, I have tried to show how free action in a deterministic – law-bound – material universe need not be paradoxical. It is possible to satisfy both requirements for freedom of the will – the actor should be the origin of the action; and that alternative outcomes to those which have actually resulted from the action should have been truly possible – without denying the unbreakability of the laws of nature. The identity of the agentive self – achieved through the intuition 'I *am* this' – secures both of these requirements. Existed identity makes of the organism an independent point of departure and a potential origin of events, planting the flag of 'here' and 'now' in a universe otherwise without egocentric markers. The unfolding of existed identity over the many hundreds of thousands of years since the first awakening of the Existential Intuition, is the basis of an ever more complex outside from which human agents are able to 'cherry-pick' between the laws of nature and manipulate the natural world which they share with all other living creatures, to uniquely human ends. The fundamental illusion – that 'I can do doing' – is ever more amply fulfilled. The outside of nature is the self-world of reasons built up over six million years.[46]

In seeking the origin of the first-person being (confined to hominids) I have looked to our 'handedness'. It is this which has enabled us alone among the beasts to grasp (in every sense of the word), the material world as a result of permitting us to get a grip on, to grasp, ourselves. We are able to get a purchase on the natural world because, through the tool-hand, we have a handle on ourselves. The sense that 'I am doing this' grows out of the sense 'That I am this' – that there is a part of the material world that I am. This is what we mean when we say that humans, alone of all living creatures, uniquely *lead their lives*: their behaviour is less shaped by mechanisms (tropisms, instincts, etc.) and more informed by conscious choices (latterly expressed in reasons). We are not merely sites through which genes are expressed in such a way as to secure their own replication, or conduits for the laws of biological nature or, indeed, of physics.

The argument I have developed in this chapter, which brings to a head the vision that informs this book, has emphasised: a) that human freedom did not come all at once; b) that although it is real, it is not absolute; c) that at any given time in history, the freedom of individuals is built upon the accumulative collective freedom of the species – rather as individual knowledge and know-how draws upon the collective knowledge and know-how of the human race; and d) that this collective basis and warrant for human freedom does not make individual expression any less real or individual. Indeed, being a latecomer – as we all are, after the first hominids – strengthens one's claim to being a free agent. (This touches on the question of whether we are liberated from the frying pan of physical determinism only to enter the fire of psychosocial determinism. There is more work to be done here and it will be done in Volume 3.) The story of humanity so far has been that, on the whole, the later one comes, the freer one is. Handedness initially awakens the sense of 'am', of one's body as an instrument, of oneself as subject-object (within the body), and (eventually) of the world as an array of objects related to one's subjectivity. In the case of a putative First Man, the complement of 'am' is the fleeting intuition of an inchoate self, not yet differentiated within an engaged body, linked to a human world not yet crystallised out of nature. In the case of latecomers, the intuition of the agentive-self has a ready-made world (of artefacts, institutions, discourses) into which it can unfold. To an ever greater extent, we are engaged in activity that is truly self-expressive: what I do is an increasingly complex expression of the increasingly complex self that I am.

Although free will may have begun as an intuition that was at least in part an illusion, it eventually became collectively true; indeed, it is always in the process of making itself ever more elaborately true – bringing about the grounds of its reality – not only for the collective but also for the individuals who make up successive generations of the collective. It is the expansion, over the generations, of the theatre of distinctively human action that has enabled reasons gradually to displace, override, requisition, biologically inflected causes as the basis of human activity and material causes to be displaced by human intentions. The many-layered human world of explicit reasons, artefacts and institutions buffers human freedom from the deterministic material universe with which it seems to be in direct conflict.

It is important to emphasise, as I did at the outset, that what has been presented is an hypothesis. As such, it has severe limitations because it is difficult to see how it could be tested. For a start, we are talking about a process that has occurred only once, so we have the historian's difficulty in allocating causal responsibility. We cannot re-run the history of primates without the opposable thumb to see whether free creatures fail to emerge. It would, however, be interesting to look at childhood development and examine the extent to which the sense of self, the sense of agency, and the manipulative capability and range of the hand grow in parallel. Second, we cannot attach dates to the maturation and elaboration of the Existential Intuition. There is a huge gap in the fossil record round about the crucial time – between eight million and four million years ago. But, more importantly, there is no conceivable way of checking the putative process or the role of various drivers because intuitions have no fossil records; or, at any rate, the chain of inference linking fossils – and artefacts – to unfolding intuitions must necessarily be rather tenuous.

If this hypothesis has any value, it is because it addresses the challenge, made more formidable by the justified ascendancy of Darwinism (though not of Darwinosis), of how we shall reconcile (in Kenan Malik's words) 'a vision of Man as a natural being with an understanding of him as a conscious agent'.[47] The resolution of this tension rests, I submit, with a proper understanding of the peculiar properties of the human hand. It is courtesy of the hand, brought to full handiness by the thumb, that we humans have learned to hitch ever longer rides on the laws of nature and become increasingly competent to manipulate those laws to our specifically human ends. This is how we – alone of the beasts brought into existence by the process of evolution – came to write *The Origin of*

*Species*. How it has come to be that human freedom, in part a self-fulfilling illusion, was bootstrapped into existence.

First-person being creates new places in the universe, without anything objective having to be changed, vantage points from which the universe can be changed. Nothing has altered the fact that, individually, we begin and end as helpless animals; but between these limits we have our brief arc through which the light burns more brightly for the more enduring collective freedom it partakes in. For each generation, the original, partly illusory, intuition of freedom is realised with ever more complexity and completeness.

NOTES

1. Edward Gibbon, *Memoirs of My Life*, quoted in Roy Porter, *Enlightenment: Britain and the Making of the Modern World* (London: Penguin, 2000), p. 184.
2. Thomas Nagel, *The View from Nowhere* (Oxford: Oxford University Press, 1986).
3. For unbelievers such as myself, this is a good example of how human freedom might be a self-fulfilling illusion. According to Gideon Yaffe (*Liberty Worth the Name. Locke on Free Agency*, Princeton, NJ: Princeton University Press, 2001), Locke argued that 'the degree to which we are free agents ... is a consequence of the degree to which we imitate the agency of God'.
4. This is not as impressive – or alarming – as it sounds. For example, as has often been pointed out, the fact that half my genes are also found in bananas does not mean that I am half-banana. Moreover, genetic determinism has recently lost ground with the recognition that experience influences gene expression: nature is expressed courtesy of nurture. The interested reader might want to consult my article in *Prospect* (August 2003) on Matt Ridley's *Nature via Nurture. Genes, Environment and What Makes us Human* – 'Customised Humans'. Ridley's arguments, however, still remain within a biologistic/deterministic framework.
5. For arguments against 'neurophilosophy', see Raymond Tallis, *The Explicit Animal*, 2nd edn (Basingstoke: Palgrave, 1999) and *On the Edge of Certainty* (Basingstoke: Palgrave, 1999) and the bibliography contained therein. For a critique of 'gene-eyed' sociobiology and other manifestations of genetic determinism, see Kenan Malik, *Man, Beast and Zombie* (London: Weidenfeld and Nicolson, 2000). We shall return to the critique of neurophilosophy – and the problems of anti-neurophilosophy – in Volume 3.
6. See in particular, Malik, *Man, Beast and Zombie*.
7. See Stephen Pinker, *How the Mind Works* (London: The Penguin Press, 1997) for a comprehensive and accessible account of human behaviour understood from the standpoint of evolutionary psychology. The epistemological blunders of evolutionary psychology are examined in Tallis, *On the Edge of Certainty*, pp. 32–44.
8. Quoted in Mary Midgley, 'Do We Ever Really Act?' Unpublished MS.
9. See Tallis, *The Explicit Animal*, pp. 161–210, 'Man, the Explicit Animal'; and Raymond Tallis, 'Carpal Knowledge. The Natural Philosophy of the Caress', *Philosophy Now* 33 (September/October 2001): 24–8.
10. Quoted in Midgley, 'Do We Ever Really Act?'.
11. David Lewis, 'Are We Free to Break the Laws?' *Theoria* 47 (1981): 113–21.

12. In the last century, there were many other attacks on 'the illusion of freedom' unconnected with science – indeed, often emanating from thinkers who were dismissive of science and of its claims to objective truth. These include post-Saussurean theorists, anthropologically-inspired sociologists, psychoanalysts and others. They are not dealt with here partly because I have already addressed them at length elsewhere – in Raymond Tallis, *Enemies of Hope. A Critique of Contemporary Pessimism*, 2nd edn (Basingstoke: Palgrave, 1999) – and partly because they are rooted in theory whereas the biological attacks on freedom at least seem to be rooted in facts.

13. I could just as well have used 'delusion'. An illusion is a false perception; a delusion is a false belief. As will be evident, freedom begins as a perception (or, more precisely, a sense or intuition) which then unfolds into a belief that is ever more elaborated in its expression.

14. I am not alone in thinking this. Merleau-Ponty, for example, believed that human consciousness 'is in the first place not a matter of "I think that" but of "I can"' (Eric Matthews, *The Philosophy of Merleau-Ponty*, Montreal and Kingston: McGill-Queen's University Press, 2002, p. 83). In the beginning, as Faust famously said, is the deed.

15. A much shorter version of the arguments of this chapter has already been published as an article: 'Human Freedom as a Reality-Producing Illusion', *Monist* 86(2) (2003): 200–19.

16. Robert Kane, *The Significance of Free Will* (Oxford: Oxford University Press, 1996), p. 4. I am deeply indebted to Kane's wonderfully comprehensive treatment.

17. That humans really do bring about things that would not otherwise occur is not (really) in doubt: the sum total of human culture – its artefacts, its institutions, its way of life insulated by so many layers from the state of nature – is a monument to collective human freedom.

18. There are occasional more impressive examples. Jeremy Rifkin, 'Man and Other Animals', *Guardian* (16 August 2003), reports how an orangutan at the Atlanta Zoo used a mirror to groom his teeth and adjust his sunglasses. Brief arias like this prove nothing. What we are interested in is what orangutans typically do for most of their lives in the wild. Pretty well all humans are able to use mirrors to help with grooming and do it all the time and think nothing of it. Very few orangutans do it and it is not part of a massively complex nexus of related activities. (Humans, by the way, created the non-wild.)

19. For a definitive demolition of microphysical randomness as a source of freedom, see Owen Flanagan, *The Problem of the Soul. Two Visions of the Mind and How to Reconcile Them* (New York: Basic Books, 2002). Kane tries out a more macroscopic version of randomness as a way out of determinism: he adopts offers something he calls 'Chaotically Amplified Indeterminacy' – that is to say, indeterminacy upscaled from the subatomic world of quantum randomness to the nervous system – as the basis for actual freedom. Kane locates the *feeling* that certain neural events are things done by us, rather than merely happening, in the superimposition of what he calls 'self-networks' – 'synchronised wave patterns (or patterns of oscillation of neural firings)' (*The Significance of Free Will*, p. 140) – on those events. The problem with localising the self in a sub-set of neural impulses is that it doesn't explain why they should be so privileged – over other nerve impulses and over other parts of the body. The self, whether we like it or not, is an intuition of the engaged individual addressed to a world. Localisation in the brain doesn't seem to capture this. There is,

moreover, nothing in *any* nerve impulses to explain why they should be first-personal in the way that Kane requires. As we discussed in Chapter 6, not even the body as a whole, *qua* organism, has a point of view. There seems little hope in finding a point of view in a conceptually isolated brain or bit of a brain. Kane's model of 'indeterministic decision-making' is also criticised by Daniel Dennett, in *Freedom Evolves* (London: Allen Lane, 2003), pp. 108–22. Dennett's specific criticisms, though well made, overlook this fundamental problem: that accounts of anything are third-personal while free will begins with 'I'. In common with many neurophilosophers, Kane is trying to stuff back into the brain what actually grew beyond it following the Existential Intuition and the pooling of sentience in knowledge and other manifestations of the collective. Trying to find free-willers, or moral agents, or citizens in neurones is worse than trying to find the leaves in the seed, because the human seed, as it were pooled its resources and participated in a forest as a whole. The Existential Intuition is the seedbed for a self that cannot be intelligibly confined to the isolated body. We shall return to this in Volume 3. In the meantime, we may confidently expect that if we leave the first person out of our account of the self, we shall fail to find its freedom.

20. And if, as I will argue in Volume 3, it is a necessary condition of there being object knowledge, objective knowledge and empirical truths, it is arguable that the Existential Intuition is *prior* to the objective world of empirical facts. Therein lies the basis of its incorrigibility.

21. Psychosocial determinism will be discussed in Volume 3, when we examine the role of knowledge, reasons and other higher-level influences on human behaviour. To swap physical determinism for a cultural prison would scarcely be an advance. The am-soil of the self is not just a skip-ful of the general am-soil of humanity which has been stuffed into passive individuals.

22. The purpose of an action defines what its component events consist of.

23. Of course, we may suspend judgement as to whether an-out-of-character action is unfree or an expression of a hidden aspect of the agent's character. When a man starts beating his wife, we may wonder whether this is a free expression of his true but otherwise unexpressed feelings towards her, or whether it is the first sign of, say, a neurological disease.

24. I owe this lovely phrase to Robert Kane.

25. Incidentally, brainwashing doesn't demonstrate the unreality of human agency. First of all, humans agents do, and organise, the brainwashing, to their own abstract and explicit purposes. Second, the brainwashed has lost his agency only with respect to certain things. Brainwashing does, however, demonstrate that particular expressions of agency are contingent but then we knew that already. The impact of head injuries and anoxia tell us as much. The fact that our freedom is in part dependent on things we have not chosen is the condition, as we have already pointed out, of its having actual content. It remains freedom none the less.

26. Mary Midgley has expressed similar thoughts in *Science and Poetry* (London: Routledge, 2001). She points out (p. 13) that the force of 'determine' (in determinism) is unclear: 'The sense in which a general "determines the fate of a private" describes outside compulsion. The sense in which "three points determine a plane" does not involve it. It is this outside compulsion we need to be free from.' Psychosocial determinism effectively regards everything that makes me be something definite as if it were a similar kind of outside compulsion. There is, however, a difference between undue and due influence. Education is 'due influence' not because (in the time

honoured sense) it 'brings out' what is already within – though it may do that – but because it is an interaction with (indeed, a refining and improving and enrichment of) what I am rather than an imposition of something that I am not.

27. See 'Ontoological Anthropology', in *The Hand*, pp. 268–73.

28. This 'principle of alternative possibilities' is necessary to avoid the Frankfurt controller scenario in which we can do what we like only so long as it coincides with what was going to happen anyway (see Kane, *The Significance of Free Will*, pp. 40–3).

29. John Stuart Mill, 'Nature'. Published posthumously in *Nature, the Utility of Religion, and Theism*, 3rd edn (London: Longman, Green and Co., 1885). I have drawn on the selections in Henry D. Aiken, *The Age of Ideology. The Nineteenth-Century Philosophers* (New York: Mentor Books, 1956).

30. This is close to the Aristotelian position that the soul is not an extra-spiritual substance but the form of the body itself. For me, the form of the body comes into being when the body is appropriated in self-consciousness as a unity that 'I am'.

31. We can also evade the problems that are associated with agent causation as it is usually understood. The first problem, pointed out by C. D. Broad, is that it is impossible to see how an agent, which seems to be outside of space-time and in itself unchanging should either engage with a particular point in space-time or bring about particular events in space-time. Smooth and unchanging, it is difficult to see how it could dirty itself with particular doings or how, as a 'standing' entity, it could bring about, or be expressed in, or engage with occurrent events. The second is that the agent has somehow to be free of the causal net when initiating actions – the action is not caused by prior events – but still able to call on it when the actions are under way. This asymmetry between input and output conditions seems highly suspicious. The present account does not require that there should be some substantive creature that is above the causal network it depends on to bring anything about but that there should be an 'outside' from which causes can be used. The process of growing that outside did not start immediately before the action but about six million years ago. More importantly, the self isn't a cause in which causation and selfhood are separate: selfhood and agency (and the collective world of agents) co-emerge. The reason for my action is not a cause in the narrow sense: it reaches beyond the immediate circumstances but does not by-pass them. Free agents are the origins of their actions but not the causes of them – in the sense of being special (uncaused) causes.

32. See Tallis, *The Explicit Animal*; and Volume 3.

33. The complex interaction between narrative and basic appetite in the generation of desires – a manifestation of uniquely human propositional awareness – will be discussed in Volume 3.

34. We must also acknowledge the limitation to free willing that comes from the fact that, though each of us is a new point of departure, the scope of my current responsibility is not coterminous with current volition. There is a deposit account of past (dead) choice; there are given circumstances that I once embraced as my world; and there are necessary mechanisms. 'Am', in short, has a penumbra (and/or a subsoil) of 'not-quite-agency': one's past, one's world, one's body.

35. Reasons are no more special kinds of causes than is agency. They are not rival types of causes that somehow break into the charmed circle of law-like material causation. They shape patterns of engagement with the causal matrix. Reason informs choices among causes transformed into handles. They are not lawbreakers but law-users.

While reasons may themselves be informed by subjective needs, they are addressed to objective goals seen as achievable by means revealed to objective understanding.

36. Quoted in *The Age of Enlightenment*, selected, with an introduction and interpretive commentary by Isaiah Berlin (New York: Mentor Books, 1956), p. 276. The power of illusion to bring things about should never be underestimated. Some of the potent motors of history have been beliefs that have proved to be false. Think of the glorious, mighty and terrifying products of collective subscription to the belief in non-existent gods. There is a more cheerful example, derived from William James in *The Will to Believe*. Two people have to jump a wide gap. One of them believes he can do it, the other is quite sure he cannot. And of course they are both right. (I am grateful to Mary Midgley for drawing my attention to this story.)

37. Quoted by Peter Reynolds, in Kathleen Gibson and Tim Ingold (eds), *Tools, Language and Cognition in Human Evolution* (Cambridge: Cambridge University Press, 1993), p. 8.

38. The sense that the world has handles which enable us to change it, and the ceaseless search for handles to bring about change, links another of Lichtenberg's aphorisms – that 'Man is a cause-bearing animal' – with the notion of causes as handles.

39. Making (of artefacts) is predicated on the intuition of agency. Animal constructions (hives, nests, dams, etc.) are not artefacts in this sense, as they are the product of pre-programmed behavioural sequences.

40. We need to think or imagine beyond what is in order to act on it. Iris Murdoch (quoted in Christopher Hamilton, *Living Philosophy*, Edinburgh: Edinburgh University Press, 2002, p. 63) puts this very well: '[O]ur fantasies and reveries are not trivial and unimportant, they are profoundly connected with our energies and our ability to choose and act.'

41. Alf Brodal, 'Self-Observations on Recovery from a Stroke', *Brain* 96 (1973): 675–94.

42. V. S. Ramachandran, D. Rogers-Ramachandran and S. Cobb, 'Touching the Phantom Limb', *Nature* 377 (1995), 489–90.

43. Christopher Frith, Sarah-Jayne Blakemore and Daniel M. Wolport, 'Abnormalities in the Awareness and Control of Action', *Philosophical Transactions of the Royal Society of London B* 355 (2000), 1771–8.

44. Eric Lewin Altschuler, Sidney B. Wisdom, Lance Stone, Chris Foster, Douglas Galasko, D. Mark, E. Llewellyn and V. S. Ramachandran, 'Rehabilitation of Hemiparesis after Stroke with a Mirror', *Lancet* 203 (1999): 2035–6.

45. The notion of self-expression is central here. It is important that we should not assume that we can be free only if we are *self-made*. At the heart of what we are as human beings is an act of appropriation, though what we appropriate is in part self-given; this means that, while we are not self-made (how could I, for example, determine the objective facts of my existence – such as that I do exist and that I was born in the twentieth century), our growth is the result of an interaction with, an assimilation of, and resistance to, parts of the given. We are thus neither self-made nor purely products: the growth of the self is, as it were, 'in the middle voice'. (Products belong to the third-person, or strictly the no-person, world of material objects.) In order to be free, we have only to be self-expressive. (This need not mean self-centred either: one can be altruistically self-expressive.) This, I believe, deals with a very influential and seemingly persuasive argument put forward by Galen Strawson to demonstrate 'The impossibility of moral responsibility' (*Philosophical Studies* 75/1–2 (1994): 5–24): '(1) Nothing can be *causa sui* – nothing can be the

cause of itself. (2) In order to be truly morally responsible for one's actions, one would have to be *causa sui* ... (3) Therefore no one can be truly morally responsible.' Strawson's error is in the second step: that freedom and responsibility require that the agent should be self-caused. The truth is, the agent is neither an effect of something outside of herself nor self-caused. First-person being is outside of the realm of causes and effects. Self-appropriation is neither passive nor active; neither an effect nor a cause. Once we have assumed ourselves we can assume responsibility for certain events and for creating a context in which we can assume responsibility for more and more events. Animals are not selfish (or irresponsible, or immoral) because they are not selves: you have to be selved to be selfish. (That is why talk of 'selfish genes' is so daft.) A free self is not one that is self-made but which is self- expressed. The self is a point of origin and actions that are free are ultimately traceable back to that point of origin.

46. It is only in the context of first-person being that the material world becomes something in, on, against and for which actions act and upon which there are patients of events. It is the self-appropriation of the body that, ultimately, transforms the material world into circumstances, substrate, opportunity and constraint.

47. Malik, *Man, Beast and Zombie.*

# Epilogue

In this volume, we have examined the nature and some consequences of the Existential Intuition which first awoke in hominids several million years ago. Many organisms are conscious, at least in the sense of experiencing interactions with their surroundings and some of the events inside their bodies; only humans are conscious of their bodies as a whole and, what is more, as something that they themselves *are*. This global organic self-awareness goes beyond the patches of proprioception, and the episodic aches and pleasures associated with activity and with the fulfilment of appetites, afforded to non-human animals. The emergence of the subject within the organism, the sense of 'me' in a body that is 'mine', the intuition 'That I *am* this [body]', had to await the development of a full-blown hand, which carried one primate over the low threshold separating the complex consciousness and fleeting self-awareness of other primates from the selfhood enjoyed by humans.

The Existential Intuition 'That I am this …' – where 'this', in the first instance, may be thought of as the engaged, active, aware, appetitive body – had momentous consequences. The human body is the only object in the world that has first-person being. First-person being introduces new possibilities into the material world: 'In man,' Schelling said, 'nature opened its eyes and noticed that it exists.'[1] But beyond that, the emergence of first-person being imports a new source of change in the universe: mankind, working with the laws of nature, has brought about new kinds of reality, configurations of matter not prefigured in the original specification of the material world. The Blind Watchmaker has brought forth The Sighted Watchmaker; and The Sighted Watchmaker – self-conscious humanity – has brought forth an intricate world of artefacts, conventions, institutions, concepts and sensitivities; watches unforeseen (and unseen) by The Blind Watchmaker.

This book has been in many respects affirmative action for first-person being. In the present intellectual climate where not only science but also scientism reign supreme, one could be forgiven for thinking of third-person being as the real stuff and first-person being as secondary, a chimerical shimmer, the steam off the pie rather than the real dish, as insubstantial as the Cheshire Cat's smile. When Daniel Dennett 'declares his starting point' for his philosophical investigations 'to be the objective, materialistic, third-person world of the physical sciences', adding that 'this is the orthodox choice today in the English speaking world',[2] the need for such affirmative action is manifest. In Volume 3, I will argue that third-person being and the material world of the physical and other sciences are themselves understandable only in the context of a coexistent first-person being. The implicit assumption that 'being in-itself' is in the third-person and first-person being is merely a perspective on it, or the equivalent assumption that third-person being is the no-person being pursued as the regulative idea of the quest for objective knowledge, appears shaky as soon as it is spelt out. There are no grounds for believing that third-person being is being itself and first-person being merely an inflection of it.[3]

We have explored first-person being from different directions. In the first chapter, we tried to define the Existential Intuition more precisely, treating it as if it were a proposition, though one with a subject and complement rather than a subject and predicate. In some respects this was heroically anachronistic, given that language has been around only for a minute proportion of the millions of years that have elapsed since the Intuition awoke in hominids. But presenting it in this way enabled us to use it as a point of entry into the most influential discussion of first-person being in the last 500 years – the *Cogito* argument.

We approached Descartes' proof of his own existence – and as a recipe for a proof of their own existence anyone might like to try out for themselves – from an unusual angle. (Some readers may indeed have had the feeling of muddle associated with looking at a tapestry from the back.) Descartes tried to recover, from the maw of systematic doubt, one piece of certain knowledge. The only piece he did recover – at least before he invoked a helpful God – was rather unimpressive and certainly less impressive than he thought. It seemed, on close inspection, that all his argument saved from universal doubt was his present moment of thought. Without recourse to a *deus ex cogito*, nothing else was recovered: no substantive 'I', no body, no world.

This meagre harvest was the inevitable consequence of placing the cart before the horse: the search for knowledge *presupposes* something called knowledge – and, along with this, the notions of justified certainty and doubt that separate knowledge from delusion or illusion; knowledge that one has been misled in the past; the language in which the search characterises itself; and, consequently, the society which is presupposed in the existence of a language, even in the language in which a solitary thinker talks to himself, if (as is certainly the case) he is talking to himself in order persuade others. (In reporting his own intuitions, he is appealing to others' intuitions, to be mobilised by their voluntarily the *Cogito* performance.) If he really does want to start from scratch, Descartes cannot presuppose all these things.

This means that he cannot really start from scratch. He cannot actually enter the solitary prison created by systematic doubt. He is inescapably accompanied by his self, his language and the society to which the words in which he formulates his doubts owe their meaning. He is too fat for the little-ease he has prepared for himself. Not surprisingly, he leaves the same prison resourced with all the things that he brought on entry. This, as we discussed in a later chapter, inescapably included his body, the necessary basis for the individuation that gives his 'I' the distinctive referent that is bundled into its having a meaning.

What added value, then, does the *Cogito* argument bring? This became apparent when, recognising its essential nature as a *performative*, as was pointed out by Hintikka forty years ago, we looked beyond the type-argument on the page to the token rehearsal off the page. Descartes had stumbled upon something rather extraordinary: a place where it was possible apparently to demonstrate by purely logical means the existence of a definite, singular existent – 'I'; a bridge across the gap between logic and empirical reality; necessity where contingency normally reigned. This was not the specific result of the *Cogito* argument. '"I" therefore I am' would have sufficed; or, indeed, 'I!' Representing it in this way shows the close affinity of the Cartesian argument/intuition/performative with the Existential Intuition. I argued that the *Cogito* argument was a reflection at a higher and more sophisticated level, of the Existential Intuition. Whereas the former was primarily an ontological blush the latter was inescapably cast in propositional form: Descartes led (so long as his argument was confined to the page) with a proposition. His *Cogito* argument – or intuition – actually had, notwithstanding his attempt to shed it by means of systematic doubt, a much bigger 'starter pack', a more generous dowry, than the hominid organism awakening to its (his/her) own existence. The Existential Intuition starts with the self-presentation of the body. There is less risk of error in the basic human sense of being 'this' – where 'this' is its own sentient and self-sentient body – than in the Cartesian conclusion that he is a mind, a thinking substance or a moment of thought. Indeed, the question of error could not arise.

This led us to the question, addressed in Chapter 3, of how far the Existential Intuition could take us: where the authority of the first person could reign unchallenged. We introduced the notion of subject-truths that were neither objective facts (and thus vulnerable to refutation) nor 'mere' subjective truths (and thus regarded as intrinsically unreal, or of dubious standing). The basis of the subject truth was that 'I' could not be mistaken, at some level (below that of factual knowledge) as to the 'this' that I am: the Existential Intuition is both a logical (or necessary) and a carnal assumption – primarily of one's body as one's own and as one's self.

Descartes' *epoche* opened up the possibility of his being a thinking being without a body: disembodiment was imaginable without self-contradiction; indeed that there was a moment of thought that was the only unassailable output from the *Cogito* argument, once the implicit but overlooked input had been set aside. This conclusion is turned upside down if the *Cogito* argument is viewed as a late expression, or reflection, of the Existential Intuition. The latter is rooted in the body from which the Intuition 'That I am' takes its rise: it is the apprehension of the body by itself. 'I' cannot be separated even conceptually from embodiment.

It could be argued that these are not rival, or opposing, views and one does not have to adjudicate between them. They are simply different intuitions that result when one starts from different places. The former is a claim about the roots of human experience and the latter is the self-reflection of a special kind of human being, a philosopher. Or the former is a pervasive sense of human being-there at the deepest level and the latter is an immediate given of an individual human being examining himself in a certain way. (And at a certain – late – stage in hominid history.) Or again, the former is the necessary context, in the widest sense, of the latter. Or finally, if this is drifting too far from Descartes' starting point and too close to mine (as it surely is), the one is a performative taking place at a high level of human consciousness (which, despite itself, implicitly allows in many things the Cartesian *epoché* specifically claims to bracket off) and the other is an empirical assertion about the nature and origin of my self-awareness. To place them head to head is to muddle logic with conceptual genesis – a danger that has haunted the 'bio-logic of am'.

All these objections have their merits. Even so, there remains an argument about the necessity of embodiment to which both approaches, albeit coming from radically different starting places, have a kind of answer. Is Descartes right in thinking that he is primarily a thinker and only accidentally embodied? Am I right in thinking that my sense of myself – as a thinker or as self-experienced in a mode closer to meatiness, such a feeling tired or in pain – is not only inseparable from my feeling that I am embodied but also provides irrefutable evidence that I am in fact embodied?

In Chapter 4, I drew on literature which has argued that the sense of identity, the ascent from consciousness to self-consciousness, necessitated embodiment. Without embodiment 'I' would have no point of application, no referent for its sense to get a purchase on. Embodiment was necessary, for example, in order to collect successive and simultaneous components of consciousness – sensations, perceptions, memory, thoughts – in a unity. 'I am thinking' can be coherently thought only of, indeed by, an embodied individual; or by an object that intuits itself as an object 'in the weighty sense' of something that exists when it is not being perceived or thought of.

Heidegger inaugurated his inquiries from a different starting point. He began with *Da-sein*, being-there, as a primordial form of being. Systematic doubt and the Cartesian epistemological prison were beside the point, since our mode of being is being-in-the-world. Being-in-the-world is *constitutive* of *Da-sein* and what is 'out there' is not externally related to us as a subject to an object, or a material object which has mysteriously to be accessed (or proven to exist) by an 'I-thing encumbered with a body'. Bypassing the Cartesian challenge, Heidegger goes on to think of other things. Unfortunately, he seems almost to bypass the body. The absence, or insufficient presence, of the body in his ontology highlights, by default, its necessity. There can be no particularised *Da-sein* (being there) without a particularising *Fort-sein* (being here). In Chapter 5, I argue the case for the body as a necessary underpinning for 'here'.

The trouble is, our relationship with our body is very unclear. The intuition 'That I am this …', where 'this' is the body that carries my name, encompasses a multitude of complex relationships: being, suffering, using, having, knowing, etc. Each of these has many facets. The deepest mystery of bodily being is that 'what it is like to be' my body is not related in any kind of straightforward sense to the objective (physical, physiological) properties of the organism. 'What it is like to be Raymond Tallis' is not, as it were, the 'inside story' of Raymond Tallis's body. There is no 'what it is like to be Raymond Tallis's body'. Moreover, the body seems for a variety of reason to be remarkably poorly qualified for the job of making 'I' be 'here'. While a self-conscious body seems a primordial example of 'this', it is difficult, in view of all the various jobs it has to do (most notably looking after itself), to see how it can underpin the 'here' that is the necessary point to counterpoint 'there'. Nevertheless, such a counterpoint seems necessary and no alternative candidates seem to be forthcoming.

The necessity of the body, then, is established and the Existential Intuition 'That I am this ...' seems correctly to intuit its own grounds. The question of what I, in fact, am – a what question that first-person being turns into one of identity – has not, however, been fully addressed. I am not solely or entirely my body; even less am I physiological states of it. In Chapter 7, we examined the various candidates for the basis of personal identity. Lockean and neo-Lockean accounts of personal identity based on psychological continuity secured through memory ran into difficulties, the most serious of which was their circularity: I could not be sure that a memory was validly a memory of something *I* had experienced, without a sense of myself – and criteria for attributing or incorporating entities into myself – being already presupposed. First-person memories, the core of personal identity over time, cannot be authenticated from within. There was also the problem that a single thread of memory did not reach from one end of one's life to another; connectedness was ensured only by the overlapping of the memory store at different phases of one's life. This then raised the question – to which there was no principled or even defensible answer – as to how much overlapping should there be in order to preserve identity.

I argued that Locke and his successors were looking for identity in the wrong place; or rather that they were trying to find identity-over-time before finding identity at a particular time, which latter depended upon the Existential Intuition. This, combined with the spatio-temporal continuity of the body was necessary to provide – and validate – the sense of enduring personal identity and the threads of auditable memory to support it. At the origin and core of personal identity is a sustained awakening of the body to itself, the sense 'That I am this ...' that makes 'itself' into 'myself'.

In the final chapter, we looked at agency and its relationship to the sense of self. It was argued that human beings are free because the awakening of first-person being, the appropriation of part of the material world as what I *am*, creates a new point of origin in the material world. 'That I am this ...' is the most profound, pervasive and efficacious enabling assumption. 'Me' plants the flag of 'here' and 'now' in the impersonal universe. The first requirement of freedom, that an individual can be the *source* of her acts, is therefore satisfied. The second requirement, that she should be able to make things turn out otherwise than they would have done anyway – that she should make a difference – is met by seeing exercising free will not as breaking the laws of nature but as (directly or indirectly) using those laws. In order to 'cherry-pick' between the laws of nature, several of which may be seen to be operating at any given time, it is necessary to approach the natural world as it were from outside. This outside is provided by the Existential Intuition as it expands into a self. The pooling of sentience in collective understanding, developing over the history of hominids and in individuals growing up in a shared world, deepens and widens the 'am-ground' of the self which provides the springboard for action on the natural world. At any given time, the sense of agency outreaches actual agency and in this sense is partly illusory; it is, however, an illusion that is self-fulfilling or reality-producing.

This, then, has been the story of the present volume. I am not too sure how much it explains that was before unexplained. In many ways it is a re-description of what no one is likely to quarrel over. In some places, an attempt to make visible what Wittgenstein said that philosophers tend to miss: what is in front of our noses. Foremost among these things at the present time are the fundamental differences between animals and human beings. Building on the observations made in Volume 1, I have tried to make biological sense of our partial escape from biology; in particular of our sense of self and our ability to bring things about that have resulted in humans creating for themselves a place apart that stands outside of nature.

Beyond this, I am conscious only of what has not been made sense of; most notably our bodily being, and what Merleau-Ponty called our 'ambiguous' status as embodied subjects. There is, that is to say, much outstanding business, some of it unfinishable but some merely unfinished. The latter will be taken up in the final volume of this trilogy attempting to characterise 'handkind'. I should like to conclude by indicating in very rough outline the issues that are now most pressing.

I have discussed personal identity but said little or nothing about its complexity and about the complex interactions between self and world in ordinary lives. Connected with this, there is much work to be done looking at how human freedom actually operates; in particular the role of reason, as opposed to causes, in shaping human lives. My take on both personal identity and freedom has very much been from the standpoint of a single individual. This is manifestly wrong: neither what I am or what I can do may be understood except in the context of the society in which I live, of which I am part, and the massive archive or deposit account of past human experience and achievement I inherited at birth and which it was the primary task of my early years to acquire; the collective world, in other words, which formed the fabric of my developing self.

The emphasis throughout this book on the isolated individual has in part been a reflection of its reference points: the solitary thinker in a Cartesian prison on the one hand and the solitary organism bounded by its epithelium on the other. A better book would have had the title *We Am: A Philosophical Inquiry into Human Being.* My lop-sided emphasis has also enabled me to bypass a central concern of those who worry about human freedom: the extent to which other human beings, individually or collectively, are a constraint on our power to choose. Is the collective constraint on our freedom from others (and indeed from our past selves and their choices) another form of determinism – a psychosocial variety which is just as bad, or as depressing, as the physical variety we have in part escaped? We need to think about how freedom is actually expressed in the real (human, social, historical) world. There is an equally important, but in a sense opposite, piece of work: connecting the present conceptions of freedom and selfhood with more formalised approaches to both autonomy and the human subject. Part of this will be trying to relate the quasi-logical Kantian subject with the empirical subject implicit in the Existential Intuition, linking the odourless transcendental ego with the sweaty armpits of real people.

The failure sufficiently to acknowledge the collective dimension of identity and freedom is linked with the most conspicuous absentee in the present volume – knowledge, the most extraordinary product of the pooling of selves, of freedoms, indeed of sentience. We have discussed neither its character nor its origin; and yet knowledge is what above all separates humans from other creatures. All animals, including humans, have sentience; only humans have knowledge. The exploration in Chapter 6 of our relationship to our own bodies (from which, I will argue, knowledge arose) throws an indirect light on the strangeness of knowledge as a mode of awareness: the impersonal knowledge I have of the body that I am (suffer, have, etc.) is curiously divorced from the immediate awareness of my carnal being, though of supreme importance for my physical well-being. The limits to my knowledge – and my sense of these limits (that there are things that are unknown about my body and there are things that are known about my body which I do not know) – reveals how little this mode of awareness is dissolved into organic life; and just how remote it is, at any rate, from the sentience, the mode of awareness we have in common with animals. The extent of the divide between present knowledge and sentience (several million years of human evolution separate them) has often been underestimated; indeed, empiricism has attempted, through reducing knowledge to heaped up sense experience, to close the divide altogether.[4] This is absurd, of course: there are things that I know, even things that I know about my body, that I cannot cash as sentience, as experience, as being. The distance between my knowledge that the sun is 93,000,000 miles from the earth and the feeling of warmth as I sunbathe; or, to take an example nearer to home, the distance between my feeling of gut-ache and my knowledge that the peristaltic activity of my colon has increased due to central up-regulation of the relevant autonomic nerves – illustrate the profound gulf between sentience and knowledge. The tension between these two realms – what is revealed to immediate experience and the world made manifest through knowledge (notably scientific knowledge) – requires closer examination. In particular, we need to develop a clearer idea of how it is that we humans are (uniquely) situated in a world of facts and physical objects perceived as having an independent existence 'out there'.

This will occupy a central position in the third volume, where I shall examine the features of what I call 'propositional awareness', and its most characteristic manifestation *the fact* – in which are merged the most highly developed symbolic system and the most complex sense of what is there. The fact, and the objective knowledge which it captures, is the supreme expression of the human intuition 'That X is the case', itself the result of the Existential Intuition 'That I am ...'. They are both fundamental manifestations of H. sapiens whom I have in a previous book dubbed 'the Explicit Animal'.[5]

Our examination of first-person being has laid the foundations of this inquiry into knowledge and truth (which aims, incidentally, not only to analyse but also to celebrate these remarkable achievements). In the present volume, I have tried to show how genuine agency can arise in a deterministic universe and how this is connected with the emergence of first-person being in a third-person, or personless, physical world. 'Am' is the knot at the heart of the world we know, making it possible for the causal network of the physical universe to be woven into the more (or less) freely chosen lives of human beings. The Existential Intuition inaugurates the (never complete) uncoupling of the human person from the human organism, permitting the latter to engage with the natural world on more favourable terms than are allowed to all other creatures. This uncoupling becomes more extensive with the growth of objective knowledge out of first-person awareness.

The Existential Intuition, which marks the point at which human consciousness starts to deviate from animal consciousness, is present throughout the remarkable journey, taken by one species alone, from sentience to sentences – from the experiencing organism to the human being asserting '*That* X is the case'. Tracing that journey, in the volume to come, and observing the distances that have opened up between its beginning and its present position will, I hope, amply confirm Karl Popper's assertion that 'human knowledge is the greatest miracle in the universe'.[6]

## NOTES

1. Quoted in Rudiger Safranski, *Martin Heidegger. Between Good and Evil*, transl. Evald Osers (Cambridge, MA: Harvard University Press, 1998), p. 369.
2. Daniel C. Dennett, *The Intentional Stance* (Cambridge, MA: Bradford Books, 1987), p. 5.
3. One of the attractions of Sartre's *Being and Nothingness* is that notwithstanding all its deficiencies, it does at least give being-in-itself and being-for-itself ontologically equal status.
4. There is, of course, an even more venerable tradition (though requiring less attention because it is hardly in the ascendant) of overestimating the gap between sense experience and knowledge. The tradition, stemming from Parmenides and given its decisive expression by Plato, placed sense experience below knowledge in terms of truth value and gave it an entirely different origin. This expression of the astonishment of human beings first coming to explicit consciousness of their distance from the natural world is something we shall discuss in Volume 3.
5. Raymond Tallis, *The Explicit Animal. A Defence of Human Consciousness*, 2nd edn (London: Macmillan, 1999).
6. Karl Popper, Introduction to *Objective Knowledge* (Oxford: Oxford University Press, 1972).

# Index